THE CHALLENGE OF CHILD WELFARE

THE CHALLENGE
OF CHILD WELFARE

edited by
Kenneth L. Levitt and Brian Wharf

University of British Columbia Press
Vancouver
1985

 # 12996119

The Challenge of Child Welfare
© The University of British Columbia Press, 1985
all rights reserved.

Canadian Cataloguing in Publication Data

Main entry under title:
The Challenge of child welfare

Includes bibliographical references.
ISBN 0-7748-0227-8

  1. Child welfare — Canada. 2. Child welfare —
Government policy — Canada.
I. Levitt, Kenneth L. (Kenneth Leslie), 1937-
II. Wharf, Brian.
HV745.A6C49 1985   362.7 '95 '0971   C85-091394-2

ISBN 0-7748-0227-8
Printed in Canada.

CONTENTS

FOREWORD

I had the opportunity, in 1974 and 1975, of serving as Chairman of the British Columbia Royal Commission on Family and Children's Law. We studied and made recommendations on virtually every aspect of family and children's law.

Although our work at the time was confined to our own province, we felt the need of a complete examination of child welfare throughout Canada. There has been a good deal of writing in journals and periodicals, but no attempt to analyse Canadian social policy in the field of child welfare.

This book is written for social work practitioners. But their work is carried on within a framework of statute law — statute law founded on assumptions which have very often not been re-examined since the statutes were passed. This book undertakes that task.

In reality the family is less protected than corporations or trade unions. The law does, of course, recognize, as a matter of public policy, the need for the maintenance and protection of the family. Yet the most profound questions of human rights arise within the family and within family law: questions relating to the custody of children, the obligations of the marriage partners, artificial insemination, and so on.

Then there is the question of state intervention. When can the state take a child from its parents? When the law perceives people as dependent, it usually endows a guardian appointed by the state with substantial powers over their lives. Women used to be treated this way. Native people are. And children are. Such measures have historically been the product of liberal reform, and their purpose has been entirely benevolent. But children are the most helpless of such special interests. If the family cannot care for the child, or if the family unit itself breaks down, the law allows the state to intervene and assign the child to parental substitutes. These may include foster parents, adoptive parents, group homes, or institutions.

A number of questions arise: When ought the state to be allowed to intervene to remove a child from its parents? We would all no doubt agree there are cases where this should be done. But then there are cases where we might disagree. Take the case of alleged neglect of a child. Who is to say that a child's parents are not bringing the child up properly? By whose standards should the care that parents are providing to a child be measured?

In my view, what occurs in the early years of life will determine much that occurs afterward. These years are vital to children's growth or their failure to grow in pre-adolescent and adolescent years. The provision of love, security, and direction in the early years is essential to a child's development of a sense of identity and to a child's notion of self-worth. If a child's emotional development in those very early years is impaired or injured, the consequence may well be an attempt by the child in pre-adolescent or adolescent years to assert his identity in anti-social behaviour. The child may be a failure at school; he may be a failure among his peers; it may be that the only way in which he can attain a sense of identity, or achieve any kind of recognition, is by an overt violation of the norms that we have come to think should govern us all. These formative years are crucial; when the full story is told, the Child is father of the Man.

Any rational approach to the breakdown of the development process is one which seeks to deal not only with the effects, but with the causes as well. The causes often lie within the family and so does the remedy. Thus we have seen the development of new perceptions in the field of child welfare. Indeed, these perceptions brought the reforms of the 1970's: unified family courts, family advocates, modernized definitions of neglect, changes in custody, guardianship, and adoption, and a greater measure of community control over resources, especially for Native communities. Some of these have been implemented, some not.

Legislation ought to set out the needs and rights of children. What are their needs? I do not think it is all that difficult to spell them out: the need for food, clothing, and shelter, for warmth and affection, for emotional security and mental health, and for education. The position of our Commission was that a child, as a human being, is entitled to certain rights.

Should these needs be spelled out as legal rights? Should children have a legal right to a permanent home, or to adequate services in their home, or to decent care and treatment if they are institutionalized? We said they should be. Moreover, where a child is handicapped, his handicap should in no way diminish his rights. Legislation dealing with children's rights should be sufficiently elaborated to indicate the application of such rights to handicapped children. Children's rights should apply equally to any children who may be institutionalized or who may be in care.

It is, of course, the primary responsibility of the family—of the parents— to provide for these needs. The function of governmental institutions and agencies is to supplement the family in meeting these needs whenever the family is either temporarily or permanently unable to meet them. Provision of resources by the state should not be regarded as a last resort.

So where are we now? The period of reform has been overtaken by the era of diminished resources and a withdrawal of sympathy in matters of child welfare. But the era of reform did affect the way people think about these questions. I know that in British Columbia, although our Commission's recommendations were not all adopted, our hearings and our recommendations made an impact on the way social work administrators and social work professionals think.

The 1970's were productive of social experimentation and change. Some may be sceptical of what was achieved. Those of us seeking to implement reform found that both the legal and social work professions were inclined to resist change. But, on the whole, there was progress in acceptance of new ideas and in the establishment of innovations on the ground. These are explored in this book.

I think this book, in assembling the views of a distinguished group of professionals, can have a profound effect on child welfare theory and practice. These practitioners, critics, and academics have much to say. I for one am grateful that their views are now conveniently available to all of us in this book.

Thomas R. Berger

PREFACE

K.L. Levitt

Child welfare has been a longstanding and significant aspect of social welfare in Canada. However, Canadian material in child welfare is largely restricted to articles in journals such as "Perceptions"[1], "The Social Worker"[2] (Le Travailleur Social), The Journal of Ontario Children and Society[3] and the Journal of Child Care.[4] There are no text books on child welfare policy and practice, and hence schools of social work, child care, and other human services teaching units rely on U.S. publications. This dependence inevitably influences what is taught, what is learned, and what becomes professional practice.

Three recent landmark Canadian publications have dealt with different aspects of services to children, including education, the place of children in Canadian society, and the law as it relates to children and family relationships. These publications showed that no single profession has a monopoly on these services, and, in fact, child welfare has not been the exclusive domain of social workers, for some time. Child care workers, family support workers, lawyers, pediatricians, educators, and many others have played a significant role in the manifold aspects of child welfare.

The first of these important publications was the Commission on Emotional and Learning Disorders in Children,[5] known as the CELDIC Report. The report dealt with special needs children with physical, mental, social, or emotional handicaps. Too frequently, these children were denied an adequate education because of failure of provincial legislation to specify responsibilities, commit resources, and develop programmes. Barriers of mistrust frequently separated service-providers, and gaps in service resulted in failure to accept ownership of an issue and failure to achieve its resolution. By its inability to modify its policy, practice, and regulations, a service system can exclude the most needy. The commitment of policy-makers to fund adequately, to develop structures for co-ordination, and to enhance trust among service-providers is required to overcome these barriers. One important attempt to develop local responsibility for the delivery of social and health services was the development of Community Resources Boards in British Columbia. This short-lived experience is well documented in a new publication, *Reforming Human Services.*[6]

In December 1973, a second significant study, the British Columbia Royal Commission on Family and Children's Law,[7] was established. This commission, popularly known as the Berger Commission, was so called for its chairman, Mr. Justice Thomas R. Berger. It was an inquiry that investigated "all aspects of laws in force in the Province which relate to children and family relationships; into the administration of justice relative to these laws"[8], and the need to augment services and agencies involved in these laws. During a nineteen month period, the commission produced thirteen reports, drafted a children's statute, and established a working Unified Family Court Project. The findings of the Berger Commission have had great impact outside British Columbia.[9]

The third important document, "Admittance Restricted: The Child as Citizen in Canada,"[10] was published in 1978. This publication was an attempt to determine how national and provincial policies and practices affect the quality of childhood in Canada. Four principles formed the cornerstone of the report: the rights of children; support for the family; equality of opportunity; and the individuality of the child's interest. The authors hoped to spark a debate that would enable communities to "identify their own issues, set their own priorities and press for changes at the community level that will affect children living there."[11]

These three contemporary publications were provocative, relevant, analytical, and critical. They made a significant advance not only in defining existing problems but also in providing direction for their resolution. They also added to the development of Canadian child welfare literature, and in many ways this publication represents a continuation of these reports.

The task of editing a book in child welfare presented a formidable challenge.[12] This book presents a selection of issues which represent the state of the art of child welfare in Canada. However, it was not possible to have chapters portraying every aspect of child welfare in each province. The contributors are predominately from Western Canada, but while the material is largely drawn from the experiences in Western Canada, much is relevant to child welfare across the country.

Several themes inform this book. A major one is the lack of standardization of child welfare policy and practice in Canada. Each of the ten provinces and two territories has its own acts, regulations, and policies. While there are certain common factors, there are no national standards and no accreditation mechanism. A second theme is the availability of social services. The current recession has witnessed the dismantling of some social service programmes and the questioning of the universality of others. A third theme concerns child welfare services to the native Indian community. A great deal remains to be done with native Indian leadership on the reserve and in the urban setting. Two chapters comment on the development of native control of child welfare services.

A fourth important theme concerns children in the care of child welfare agencies. To what extent are the range and quality of services adequate? How well do we measure the effect of these services? The final theme deals with prevention, early identification of families whose children may be at risk without certain services. What constitutes preventive intervention? How successful are preventive programmes? These and other ideas are discussed in subsequent chapters. Brian Wharf summarizes the issues raised and suggests some directions for resolution.[13]

This publication should interest a wide range of readers, particularly social work and child care students and child welfare practitioners. Law students and lawyers dealing with child welfare legislation will find a number of useful chapters. People in social welfare management positions, and legislators, will find information and points of view against which to measure current practice and legislation. Foster parents, child welfare advocacy groups, and the general public will find material that is significant to their interests.

The point of view which transcends the chapters supports an institutional rather than residual approach to service provision. The former advocates that a range of services be available so the family can choose the one which best meets its need at any given time. In contrast, the residual approach assumes the family is self-sufficient and turns to government agencies only when its own resources are exhausted. The residual approach dominates the policies of most provincial governments in Canada today, but in the view of most of the contributors, it represents a penny wise but pound foolish approach not only to child welfare but to the broader field of social welfare.

NOTES

1. *Perceptions* is published by the Canadian Council on Social Development.
2. *The Social Worker* is published by the Canadian Association of Social Workers.
3. *Journal* is published by Ontario Association of Children's Aid Societies.
4. *Journal of Child Care* is published in Calgary, by the University of Calgary.
5. *One Million Children,* The Commission on Emotional and Learning Disorders in Children (Toronto: Leonard Crainford, 1970).
6. Michael Clague, Robert Dill, Roop Seebaran and Brian Wharf, *Reforming Human Services: The Experience of the Community Resources Boards in B.C.* (Vancouver: U.B.C. Press, 1984).
7. The Royal Commission on Family and Children's Law, Province of British Columbia (Vancouver, 1973-1975).
8. Extract from Order-in-Council No. 4043 as amended by Order-in-Council No. 208, Province of British Columbia, 17 January 1974.

9. See Chapter 11, "The Berger Commission Report on the Protection of Children: The Impact on Prevention of Child Abuse and Neglect" in this volume. For an analysis of the problems in implementing the commission's recommendations, see Marilyn Callahan and Brian Wharf, "Demystifying the Policy Process: A Case Study of the Development of Child Welfare Legislation in B.C." (Victoria: University of Victoria School of Social Work, 1982).

10. Canadian Council on Children and Youth, *Admittance Restricted: The Child as Citizen in Canada* (Ottawa: The Council, 1978).

11. Ibid., p. 3.

12. The content of each chapter is the sole responsibility of its author.

13. Some concrete propositions are contained in a recent position paper: "The Child and Family Services Act: Legislative Proposals" (Regina: Queen's Printer, 1985).

1

PUBLIC APATHY & GOVERNMENT PARSIMONY: A REVIEW OF CHILD WELFARE IN CANADA

Marilyn Callahan

Children's needs are relatively unchanging, but attempts to meet them differ substantially between cultures, nations, and generations. How groups care for children is a fundamental indicator of their concern about the future of their most vulnerable members. The purpose of this chapter is to examine Canadian efforts to care for some of its children, those who have no parents or whose families are unable or unwilling to provide for them. The central theme of this discussion is that progress has been difficult to achieve because of conflicting and deeply held beliefs about children, the role of the state and parents in their care, and the value of reward and punishment in changing behaviour. As a result, the political constituency for child welfare is small and relatively powerless. The intent of this examination is to provide some directions for reform. Subsequent chapters will analyse these issues more thoroughly and recommend specific actions for practitioners, students, and scholars.

The chapter begins by defining child welfare and placing this definition in the context of differing perspectives on social welfare. An examination of major legislative changes in the last decade and the service delivery system in child welfare shows that progress has been slow, although some significant innovations taking place at the federal, provincial, and local levels will also be noted. The chapter concludes with some of the profound dilemmas confronting child welfare workers in their daily practice which reflect the nationwide ambivalence about the purpose of the child welfare system.

PERSPECTIVES ON CHILDREN AND CHILD WELFARE

Few would dispute the fact that the future of this country will be determined by the children or that a nation's strength lies in its capacity to nurture and prepare children for this responsibility. Beyond this lofty goal, there is little agreement. Three fundamental issues create dissension: what is the status of children as members of the state, what is the appropriate division of responsibility between the state and parents in the stewardship of children, and how are parents and children best motivated to carry out their responsibilities? Each question prompts strongly emotional and very different responses. Morrison, for example, has suggested a range of public opinions on the status of the child: as an afterthought or chattel to be considered only as the need arises, as a person in a vulnerable lifestage requiring special care and consideration, as a social problem or potential problem requiring punitive and controlling measures, or as an adult in miniature with the same needs and responsibilities.[1] A recent report from the Canadian Council on Children and Youth states that these are typical attitudes towards minority groups and result in inadequate, ad hoc, and discriminatory policies.[2] In the view of the council and others, children should be first considered as individual citizens with the same guarantee of human rights as other citizens and second as children who require special policies and services because of their lifestage.

The second question, the responsibility for meeting basic needs and guaranteeing rights, raises several contentious issues: how to define the boundaries between the state and parents in the care of children, how to balance the rights of parents, children, and the state, and whether some children by virtue of their abilities, race, or economic status should command more resources of the state for their development than others. The final question, on human motivation, is probably the most provocative. Some argue bluntly that parents who fail their children should not be rewarded with government services since this will undermine their commitment to improve. Ellen Goodman has observed that there are very contradictory views on reward and punishment, which she calls the two-track work ethic.

> According to the politics of the new fiscal year, the rich have lost their willingness to work hard because the government has taken too much money away from them. The poor, on the other hand, have lost their willingness to work hard because the government has given too much money to them. In response to this grave situation as of October 1 we have cut the taxes of the rich most lavishly, giving them more money and more incentive to work. We have cut aid to the poor, giving them less money and therefore more incentive to work. . . . Now no one has explained to me exactly why the rich need money to make them labor while the poor need desperation.[3]

Opinions on these issues can be loosely grouped into three perspectives which have shaped the course of child welfare in Canada. For the most part, these perspectives differ significantly from one another, although Canada as a nation has struggled to develop a system which pays lip service to each of them.

The Residual Perspective

There are many who believe that the care of children, while important, is not the proper business of the state. Parents have the primary responsibility for meeting the basic needs of their children, although health and education are shared concerns. In this view, the best way to ensure the proper care for children is to guarantee the rights of parents to carry out their job and to emphasize their responsibility to do so. The child welfare system should intervene only when the life of the child is threatened or the level of care or behaviour of the child is well below community standards. Even in these cases, it is preferable to wait for neighbours and community groups to respond prior to government action.

According to this perspective, the purpose of government child welfare services is to ensure the child's safety and to provide alternative care where necessary. In some cases, the purpose is to protect society from certain children through their incarceration and, if possible, their eventual rehabilitation. Services are necessary and justified for a few and are symbols of government compassion. They are carried out by a small group of professionals such as lawyers, social workers, child care workers, and police who are expert in dealing with individual problems. There are many examples of child welfare programmes with a residual focus: counselling for abusing parents, juvenile training centres, foster home care, and refuges for street kids.

The compelling aspects of the residual approach are its simplicity in analysing the causes of problems and its faith in the inherent goodness of the social system. It demands little in the way of change, except for a relative few. Critics of the residual approach find these very attributes its failures. Most social workers reject the residual approach because of its punitive philosophy and failure to come to grips with fundamental causes of family problems. However, it gains wide support among others, particularly during economic hard times.

The Institutional Perspective

This perspective is founded on the belief that rather than being chattels or problems, children are a vulnerable group with special needs and rights. Regardless of the capabilities of their parents, all children will require government service at some time. The emphasis is on the normalcy of child welfare services and the realization that no one individual or family can be expected to soldier on alone in a complex and rapidly changing society. This comprehensive view of child welfare includes economic, legal, educational, housing, health, and social welfare policies and involves the contribution of many different professionals as well as social workers and child care workers. Some proponents of this perspective recommend more modest objectives for social programmes, particularly during the present fiscal crisis. They suggest that rather than directing services to all families, it is important to identify those most in need of additional supports and deliver service to them as soon as possible to prevent such problems as family breakdown, delinquency, poor nutrition, and inadequate education. They argue that while it may be desirable for government policies to maximize the full potential of all children in the long run, the present objective should be to ensure that most children have the basic opportunities for adequate development. Programmes such as well baby clinics, "Headstart," parent education courses, and day care are examples of this latter point of view; family allowances, public education, and public health services are ambitious illustrations of the institutional perspective.

The appeal of this approach is its faith in the basic economic and social institutions in society and in the capacity of programmes to redress inequalities. The solution to failure is to find a better programme. Those on the left of the political spectrum find the institutional approach naive in its belief that equality can be achieved by tinkering with a class-bound system. Those on the right believe that extending the role of government to achieve the full potential of all individuals will be expensive and highly intrusive in the lives of ordinary families. Most social workers support the institutional perspective. It fits with the individual rights and social justice goals of their profession and with their training in developing and implementing social programmes.

A Radical Perspective

Several writers in recent years have argued persuasively that in spite of the lofty objectives for the child welfare system set out in the preceding perspective, its fundamental purpose as a part of the larger social service system is to control children and families who might otherwise embarrass those in power or seriously threaten the status quo of Canadian society. Services directed to undesirable parents are designed to undermine their parental role and acculturate their children into more mainstream values. Native Indians and the poor have been identified as two groups for whom this analysis particularly applies. McKenzie and Hudson describe this process as structural and cultural colonialism, which involves a systematic devaluation of the norms, values, and opinions of the native groups. In another chapter, Wharf suggests that preventive child welfare programmes directed towards the poor may have the best of intentions and the worst of results:

The family attempting to cope with a limited income, inadequate housing and other problems might, on learning that they were classified as being potentially neglectful parents, simply give up the struggle and request that the appropriate child welfare agency assume the responsibility for the care of their children. The label might be the last straw for the inadequate parent.

Proponents of this perspective recommend the dismantling of the current child welfare system, the introduction of economic policies designed to redress inequality, and a stringent guarantee by government of essential human rights for disadvantaged groups, including women and children. In a curious way the radical and residual perspective share several common elements: a suspicion of government programmes to remedy family problems, an antipathy towards professionalism, and, at times, a romantic faith in the capacity of individuals to care for one another if given the right circumstances. For the residualists, this means freedom from government interference; for the radicals, a government plan which achieves economic and social justice.

Most examples of the radical perspective in action have been implemented at a group or community rather than national level. Native Indians, for example, have concentrated most of their efforts on carving out a new economic arrangement with government in the lands claim issue and in fighting for assurance of their aboriginal rights in the development of the Constitution. Although they have made some strides in assuming control of their own child welfare system in recent years, their fundamental belief is that these services will be largely unnecessary once the other policies are in place.

Some communities across Canada have implemented the "green dollars" system, a co-operative venture which substitutes the exchange of individual efforts for money.[4] Day care, dental work, housing, fresh vegetables, and countless other goods and services are exchanged to help equalize economic opportunities, at least within the community. The National Action Committee on the Status of Women and other feminist organizations have argued for fundamental economic reforms on a large scale. Equal pay for work of equal value, pensions for homemakers, guaranteed annual incomes, and changes in human rights legislation are fundamental platforms of these groups. They maintain that until women have equal economic and political opportunities, the insurmountable problems that many face in raising their children will not be overcome.

Although most social workers accept the analysis of the radical perspective, they do not embrace it as a blueprint for action. Valentich and Gripton suggest that the radical analysis "is not sufficiently developed to serve as a practicable guide for societal transformation" and that "social workers are pragmatists who understand the limits of their political power. . . and are committed to alleviating individual distress in the context of present micro-realities."[5] There are few jobs for radical reformers. However, as the above examples indicate, it is possible to create radical changes on a small-scale level, even with individuals and families.

The following story illustrates this possibility and the differences between the three perspectives. During a cholera outbreak, a physician was asked to investigate:

> he was anxious to do and to help, but he was also a good social analyst. He discovered that a greatly disproportionate number of cholera victims got their water from the pump on Broad Street. He concluded that there was something about the *pump* (not those who drank the water) that was causing the disease. Now, the next part of the story is very crucial.
>
> What did he do? He did not apply for a research grant to study the characteristics of the pump and its water in order to develop a theory of the etiology of cholera. Nor did he publish a pamphlet urging people not to get their water from this pump. *He ripped the handle off the pump*. That particular cholera epidemic subsided.[6]

CHILD WELFARE: A DEFINITION

Clearly, these different perspectives create different objectives and boundaries for the child welfare system. The following definition attempts to combine elements of all three and to recognize the reality as well as the aspirations of child welfare.

It is a system designed to guarantee to children the resources required for their development and the rights essential for their fair treatment by providing supportive, supplementary, and substitute services to children and their families and advocating changes in economic, health, education, and social policies which have a significant impact on their well-being. In Canada, it is best viewed as three concentric circles. In the centre are those policies designed to ensure economic equality and freedom from discrimination. The next ring contains universal programmes which serve many more children: day care, well baby clinics, public school education, family allowances, and child tax credits. They are generally delivered with little stigma and provide for a wide variety of needs. On the outer ring are those policies and services designed to meet the basic needs of some children and families: protection programmes, emergency shelters, foster care, and so forth.

There are several advantages of such a broad definition. It encourages an integrated view of children's development and relates children and family needs to a broad range of economic and social issues. It also attempts to create a unity of purpose among professionals and the diverse groups concerned with children's welfare. However, most of the articles in this book deal with children and families in the outer circle and the struggle to define their needs in a more universal fashion. This has been the challenge for the child welfare system in Canada since its inception.

THE NUMBERS OF CHILDREN IN THE CHILD WELFARE SYSTEM

At the broadest level, of course, all Canadian children are served by the child welfare system. But identifying the precise number requiring and receiving care and guidance is difficult. Provinces have different systems for reporting their activities, and Health and Welfare Canada publishes only those figures where cost-sharing has been provided under the Canada Assistance Plan. There are no national voluntary organizations which compile statistics on child welfare on a regular basis. However, it is possible to provide some estimates of children receiving government-funded services for alternative care or for counselling and support to remain in their own homes.

TABLE 1

Children in care of government permanent/temporary [1]	74,295	
Children in homes for special care [2]	40,910	
Children receiving protective service in their own homes [3]	145,992	
Children in licensed group or family day care who receive subsidy [4]	69,535	
Children convicted of delinquencies and sentences to correctional institutions or probation [5]	44,149	
	374,881	(4.8 per cent of all Canadian children)

1. *Basic Facts on Social Security Programs* (Ottawa: Health and Welfare Canada, October, 1983), p. 5.
2. *Ibid.* May be some overlap with above category.
3. Corinne Robertshaw, *Child Protection in Canada* (Ottawa: 1981), p. 21. This figure is based on estimates from some provinces, actual statistics from others for 1980.
4. *Status of Day Care in Canada,* National Day Care Information Centre (Ottawa: 1983), p. 6. 139,070 children are in licensed group or family day care. Approximately one-half of these would be subsidized.
5. Juristat Service Bulletin (April 1984): 5.

Excluded from this estimate are children receiving services from voluntary organizations such as alternative schools, family-planning clinics, neighbourhood organizations, and government and voluntary mental health services. Also excluded are the estimated one million children receiving day care in unlicensed facilities and other children in day care whose families do not receive subsidies.

There are two major trends in these figures in the last two decades. More children are coming to the attention of the child welfare system for assistance, protection, and guidance. The Report on Sexual Offences against Children, for example, indicates a 431 per cent increase in reported cases of sexual abuse between 1977 and 1980 in Canada.[7] Most provinces have noted an overall increase in the numbers of reports on child abuse and neglect since mandatory reporting laws were enacted and the wide publicity that has been given these subjects in recent years. However, other categories of service have been falling. There has been a sharp decline in the birth rates to adolescents — from 58.2 per 1000 for 15 to 19 year olds in 1961 to 26.4 in 1981 and a dramatic rise in the numbers of these young women who are unmarried and raising their children from 30 per cent in 1970 to 85 per cent in 1981.[8] This has shifted demands from adoption services to day care and family support services. Charges of delinquency have also been declining, 5.2 per cent from 1981 to 1983, probably in part a result of the decreasing number of teenagers and the addition of preventive programmes.[9]

The second trend is the change in services for children once they are involved in the child welfare system. Fewer children are taken into government care, and more remain with their own families for supportive and supplementary service. (See Table 2.) There is growing evidence that there is a relationship between these two types of service. In Hepworth's chapter, he notes that in Ontario, for example, with the lowest percentage of children in care, the number of child welfare workers has increased by 71 per cent between 1966 and 1980, and the numbers of children receiving assistance in their own homes has almost doubled in the last two decades. In B.C., the percentage of children in government care decreased consistently after the introduction of in-home services in 1973.[10]

DEVELOPMENTS IN CHILD WELFARE LAW

Legislation is the clearest written statement that a society makes about its commitments, and for that reason it is useful to examine recent reforms in child welfare law. The law is also a good reflection of the will of those governed. As Mohr states:

> The revolution in family law which has occurred during the past decades shows itself now (as most revolutions eventually do) to have been an adaptation to what was going on in our minds and between us. . . . As the Jesuit philosopher Bernard Lonergan once said about the Church, the Law too arrives at the place of action always a bit late and out of breath.[11]

TABLE 2

NUMBER OF CHILDREN IN CARE AS PERCENTAGE OF TOTAL POPULATION OF CHILDREN UNDER 19

Province/Territory	1977			1981			
	No. of Children in Province[1]	No. of Children in Care[2]	%	No. of Children in Province[1]	No. of Children in Care[2]	%	% Change
Newfoundland	250,400	4,803	1.92	230,350	2,500	1.09	− 0.83
Prince Edward Island	46,085	277	0.60	43,325	200	0.46	− 0.08
Nova Scotia	310,455	2,294	0.74	284,240	1,400	0.49	− 0.25
New Brunswick	266,870	2,752	1.03	245,700	2,000	0.81	− 0.18
Quebec[3]	2,216,620	31,200	1.41	2,015,795	33,300	1.65	+ 0.24
Ontario	2,881,775	13,710	0.48	2,695,535	12,200	0.45	+ 0.03
Manitoba	365,480	2,936	0.80	334,475	2,300	0.69	− 0.11
Saskatchewan	344,940	2,715	0.79	333,555	2,700	0.81	+ 0.01
Alberta[3]	696,345	10,981	1.58	756,110	5,100	0.67	− 0.91
British Columbia	883,030	10,200	1.16	827,585	8,500	1.02	− 0.14
N.W. Territories & Yukon	29,380	1,030	3.51	29,295	600	2.05	− 1.46
Total	8,291,380	82,898	1.27	7,795,695	73,901	0.95	

1. National Census, 1976, 1981.
2. Health and Welfare Canada
3. Includes children requiring protective services but remaining in their own homes.

There are many different statutes governing child welfare, but they have three ingredients in common: they are concerned with who shall have custody and guardianship of children; they reflect, often indirectly, the minimal standard of care and behaviour permitted for children; and they define the process by which custody and guardianship will be changed if minimal standards are not met. Most of these statutes are provincial responsibilities and include acts such as Family Relations, Adoption, Child Paternity and Support Act, Family and Child Services, and Mental Health legislation. The federal government remains in charge of the Young Offenders Act because of its responsibility for the Criminal Code, although provinces are assigned the task of administering juvenile justice through Family Court, Probation, and Training Schools legislation. The Criminal Code (Section 197) also defines the responsibilities of parents towards their children and the penalties for those who fail to meet these obligations. This section of the code is rarely used in child abuse or neglect situations because of the vagueness of the charge and the limitations available to the court in determining penalties (prison or summary conviction). It is also deemed to be too punitive to be effective in most child protection situations.

Child protection legislation has been selected for particular examination in this section of the chapter for several reasons. It is the statute that is most important for child welfare workers in many different settings; it contains many powerful and controversial sections with far-reaching implications for workers and families; and yet there has been very little examination and comparison of the twelve statutes in Canada and the Territories. Most of these statutes have been revised during the last decade, and during their revision, there was much debate on the basic questions in child welfare proposed at the beginning of this chapter. (See Table 3.)

When should the state intervene in family life?

All child welfare acts list the reasons for state intervention on behalf of children. These reasons are, in effect, a statement of an acceptable minimum of care that each child has a right to expect and reflect the degree to which Canadians are committed to any one perspective about children and families.

Robertshaw has summarized these as follows:
1. children who have been abandoned or whose parents wish to divest themselves of parental responsibility towards them,
2. children who are habitually absent from home or school or whose parents fail to provide for their education,
3. children whose parents are unwilling or unable to control them,
4. children who are not getting necessary medical attention,
5. children who are living in unfit or improper places, unfit or improper circumstances, or with unfit or improper persons,

TABLE 3
CHILD PROTECTION LEGISLATION IN CANADA

Name of Act	Assented to	Matters included	Grounds for Apprehension	Preventive Services	Special Status for Native Indians	Child's Right to Testify	Right to Counsel
Family and Child Service Act (B.C.)	1980	Protection of children	Basic reasons (excluding emotional neglect)	Not included	In notification of hearing—One band has assumed control of child welfare—not in Act	Not mentioned	Not mentioned
Alberta	1984	Protection of children, adoption, juvenile justice, compulsory care	Basic reasons: sexual abuse & potential abuse, emotional development *threatened*	Included "as long as reasonably practicable"	In providing a copy of any orders made on Native Indian children	Children over 12 must be consulted about temporary custody order	Child may be granted counsel
The Family Services Act (Saskatchewan)	1981	Protection of Children, adoption	Basic reasons	Included, not mandatory	No	Court's discretion	Parents may be granted counsel
The Child Welfare Act (Manitoba)	1984	Protection of children and juvenile justice, children of unmarried parents, adoptions, guardianship of children	Basic reasons & minor parent, sexual abuse, injurious environment	Included, not mandatory	In adoption. Although not specified in legislation, bands can and have applied to form their own Children's Aid Societies under the Act and assume control for child welfare	Court's discretion: specifies importance of views of child	Child and parent may be granted counsel

TABLE 3 *(continued)*
CHILD PROTECTION LEGISLATION IN CANADA

Name of Act	Assented to	Matters included	Grounds for Apprehension	Preventive Services	Special Status for Native Indians	Child's Right to Testify	Right to Counsel
Act Respecting the Protection & Well-being of Children & their Families (Ontario)	1984	Protection of children, Young Offenders Adoption	Basic reasons & substantial risk of physical harm, sexual abuse, emotional harm & risk of harm	Included, not mandatory	Allows for specific development of Native children's Aid Societies. Also notification of hearing	Court's discretion: specifies importance of views of child. Child also has a right to notification of hearings and to be present in court if over 12 years with court's discretion. Child has right to a plan for care.	Child may be granted counsel
Loi sur la Protection de la jeunesse (Quebec)	1977	Protection of children	Basic reasons & sexual abuse, serious behaviour disturbances, mental or emotional development is *threatened.*	Included, not absolutely mandatory but worded forcefully	No	Mandatory that court give child opportunity to be heard. Child also has right to know of planning for his care.	Child and parent have right to counsel
Child Welfare Act (New Brunswick)	1966	Protection of children	Basic reasons & *tending* to become incorrigible	Mandatory, the Director "shall provide preventive welfare services to chil-	No	Not mentioned	Not mentioned

				...dren and families."			
Children's Services Act (Nova Scotia)	1976	Protection of children, adoption, juvenile justice	Basic reasons	Not included	No	Not mentioned	Not mentioned
Family and Service Act (P.E.I.)	1981	Protection of children	Basic reasons & sexually abused, domestic violence, inappropriate work, refused proper services, minor parent, injurious environment	Included, not mandatory	No	Court's discretion: specifies importance of views of child	Not mentioned
The Child Welfare Act (Nfld.)	1972	Protection of children	Basic reasons & severe domestic violence, sexual abuse, child dangerous to himself or others	Not included	No	Court's discretion: specifies the importance of views of child	Not mentioned
Child Welfare (Yukon Terr.)	1970	Protection of children, children born out of wedlock, adoption	Basic reasons & *tending* to make him idle, *hinder* his emotional & mental development	Mandatory, the Director is responsible for the amelioration of conditions that lead to neglect	No	Court's discretion: specifies the importance of the views of the child	May be provided
An Ordinance to provide for the welfare of children (N.W.T.)	1961	Protection of children, children born out of wedlock, adoption	Basic reasons	Not included	No	Not mentioned	Not mentioned

6. children who are not receiving adequate care because of the inability of their parents to provide such care,
7. children whose lives, health or morals are endangered; (in some statutes linked to the conduct of their parents); and
8. children whose emotional or mental welfare is endangered because of emotional rejection, deprivation of affection, isolation or lack of appropriate parental care, (in some statutes requiring the evidence of a psychiatrist). Only B.C. does not include this.

In addition to the above, the following four definitions are found in a minority of statutes:

9. children who are sexually abused, assaulted or exploited (Manitoba, Quebec, Newfoundland and P.E.I. definitions),
10. children whose environments are injurious to them or whose parents fail to protect them adequately (Manitoba and P.E.I. definitions),
11. children living in a situation where there is severe domestic violence (Newfoundland and P.E.I. definitions), and
12. a pregnant child who refuses or is unable to provide properly and adequately for the health and welfare of herself or child both before and after the birth of the child (P.E.I. and Manitoba definitions).[12]

In reforming legislation, several provinces have attempted to identify very specific reasons for intervention such as those in 9, 11, and 12 of the above list and to eliminate clauses such as 5 and 6. In this way judges and social workers have a clear mandate for protecting children, and there is less opportunity for discrimination on the basis of race, sexual orientation, economic status, cultural background, or the moral behaviour of the parents. The result for the child rather than the lifestyle of the family is made the paramount issue for the court. Another argument for specific reasons for apprehension relates to the legal rights of parents. It is very difficult to mount a defence against vague charges. In fact, the tradition of jurisprudence has been to clarify the precise meaning of offensive behaviour, not only to provide some consistency in the courtroom, but also to help potential offenders avoid illegal behaviour.

One of the most controversial clauses found in most statutes (with the exception of British Columbia) deals with emotional deprivation and abuse. Such clauses extend the definition of child welfare beyond the physical and moral development of the child and, in most provinces, require the testimony of a psychiatrist. Some believe this extension is unwarranted. They believe it is too difficult to define emotional neglect or to predict with any certainty the results of such deprivation. Others have forcefully argued that experts in child care and psychiatry are as able to identify emotional deprivation as physical or sexual abuse and that the long-term results can be more devastating for the child. Ontario has had the longest experience with this clause. It has been used successfully as a last resort for the handful of parents who refuse voluntary assistance in meeting their children's emotional needs and where this deprivation has not resulted in obvious physical symptoms covered in other clauses for apprehension.

WHAT IS THE STATE'S ROLE IN ASSISTING FAMILIES TO PROVIDE FOR THEIR CHILDREN?

Most statutes require intervention only after children have suffered some kind of substantial harm and may be at further risk. However, Quebec, New Brunswick, and the Yukon Territory statutes include such phrases as "threatening or hindering mental or emotional development" and "tending towards undesirable behaviour." In effect, in these provinces intervention could be mounted for children at risk of abuse or neglect. There has been much debate on this subject, and those with an institutional perspective have argued for more comprehensive clauses allowing parents and workers to call on the authority of the court and legally demand services well before the child is in serious jeopardy. Opponents of this position argue that families in need could include an astounding number and that it would involve an unpredictable and expensive undertaking. For example, the rapidly rising number of single-parent families headed by women earning less than poverty line wages could potentially mount a powerful lobby and demand assistance in parenting.

Few provinces in Canada have enacted a preventive approach to child welfare. Only the New Brunswick and Yukon Territory statutes state clearly that the duties of the director of child welfare must include the provision of preventive services when required. In Quebec, when a child's circumstances are threatening to hinder development and the situation is not urgent, the director must contact the parents and attempt to arrange voluntary measures to improve the situation. Several other provinces, including P.E.I., Saskatchewan, Manitoba, and Ontario, outline an impressive array of services to assist parents in providing for the care of children who may be in need of protection but who do not require the authorities to provide these services. Most statutes also provide for voluntary short-term custody and care agreements which can be arranged between the child care agency and the parents without court intervention. However, the parent must demonstrate special needs and must relinquish custody in whole or in part for the period of time of the agreement. Parents who are fearful about losing custody of their children may be very reluctant to relinquish it voluntarily. All child welfare statutes provide for at least secondary prevention through the range of dispositions open to a judge upon finding a child in need of protection. As one option the judge may return the child to the parents under supervision of a child care agency. During this time, resources for improving the child's care and preventing further breakdown can be mounted. The article by David Cruickshank examines legislation for prevention more fully.

In practice, child welfare workers are constantly mobilizing preventive services for children before legal intervention, but there is no statutory requirement that they do so. Many fear that preventive services are the easiest to abandon when funds and time are limited.

How to balance the rights of children, their parents, and the state

One of the most difficult dilemmas facing legislators is the need to achieve an optimum balance of rights in the legal process, recognizing that the needs of each party may in fact conflict. For example, the Royal Commission on Family and Children's Law in B.C. explored the often neglected topic the child's sense of time.

> From our discussions with professionals who have studied this field, we know that time runs out quickly for children. The longer the delay, the longer the child is moved around, left in a temporary situation, or left with his neglecting or abusing family, the less likely he is to enjoy mental health as an adult.
>
> Emotionally, the infant cannot stretch his waiting more than a few days without feeling overwhelmed by the absence of his parents. During an absence he may quickly latch onto another adult or adults, and begin to put down roots. He cannot appreciate the concept of temporary care. For most children under the age of five, an absence of parents beyond two or three months is beyond comprehension.[13]

Yet, in order to protect the rights of parents, it is important to provide ample time for them to improve their family situation sufficiently to offer an adequate home for their children and to prepare their case for the court. Time is also required for professionals to carry out social assessments and to explore possible resources for children and their families. Court dockets are consistently overloaded, and practical reasons often demand that cases be held over to a later date. In recognition of this dilemma, most child welfare statutes impose severe limitations on the time in which the court must be notified if a child is brought in to care (usually five days), limitations on the court in setting the date for the hearing (often twenty-one days after the first court appearance), and restrictions on the length of court orders for temporary care of children (usually twelve months). Three statutes provide for the rights of parents to counsel, and all include parental rights to appeal. However, in spite of the best intentions of legislation, its implementation often falls short of expectations, and it is frequently the child's sense of time that is most disregarded.

Probably the most significant change in court process in recent statutes is the recognition that while parental and professional opinions are important, children also have a right to be heard in proceedings affecting their lives. Several statutes make specific reference to the importance of such testimony and allow the court discretion in determining appropriateness given the circumstances and age of the child. The Quebec statute requires that children be given an opportunity to be heard, and Ontario makes provision for children over 10 to be provided with copies of hearing dates and custody reports where appropriate. Only Quebec provides the right of the child to counsel in statute.

In spite of these developments, child protection legislation remains primarily residual in its philosophy and intent. Most statutes include statements about the needs of families for support in caring for their children and the rights of children as citizens of Canada, but with some notable exceptions, they guarantee only that the most basic of these will be met. The law is almost silent on the needs of native Canadians in spite of the shocking numbers of native children in care and the clear evidence that poverty, poor housing, malnutrition, and discrimination have precipitated this crisis.

CHILD WELFARE SERVICES

Child welfare services in Canada emerged from ad hoc groups of volunteers funding and delivering assistance to poor and homeless children and shifted gradually to government funding for a broader base of protection and prevention services delivered primarily by professionals. Government funding has changed as well, from municipalities bearing the major costs, to provincial governments, and finally to a shared arrangement between provincial and federal governments. The aim of this section is to unravel the complex system of child welfare services, assess its strengths and weaknesses, and document some of the recent initiatives which could make these services more responsive.

Child welfare services were originally thought to be such an insignificant matter that they were not really mentioned in the B.N.A. Act but assigned to the provinces in a general clause covering similar issues. This was probably appropriate for a sparsely populated, largely agrarian country where children were an integral part of the family enterprise. By the 1940's and 1950's, however, provinces were struggling to meet their commitments to a much larger number of children and families primarily living in urban and industrialized areas.

The Canada Assistance Plan of 1966-67 was a landmark piece of legislation for income, child welfare, and family services. Its purpose was clearly to redress inequalities between the federal and provincial governments — the federal ability to tax and the provincial responsibility to provide services. Effectively it provides 50 per cent cost-sharing for all basic income services, which includes payments for children in institutional care and foster homes. In addition, the federal government shares the costs of other social services such as counselling to families and preventive services upon provincial request. As the following figure indicates, general assistance (primarily social assistance payments) demands the greatest percentage of federal monies while child welfare, which includes children in care as well as preventive services, receives one of the smallest amounts. (Homes for special care and welfare services include some expenditures on children.)

Figure 1

ESTIMATED DISTRIBUTION OF EXPENDITURES FOR 1983-84
WITHIN THE CANADA ASSISTANCE PLAN BY PERCENTAGE

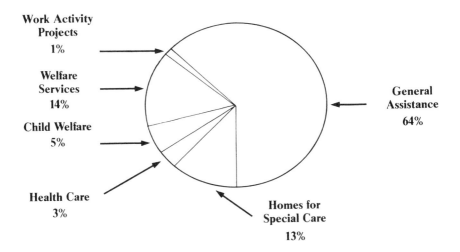

From: Canada Assistance Plan Annual Report, 1983-84, p. 2-31.

Despite attempts to revamp C.A.P. in 1976-77, which included recommendations to expand the range of services eligible for cost-sharing and another suggestion to scrap the whole plan and institute block-funding, C.A.P. has remained virtually intact. It has largely accomplished its original purpose but, like every solution, there have been unanticipated consequences. First, it has left the federal government in the position of paying at least half the piper, yet calling few of the tunes. Although C.A.P. delineates in a relatively broad way the services eligible for cost-sharing, it does not demand that the provinces produce programme evaluations for continued funding or that a specific range of services be offered. It has also maintained the connection between the poor and child welfare services. The overall target group to be served under C.A.P. is "persons in need or likely to become in need," and need is defined in financial terms. In reality, this sometimes means that workers attempting to offer more preventive services are required to estimate income levels of their clientele. The essential inequities in the distribution of wealth are not addressed in C.A.P. — the richer provinces can spend more on services and, in turn, receive more federal money. Overall, however, C.A.P. remains as an innovative attempt to remedy problems unforeseen in the B.N.A. Act.

The federal government's role in financing child welfare has extended beyond C.A.P. to direct payments to families through family allowances and indirect benefits through the income tax system such as child tax credits and deductions for children and child care. All of these cash programmes have a major impact on many Canadian families and certainly earn political kudos for the federal government.

In addition, the federal government has initiated many innovative services through National Welfare Grants and Canada Works. It would probably be accurate to state that many day care and family centres in Canada began from the latter programme, often to the consternation of provincial authorities, who were left to pick up the on-going tab when federal funding ceased. The federal government has also sponsored some effective policy review mechanisms such as the National Welfare Council and the Advisory Council on the Status of Women. The publications from these two sources are often the only national research on family welfare that is thoroughly executed and widely distributed.

But the nuts and bolts of child welfare services are designed and delivered at the provincial level. These systems differ in three dimensions: the degree of decentralization, integration, and community control. (See Table 4 for a summary). Economic, geographic, and ethnic differences have greatly influenced the way services have developed in each province, but different perspectives on child welfare have also played a significant role.

Some provinces have adopted a structure which best delivers residual child welfare services. In this model, the mandate of the organization is narrowly focused on the safety and control of a small number of children and families. Although services may be decentralized, decision-making remains highly centralized at the top management and political levels. Professional autonomy is limited primarily through narrow job descriptions and a plethora of policy directives governing day-to-day decisions. Highly specialized professionals and those with community development expertise are largely unnecessary. For the most part, in-service trained staff are preferred. The organization usually delivers bare bones protection services, exclusive of other government services for children. Community involvement in the development of government services is discouraged, although voluntary and profit-making organizations are encouraged to deliver specialized and preventive services and in some cases to contract protection services from government.

This lean structure makes sense for the delivery of residual services. It ensures that politicians and top management can control information and carefully monitor government expenditures. It limits the influence of professionals and community groups in demanding an expanded mandate for child welfare services. It further limits costs by reducing the need for highly trained staff and by contracting specialized services. Although the disadvantages of this system are obvious for the development of services, the stress it creates for management and politicians is often overlooked. They have no buffer zone between themselves and public criticism, particularly when a child dies unnecessarily or major child welfare problems plague a particular community.

The institutional model is characterized by an expanded mandate for child welfare services frequently integrated with other government services for children. Decision-making and services are decentralized to local units, although there is a wide variety in the degree of decentralization and a chronic tension between local decision-making and coherence at the provincial level. Frequently, there is a distinction between the policy-making role of the local units and their headquarters. Local units are primarily in charge of service-delivery decisions, while headquarters determines overall directions, funding guidelines, and the setting of standards. Professionals are required to work co-operatively with one another and with local community workers and groups. The voluntary sector is involved in the development as well as delivery of services. Community involvement and sometimes control of services are encouraged through local planning councils and decision-making boards, similar to the school board model.

Some provinces have attempted to overhaul their organizations to fit the institutional model. B.C. initiated Community Resources Boards in 1974 in an attempt to combine income, services, and statutory and preventive services for children and families and to inject public participation in the management and delivery of services. Although the Resource Boards have been disbanded a recent evaluation concluded that they served to unite local participants and provincial politicians in a common cause, and developed more streamlined service delivery systems, and more appropriate local programmes.[14]

Quebec has had the most experience in the institutional service delivery system. After the Castonguay-Nepveu Report in 1970,[15] the government of Quebec developed a single Ministry of Social Affairs to deliver health and social services at a local level and to create regional citizen boards to direct and monitor local operations. In the Quebec plan, income assistance is delivered through another ministry. In 1984 New Brunswick indicated its intention to develop a similar resource board model of services, and Manitoba has recently developed a community based child welfare system in the Winnipeg area. It is interesting to note that these provinces have made a firm commitment to preventive services in their legislation.

Ontario and Nova Scotia have a unique system of citizen involvement and local service delivery through children's aid societies, funded almost totally by government but with some local autonomy. In spite of these developments, several provincial and national reports in the last few decades have

TABLE 4

PROVINCIAL CHILD WELFARE SERVICE SYSTEMS

Province	Ministry and Division Responsible for Child Welfare	Children's Services Integrated with This Ministry		Delivery System
		Juvenile Corrections	Health	
Nova Scotia	Department of Human Resources	X	—	13 Children's Aid Societies; 5 govt. offices
New Brunswick	Department of Social Services, personal Social Services Division, Child and Family Services	—	—	Government offices changing to local resource boards and integrated system in 1985
Nfld.	Department of Social Services	X	—	Government offices
P.E.I.	Department of Health and Social Services, Social Services Branch	X	X	Government offices
N.W.T.	Department of Social Services, Family and Children's Services	X	—	Government offices
Yukon Territory	Department of Health and Human Resources	X	X	Government offices
B.C.	Ministry of Human Resources, Family and Children's Services	—	—	Government offices (formerly Resource Boards, similar to Quebec)
Alberta	Department of Social Services and Community Health, Child Welfare Branch	X	X	Government offices
Sask.	Department of Social Services, Family and Community Services	X	—	Government offices
Manitoba	Department of Community Services and Corrections, Child and Family Services	X	—	Government offices 4 Children's Aid Societies; Native Children's Aid Societies
Ontario	Ministry of Community and Social Services, Children's Services Division	X	Mental Health	Over 50 Children's Aid Societies (Native Children's Aid Societies to be started in 1985)
Québec	Ministère des Affaires Sociales; Direction des Politiques de services sociaux, Services des politiques à l'enfance et à la famille	X	X	Local government social service centres with Regional Boards

reached similar conclusions.[16] Children's services in Canada require significant changes. Some of the major recommendations are:

1. Children's needs must take precedence over the demands of the service system. Services have developed to address different problems or apply different methods. Frequently children are bounced from service to service, because they have multiple needs and the agency has a limited mandate. Alternately, children are labelled to fit the mandate of the particular agency serving them. A telling example is delinquent, neglected, or disturbed children. Some are served by the correction system, others by child welfare, and others by mental health services even though their needs may be very similar. Some children move through all three systems according to different professional diagnoses of their problems. Children are frequently adrift in the service system, particularly in foster or institutional care. They may be moved to several different placements with little long-range planning not on the basis of their needs but because of the resources and expertise of staff and foster parents.

Several initiatives have been undertaken to deal with these deficiencies. Most provinces have recently developed case-tracking systems to monitor the planning for children in care. Multiservice centres at the local level are another attempt to match needs to services. However, at the heart of this problem is the challenge to professionals to tailor their methods to match client needs and to overcome the fear that if this were done services might expand greatly.

2. Community-based preventive programmes should be expanded and adequately funded. As noted at the beginning of this chapter, the most signigicant expansion in child welfare services has been in the development of home-based services. This has been an important achievement but one that may need careful nurturing to survive in times of budgetary restraint. Services for children in care usually have a more open-ended budget because they are legislated. Budgets for in-home services are usually fixed. When government contracts with voluntary agencies for the care of children, these agencies are only paid as long as they keep the children. There is a built-in incentive to prolong care. Further, an Ontario report states:

> Once residential places had been developed there was a natural tendency to use them rather than to seek more creative and less destructive alternatives. Caseload pressures predisposed a frontline worker to place a problem child in a group home and then turn to other children, even if a more rigorous examination of the first child's needs might have led to an alternative course of action.[17]

In addition, Rino Patti notes the phenomenon of "sunk costs."[18] Expensive buildings, equipment, and a full complement of unionized staff are much more difficult to dislodge than a few streetworkers headquartered in a church basement. More funds are required for in-care services. A review of the child welfare budget in B.C., for example, from 1978 to 1981 indicates that funds for 8,700 children in care demanded at least 65 per cent of the budget while preventive programmes including infant development, day care, rehabilitation, special services, and homemakers for 25,000 children received the remaining 35 per cent.[19] Altogether, many forces conspire to maintain in-care costs and reduce those funds available for more preventive work.

3. Consistent policy-making and funding is required within provinces and at a national level. The services of psychiatrists are free of charge, but counselling at a child guidance centre may cost a fee. Children may be served according to these practical considerations rather than according to their needs. Many different ministries with contradictory policies have been involved in planning children's services but frequently without consultation. Although in some jurisdictions local planning groups include representatives from these various ministries, their co-operative efforts are confounded by divisions at the headquarters level. The policies of the federal government should complement provincial efforts and provide national leadership to improve provincial programmes.

Although proposals have been put forward to implement these recommendations, they have been largely ignored. This inertia is not caused by professional disinterest or management ineptness, but by the lack of a political constituency for child welfare. Most policy-makers in child welfare are far removed in age, economic status, and social experience from the families and children involved in these services. Professionals who lobby on behalf of their clients appear self-protective, and voluntary family agencies risk retribution if they vigorously oppose the policies of the government which funds them. The public is generally unconcerned about child welfare matters unless a poignant case is highlighted in the media. Finally, their relatively small numbers, their poverty, and the highly sensitive nature of their problems make it unlikely that children and families in crisis would or could take political action on their own behalf.

This may be changing as a wider range of families require assistance from the child welfare system. Divorce, missing children, adolescent alcohol and drug abuse, and sexual assault are growing problems which cross economic boundaries. The child welfare system which has served middle class families in the past—babysitters, grandparents, friends, playschools, summer camps, boarding schools, private counsellors, and family allowance and tax deductions—is stretched to capacity as well. Whether this will result in more public pressure to improve government-funded services or the further development of a private child welfare system remains to be seen.

PRACTICE AND CHILD WELFARE

This chapter began with a discussion about differing attitudes towards children and their care. Although these perspectives provide the fuel for public debate on social issues, they also have a direct impact on the practice of child welfare workers. In their day-to-day practice with individual clients, workers must have the ability to deal with the ambiguity of their role and the ponderous process of institutional change in their organization, two direct results of our uncertainty about the purposes of the child welfare system. The last section of the paper will explore the classic conundrums of child welfare practice and offer some suggestions for coping with these demands.

1. How to Speak Softly Yet Carry a Big Stick.

Most child welfare workers regardless of their training and experience find the tasks of balancing their concern for the child, the parents, and the state a challenging one. Not infrequently they must confront parents they may have never met before with complaints about their child-rearing. In the opening minutes of such an interview, workers must convey their respect for the parents, yet face them with the right of the state to intervene, if only briefly, in their private family life. They may also have to cope with their own feelings of anger and helplessness in circumstances where parents have injured, abandoned, sexually assaulted, or exposed their children to serious emotional and physical hazards. In the final analysis, the worker's task is to engage parents in working together to improve the situation for their children with the full knowledge that if they do not, the worker has the authority to remove the child from the home. This threat can seriously jeopardize forthright communication and genuine work. It can be used as unwisely as the parents may have used their authority with their own children, thereby surreptitiously confirming that "might is right."

Workers most successful with this dilemma are those who feel comfortable with their own capabilities and limitations and who are clear about their role and their agency's obligations. Frequently, these workers find that their role with parents involves teaching them about their rights and responsibilities and about the law and policy governing their situation, assisting them to find the necessary legal, medical, and social support and evaluating overall progress in the family. Often workers cannot serve as parental confidants, but they can ensure that parents find capable counsellors. Their role with the children may involve direct counselling and support to assist them in coping with their own guilt about the family breakdown. As Shields and Turner suggest in this volume, many workers report that their best results occur when they are clear about their power and use it with the knowledge that in most cases the child's best interest is served when the parents are able to be the caregivers.

2. *How to See the Forest and the Trees.*

Few workers enter child welfare education or practice without a great deal of compassion for children and strong commitments to make changes for those who are most disadvantaged. After a cursory exposure to practice, it is evident to most that troubled families benefit from help the sooner it is offered, often before they have children and certainly before the apprehension of these children is a likely alternative. In fact, workers know that when they are assisting families to prevent serious problems, there is less chance that their authoritative powers will interfere with the helping process.

However, when economic forces create crises in families and cutbacks in workers, it is likely that preventive approaches will be put aside for the day when the desk is cleared and the phone is silent. The effect is profound for many workers. Some lose their commitment, some become experts in crisis management, and some protect a small portion of their professional practice, often after hours, to start such community initiatives as single parents' support groups, drop-in nurseries, or voluntary grandparents. Overall prevention becomes dependent upon the extraordinary initiatives of a few workers, and this feeling of powerlessness can exact a high toll. Burnout, withdrawal, cynicism, and depression are common to workers and clients alike. Perhaps those workers who continue to practice effectively are those who set and live with modest objectives and who are able to gain reward from the cumulative results of their efforts over time.

3. *How to Rub Your Belly and Pat Your Head.*

The problem of ministering to clients and meeting the administrative demands of an agency have become increasingly problematic for child welfare workers, particularly as management increases its demands for accountability. Often workers who used to have authority to make most of their own decisions must now consult with several levels of management and prepare supporting documentation. Again, this loss of autonomy can have negative consequences, particularly for those whose practice wisdom greatly exceeds that of the final decision-maker. For many workers, their need to help is not satisfied by paperwork, and those who survive best often have excellent case management skills and the ability to use their political strength effectively within the organization.

4. *Old Wine in New Bottles.*

Child welfare workers are concerned about the pragmatic issues of public policy. Some of these are permanent planning for children in long-term care, the rising number of troubled teens unsuitable for foster homes, and possible alternatives to government care for native Indian children. Politicians and the general public, on the other hand, express far more interest in analysing new problems and proposing possible solutions. In the last few years, for example, public attention has focused on child abuse, family violence, pornography, and sexual offences. A child welfare worker commented recently that child welfare problems remain relatively the same under different labels. In the sixties, recalcitrant youth were transients; in the seventies, street kids; in the eighties, teenage prostitutes. In order to attract public and media attention, the problem has to appear novel and somehow threatening to social order. However, implementing and evaluating programmes to address these problems receive scant attention unless some tragedy occurs. The painful suicide of Jimmy Cardinal of Alberta in 1984 is one example.[20] He was apprehended at four years of age and had sixteen foster homes prior to his death at seventeen. A full review of all permanent foster children took place as a result. But this is still an exception. The resources and interest remain concentrated on problem analysis rather than solutions. The challenge for child welfare workers is to find ways to convince the public that the care of the least advantaged children is the urgent concern of the whole community.

Much has been said about these dilemmas, and often they are thought to be the particular problems of one agency or certain workers. But they are not. They are reflections of the fundamental uncertainties in Canadian society about the responsibility of the state, the sanctity of the family, and the value of children. In theory, we care about all three; in practice, we hope that the individual worker counselling the individual family will sort out the priorities and make the right decision.

NOTES

1. T.R. Morrison, "Ways of Seeing Children," in *Children and the State*. ed. S. James Albert. Proceedings of a conference held 16-18 April 1978, at the School of Social Work, Carleton University, Ottawa, Canada.
2. Canadian Council on Children and Youth, *Admittance Restricted: The Child As Citizen in Canada* (Ottawa: The Council, 1978).
3. Ellen Goodman, "The Two-Track Work Ethic," *Victoria Times*, 5 May 1981, p.5.
4. Tom Linton, *Vancouver Sun*, 24 July 1984.
5. M. Valentich and J. Gripton, "Ideological Perspectives on the Sexual Assault of Women," *Social Services Review* 58 (1984): 457.
6. William Ryan, *Blaming the Victim* (Toronto: Random House, 1976), p. 257.
7. *Report on Sexual Offences against Children* (Ottawa: Minister of Supply and Services, 1984), p. 127.
8. "Adolescents Face Stressful Life Changes," a report prepared by the Health Promotion Studies Unit of the Health Promotion Directorate, Health and Welfare Canada, 1983, p. 10.

9. *Juristat*, Statistics Canada, vol. 4, no. 7 (1981): 1.
10. Janet Currie and Fred Pishalski, *Loosening the Fabric* (Victoria: B.C. Association of Social Workers, Southern Vancouver Island Chapter, and the B.C. Childcare Services Association, 1983), p. 5.
11. J.W. Mohr, "The Future of the Family, the Law and the State," Keynote address: The People's Law Conference: The Family and the Law, Ottawa, 9 and 10 April, 1984.
12. Corinne Robertshaw, *Child Protection in Canada* (Ottawa: Health and Welfare Canada, 1981), p. 5.
13. *Royal Commission on Family and Children's Law,* Part 5 (Vancouver: 1975), p. 33.
14. Michael Clague, Robert Dill, Roop Seebaran and Brian Wharf, *Reforming Human Services* (Vancouver: University of B.C. Press, 1984).
15. Quebec Commission of Inquiry on Health and Social Welfare, Report of the Commission, [The Castonguay-Nepveu Report] (Quebec City: Official Publisher, 1970).
16. See Joe Ryant, *A Review of Child Welfare Policies, Programs and Services in Manitoba* (Winnipeg: July, 1975); *Consultation Paper: Children's Services, Past, Present and Future* (Ontario: Minister of Community and Social Services, 1980); *Admittance Restricted: The Child as Citizen in Canada*; The Commission on Education and Learning Disorders in Children, *One Million Children: The Celdic Report* (Toronto: Leonard Crainford, 1970); Mr. Justice J.E. Cavanagh *Board of Review. The Child Welfare System* (Alberta, 1983), Chap. 3, pp. 26-32.
17. *Consultation Paper: Children's Services Past, Present and Future,* p. 14
18. Patti Rino, "Organizational Resistance and Change: The View from Below," *Social Services Review* 8 (1974): 367-383.
19. *Annual Reports*, Ministry of Human Resources, B.C., 1978, 1979, 1980, 1981. Numbers of children in care and children served in their own home varied during this period. Figures given are for 1980 (in-care), 1978 (in-home).
20. R.J. Thomlison, *Case Management Review: Northwest Region, Department of Social Services and Community Health* (Alberta, 1984).

2

CHILD NEGLECT AND ABUSE

H. Philip Hepworth

The Persistence of Apprehension

Today's child welfare services manifest the basic apprehension or rescue philosophy underlying the original child protection legislation introduced at the end of the nineteenth century. There are still many children removed from their homes who spend greater or lesser periods of time in some form of substitute care. However, there are basic resource constraints, namely, workers and placement facilities, which determine how many children can come into care. In recent years there have been more attempts to provide protection and prevention services to children in their own homes and so to avoid or delay the need for apprehension. Nevertheless, the apprehension provisions remain an integral part of child protection legislation, an ultimate sanction, which affects thousands of children and families every year.

Changing Definitions of Neglect and Abuse

In seeking to explain why children are apprehended or taken into care, it is necessary to stress another determining factor or constraint, the existence of legislation and machinery for this purpose. It follows that the actual reasons for apprehension are socially defined and depend on the interpretations of social workers, judges, and other persons who themselves reflect the prevailing values of society. As material standards have risen during the last eighty or ninety years, so views have changed on what constitutes poverty. Similarly, views about child-rearing and child-handling have tended to change. Just as poverty was thought to have disappeared by the mid-1950's (Harrington, 1962), so the more blatant forms of child neglect and malnutrition had apparently disappeared. On closer examination, though, poverty was still found to be a major problem, and the evidence of increasing demand for child welfare services suggested that child neglect was still a problem (Canadian Council on Social Development, 1973). It is, however, necessary to distinguish between the persistence of a social problem and a conclusion that it is getting worse. The focusing of public attention on child abuse during the past two decades has raised precisely this question. Are child neglect and abuse getting worse, or are we seeing a persistent phenomenon more clearly? Or, indeed, are our perceptions changing and becoming more stringent?

There is evidence that public tolerance of violence towards children is falling, partly because of well-publicized cases of children dying after being badly hurt and partly because of a well-orchestrated campaign to make child abuse an issue of public concern (Nelson, 1978). Such publicity does not itself indicate anything about the actual incidence of child abuse, but it does show something about public willingness or unwillingness to tolerate violence towards children. One logical consequence is continued pressure on child welfare services to intervene where child abuse may be present. The overall level of activity of work in the child welfare services has therefore tended to grow or be maintained even in a period when the child population aged 0 - 14 years has fallen from 6.6 million in 1966 to 5.5 million in 1981.

In looking at who the children are who come into care, it is necessary to recognize that demographic trends play a major part in determining the target populations from which the child welfare services draw. Child welfare services grew to keep pace with rising demands from a growing child population during the post-war period. Moreover, the peak years for number of children in care and number of completed adoptions 1969 and 1970 coincided with the peak years for recorded illegitimate births (Hepworth, 1980).

Who are the Children in Care?

Much has been said in recent years about older, more difficult children coming into care and the problems posed in placing such children in appropriate settings. It is almost impossible to know whether the children admitted to care really are more difficult to handle than children admitted twenty or even fifty years ago. Similar assertions were made in the past (Hepworth, 1980, p. 85). Moreover, reduced use of institutional care may mean that more difficult children are cared for in "less secure" settings such as foster and group homes. We do know that demographically the child population has aged since 1959, but this is a function of the baby boom peaking and births falling steadily until the mid-1970's.

We should look at what we do know about the children in care from official statistics. One characteristic worth noting is that more boys than girls are in care, and after allowing for normal sex distribution (51:49) in the general population, boys are overrepresented on average by about 5 per cent.

(See Table 1.) In Ontario this discrepancy holds true for children of unmarried mothers, even though about half of these children are under 5 years. (See Table 2.) It is, however, still possible that boys manifest behavioural problems more frequently than girls and that, especially in the case of delinquency, this accounts for most of the overrepresentation.

The age configuration of children in care does not appear to vary by legal status. In Nova Scotia, where figures are available only for wards, 52.3 per cent of children in care were over the age of fourteen in 1980-1981. In Ontario, in 1980 53.3 per cent of crown wards were over twelve, as were 54.6 per cent of society wards and 52.8 per cent of non-wards. However, in the case of voluntary agreements in Ontario only 31.0 per cent of children were over twelve years, compared with 48.4 per cent under the age of seven years. (See Table 3.) In Saskatchewan, 71.2 per cent of permanent ward admissions in 1980 -1981 were children under the age of five, and of these 263 of 331 were under one year. (See Table 4.) Differences in legislation and procedure account for some apparent discrepancies between provinces. In some cases children relinquished for adoption are never shown as being admitted to care, whereas in Saskatchewan, they are.

But allowing for legal and procedural differences, the dynamics of the child welfare process remain the same. The more permanent the contact between the child and the child welfare services, the older the child is likely to be.

The ethnic and demographic characteristics of particular sub-groups within a province may affect the age distribution of children in care. In the case of admissions to permanent ward status in Saskatchewan, whereas 75.6 per cent of non-Indian children admitted to care were under one year, only 23.5 per cent of Indian and Metis children admitted were under one year. (See Table 4.) At the same time, 62.5 per cent of Saskatchewan children in care were of native origin. (See Table 5.)

If we look briefly at ethnic status, we find that of 276 children of unmarried parents admitted to care in Saskatchewan in 1980-1981, 55 (19.9 per cent) were of native origin. By contrast, of 1,964 children admitted to care for reason of protection, 1,154 (58.8 per cent) were Indian and Metis children. (See Table 6.) The overrepresentation of native children in care in relation to their distribution in the general child population is a major characteristic of services in western Canada and must be borne in mind when attempting to assess the type of placement arrangements made (Johnston, 1983, pp. 37, 55).

Family Size

The Saskatchewan data indicate that 1.3 children per family are involved in protection (i.e. in care) cases; in other words quite a large proportion of admissions involve several children from the same family.

In 1977 the average number of children under the age of 16 in single parent families in Canada was 2.1. This number is higher than the Canadian average for families with children under 25 which was 1.6. The figure of 2.1 children coincides with the number of children involved in protection and prevention cases in Ontario (Hepworth, 1980, p. 42). A Quebec study of all children in care tends to confirm the finding that children in contact with the child welfare services come from families of above average size, 25 per cent from families with two or less children, 46 per cent from families with three to five children, and 29 per cent from families of six or more children. (Québec, 1979, p. 78(b)). The Quebec study also reports that 11 per cent of the children have a deceased father and 12 per cent of children have a deceased mother (Québec, 1979, Annexe Statistique, tableaux B-13-1, B-13-2a).

REASONS FOR ADMISSION TO CARE

As may be seen in Table 7, the primary reason for children being admitted to care in British Columbia in recent years is stated to be parental failure or neglect, over 40 per cent of admissions. The next largest category is desertion or abandonment in about 8 per cent of cases. Other reasons for admission also involve parents, the death of one or both parents, physical or mental illness of parents, the single-parent status of mothers, the failure to provide medical treatment, and the imprisonment of one or both parents. Physical abuse is stated to be the reason for admission in between 2 and 4 per cent of cases. Lack of housing is stated to be the reason in around 1 per cent of cases, but no mention is made of poverty or lack of income.

The characteristics of the children therefore account for only a small proportion of the reasons for admission. Between 4 and 5 per cent are children awaiting adoption placement. Around 1 per cent have physical handicaps, and between 3 and 7 per cent are mentally retarded. Finally, just over 2 per cent are delinquent and 1 per cent are transient.

Parental Incapacity and Vulnerable Families

Thus the predominant reason for children being admitted to care appears to be parental failure or incapacity of one kind or another. But how should such failure or incapacity be judged? Are we dealing with sins or errors of commission or omission? Are we dealing with factors or characteristics quite beyond the parents' ability to control?

As already indicated, there is strong presumptive evidence that many children entering care come from one-parent families. Moreover, we know that single-parent, and especially female-led, families are concentrated in the lowest income quintile (Statistics Canada, 1979, p. 21). We know that about 20 per cent of children in care are of native origin and that a high proportion of native people, whether status or non-status Indian or Métis, are in receipt of social assistance. In the case of status Indians, there is also documented evidence of poor housing conditions, one in three Indian families being estimated to live in crowded conditions in 1977 (Canada, Indian and Northern Affairs Canada, 1980, p. 30). What emerges from the available data is a picture of vulnerable families buffeted by cumulative vicissitudes.

The Quebec study of all children in care tends to confirm the picture of family vulnerability, with 11 per cent of fathers and 12 per cent of mothers dead and the whereabouts of only 56 per cent of fathers and 69 per cent of mothers known (Quebec, 1979b, p. 107). Parental behaviour or characteristics were said to be the reason for 53 per cent of the children being in care (ibid., p. 86). At the same time, the fact of over half the children having siblings also in care, and this *not* being linked to delinquency or abuse, leads the Quebec researchers to the following conclusions. "We are able to deduce that the children most often placed also have more brothers or sisters in care and come from families more damaged or with multiple problems" (ibid., p. 80, author's translation). In Quebec then, as in British Columbia, parental behaviour, characteristics, or circumstances appear to play a major role in the reasons for admission to or being in care.

Further analysis of the Quebec data on children in care and the British Columbia data on admissions to care suggests that in at least two-thirds and possibly over three-quarters of cases, it is parental factors which are the predominant reason for substitute care being provided. The behaviour or condition of the children themselves are secondary reasons, and even so it is parental inability to care for a child with mental or physical handicaps or to cope with misbehaviour which dictate the admission of children to care. (See Tables 8 and 9.)

But while parental factors or circumstances are the primary reason why children are in care, many of the circumstances identified appear to be beyond parental control. At the same time, terms such as serious neglect, abandonment, and moral, mental, and physical danger raise a number of questions not readily answerable using the available data.

Protection and Prevention in Ontario

The protection and prevention statistics for Ontario illustrate the extent to which child welfare problems are perpetuated over time. Of 26,429 cases opened in 1980, 8,308 were reopened cases, the latter involving 16,131 children. What these Ontario figures also show is the prevalence of child neglect (as defined by contact with the child welfare services) in the community. The 102,177 children involved in protection and prevention cases in 1980 represented 5.3 per cent of the child population aged 0-14 years inclusive. This proportion does not include children of unmarried mothers receiving services during the year, children remaining in care, or the 46,165 cases receiving "brief" service. (See Table 10.)

Such large numbers of children would not be so alarming, if the primary responsibility and resources of the child welfare services were supportive and preventive in nature. But most of the child welfare involvement arises because children are or are potentially at risk of neglect. At the same time, the services are limited in the type or quantity of material help they can give. Consequently, much child welfare work boils down to visits of inspection to see that everything is going well in the child's home. Certainly, such visits can be supportive and helpful, but the powers of apprehension resting with the social worker and the courts may simply add to the tension and stress already existing in the home.

Both child neglect and child abuse are socially defined phenomena, and how, and whether, particular cases come to be identified or counted is a function of complex interactions between social mores, legislative enactments, the structure and operations of such institutions as the courts and child welfare agencies, the level of staffing and resources available, and many other factors. Inadequate or inexact as the resulting incidence and prevalence data may be, we are able to learn a great deal about Canadian child welfare services and about the children who are in care or who are receiving protective and preventive services by closely examining the records and reports which are available.

Child Neglect and Children in Care

As a percentage of the child population, there were more children in care in 1971-72 (1.44 per cent) than in 1961-62 (0.94 per cent). Two factors appear to account for this occurrence: illegitimate births continued to rise until 1970, and the child welfare services expanded to cope with the demands arising from the growing child population. After 1971-72 the percentage of children in care stayed at higher levels than those prevailing throughout the 1960's. Generally, the child welfare services continued to grow during the early 1970's at a time when the child population began to decline (Hepworth, 1980, 1982).

Ontario has consistently shown a higher level of activity in terms of children entering and leaving care than is apparent in other provinces. At the same time, it has consistently had the lowest proportion of its child population in care (Hepworth, 1980, pp. 76, 77, 124). The level of activity is determined at least in part by the level of staffing. Ontario child welfare positions increased by 71 per cent between 1966 and 1980, and social workers alone by 58 per cent (Hepworth, 1982, pp. 36-38). This development occurred against a background of comprehensive geographic coverage of the province by children's aid societies.

Between 1960 and 1980 the proportion of children admitted to care in Ontario after previously receiving protection and prevention services in their own homes has steadily risen from 48.8 per cent to 75.6 per cent. In addition, a number of children of unmarried mothers are admitted to care (i.e., relinquished) after their mothers have received services. Consequently, the majority of children are admitted to care after some kind of systematic contact between the services and the children has already taken place, though the extent to which admissions to care can then be called "planned" is not apparent.

One other salient feature of the Ontario child welfare services is the steady growth of the protection and prevention services in the child's home. The number of children involved in these cases has risen from 54,086 in 1961 to 102,177 in 1980. As a proportion of the child population aged 0-14 years inclusive, these numbers represent an increase from 2.7 per cent to 5.3 per cent. The available figures do not permit an analysis of the extent to which children recur in successive years, though children in new cases represent about one-third of all children receiving these services in any one year. (See Table 11.)

The average number of children involved per protection and prevention case has fallen from 2.85 in 1961 to 2.11 in 1980. In new cases, the fall has been from 2.61 to 1.88, and in reopened cases, from 3.04 to 1.94. As is apparent in these figures, on average more children per case are involved in reopened cases than in new cases. (See Table 14.)

In conclusion, as a proportion of the child population aged 0-14 years, children in care at the end of the year in Ontario were at the same level in 1980 as they were in 1961 after falling slightly in the mid-1970's. By contrast, children receiving protection and prevention services in their own homes have almost doubled in number and proportion in the same period. At the same time, the average number of children involved in each protection case has steadily fallen. (See Table 11). The evidence available for other provinces supports the same broad picture, though there are interesting and important differences between provinces.

The Ontario protection and prevention figures have shown the tendency in recent years for the child welfare services to have contact with a higher proportion of the child population. On preventive grounds there is little reason other than obvious resource constraints why this trend should not continue. Something similar appears to have happened with child abuse, which ought to be regarded as a sub-category of child neglect.

CHILD ABUSE: PROBLEMS OF DEFINITION

Child abuse is no easier to define than child neglect, and the provinces do vary in this respect. Over the period 1971 to 1981, the number of verified child abuse cases in Manitoba, for example, rose from 49 in 1971 to 330 in 1981, but in each of the eleven years the majority of children involved were left in their own homes or returned with agency supervision. In a small number of cases there was temporary loss of parental rights, and in an even smaller number there was permanent loss. During the same period the number of children in care in Manitoba fell from 5,087 in 1970 to 3,621 in 1980. The main point to be made here is that, even with and after verification, child abuse constitutes a small sub-sample of child neglect cases, which are themselves subject to variable definition. Moreover, serious though child abuse is, in only a minority of cases was removal of children from their own homes thought necessary by the courts and child welfare services in Manitoba.

There is a similar picture in Alberta where the child protection registry for the period 1974 to 1978 received all child neglect and child abuse reports. (See Table 12.) However, in 1979 Alberta changed the way it coded neglect and abuse reports and has since shown all abuse reports, specifying the number of children involved, rather than only verified cases as had been the case previously (Alberta Social Services and Community Health, 1981, p. 5). As a consequence, the numbers shown are the children involved in alleged cases of abuse, and do not necessarily reflect any basic change in the prevalence of child abuse, but they do show changes in the rate at which different types of alleged neglect or abuse are reported. (See Table 13.)

A similar picture on the reporting of child abuse appears in Quebec after the establishment of the Comité de la protection de la jeunesse in 1975. In the three years 1976, 1977, and 1978 the number of reports retained after investigation was 1,902, 2,295, and 2,781 respectively; these represented 36.6, 25.0 and 24.0 per cent respectively of all requests for aid received. (See Table 14.)

Revised procedures led to a different statistical picture being presented for Quebec in 1979. The directors of child protection (les directeurs de la protection de la jeunesse) in each Social Service Centre (C.S.S.) were required to report all cases of mistreated children received to the Comité de la protection de la jeunesse. Consequently, the 4,177, 3,697, and 2,999 reports made in 1979, 1980, and 1981 respectively were more akin to the previous totals of aid requested, though with some screening out of obviously inappropriate cases. The change in reporting procedure led to some increase in the proportion of apparent sexual abuse cases and a fall in the proportion of neglect cases. However, the key feature is the majority of cases in which physical abuse is involved. The other fact of some note is that 83.3, 88.4, and 90.9 per cent of cases had not been reported to the comité previously. (See Table 15.) Just over a quarter of reports involved children under six years old, and a similar proportion children over fourteen. (See Table 16.)

The change in reporting procedures in Quebec requires careful interpretation of the available figures. Reporting rates between the regions (C.S.S.) and the comité varied widely in relation to population. It is possible that the same problem of reporting to a central point has occurred in Quebec as it did in Ontario a few years ago; fourteen social service centres have to report to the comité, and the variations in reporting appear to reflect underreporting in rural areas and overreporting in urban areas; this may reflect the extent to which the service network is developed in Quebec, rather than say anything about the underlying incidence of child neglect and abuse. Other data for Quebec show that larger families tend to occur in rural areas (Quebec, 1979, p. 110(b)). Also, the proportion of children in care who are orphans is higher in rural areas than in other parts of Quebec (Quebec, 1979, Annexe Statistique (a), A-49, A-50). On average 53 per cent of children in care have at least one brother or sister also in care, and again this proportion is higher in rural areas (Quebec, 1979, Annexe Statistique, (a) tableau A-57).

Some of the difficulties of accurately verifying and recording child abuse cases are apparent in the 1978 Annual Report of the British Columbia Ministry of Human Resources. In a table headed "Cases of Probable Child Abuse — A Comparison," a steady increase in the number of substantiated child abuse cases is shown from 122 in 1973 to 578 in 1978. (See Tables 17, 18.) A footnote indicates that unsubstantiated child abuse and child neglect cases were included in earlier figures published for 1973 and 1974 (British Columbia, Ministry of Human Resources, Annual Report, 1978, p. L. 33). Notwithstanding this revision, the heading of "probable child abuse" indicates some uncertainty that the "substantiated" figures accurately reflect a discrete and measurable phenomenon. A change in the forms used for reporting in January 1978 is said in the 1980 Annual Report of the same department to have led to more reports being received, 605 in 1978 (revised from the previous figure), 791 in 1979, and 987 in 1980 (British Columbia, 1980-81, p. 30). The figure for 1981 is 1,286. (See Tables 17, 18, 19.) At the same time, the 1980 report notes that notwithstanding receiving more reports of child abuse or neglect cases, fewer children needed to be admitted to care, and fewer deaths resulted from abuse or neglect (British Columbia, 1980, p. 32).

It is obviously necessary to avoid placing too much reliance on recorded child abuse figures. It is certainly true that most provinces record an increase in the number of reported child abuse cases during the 1970's. But most provinces only introduced child abuse registers during the same period, so that an apparent increase in cases may only reflect a new set of reporting procedures being implemented. Moreover, some provinces have not been satisfied with what was being recorded and have either further modified their procedures or changed the criteria being used; this almost certainly accounts for an apparent surge in sexual abuse cases, though this does not gainsay the fact the general public may feel freer than in the past to report cases of suspected abuse or neglect.

It is obviously extremely difficult to separate child neglect and child abuse. Moreover, it is not particularly useful to do so. Child neglect is a much larger phenomenon than child abuse, and in concentrating resources on the latter, there is a risk of diverting attention away from the bigger problem. We come back at this point to the question of whether the real issue is one of parental capacity or incapacity to care for children or whether we are dealing with a societal issue, which can only be dealt with at the societal level. Moreover, there is little if any documented evidence of the use made of child abuse registers, how effective they are in helping trace children at risk, and how confidential they are. In the case of Ontario, a person thought to be an abuser can have his or her name on the register for 25 years. There are obvious serious human rights issues involved here when the circumstances giving rise to the original report may have been extremely short-lived and when, as argued here, the actual determination of what constitutes abuse is so difficult to make (Frank and Foote, 1982; Schwartz, 1977; New Society, 1980).

APPREHENSION VERSUS PREVENTION

In recent years the pendulum has swung uneasily between more or less coercive powers in the child welfare services. Cost has always been a concern since child welfare services were started, and hence there has always been a corresponding reluctance or inability to bring children into care. For many years the designation "free homes" was used to describe foster situations where no cost was involved. Maintenance payments for children in foster homes were slow to be introduced and usually lagged behind the real cost of keeping a child. Demographic trends brought increased demands for services after 1945, and this brought a steady expansion in the services and a new emphasis on professional practice. Professional social workers were imbued in the main with an ideology that the preservation of the family unit ought to be a primary objective of good child welfare practice. Such a view coincided with the desire of governments to limit expenditures, and, consequently, protection and prevention services to children in their own homes became a major feature of the child welfare services.

Nevertheless, the growing number of children relinquished for adoption in the period up to the early 1970's brought a new emphasis on the creation of new family units. When the supply of babies for adoption diminished, the possibility of placing for adoption older children in care, or those with special needs, was explored. To do this, children had to be full legal wards of the child welfare services, and thus a situation developed where, on the one hand, more children were "supported" in their own families and, on the other, more children in care were placed in adoptive homes wherever possible. On the face of it, such developments have made sense, but how beneficial the results have been is not always apparent. Expanded child welfare services have "detected" more children in apparent need of protection, but traditional modes of operation have not changed radically. Thus, the ultimate sanction of apprehension has remained in force, and the resources available to provide adequate support for children in their own homes have remained in short supply.

A new way of looking at the rights and needs of children has raised serious questions about the justification for, and efficacy of, radical child welfare interventions. At the same time, public concern about child abuse has brought more pressures on child welfare agencies to take children into care and to retain them there. Thus there are multiple contradictions besetting the child welfare services when the lack of resources, the need to economize, and the desire to preserve the family unit coincide on the one hand, and, on the other, poor material conditions, suspected neglect and abuse, and public opinion combine to suggest that apprehension is necessary (Ontario, 1982).

There are parallels with other social control agencies such as the police and the courts. Contacts with such agencies carry their own risks; probation orders and suspended sentences, when breached, can soon lead to imprisonment. So too the coercive powers of the child welfare services may bring results not desired or intended. It is a sad fact that many children graduate from child welfare services to training schools and even ultimately to prison; this is particularly true for native children (Native Council of Canada, 1978).

Nor should it be supposed that the road for children receiving foster care or being adopted is always smooth. Rather, the radical intervention in children's lives necessitated by poor family circumstances may simply compound previous difficulties and add further hurts to those already sustained. We ought not to confuse motivation to do the best for children with what actually transpires for them. Certainly, what is sometimes achieved is the best that could be hoped for in the circumstances, but there is accumulating evidence that children receiving substitute care know that for them this is second best, and sometimes it is not even as good as that.

The dilemma may be insoluble, but an attempt should be made to rethink the philosophy on which child welfare services are based. There have been major social and demographic changes since child welfare services were first introduced. In the early years of the century, single-parent or parentless families resulted in the main from the death of parents. Today single-parent families are often the result of personal choice, separation or divorces. Certainly some of the original reasons for having child welfare services persist, but there may be fewer justifications for severing family ties on a permanent basis. Put more positively, there is a strong case for putting more resources into an array of family support services and rendering help as circumstances warrant. In fact, child welfare services are in contact with so many children and families that support services provided to all families may be the only effective alternative.

REFERENCES

Alberta Department of Social Services and Community Health. *Annual Report*, 1979-80. Edmonton, 1981.

Allen, His Honour Judge H. Ward, *Judicial Inquiry into the Care of Kim Anne Popen by the Children's Aid Society of the City of Sarnia and the County of Lambton, Vols I - IV.* Toronto: Queen's Printer, 1982.

British Columbia. Ministry of Human Resources. *Annual Reports, Statistical Reports and Tables, 1976/77-1980/81.*

Canada. *Canada Assistance Plan.* 1966

Canada. Indian and Northern Affairs Canada. *Indian Conditions: A Survey.* Ottawa, 1980.

Canada. Statistics Canada. Consumer Income and Expenditure Division. *Single-parent families in Canada, 1977.* Ottawa: Minister of Supply and Services, 1979.

Canadian Council on Social Development. *Guaranteed Annual Income: An Integrated Approach.* Ottawa: The Council, 1973.

Frank, A.W. III, and C.E. Foote. "Formulating Children's troubles for organizational intervention." *Canadian Review of Sociology and Anthropology* 19 (1982): 111-122.

Hagan, J., and J. Leon. "Rediscovering Delinquency: Social History, Political Ideology and the Sociology of Law." *American Sociological Review* 42 (1977): 587-598.

Harrington, M. *The Other America — Poverty in the United States.* New York: Macmillan, 1962.

Hepworth, H.P. "Family Policy in Canada: The Case of Mothers' Allowances." *SPAN Newsletter,* June 1981.

———*Foster Care and Adoption in Canada.* Ottawa: Canadian Council on Social Development, 1980.

———"Trends and Comparisons in Canadian Child Welfare Services." Paper prepared at the First Conference on Provincial Social Welfare Policy, University of Calgary, 5-7 May 1982.

Johnston, Patrick. *Native Children and the Child Welfare System.* Ottawa: Canadian Council on Social Development, 1983.

Jones, A., and Rutman, L. *In the Children's Aid.* Toronto: University of Toronto Press, 1981.

J.S. Leon. "The Development of Canadian Juvenile Justice: A Background for Reform." *Osgood Hall Law Journal* 15 (1977): 71-105.

Native Council of Canada. Crime and Justice Commission. *Méetis and Non-Status Indians.* Ottawa: Supply and Services Canada, 1978.

Nelson, B.J. "Setting the Public Agenda: The Case of Child Abuse." in J.V. May and A.B. Wildavsky, eds. *The Policy Cycle.* Beverly Hills: Sage, 1978.

New Society. "Use or Abuse?" 28 February 1980, p. 437.

Ontario. Ministry of Community and Social Services. *The Children's Act: A Consultation Paper.* Toronto: The Ministry, 1982.

Platt, A.M., *The Child Savers: The Invention of Delinquency,* 2d. ed. Chicago: University of Chicago Press, 1977.

Québec. Ministère des Affaires sociales. *Opéeration 30000, annexe statistique.* Octobre 1979 (a).

———*Opéeration 30000, rapport final.* Octobre 1979 (b).

Schwartz, D.A. "A Reappraisal of New York's Child Abuse Law: How Far Have We Come?" *Columbia Journal of Law and Social Problems* 13 (1977): 118.

Splane, R.B. *Social Welfare in Ontario, 1791-1898.* Toronto: University of Toronto Press, 1965.

TABLE 1

BOYS IN CARE AS PERCENTAGE OF ALL CHILDREN IN CARE
OF PROVINCIAL CHILD WELFARE SERVICES 1977/78-1980/81

	1977/78	*1978/79*	*1979/80*	*1980/81*
Newfoundland	56.8	56.4	55.7	—
Nova Scotia [1]	56.4	56.6	57.7	56.8
Ontario	56.6	55.6	55.6	55.8
Saskatchewan [2]	51.8	50.1	48.5	52.9

Source: Provincial departments of Social Services, *Annual Reports* and unpublished statistics.
1. Wards only.
2. Permanent ward admissions.

TABLE 2

CHILDREN OF UNMARRIED MOTHERS IN CARE IN ONTARIO
BY AGE AND SEX 1977-1980

	1977		*1978*		*1979*		*1980*	
Total children in care	2,715	100.0	2,665	100.0	2,771	100.0	2,562	100.0
Children in care by age								
Under 1 year	866	31.9	781	29.3	844	30.5	815	31.8
1 and 2 years	305	11.2	376	14.1	432	15.6	337	13.2
3 and 4 years	175	6.5	174	6.5	189	6.8	188	7.3
Total under 5 years	1,346	49.6	1,331	49.9	1,465	52.9	1,340	52.3
5 to 12 years	621	22.9	613	23.0	607	21.9	549	21.5
13 to 17 years	669	24.6	638	24.0	614	22.1	570	22.2
18 years and over	79	2.9	83	3.1	85	3.1	103	4.0
Male	1,557	57.3	1,492	56.0	1,524	55.0	1,426	55.7
Female	1,158	42.7	1,173	44.0	1,247	45.0	1,136	44.3

Source:

Ontario, Ministry of Community and Social Services, unpublished annual statistics.

TABLE 3

CHILDREN IN CARE IN ONTARIO BY AGE AND STATUS,
DECEMBER 31, 1977-1980

	1977		1978		1979		1980	
Voluntary Agreements	No.	%	No.	%	No.	%	No.	%
0- 6 years	702	5.3	745	5.4	793	5.6	667	5.1
7-12 years	290	2.2	301	2.2	347	2.5	283	2.2
13-17 years	536	4.1	587	4.2	618	4.4	419	3.2
18 years and over	—	—	—	—	11	0.1	8	0.1
Total	1,528	11.6	1,633	11.8	1,769	12.6	1,377	10.6
Non Wards								
0- 6 years	588	4.5	606	4.4	578	4.1	597	4.6
7-12 years	210	1.6	235	1.7	248	1.8	210	1.6
13-17 years	361	2.7	351	2.5	357	2.5	300	2.3
18 years and over	557	4.3	562	4.1	589	4.2	601	4.6
Total	1,716	13.1	1,754	12.7	1,772	12.6	1,708	13.1
Society Wards								
0- 6 years	788	6.0	995	7.2	892	6.4	713	5.5
7-12 years	801	6.1	888	6.5	767	5.5	720	5.5
13-17 years	1,537	11.7	1,898	13.7	1,863	13.3	1,724	13.2
Total	3,126	23.8	3,781	27.4	3,522	25.2	3,157	24.2
Crown Wards								
0- 6 years	1,170	8.9	1,259	9.1	1,472	10.5	1,432	11.0
7-12 years	1,721	13.1	1,672	12.1	1,725	12.3	1,738	13.3
13-17 years	3,870	29.5	3,715	26.9	3,744	26.7	3,593	27.6
18 years and over	—	—	—	—	4	0.1	28	0.2
Total	6,761	51.5	6,646	48.1	6,945	49.6	6,791	52.1
Total children in care	13,131	100.0	13,814	100.0	14,008	100.0	13,033	100.0

Source:
Ontario, Ministry of Community and Social Services, unpublished annual statistics.

TABLE 4

ADMISSIONS TO PERMANENT WARD STATUS BY AGE, SEX AND ETHNIC ORIGIN IN SASKATCHEWAN IN 1980/81

	Indian-Métis				Other				All Origins		
	Male	Female	Sub-total No.	%	Male	Female	Sub-total No.	%	Male	Female	Total
Under 1 year	18	22	40	23.5	117	106	223	75.6	135	128	263
1- 4 years	29	21	50	29.4	9	9	18	6.1	38	30	68
5- 9 years	19	17	36	21.2	6	7	13	4.4	25	24	49
10-14 years	18	13	31	18.2	15	11	26	8.8	33	24	57
15 years and over	7	6	13	7.7	8	7	15	5.1	15	13	28
Total	91	79	170	100.0	155	140	295	100.0	246	219	465

Source: Saskatchewan, Department of Social Services, unpublished statistics.

TABLE 5

ETHNIC STATUS OF ALL CHILDREN IN CARE IN SASKATCHEWAN, 1977/78-1980/81

	Treaty Indian		Indian		Métis		Sub-total		Other		Total	
Year	No.	%	No.	%	No.	%	No.	%	No.	%	No.	%
1977/78	278	10.6	517	19.6	750	28.4	1,545	58.6	1,093	41.4	2,638	100.0
	Status Indian (confirmed)		Status Indian (unconfirmed)		Métis and non-status Indian							
1978/79	469	19.6	303	12.7	669	27.9	1,441	60.2	954	39.8	2,395	100.0
1979/80	564	23.8	247	10.4	629	26.5	1,440	60.7	932	39.3	2,372	100.0
1980/81	548	25.3	170	7.9	636	29.3	1,354	62.5	811	37.5	2,165	100.0

Source: Saskatchewan, Department of Social Services, unpublished statistics.

TABLE 6

SELECTED STATISTICS ON THE ADMISSION OF INDIAN, MÉTIS, AND OTHER
CHILDREN TO CARE IN SASKATCHEWAN BY THE DEPARTMENTS OF SOCIAL
SERVICES AND OF NORTHERN SASKATCHEWAN IN 1977/78-1980/81

	1977/78		*1978/79*		*1979/80*		*1980/81*	
	No.	*%*	*No.*	*%*	*No.*	*%*	*No.*	*%*
(a) Indian Children								
Unmarried Parents	18	3.1	25	3.6	18	2.6	25	3.2
Protection	569	96.9	673	96.4	682	97.4	764	96.8
Total	587	100.0	698	100.0	700	100.0	789	100.0
	(26.5%)		(33.0%)		(34.6%)		(35.2%)	
Métis Children								
Unmarried Parents	34	6.3	32	7.7	27	6.5	30	7.1
Protection	502	93.7	385	92.3	386	93.5	390	92.9
Total	536	100.0	417	100.0	413	100.0	420	100.0
	(24.2%)		(19.7%)		(20.4%)		(18.8%)	
Other Children								
Unmarried Parents	303	27.7	264	26.4	247	27.2	221	21.4
Protection	792	72.3	737	73.6	662	72.8	810	78.6
Total	1,095	100.0	1,001	100.0	909	100.0	1,031	100.0
	(49.3%)		(47.3%)		(45.0%)		(46.0%)	
Total admissions to care								
(b) Type of admission								
Unmarried Parents	355	16.0	321	15.2	292	14.4	276	12.3
Protection	1,863	84.0	1,795	84.8	1,730	85.6	1,964	87.7
Total	2,218	100.0	2,116	100.0	2,022	100.0	2,240	100.0
(c) Permanent Ward Admissions								
Indian/Métis								
Male	117	20.6	96	17.7	71	15.2	91	19.6
Female	97	17.0	111	20.6	96	20.5	79	17.0
Other								
Male	178	31.2	175	32.3	156	33.3	155	33.3
Female	178	31.2	159	29.4	145	31.0	140	30.1
Total	570	100.0	541	100.0	468	100.0	465	100.0

Source:
Saskatchewan, Department of Social Services, unpublished statistics.

TABLE 7

REASONS FOR ADMISSION TO CARE OF SUPERINTENDENT OF CHILD WELFARE
AND CHILD WELFARE AGENCIES IN BRITISH COLUMBIA

	1977/78		*1978/79*		*1979/80*	
	No.	*%*	*No.*	*%*	*No.*	*%*
Physical Abuse	125	2.8	106	2.3	203	4.1
Parent failure/neglect	1,933	43.0	2,191	47.6	2,329	46.8
Desertion or abandonment	382	8.5	349	7.6	408	8.2
Emotional disturbances needing treatment	205	4.6	149	3.2	137	2.8
One parent deceased	37	0.8	44	1.0	70	1.4
Sole parent deceased	155	3.4	118	2.6	138	2.8
Parental illness, mental	130	2.9	146	3.2	117	2.4
Parental illness, physical	159	3.5	154	3.3	250	5.0
Awaiting adoption placement	214	4.8	241	5.2	202	4.1
Removed from adoption placement	—	—	8	0.2	5	0.1
Awaiting permanent plan	70	1.6	74	1.6	81	1.6
Rehabilitation plan for parents	225	5.0	197	4.3	252	5.1
Physical handicap	47	1.0	41	0.9	49	0.9
Mental retardation	322	7.2	205	4.4	164	3.3
Delinquent behaviour (Juvenile Delinquents' Act only)	115	2.6	107	2.3	109	2.2
Transient[1]	38	0.8	99	2.2	58	1.2
Unmarried mothers	64	1.4	53	1.2	49	0.9
Parental failure to provide needed medical treatment or prevention	33	0.7	28	0.6	17	0.3
Parent or parents imprisoned	51	1.1	52	1.1	61	1.2
Inability of family to provide needed education or training	78	1.7	78	1.7	78	1.6
Requested by other provinces	92	2.0	138	3.0	126	2.5
Lack of housing for family	25	0.6	24	0.5	75	1.5
Total	4,500	100.0	4,602	100.0	4,978	100.0

Source: British Columbia, Ministry of Human Resources, *Annual Reports 1977/1978-1979/80,* Statistical Tables.

1. Children in care seven days or less no longer counted.

TABLE 8

DISTRIBUTION OF CHILDREN IN OPERATION 30,000 ACCORDING TO
THE DESCRIPTION OF THE CURRENT SITUATION
OF THE CHILD AND HIS FAMILY

	No.	*%*
Physical abuse/Sévices physiques	698	2.3
Sexual abuse/Abus sexuels	241	0.8
Serious neglect/Négligence grave	2,451	8.0
Parents deceased/Parents décèdés	1,175	3.9
Abandonment/Abandon de fait	4,735	15.5
Parental irresponsibility over school attendance/ Irresponsabilité des parents vis-à-vis la fréquentation scolaire	537	1.8
Unsuitable work/Travail disproportionné	17	0.1

Sexual exploitation/Exploitation sexuelle	21	0.1
Sale and distribution of drugs/Vente et distribution de drogue	29	0.1
Situation of moral danger/Situation de danger moral	432	1.4
Situation of physical danger/Situation de danger physique	945	3.1
Danger to child's mental and emotional development/ Situation de danger pour le développement mental et émotif de l'enfant	4,296	14.1
Unsuitable behaviour marked by delinquency/ Comportements disfonctionnels marqués par des agirs délinquants	2,167	7.1
Inability of child to function in family/ Incapacité de fonctionnement de l'enfant dans sa famille	1,387	4.6
Inability of child to function in school/ Incapacité de fonctionnement de l'enfant à l'école	284	0.9
Inability of child to function with peers and in community/ Incapacité de fonctionnement de l'enfant avec ses pairs et le voisinage	115	0.4
Running away/Fugue	137	0.5
School absenteeism/Absentéisme scolaire	115	0.4
Difficulty of family setting to meet specific needs of physically handi- capped child/Difficulté du milieu familiale de satisfaire aux besoins spécifiques de l'enfant handicapé physique	555	1.8
Difficulty of family setting to meet specific needs of mentally handi- capped child/Difficulté du milieu familial de satisfaire aux besoins spécifiques de l'enfant handicapé mental	1,877	6.2
Temporary difficulty to care for child due to physical or mental illness of one or both parents/Difficulté temporaire de s'occuper de l'enfant par suite de la maladie physique ou mentale de l'un ou l'autre des deux parents	859	2.8
Temporary difficulty of surviving parent to care for child due to death of other parent/Difficulté temporaire du parent survivant de s'occuper de l'enfant par suite du décès de l'autre parent	719	2.4
Temporary difficulty of parent with custody to care for child following separation/Difficulté temporaire du parent ayant la garde de l'enfant de s'en occuper à la suite d'une séparation conjugale de fait	695	2.3
Temporary difficulty of parent with custody to care for child following divorce or legal separation/Difficulté temporaire du parent ayant la garde de l'enfant de s'en occuper à la suite d'un divorce ou d'une séparation légale	936	3.1
Permanent inability of family setting to care for child due to a physical or mental illness or the imprisonment of one or both parents/ Incapacité permanente du milieu familiale de s'occuper de l'enfant par suite d'une maladie physique ou mentale ou de l'incarcération de l'un des parents ou des deux parents	1,764	5.8
Long-term difficulties in parent-child relationships/ Difficultés chroniques dans les relations parents-enfants	1,548	5.1
Inaccessibility of community resources/ Inaccessibilité des ressources communautaires	83	0.3
Other factors		
Inaccessibility of health services/Inaccessibilité des services de santé	24	0.1
Inaccessibility of school services/Inaccessibilité des services scolaires	323	1.1
Information missing/Information manquantes	1,173	3.9
Sub-total		5.1
Total	30,338	100.0

Source: Québec, Ministère des Affaires sociales, Opération 30000, annexe statistique, Octobre 1979, Tableau A-62.

TABLE 9

REASONS FOR BEING IN CARE IN BRITISH COLUMBIA
AND QUÉBEC IN PERCENTAGES

Parental Factors	British Columbia	Québec
Physical Abuse	4.1	2.3
Sexual Abuse	—	0.8
Sex Exploitation	—	0.1
Serious neglect	46.8	8.0
Abandonment	8.2	15.5
Moral, mental, physical danger	—	18.6
Parental illness/imprisonment	8.6	8.6
School attendance (parental failure)	1.6	1.8
Unmarried mother	0.9	—
Inability to care due to separation/divorce	—	5.4
Rehabilitation of parents	5.1	—
Death of one or both parents	4.2	6.3
Sub-total	79.5	67.4
Behaviour or Condition of Children		
Sale of drugs	—	0.1
Delinquency	2.2	7.1
Inability to function in family	—	9.7
Inability to function in school	—	0.9
Inability to function in community	—	0.4
Running away/transient	1.2	0.5
School absenteeism	—	0.4
Unsuitable work	—	0.1
Physical handicap	0.9	1.8
Mental handicap	3.3	6.2
Emotional disturbance	2.8	—
Sub-total	10.4	27.2
Other Factors		
Lack of community, health, education services	—	1.5
Lack of housing	1.5	—
Requested by provinces	2.5	—
Information missing	3.9	—
Subtotal	4.0	5.4
	100.0	100.0

Source:
British Columbia, Ministry of Human Resources, *Annual Report 1979/80.* Québec, Ministère des Affaires sociales, Opération 30000, annexe statistique, octobre 1979, Tableau A-62.

TABLE 10

PROTECTION WORK CASELOAD IN ONTARIO CHILD WELFARE SERVICES IN 1977-80

	1977		1978		1979		1980	
	No. of Cases	Children Involved	No. of Cases	Children Involved	No. of Cases	Children Involved	No. of Cases	Children Involved
Carried over	16,050	36,599	18,226	39,531	20,696	42,677	22,060	43,851
New cases	14,023	28,290	16,631	32,270	17,697	33,685	18,121	34,095
Reopened cases that were opened in former years	7,244	16,190	8,223	17,766	8,308	15,938	8,308	16,131
Children transferred to own home from care of society	—	7,131	—	7,261	—	7,580	—	8,100
Total open cases during year	37,317	88,209	43,080	96,768	46,481	99,880	48,489	102,177
Children transferred to in-care service from protection	—	8,450	—	9,219	—	9,219	—	8,953
Cases closed	19,091	40,028	22,384	44,852	24,422	46,791	27,195	52,104
Total cases and children at end of year	18,226	39,731	20,696	42,697	22,059	43,870	21,294	41,120
Service to unmarried parents' cases	2,447	—	2,148	—	—	—	—	—
Brief services	—	—	32,990	—	35,976	—	46,165	—

Source: Ontario, Ministry of Community and Social Services, unpublished annual statistics.

TABLE 11

PROTECTION AND PREVENTION CASELOAD IN ONTARIO BY NUMBER OF CHILDREN PER CASE, 1977-1980

Year	New Cases	Number of Children	Number of Children per Case	Re-opened Cases	Number of Children	Number of Children per Case	All open Cases	Number of Children	Number of Children per Case
1961	8,170	21,332	2.61	2,409	7,332	3.04	18,969	54,086	2.85
1966	11,579	30,584	2.64	3,680	11,260	3.06	23,387	67,819	2.90
1971	10,863	26,584	2.45	5,880	16,205	2.76	28,323	77,956	2.75
1976	12,320	25,591	2.08	6,480	15,175	2.34	34,196	83,056	2.43
1977	14,023	28,290	2.02	7,244	16,190	2.23	37,317	88,209	2.36
1978	16,631	32,270	1.94	8,223	17,766	2.16	43,080	96,768	2.25
1979	17,697	33,685	1.90	8,308	15,938	1.92	46,481	99,880	2.15
1980	18,121	34,095	1.88	8,308	16,131	1.94	48,489	102,177	2.11

Source: Ontario, Ministry of Community and Social Services, unpublished annual statistics.

TABLE 12

NUMBER OF REPORTS RECEIVED BY CHILD PROTECTION REGISTRY IN ALBERTA, 1974-1978

	1974		1975		1976		1977		1978	
	No.	%	No.	%	No.	%	No.	%	No.	%
Child Neglect	4,839	91.6	4,812	92.9	5,185	95.6	6,454	96.5	8,108	96.8
Child Abuse	446	8.4	369	7.1	237	4.3	232	3.5	270	3.2
Total	5,285	100.0	5,181	100.0	5,422	100.0	6,686	100.0	8,378	100.0

Source: Alberta, Department of Social Services and Community Health, unpublished statistics.

TABLE 13

NUMBER OF CHILDREN INVOLVED IN REPORTS RECEIVED BY
CHILD PROTECTION REGISTRY IN ALBERTA, 1979-1981

	1979		1980		1981	
	No.	%	No.	%	No.	%
Children allegedly neglected	11,307	88.8	12,301	82.8	12,688	83.0
Children allegedly abused	1,431	11.2	2,559	17.2	2,600	17.0
(Total allegedly physically abused)	—	—	(2,278)	(15.3)	(2,257)	(14.8)
(Total allegedly sexually abused)	—	—	(281)	(1.9)	(343)	(2.2)
Total children reported	12,738	100.0	14,860	100.0	15,290	100.0

Source: Alberta, Department of Social Services and Community Health, unpublished statistics.

TABLE 14

NUMBER OF REQUESTS FOR AID RECEIVED BY THE COMITÉ DE PROTECTION
DE LA JEUNESSE IN QUÉBEC, 1976-1978

	1976		1977		1978	
	No.	%	No.	%	No.	%
Number of requests for aid received by the CPJ (relevant or not to its mandate)	5,223	100.0	9,178	100.0	11,597	100.0
Number of reports retained for the purpose of verification-evaluation	1,910	—	2,295	—	2,781	—
Reports retained as percentage of requests received	—	36.6	—	25.0	—	24.0
Source of the reports retained:						
Person having an individual tie with the child	965	50.5	1,113	48.5	1,387	49.9
Person having an institutional tie with the child	945	49.5	1,182	51.5	1,394	50.1
Types of abuse reported:						
Physical abuse	1,007	53.0	1,185	51.6	1,202	43.3
Sexual abuse	94	4.0	158	6.9	202	7.4
Neglect	451	23.7	454	19.8	695	25.0
Elevated risk	95	5.0	201	8.8	271	9.7
More than one abuse	255	13.4	297	12.9	406	14.6
Total	1,902	100.0	2,295	100.0	2,781	100.0

Source: Québec, Ministère de la Justice, Comité pour la protection de la jeunesse, *First Progress Report*, May, Québec 1977; *Rapport Annuel, 1978-79*, Québec, 1979; *Rapport Annuel, 1979-1980*, Québec, 1980.

TABLE 15

STATISTICS ON MISTREATED CHILDREN REPORTED TO THE QUÉBEC
COMITÉ DE PROTECTION DE LA JEUNESSE, 1979-1981

	1979		1980		1981	
Type of problem	*No.*	*%*	*No.*	*%*	*No.*	*%*
Physical abuse	2,292	54.6	2,115	57.2	1,704	56.8
Neglect	488	11.7	260	7.0	136	4.5
Sexual abuse	541	12.9	633	17.1	690	23.0
Physical abuse and neglect	434	10.4	354	9.6	236	7.9
Physical and sexual abuse	66	1.6	102	2.8	86	2.9
Other	214	5.1	217	5.7	142	4.7
No information	142	3.6	16	0.6	5	0.2
Total	4,177	100.0	3,697	100.0	2,999	100.0
Total number of abuse cases involving sexual abuse	607	14.5	735	19.9	776	25.9
Total number of new cases reported	3,479	83.3	3,268	88.4	2,727	90.9

Source: Unpublished statistics compiled by the Comité de Protection de la Jeunesse.

TABLE 16

DISTRIBUTION OF REPORTS MADE TO THE QUÉBEC COMITÉ DE PROTECTION
DE LA JEUNESSE BY AGE OF CHILDREN INVOLVED, 1979-1980

	1979		1980		1981	
Age	*No.*	*%*	*No.*	*%*	*No.*	*%*
0- 5 years	1,173	27.7	998	27.0	723	24.1
6- 9 years	822	19.6	619	16.7	519	17.3
10-13 years	957	22.9	784	21.2	702	23.4
14-17 years	1,109	26.6	1,147	31.0	891	29.7
No information	116	3.1	149	4.1	164	5.5
Total	4,177	100.0	3,697	100.0	2,999	100.0

Source: Unpublished statistics compiled by the Québec Comité de Protection de la Jeunesse.

TABLE 17

NUMBER OF REPORTED OR PROBABLE CASES OF CHILD ABUSE IN BRITISH COLUMBIA, 1971-1975

Age and Sex	1971		1972		1973		1974		1975	
	Reported	*Probable*	*Reported*	*Probable*	*Reported*	*Probable*	*Reported*	*Probable*	*Reported*	*Probable*
Male										
under 3 years	27		34	26	34	24	34	28		50
3-10 years	8		31	24	52	37	44	36		66
11 years and older	6		9	7	21	15	15	12		25
no age reported							2	2		
Female										
under 3 years	22		17	13	29	21	27	27		31
3-10 years	16		28	22	15	11	29	24		46
11 years and older	11		17	13	20	14	20	16		4
Total	90		136	105	171	122	171	140	430	262

Source: British Columbia, Ministry of Human Resources, *Annual Reports.*

TABLE 18

NUMBER OF REPORTED CASES OF PROBABLE CHILD ABUSE
IN BRITISH COLUMBIA, 1976-1981

Age and Sex	1976	1977	1978	1979	1980	1981
Male:						
Under 3 years	58	63	48	87	64	
3-10 years	92	99	141	155	200	
11 years and older	41	46	75	81	123	
No age reported	—	2	—	—	1	
Female:						
Under 3 years	52	43	45	71	50	
3-10 years	90	93	130	164	198	
11 years and older	84	104	166	233	351	
Total:	417	450	605	791	987	1,286

Source: British Columbia, Ministry of Human Resources, *Annual Reports.*

TABLE 19

BRITISH COLUMBIA CHILD ABUSE BY TYPE 1979-1981

Year	Physical	Sexual	Neglect	Other	Total
1979	653	138	561	139	1,491
1980	740	247	684	307	1,978
1981	802	484	795	441	2,522

Source: British Columbia, Ministry of Human Resources, *Annual Reports.*

3

POVERTY AND CHILD WELFARE

Marjorie Martin

All available evidence from historical sources and recent studies indicates that poor families are disproportionately higher users of public child welfare services in Canada. This chapter outlines the three major rationales offered to explain this phenomenon — a psychological, a sociological, and a power-relationship analysis. Of these three, the first has been the most persistent. It postulates that the poor have a personality set with characteristics ill-adapted for success in our society. The second rationale proposes that economic and social stresses make the poor more vulnerable to personal, familial, and social breakdown. The third analysis focuses on the power relationship between the poor and the social intervention agencies, a relationship which puts the poor at a great disadvantage.

These three explanations can be linked to perspectives of child welfare described in Chapter 1. The residual perspective incorporates the psychological rationale. Underpinning this ideological set is the belief that our society offers opportunities for all families to provide for the physical, emotional, and social needs of their children and, consequently, that failure in these tasks is a failure of the parent(s) or possibly the family as a whole. Service intervention is thus focused on seeking change at the individual or family level.

Conversely, the institutional perspective tends to embody the sociological rationale. It assumes that family supports and resources are not fully or automatically available, but need to be consciously introduced as universal social policies. Service intervention is focused at the community or broader social system level.

The third explanation of poverty focuses on the power differential between rich and poor. This explanation parallels the radical perspective described in Chapter 1. The power differential occurs both at the individual level, where client meets agency, and at the level of social class, as characterized by the unequal distribution of wealth in Canada.

In later chapters of this book, descriptions of child welfare policy and programmes illustrate how commitment to one or the other of these rationales governs the selection and development of child welfare services, a selection which often seems divorced from the needs of families.

THE POOR

As we examine the three rationales, it is useful to keep in mind a picture of the poorest families in Canada. Firstly, all families supported by public assistance have incomes well below the low-income (poverty) lines set by Statistics Canada. In 1983, for example, the relationship of family income at the income assistance level to the low-income line[1]:

TABLE 1

SUPPLEMENTED ANNUAL INCOMES OF FAMILIES ON SOCIAL ASSISTANCE MEASURED AGAINST POVERTY LINES, BY PROVINCE, 1983

	One Adult, Child Age 4			Two Adults, Children 10 & 13		
Province	*$ Amount*	*Per Cent Poverty Line*	*Rank*	*$ Amount*	*Per Cent Poverty Line*	*Rank*
Newfoundland	7,189	64.5	6	9,122	52.9	8
P.E.I.	8,161	73.2	3	11,750	68.2	3
Nova Scotia	7,825	65.5	5	11,354	61.6	6
New Brunswick	7,105	59.5	10	8,270	44.9	10
Quebec	7,615	60.5	9	10,722	55.3	7
Ontario	7,809	62.1	7	9,738	50.2	9
Manitoba	7,697	61.2	8	13,018	67.1	4
Saskatchewan	9,313	78.0	1	13,628	73.9	1
Alberta	9,335	74.2	2	14,052	72.4	2
British Columbia	8,515	67.7	4	11,960	61.7	5

Source: Social Planning Council of Metro Toronto, *Social Infopac*, Vol. 3, No. 4, 1984.

The population supported by income assistance varies with the unemployment rates. In 1983, with its high rate of unemployment, the Canadian total of individuals receiving assistance had risen to 1,800,000 in March. In B.C., in that same month, 8.5 per cent of the population were receiving income assistance, and of that percentage, approximately 69 per cent or 177,500 were parents and children.

Of families receiving public assistance, the single-parent family is particularly vulnerable. It is the most rapidly increasing family structure and remains on income assistance relatively longer than the two-parent family; consequently, it is more deeply affected by the erosions of person and situation that are a consequence of lengthy enforced poverty.

The number of two-parent families supported by income assistance is not insignificant in B.C., and it has increased in the past year, but this increase appears to be more directly related to the general rise in unemployment rates in 1982-83 and might be expected to drop again as employment opportunities increase.

A second vulnerable group is native families, whose economic plight has been documented in Canada and the United States and who live with prejudice as well as chronic poverty. High rates of unemployment persist for natives both on and off reserve, and, correspondingly, natives are high users of income assistance. This situation is described more fully in a later chapter by McKenzie and Hudson.

Not all, or even a majority of poor families become involved in the child welfare system, but they represent a disproportionately high percentage of the families who do. The evidence is particularly clear with respect to native families. Patrick Johnston, who completed a history of native involvement in child welfare, states that in 1980, while 0.96 per cent of all children in Canada were being cared for by the government, the level of native children in care was 4.6 per cent of the native child population.[2] These percentages, as alarming as they are, represent an improvement from the 1960's when, in B.C., one-third of the children in care were "saved from the effects of crushing poverty, unsanitary health conditions, poor housing and malnutrition. . .on many reserves" by an all-too-ready use of apprehension and placement in non-native foster or adoption homes.

For the non-native poor, specific nationwide evidence of rate of involvement in child welfare is not available because consistent information on the income of clients is either not documented or not collated nationally. However, using the few studies available, the National Council of Welfare stated flatly in 1979: "One fundamental characteristic of the child welfare system, however, has not changed appreciably over the years: its clients are still overwhelmingly drawn from the ranks of Canada's poor."[3] As an example, the council cites a 1979 Quebec report which indicated that two in every three children in care in the Province came from low-income families. Across the country, a B.C. research project completed by Neave and Matheson in 1968 found that of children admitted to care, 57 per cent were from families supported by income assistance.[4] A later study, conducted in 1972, surveyed 876 clients of Vancouver's Children's Aid Society, 35 per cent of whom had children in care. It found that 41 per cent of the families involved were supported by income assistance.[5]

Changes in the child welfare client population might be expected, for example, as native governments assume control over native child welfare, or if significant improvements are made in financial assistance,[6] however, we do not have procedures in place to track these developments accurately.

THE PSYCHOLOGICAL RATIONALE

The earliest and most persistent explanation for chronic poverty is that of a personality set or character defect. While society accepts that some of its members will experience temporary or voluntary poverty in the normal course of a lifetime, the persistently poor are seen as having personality traits which prevent their moving on to economic success. Common wisdom and professional belief is that these traits can be modified. While the method of modification has varied, the strength of this explanation is evident with even a cursory look at the dominant professional methodology and service focus — individual and family counselling and behaviour adjustment services are paramount. Service contracts, for example, a newer technique of planned intervention, typically have objectives committed to change of individual personality and behaviour or to change in internal family relationships.

One hundred years ago, the language was different but the phenomenon observed was not. The chronic poor were "paupers" with moral defects — "demoralization, ignorance, criminality and a wide array of other inadequacies," including those of family mismanagement and lack of parenting skills.[7] The pauper suffered from "the indisposition to do manfully [his] appointed task in life."[8] Amelioration of these personal inadequacies was sought through the "elevating influences" of members of successful middle-class society. Failing family change, children were then rescued from the evils of pauperism by removal from parents and placement in a home which would teach new values, attitudes, and behaviour.

Over time, the words to describe personal inadequacies has changed, but little else. The culture-of-poverty writers of the 1960's restated these ideas in a new form. In their view, a sub-culture existed among the chronic poor which engendered in them such traits as sense of resignation or fatalism, strong orientation to present time and place, need for immediate gratification, marginal social involvement (alienation), predisposition to authoritarianism, cynicism, and mistrust of authority, and so on.[9] These traits worked against economic independence and advancement and against family stability. The belief that negative traits had a genetic root was abandoned and replaced by the theory that they were a product of a longstanding poverty culture, which, although it may have come into existence in response to external conditions, now existed independently and was self-perpetuating — handed down from parent to child. The focus of treatment continued to be change in the character and behaviour of the client.

A more modern version of the same theory would use different words and tend to locate more of the source of personality inadequacy within the immediate family and in family interaction. Poor communication skills, lack of competence in developmental tasks, low self-esteem, low ability to conceptualize, lack of life goals are more current ways of expressing negative features of personality.

The helping service offered in response to this rationale has become more sophisticated and "scientific," but it has not changed significantly over the years. Its model is the one-to-one helper/helpee relationship focused on the individual (family) and seeking to modify particular coping and problem-solving behaviours through counselling, parent skill training, life skills management, assertiveness training, and other techniques.

THE SOCIOLOGICAL RATIONALE

The second major constellation of explanations for the overrepresentation of the poor in child welfare are those grouped under a sociological explanation. This explanation revolved around the concept of aspects of poverty as sources of stress — poor nutrition, inadequate housing, limited medical resources, lack of access to intellectual and cultural stimulation, and negative judgments from the community at large (being tarred with the 'welfare bum' brush, for example).

Medical researchers point out that from the moment of conception, a child experiences the direct consequences of poverty and faces a higher risk in physical and intellectual development.[10] *One Million Children*, a report which was the culmination of four years of research on the unmet needs of children with emotional and learning disorders states, "it would be naive and unscientific to omit from this report a discussion of the relationships between material poverty, inadequate housing and malnutrition and the presence of emotional and learning disorders in children."[11]

Nutrition problems are critical. Poor nutrition of the mother results not only in low birth weight and higher incidence of premature delivery and infant mortality, but cellular growth may be significantly affected. Retarded brain growth (capacity for intellectual development) and cell development predisposing individuals to later diseases are two major consequences.[12]

Undernourishment which persists after birth continues to interfere with physical and mental growth. When the child enters school, growth problems result in low energy and attentiveness which can then affect learning and development of positive relationships with peers and with the school as a system.[13] In addition to nutrition, other components of stress are identified as housing, inadequate medical and dental attention, and the middle-class material value demands of the school and social environment.[14]

Housing inadequacies are commonly depicted as problems of overcrowding and limited heat and light, all of which interfere with family comfort and study/work habits necessary for success at school. In addition, however, a high level of mobility is caused by the search for affordable and adequate housing, a pattern most particularly evident in the recent years of escalating housing costs. For some urban poor families, particularly those headed by female single parents, frequent changes of housing are common. The life of a single-parent family will often begin with a move from the original family home to a temporary shelter. Subsequently, the parent moves again in a search for both affordable housing and an environment that supports and accepts her and her family. One small explanatory study of single parents supported by income assistance found that families moved in a range of 2.6 to 3 times in a two-year period, citing cost and lack of satisfaction with the neighbourhood as major factors.[15] Each move adds stress to the whole family, but most particularly to the child. While adults are mobile and can sustain a social and work life over a relatively wide geographic area, the child likely faces a total life change covering school, peers, significant adult figures, and social environment.

Limitations of the poor family in securing and using medical attention are evident and persistent. Although the introduction of medical, hospital, dental, and pharmaceutical coverage in various jurisdictions has been a major improvement over earlier years, the poor family still has to cope with costs of accessing and utilizing medical attention, such as bus fare, non-subsidized drugs, and dietary extras.

A further major stress component is the predominance of middle-income material norms, most particularly in the school system. Lack of acceptable school clothing is a first basic problem; even though an onlooker would not judge current school attire to involve much cost. Further, the child may not have developed confident social and learning attitudes and adequate language, perceptual, or symbolic skills because of lack of resources in a home where magazines and newspapers are a luxury. The problems are all-pervasive — children who are granted free admission to summer camps will balk at the prospect of not having a real sleeping bag or the "correct" sneakers. Children who have free tickets to a concert resist going unless they have not only bus fare, but money for snacks and drinks. In 1970, the CELDIC report suggested that the outcome of such stress is that the child tends to become either a troublemaker or withdrawn and neurotic.[16] Extreme behaviour at either end of the range, although perhaps more frequently acting-out, will evoke the attention of significant adults, and not unusually, the child welfare system.

For the family as a whole, the stress of poverty is seen as eroding the ability to nurture, to support, and to foster confidence and hope. On a day-to-day basis, the parent must be responding to survival demands rather than the less pressing tasks of family development. An American study on the urban poor states, "their goals. . .are the same as those of families with adequate income, but their priorities focused on the bare essentials."[17]

The cumulative effects are described by the National Council of Welfare, who point out that stress levels are highest and the impact is felt most strongly by single parents, native families, and families with physically and mentally handicapped children, and that the results are increased physical illness as well as personal and family breakdown.[18]

The proponents of this explanation for the high involvement of the poor in child welfare seek a helping strategy of improvements in the family environment, such as: (1) increase in income, either with actual dollar increase (if the source of income is public assistance) or indirect dollar increase through subsidized housing, medical care, recreation, and so forth, and (2) increase in the participation of parents in school and neighbourhood in order to broaden society's definition of the range of acceptable values, attitudes, and behaviours. (Multicultural programmes are an example of this approach.)

THE POWER RELATIONSHIP

The third constellation of explanations for the poor family's over-representation in child welfare can be clustered under a power differential explanation. The problem here is two-layered: the poor have no power in society as a whole, and they have no power within the child welfare system in particular.

Poverty in Canadian society is commonly equated with failure, although poverty voluntarily sought and independently supported or well-managed can be acceptable. For example, we applaud religious leaders who seek poverty or self-sufficient small farmers without a cash income. Those who turn to government support in the form of income assistance are viewed with a negative or jaundiced eye, at best with ambivalence. From time to time, the poor gain more respect or power and are "consulted" or encouraged to "participate in decision-making." In all, however, the record of actual influence on significant policy and programmes is dismal, as the history of welfare rights action in the United States and Canada attests. Presently, the dominance of a neo-conservative philosophy in federal and some provincial governments has reinforced the view of poverty as personal failure. Recent changes in income assistance have reduced benefits for employable persons (including single parents) and offering, rather than job creation programmes to increase opportunities, job-finding programmes built on an assumption that lack of job-seeking skill is causing unemployment.

Single parents and natives are doubly damned. The female single-parent carries not only the lower status of women but also that of failed marriage. Native families are confronted at best by society's ambivalence about special status and at worst by the stigma of being perceived as dependent. They are now viewed as seekers of both public funding and public understanding.

At the more specific level of the child welfare system, poor families confront a paternalistic service, characterized by entrenched power differentials between client and service worker. The National Welfare Council states, "the poor are as much at a disadvantage when they look for help as when their troubles are developing."[19]

The first component is that the poor, unlike the non-poor, who can access a variety of public and private supports, must rely heavily on public services. Very often the public welfare system is used, and as well public housing, public health, subsidies in day care, school counselling services, budget counselling, detoxification centres, provincial mental hospitals, jail (when fines cannot be paid), transition houses, youth service projects such as Katimavik, and particularly in the case of natives, government grants for various programmes. This makes the poor very visible to government authorities, and the visibility in one part of the system carries over to other parts. The evidence is particularly clear in respect to recipients of income assistance whose home management inadequacies are quickly evident to government services and who are referred to other services, including the public child welfare system.

The dilemma of the poor help-seeker is compounded by the demand of the public helping system for presentation of a significant problem. Simple neurosis, ordinary worry over child development, low income (rather than poverty), feelings of personal unease, beginning of marriage stress — none of these problems evoke much help. For a number of years, for example, families applying to B.C. public housing were admitted only if they faced eviction and many, very sensibly, arranged for that to happen. Income assistance policy in B.C. ensures that the "careful manager" will only receive the basic monthly grant; overages are reserved for persons in crisis, who, for example, run out of food or fuel or lose children's winter clothing. The good manager who needs more money and knows that a crisis situation will secure it, is in anguish. Should she provoke a crisis and risk a judgment from the helping system that she is a poor manager and perhaps a negligent mother?

Once the family has come to the attention of the child welfare system, it faces the judgment of an organization with overwhelming middle-income values and behaviour standards. At the point of entry, this may not be clear to the client because the first marked power differential is in the control of information. Clear statements of expectations, standards, helping mode, agency procedures, and judgments are not typically made available and often are only presented verbally in the intake interview. Lack of information fosters fear and uncertainty, undermining the client's confidence and capacity to engage with the helper to set mutually developed goals and strategies. This enhances the client's dependency on the worker as a personality, rather than on her competence as a manager of agency policy and resources to solve family problems. It is an instructive contrast to compare the entry of the new student into university with that of a new client into the child welfare system. The student has, in addition to a calendar containing all significant policy (and often a handbook of student course evaluations), a student counselling centre and a student union. Finally, if serious questions persist, the student ombudsman is available. The child welfare client will have a verbal explanation from a social worker and might have a descriptive pamphlet but is unlikely to have any other information or support system.

Paternalistic, middle-class judgments of client behaviour have persisted from the first child welfare services to the present. The first relief societies and children's welfare organizations are described by some writers as instruments of social control and means by which the middle class sought to stabilize the class structure and control pauperism.[20] Evidence of middle-class judgment persists. T.R. Morrison speaking to a 1978 conference on children and the state, commented: "An assumption underpinning the many policies and programs in child welfare is that an increase in the number of professionals and concomitant growth in their skills and years of formal training will enhance the quality of care for children. These social work professionals, as the middle class reformers from which they emerged, however, really provide a labelling and policing service for a child welfare system which is directed primarily at the poor, but designed in accordance with the twin standards of "professional practice" and middle class family norms."[21]

In B.C. research by Matheson and Neave gives a more specific illustration of this point. In examining planned and unplanned admissions to care, they noted that the treatment mode seemed more suitable for the white, young, better educated, average or above average income, and semi-skilled or better. They summarize: "It would be of more than passing interest to determine the role of child welfare agencies in the entire process of child separation, since they appear to be consistently more successful in their relations with some segments of society than with others."[22]

A more current and vivid example of middle-income judgment is available in the description of an American project to develop an "Urban Scale to assess the adequacy of child care."[23] Many of the judgments on the scale clearly equate positive parenting with the lifestyle of a better-than-poverty income. Some examples:

State of Repair of House: Windows are caulked or sealed against drafts. Doors are weatherproofed. There are window screens in good repair on most windows.

General Positive Child Care: Mother plans for variety in foods. Mother plans meals with courses that go together. Child is taught to swim or mother believes child should be taught to swim.

Negligence: Mother plans special meals for special occasions. Clothing appears to be hand-me-downs (score positive for "no").

Quality of Household Maintenance: There are leaky faucets. Mattresses are obviously in poor condition (score both positive for "no").

Quality of Health Care and Grooming: Ears are usually clean. It is obvious that mother has given attention to child's grooming at home.

The poor family, confronted with an articulate and knowledgeable child welfare and court system, cannot marshal the information and effective response as well as a family with better income. The latter can consult and use a lawyer of its own choice, can consult and use experts in child-rearing such as psychologists, can purchase outside supports such as home help or a place in a residential school or camp. One American study, completed in 1980, reviewed decision-making in protective services and examined situations where service was recommended but not accepted by the family. The authors state,

> Those who refused service fell into two groups: those who ran away or moved, and those who stayed and refused service after investigation had validated the complaint. Those who refused service seemed to be more middle class and less disorganized as families than either those who received services or those who left to avoid them. If a case came to court, these families often hired a lawyer to contest the charges. Sometimes they simply refused to cooperate with the worker.[24]

The power of the judgment of the system is affirmed in Canada by Hepworth, who states: "On the evidence available, it is not so much the changing characteristics of neglected or delinquent children that has determined how they are cared for, but rather a continuation of changing administrative and legal arrangements and of changing public attitudes toward the treatment of children."[25]

The proponents of this third rationale argue that strategies should be designed to redress the balance of power. For natives, this strategy would be to transfer child welfare to native organizations. Other strategies include provision of more information to parents about child welfare rights and responsibilities, support to client groups or natural parent societies, improvements in legal aid, and re-evaluation of standards used to judge not only natural homes but foster homes.

Of the three rationales outlined, the first dominates present practice. While the seventies saw some opening up and consideration of the other two rationales, T.R. Morrison gives a sobering warning for the eighties:

> In a recent report on classification of exceptional children, a suggestive theory was proposed concerning society's response to deviancy. When society is experiencing economic difficulty, when it is in a conservative mood, when traditional values and institutions are supported, then the difficulties facing individuals are likely to be attributed to personal weaknesses or deficiencies. The child who evidences problems will be seen as somehow inadequate, or unable to take advantage of existing opportunities, until those inadequacies are remedied. Approaches to

these problems will be oriented towards the elimination of deficits within the individual and blaming the person if that effort fails to work . . . . When the economy is more buoyant, when existing norms, institutions and values are subjected to criticism, then the individual will be viewed as basically good and his or her problems will be seen as due largely to inadequate circumstances, rather than to personal failings. Help will take the form of modifications of institutions and attempting to increase their relevance to the person and society. Approaches to problems will be political, oriented towards such social policies as improving opportunity rather than remedying personal defects.[26]

If this pattern holds true, we can expect the recession and growth of neo-conservatism of the beginning of the 1980's to force an even greater emphasis on the "personality inadequacies" rationale and relative dismissal of the other two formulations, a narrow approach which would seem to ensure that the poor will continue to be the target of child welfare programmes.

What could be the response of the child welfare system to this situation? A number of remedial actions are suggested by this analysis, ranging from increasing self-awareness to refocusing direct action and from direct client work to influencing strategies directed at national policy-makers.

Although the energies of the child welfare services are drained by the high demand of day-to-day service, it is essential that they continue to raise awareness of the causes of child neglect and abuse and redirect energy into prevention. A critical problem impeding analysis and confounding remedial action is the lack of accurate comparative research data which looks across Canada and across income lines to highlight and target effective action. The data gathered concerning native child welfare is an excellent example, and the outcome actions illustrate the value of such documentation in influencing change.[27]

Child welfare agencies can seek to reverse the trend described by Morrison by bringing to public and political attention the evidence of the extent to which poverty creates child welfare problems. They can join with other professional, client and community agencies in the lobby for improvements in broad income security policies which slow down and seek to reverse the spread of poverty.

At the direct service level, child welfare agencies should examine their own policy and programmes, both to ensure maximum direct effort to relieve the poverty of clients and to address the dynamics of the power relationship which work against the poor gaining maximum benefit from the agency. A simple base for the former is to ensure that the agency has available all information about rights of resources for clients — income assistance, unemployment insurance, housing subsidy, medical benefits, and so on. The evidence in B.C., which may well be indicative of national trends, is that the take-up rate for such benefits can be well below maximum use. Such information can foster assertive and planned activity on the part of clients and workers to bring more material security into the family home.[28]

A second thrust of the direct service agency could be an examination of information systems and service patterns to determine the extent of the imbalance of power between clients and the agency. Does the agency have adequate, available, and appropriately written information for clients? Is the agency pro-active in seeking to educate and support the rights of the family? Does the agency have an appeal system for re-examination of service decisions? Has the agency introduced modes of service, such as mutual support groups, which empower the client?

Because agencies now face reduced budgets and higher workload, any changes in their policy and programme must be low cost and energy-effective. This analysis of the role of poverty and child welfare suggests that there are such changes which agencies could introduce which hold potential for enhancing service and reducing workload and which could improve the lot of the poor as users of service.

NOTES

1. Social Planning Council of Metropolitan Toronto, *Social Infopac,* vol. 2, no. 4 (October 1983): p. 5.
2. Patrick Johnston, *Native Children and the Child Welfare System* (Toronto: Canadian Council on Social Development, 1983), p. 57.
3. National Council of Welfare, *In the Best Interests of the Child* (Ottawa: The Council, 1979), p. 2.
4. K. Douglas Matheson and David C. Neave, *Child Separation in B.C.,* M.S.W. thesis, University of B.C., 1971, p. 55.
5. Ruth Chisholm, *Family Service Survey* (Vancouver, Children's Aid Society, 1972), p. 3ff.
6. H. Philip Hepworth, *Foster Care and Adoption in Canada* (Ottawa: Canadian Council on Social Development, 1980), p. 99.
7. Joey Noble, "Saving the Poor and Their Children." unpublished paper, p. 15.
8. Roy Lubove, *The Professional Altruist* (Cambridge: Harvard University Press, 1973), p. 5.
9. Eleanor B. Leacock, *The Culture of Poverty* (New York: Simon and Shuster, 1971), p. 239ff.
10. Thomas J. Ryan, *Poverty and the Child* (Toronto: McGraw-Hill Ryerson, 1972), p.19ff.
11. Commission on Emotional and Learning Disorders in Children, *One Million Children* (Toronto: Leonard Crainford, 1970), p. 32.
12. Ryan, p. 19ff.
13. Commission on Emotional and Learning Disorders in Children, p. 32.
14. National Council of Welfare, p. 4.
15. Catherine Luke, "Community and Mobility: A Comparative Study of Single Parents in Victoria West and James Bay" (Victoria: Ministry of Human Resources, 1979).
16. Commission on Emotional and Learning Disorders in Children, p. 32.

17. Communicating Research on the Urban Poor, *Poverty's Children* (Washington, 1966), p. 9.
18. National Council of Welfare, p. 5ff.
19. National Council of Welfare, p. 9.
20. For example, Lubove, p. 39; Noble, p. 38.
21. S. James Albert, *Children and the State,* Proceedings of a Conference 16-18 April 1978, School of Social Work, Carleton University, Ottawa, p. 10.
22. K. Douglas Matheson and David C. Neave, "Directions in Research," *Child Welfare* 57 (1978): 17ff.
23. Norman A. Polansky, Mary Ann Chalmers, Elizabeth Buttenweiser and David Williams, "Assessing Adequacy of Child Caring: An Urban Scale," *Child Welfare* 57 (1978): 443ff.
24. Joan W. DiLeonardi, "Decision Making in Protective Services," *Child Welfare* 59 (1980): p. 361.
25. Hepworth, p. 73.
26. Albert, p. 31, 32.
27. See also, Sheila B. Kamerman and Alfred J. Kahn, "Child Welfare and the Welfare of Families with Children," pp. 147-168, in Brenda G. McGowan and William Meezan eds., *Child Welfare Current Dilemmas Future Directions,* (Itasca, Illinois: Peacock, 1983).
28. M. Callahan and M. Martin, "Developing Consumer Information — A Strategy for Service and Policy Change," *Social Worker* 49 (1981): 161-73.

4

CHILD SEXUAL ABUSE:
A CHILD WELFARE PERSPECTIVE

Chris Bagley

In the last quarter of the twentieth century, Canada faces three profound problems of child welfare. The first concerns the disorganization of the childhood of so many aboriginal people, a direct result of the imperial legacy which devastated so many aspects of native economy and culture and which resulted in the continued and often desperate economic poverty of these people.[1] The second major problem concerns the alienation of the aspirations of many young people through the disruption of their families through divorce, economic misfortune, and the failure of many institutions to meet their needs in a positive way and linked to this, the alarming rise in suicidal behaviours in young people.[2] The third major problem concerns the abuse and neglect of children and adolescents.[3] One aspect of this abuse — sexual abuse — has the most devastating long-term effects and is almost certainly the cause of a significant proportion of the more serious problems of adolescent adjustment which are of major concern of child welfare and child care case loads. If the incidence of child sexual abuse can be reduced, the incidence of many other child welfare problems will be significantly reduced also.

BASIC ISSUES IN CHILD SEXUAL ABUSE

Although the term "incest" persists to describe sexual assaults on children within the family, incest and child sexual abuse are not synonymous. Incest should be defined in anthropological or socio-biological terms and concerns the aversion towards and the rules and taboos concerning continued sexual relations between closely related people which are likely to result in pregnancy and an alternative family.[4] Incest in the anthropological sense always concerns sexually mature individuals engaging in consummated sexual intercourse, usually in a consensual union. The large majority of cases of child sexual abuse do not fulfil these conditions, but instead involve the sexual coercion and domination of young children of both sexes by adults fulfilling neither the legal nor the anthropological definition of incest.[5] Sexual abuse of children is usually the act of someone known to the victim, most often a family member.[6] However, stepfathers or cohabitees are more likely than biological fathers to assault children. Legally, incest involves an individual having sexual intercourse with a close relative, but many sexual assaults on children by both relatives and non-relatives stop short of actual intercourse. This does not usually make the psychological trauma of the assault any the less, however.

Another problem concerns the incest taboo itself: since sexual assaults on children are widespread, either the taboo is frequently violated or else incest applies to a different category of adult relationships. The latter is a much more plausible possibility. In her historical review of the "best kept secret,"[7] Florence Rush produces a mass of evidence to show that the sexual exploitation of children has been an integral but undiscussed part of Judeo-Christian culture for many centuries. This sexual concern of males with deflowering the purity and innocence of childhood led to the obsession of many Victorian males with the exploitation of children, a passion which has borne fruit in the modern obsession with nymphets and child pornography. So-called sexual emancipation, Rush argues, has led to the male image of a utopia in which, "men will never be burdened by emotional traumas, venereal disease, pregnancy, commitments, responsibilities, charges of rape, statutory rape or child molestation as the consequence of their sexual behaviour."

Rush also exposes the "Freudian cover-up," which provided a useful psychological rationale for the male-invented myth that female children fantasized and invented sexual relations with their fathers. "The demon nymphette," the satanic, lustful child who seduces the adult male, is also exposed by Rush as a male-invented myth. Unfortunately, this idea of the child as seducer of the innocent adult, which marks the clinical literature of earlier decades, still survives in some clinical accounts of sexual abuse.[8]

Sexual abuse of children takes many forms and is certainly not confined to the intercourse defined by the incest statute. Sexual abuse can range from the sexualization of children for commercial purposes (in advertisements or in mass media); to the exploitation of children through pornography; to various kinds of sexual assault ranging from exposure and manual interference to the grossest forms of sexual assault on pre-pubertal children. The feminist view, which I accept, is that this sexual exploitation of children is made possible by a deep-rooted value climate which makes females, and especially powerless females, suitable objects for all kinds of exploitation. In this context, Herman and Hirschman identify what they term "covert incest,''[9] seductive, overbearing behaviour in fathers which does not involve consummated sexual intercourse: one factor here seems to have been the role of the mother, who is able to protect her daughter against the father's assaultive intents. Outcomes for children in such families are different too:

> Covert incest fosters the development of women who overvalue men and undervalue women, including themselves. Overt incest fosters the development of women who submit to martyrdom and sexual slavery. Those who consider masochism, selflessness and deference to men desirable attributes of mature womanhood may even consider a little bit of paternal seduction desirable for proper feminine development. But for those who aspire to an image of free womanhood, incest is as destructive to woman as genital mutilation or the binding of feet.

Adults who sexually assault children, including their own, are frequently described as inadequate personalities who have created or experienced disordered marital relationships and who often abuse alcohol.[10] These clinical profiles do not contradict the argument that child sexual assault is caused, fundamentally, by a basic value principle which underpins the exploitation of all children. The argument asserts that weak and relatively powerless males use children (usually, but not always, female children) not only for sexual gratification, but for the exercise of power and status as well.[11]

The coerced silence of the child victim is frequently reported.[12] This silence is one of the many factors which devastate the self-esteem of the victim and make revelation so difficult. The child who does manage to reveal the assault to outsiders was until recently, and probably still is in many traditional communities, not believed; or if believed, she was stigmatized and the offence itself ignored.

THE EXTENT OF CHILD SEXUAL ABUSE

All the evidence until the early 1980's suggested that the true incidence of child sexual assault within a family context was largely unknown, but almost certainly has involved a significant minority of all children. Sarafino estimated in 1979 that there were 336,200 sexual offences of all kinds each year in the United States.[13] However, this figure, based on agency reports, is almost certainly an underestimate, and other figures put the figure between 5 and 15 per cent of the child population.[14]

Finkelhor surveyed a population of college students in the United States and found that 19 per cent of the women and 9 per cent of the males had been sexually assaulted by the age of sixteen.[15] More girls from lower-income families had been assaulted, as had more from socially isolated backgrounds and from family situations in which the natural mother was absent. Eleven per cent of the women in this survey had been assaulted when under twelve by someone aged eighteen and over, usually someone within their intimate social network. Finkelhor concludes that

> these figures confirm the growing suspicion that sexual victimization of children is very widespread. They also show that it is very much a family problem. If we were to extrapolate on the basis of this data, something we are not really entitled to do, given the limitations of the sample, we would estimate that about 9 percent of all women are sexually victimized by a relative, and about one and a half percent are involved in father-daughter sex.

One of the limitations of these estimates, which Finkelhor acknowledges, is that children from low-income families (a high-risk group) are less likely to become college students. In addition, a frequent result of child sexual assault in the family is disorganized behaviour, including dropping out of school. Thus, Finkelhor's estimates for the general population are likely to be underestimates.

A replication of Finkelhor's work in 1983 with a student population at the University of Calgary indicated a somewhat higher incidence of child sexual abuse.[16] However, using a more conservative definition of serious child sexual abuse than he did — handling or intercourse with the child's unclothed genital area up to age 16 by someone at least three years older or someone using force or threat — we found that 19 per cent of the 404 women and 11 per cent of the 164 men had been victims of childhood abuse. Moreover, those young adults reporting such abuse had significantly poorer self-concept than those who had not been abused. This finding held for men, who had all been the subject of homosexual abuse, as well as for women.

Another type of study — a non-random survey of a large female population in North America — provided a different perspective.[17] In 1980, 106,000 female readers of the widely circulated magazine *Cosmopolitan* returned a postal questionnaire. Of these, 11 per cent had experienced sexual relations with a relative when a child: 5 per cent reported brother-sister relations, 3 per cent father-daughter, and a further 6 per cent reported sexual assault by an uncle, grandparent, or other relative. Rape, threats, and coercion were frequent features, and only sex between siblings close in age was reported to have no harmful psychological sequels for the girl. Often the trauma reported was great and long-lasting. This interesting survey cannot give accurate estimates for the population at large, but it does confirm the widespread nature of the problem as well as the frequent trauma which the assault entails.

Random sampling of general populations using standardized measures of sexual activity is likely to produce a more accurate estimate of prior sexual abuse, though it is likely to be less accurate than asking a population of children whether they are experiencing, or have experienced, unwanted sexual activity. Paradoxically, such research is rendered extremely difficult by the insistence of school boards that parental permission be obtained before questions about sexual topics can be asked of students. But it is hardly likely that a parent who is abusing or has abused a child will give such permission. Thus, in a study of self-concept in a large population of junior high school students in both separate and public school systems in Western Canada, we were unable to obtain any personal or background data on subjects, apart from their grade and sex. We found that about 3 per cent of girls and 2 per cent of boys had devastated self-concept on three different measures. But we had no way of knowing what factors (including current or past sexual abuse) underlay their desperate unhappiness, nor did we have any way of reaching them. But, as we showed in an experimental English study, such adolescents can be identified through the school system and successfully counselled.[18]

Two random samples of urban populations also have provided useful estimates. In a survey of 930 adult women in San Francisco, Russell found that 38 per cent had experienced sexual assault of some kind before they were eighteen, and 28 per cent reported at least one such experience before the age of fourteen.[19] Five per cent of these women had been subject to serious sexual assault, amounting to rape or attempted rape by a family member. Stepfathers were the most common abusers, and 17 per cent of women who had stepfathers suffered serious sexual abuse by them.

In Calgary, a random sample of 400 adult women first studied their mental health profiles and then, in a reinterview a year later, repeated the mental health measures and also asked about sexual abuse in childhood.[20] Twenty-two per cent of women reported serious sexual assault by the age of sixteen. Chronically poor mental health (including depression, anxiety, and suicidal ideas) was significantly linked to sexual abuse in childhood, although such abuse explained only a proportion of the variance in adult mental health. As in other studies, fewer than 10 per cent of the women had been able to report the assault to anyone or to get effective help afterwards. In two-thirds of the cases in the Calgary study, the assailant was known to the victim or her family.

Consider one case from this survey: a woman was sexually assaulted over the period of a year when she was in day care by the proprietor's husband who threatened her with a gun, warning her not to tell anyone. At age seven she was sexually abused by her grandfather, and at age eleven she was raped by a family friend. At age fifteen she made a serious suicide attempt "because of what those men did to me." Even then she received no professional help, but she was at last able to talk to her mother about the sexual assaults.

This study is by no means exceptional, and it illustrates both the prevalence of sexual abuse and its long-term psychological effects.

Our own estimate for Canada, which was made before the publication of the definitive studies of the Badgley Committee[21] was that at least 5 per cent of all females would, by their sixteenth birthday, have experienced serious sexual assault, usually within a family context. We estimated, based on this conservative incidence figure and the available data on the average length of time over which assaults continue, that the *averaged* proportion of children in elementary and junior high school *currently* being assaulted (within the past week) was 0.75 per cent or about seven or eight per 1,000. Every elementary school in Canada would, on the most conservative estimate, have two or three who were currently being sexually assaulted. In addition, we estimated that about five times this number (increasing as the average age of the student increases) would be still suffering trauma as a result of past sexual abuse. None of the individuals in this estimate would have received any assistance from formal helping agencies for the sexual abuse or its long-term effects.[22]

Since we made these estimates, the Badgley Report has provided more definitive figures on the prevalence of sexual abuse in Canada which indicate that the figures above are almost certainly underestimates.[23] The report commissioned a national random survey of 2,138 individuals, 94 per cent (2,008) of whom responded. Subjects were asked, in a self-completion questionnaire, whether at any time "any unwanted sexual acts had ever been committed against them and how old they were when these incidents occurred. The questions dealing with unwanted sexual acts elicited information about exposures, threats, touching and attacks." (p. 179).

The two crucial questions concerning sexual touching and assault were:
1. "Has anyone ever touched the sex parts of your body when you didn't want this?"

The reply categories were: never happened to me; or circle as many as apply of: touched your penis, crotch, breasts, buttocks and anus; kissed/licked your penis, crotch, breasts, or anus; other types of touching (specify).
2. "Has anyone ever tried to have sex with you when you didn't want this, or sexually attacked you?"

The reply categories were: never happened to me; or circle as many as apply of: tried putting a penis in your vagina; tried putting something else (a finger or an object) in your vagina; tried putting a penis in your anus; tried putting something else in your anus; forced a penis in your vagina; forced something else in your vagina; forced a penis in your anus; forced something else in your anus; stimulated or masturbated your crotch or penis; other acts (specify).

TABLE 1

UNWANTED SEXUAL ASSAULTS

Age abuse occurred	Males (n = 1002)		Females (n = 1006)	
	Touching	Assault	Touching	Assault
Under 7	6	1	6	8
7-11	11	5	24	21
12-13	11	4	26	12
14-15	13	9	36	20
All under 16	41	19	92	61
Both categories under 16	60 (5.9%)		153 (15.2%)	
16-17	22	12	40	27
Both categories under 18	94 (9.4%)		220 (21.9%)	

Source: Adapted from Tables 6.1 to 6.3, pp. 180-82 of the Badgley Report.

These figures indicate that by the time they are fifteen, 6 per cent of boys and 15 per cent of girls have been the subject of sexual assault which violates the Criminal Code of Canada. By the time they are seventeen, 9 per cent of boys and 22 per cent of girls have been victims of such assaults.

Virtually all of the males had been the subject of homosexual assaults. Sixty per cent of the child victims had been threatened or physically coerced by their assailants. Four per cent of male victims and 20 per cent of female victims received physical injuries following the assault, while immediate psychological trauma was reported by 7 per cent of males and 24 per cent of females. No estimates of long-term psychological harm were made.

For the female victims, 18 per cent of assaults were by a stranger; 10 per cent involved a close blood relative (sibling, parent, or grandparent); 14 per cent involved other categories of blood relative or family member including a stepparent; 1 per cent involved a person in a position of trust such as a teacher; and 57 per cent involved someone else known to the victim. Both before and during adolescence, girls were also vulnerable to sexual assault by "gangs of predatory and dangerous adolescent males" (p. 219).

Fewer than a half (41 per cent) of female child victims and only 26 per cent of male victims reported the assault to anyone in authority. Reasons for non-reporting included "it was so personal," "I was too ashamed. . . too angry. . .didn't want to hurt my family. . .thought I would be blamed."

In addition to these findings, the Badgley Committee showed that sexual threats and sexual exposure were also common. Sexual exposure had a dangerous aspect because the trapped or paralyzed victim often became the subject of a more serious sexual assault.

The Badgley Committee concludes from these figures that:

> Sexual offences are committed so frequently and against so many persons that there is an evident and urgent need to afford victims greater protection than now being provided. The findings of the National Pop-

ulation Survey clearly show the compelling nature of the fears and stigma associated with having been a victim of a sexual offence. . . . What is required is the recognition by all Canadians that children and youth have the absolute right to be protected from these offences. To achieve this purpose, a major shift in the fundamental values of Canadians and in social policies by government must be realized.

The Committee is aware that these basic changes will not come about easily or quickly. If no action is taken, or if only token programs are initiated, the risk that children and youths will continue to be sexually abused will remain intolerably high. In this respect, one of the Committee's major recommendations is that the Office of the Commissioner which we recommend be established have as one of its principal responsibilities, in cooperation with the provinces and non-governmental agencies, the development, coordination and implementation of a continuing national program of public education and health promotion focussing on the prevention of sexual offences and the protection of young children, youths, and adults who are victims. (p. 193)

THE LEGACY OF TRAUMA

The legacy of the trauma can stay with an individual for a lifetime, and the extrapolation of the estimate that at least half of the 19 or 20 per cent of girls who are sexually abused will suffer some long-term harm produces the staggering estimate that perhaps half a million women in Canada are suffering impaired mental health associated with the long-term psychological legacies of childhood sexual assault. There is obviously some logic in the feminist complaint that the sexual assault of female children is an important aspect of the socialization of women for passivity and of personality problems associated with or leading to subordination.[24]

The most frequent evidence on the amount and harmfulness of child sexual abuse comes from the surveys of patient, client, and agency populations. The motivation of a number of workers (Meiselmann, Renvoize, Forward and others)[25] — to research the subject has been the realization that a large number of their female patients in unselected clinical populations had experienced sexual assault as children and that those assaults were often causally related to later clinical problems. Other surveys of runaway teenagers;[26] young drug-users;[27] young prostitutes;[28] and juvenile prostitutes;[29] have indicated that at least half of these female populations have been victims of child sexual assault. There is evidence too from a systematic clinical study that these assaults have an important causal relationship with later disturbed behaviour.[30]

Studies which show the harmful sequels of child sexual abuse and its links to other behavioural problems can be illustrated by the work of Silbert, which is quite typical both in terms of its methodology and its findings.[31] Silbert surveyed two hundred street prostitutes in San Francisco. Seventy per cent of the women she located were under 21, and 96 per cent were runaways when they began prostituting, usually as juveniles. The results, Silbert reports:

> are alarming, and contradict commonly held viewpoints on prostitution from many aspects. The excessive victimization, physical and sexual abuse, and learned helplessness, coupled with the young ages and disturbed backgrounds of the women, produce a distressing portrait of women trapped in a lifestyle they do not want, and yet feel unable to leave. Sixty percent of the subjects were the victims of juvenile sexual exploitation, and most subjects started running away from home as a result of sexual, physical or emotional abuse. Once in the streets, they were victimized by both customers and pimps: they were beaten, raped, robbed and abused.

The majority of the girls came from middle-class families with a formal religious atmosphere. This was no protection against sexual exploitation by fathers or stepfathers. Seventy per cent of the abused girls suffered repeated sexual assault by the same family member, often for a period of years. Almost all of these child victims lost their virginity as a result of the abuse; but they could only escape from their male dominated households by running away. Once in the streets the obvious means of survival was prostitution. The majority of respondents who had been sexually assaulted within their families felt that their drift into prostitution was directly related to the earlier sexual assault.

The Badgley Report also provides evidence that the situation of child and adolescent prostitutes represents the most serious kinds of sexual abuse in Canada.[32] The committee undertook a detailed and comprehensive survey of samples of juvenile prostitutes in the major cities. Such children — 229 sampled and interviewed in the survey — were not difficult to find, and their numbers illustrate the extent of the problem. Any adult wanting to have sex with a child of either sex can purchase it for as little as $20.00 for ''normal'' intercourse or oral sex. It was found that at least a quarter of the young people available for sex on the streets were boys. This reflects the findings of the National Population Survey, which indicated that one in ten boys is the subject of serious homosexual abuse at some time in his childhood, while one in five girls is the subject of serious sexual assault by a male. The juvenile prostitution system is, at present, an institution in which child sexual abuse is accepted as an underground, but largely tolerated, aspect of urban life. There are at present no legal sanctions that can be applied against adult customers and few effective sanctions against the pimps, the ''cruellest and most cold-hearted abusers'' in this unhappy scenario.

Badgley and his colleagues propose clear legal changes, based on a review of existing law and legal cases and the results of the survey. These young people were much more likely than the general population to have been introduced early in their lives to various forms of sexuality, and over one-third were sexually experienced by their eleventh year. Thirty per cent of the children were sexually initiated by a guardian, a parent, a family member, or someone else in a position of trust. However, sexual abuse, although important, was not the major factor leading to entry into prostitution.

The large majority of young prostitutes come from seemingly respectable middle-class homes filled with tension, strife, marital quarrels, and parental alcoholism. Sometimes, but not always, this parental dysfunction was associated with physical and sexual abuse of the child. Running away from home was a frequent response to these abusive families; however, children on the streets were particularly vulnerable to recruitment to prostitution and all its attendant perils. Just over half of the children and adolescents of both sexes had contracted a venereal disease, and over two-thirds of the boys and three-quarters of the girls had been the subject of beatings or torture by customers, pimps, drug dealers, and other people on the street. Normal social service and child welfare agencies seem to have entirely failed these children, yet for many of the girls especially, life on the street was a form of degradation and slavery at the hands of customers and pimps.

Badgley declares that:

> In the Committee's judgment, the relationship between young prostitutes and pimps encompasses one of the most severe forms of abuse of children and youths, sexual or otherwise, that currently occurs in Canadian society. The relationship is based on two forms of ruthless exploitation: psychological and economic. The pimp exploits and cultivates the prostitute's vulnerabilities — her low self-esteem, her feelings of helplessness, her loneliness on the street and her need for love and protection. These weaknesses are the fetters with which the pimp binds the girl to him and keeps her on the street. Economically, pimps exploit prostitutes by drawing them into a form of virtual slave labour, or at least into a relationship in which one party, the pimp, provides a service whose value is vastly outweighed by the amount which the other party, the prostitute, is required to pay for it. The cost to the prostitute of working for a pimp goes far beyond the earnings that she gives him; it amounts to the girl's forfeiture of her future. Opportunities to obtain a better education, to become free of drug and alcohol addiction, to sort out emotional problems, to return to a normal lifestyle and to enter into healthy, caring relationships, are seriously jeopardized or permanently destroyed. The relationship between juvenile prostitutes and pimps is parasitic and life-destroying. In the Committee's judgment, it must be viewed as a problem of the utmost gravity. It must be

stopped. (p. 1061)

IS CHILD SEXUAL ABUSE INCREASING?

An important issue is whether the actual incidence of child sexual assault is increasing, or whether both cultural values and professional practice are changing in ways which make it easier for victims to report abuse. It is clear that 1978 was a key year for professional understanding of the problem of child sexual abuse, with a "knowledge explosion" of books and monographs bringing an enlightened focus to understanding the problem, its consequences, and its treatment.[33] Previously, reports on the topic were sparse, and they often suggested that the incidence of sexual assault on children was low; that such assaults were the result of family dysfunctions in which mothers held a large share of blame; that often the victims of such assault were not harmed or traumatized; and that often the child victims themselves played a seductive role, leading on the weak but sexually frustrated male. It is astonishing, in retrospect, that the professional community should have accepted such myths and distortions so passively, and it should serve as a reminder that current practice and concepts in other areas of child welfare may be similarly biased. On this model then, the great increase in agency reports of child sexual abuse[34] are an indication that victims now have greater perception that such assaults are wrong, that complaining to people outside the family is legitimate, and that such complaints will bring meaningful help.

This may be an overly optimistic view, however. The authority of the family over children is still widely stressed, and in the private domain of family socialization, children may have no alternative but to believe the adult male who tells the child that conformity to sexual domination is necessary along with the other conformities required of children. The child has to be assured that the threats against disclosure are unrealistic or empty and that professionals such as teachers, ministers, police, crisis workers, and social workers will be both sympathetic and effective in bringing help. Such ideal conditions are frequently not met.

Although it is easier now for women and children to escape from physically and sexually abusive males, alternative sociological forces also make it likely that the amount of sexual abuse of children within families could be increasing. First of all, the eroticization of childhood by adults, largely for commercial purposes, may have accentuated a focus on children as suitable victims. Family changes may be important too. David Finkelhor points out that the presence of an unrelated adult male in a household is a special risk factor for children in terms of sexual assault:[35] such "blended" families are increasing as divorce and remarriage rates increase. Diana Russell's San Francisco research illustrates clearly the risks which "blended" or remarried families subject children to.[36] She found in a survey of 930 adult women that 2 per cent of women had been sexually abused as children by their biological fathers; but 17 per cent of women with a stepfather had been sexually abused by him when a child. Moreover, when stepfathers sexually abused their daughters, they were much more likely than other relatives to abuse them at the most serious level, involving attempted or achieved penile-vaginal penetration or manual interference with the child's unclothed body.

Some intriguing data on the stability of rates of child sexual abuse in Canada over the past fifty years are given in the Badgley Report.[37] Noting the possibility that sexual assaults taking place many years before may be distorted in memory or even completely repressed (perhaps leading to underreporting by older persons), Badgley showed that the number of "unwanted sexual acts" of all types hardly varied by age of the respondent — those aged sixty-one or more reported, on average, the same number as individuals aged twenty-one to thirty. However, females aged eighteen to twenty reported some 20 per cent more assaults than did individuals in any other age group. Badgley is cautious about this increase, suggesting it might be owing to sampling error or to a more vivid recall of recent events. This is an area in which repeated surveys of large samples of young adults could give data on trends over time.

A case history reported by the Badgley Committee in response to their National Survey illustrates the difficulty of getting full data on the incidence of child sexual abuse:

> Even though I am no longer a child or youth (I am 40), I would like to report sexual abuse as a child. The first rape occurred when I think I was approximately 18 months old. I was too little to speak and tell my mother. A second rape occurred when I was between two and three. From three to age seven I was raped routinely, especially in the summer when I could not be kept in the house. The rapist was my father.
>
> Until age 36, I had no recollection of my childhood. Growing up on a farm, I had assumed until then that it had been a happy one. I knew my father as a good man, religious and a leader in our small community.
>
> When he died, freeing within me the terror and rage against him, I started experiencing serious problems towards men. If any man showed any interest, I would "freeze up," be paralyzed inside, and unable to move or speak. . . .After five years of primal therapy [re-experiencing one's childhood] I am just beginning to recover my soul which had gone into hiding to survive the trauma. At age six, I had suffered a stroke (I wanted to die), but I survived. I had to relearn how to speak and walk. I forgot everything prior to that period. From age six to 36, I functioned as an average neurotic having no idea of what my past had been. During the last four years, I have been able to reattach the child in me to the functioning adult. (pp. 163-164)

If indeed some deeply traumatic childhood events are sometimes repressed, then the surveys asking adults to recall such events may be underestimates. Another possibility is that adults may deny the existence of or decline to discuss early events which they found deeply disgusting.

A potent factor in the possible increase in the amount of child sexual abuse is the development of the ideology in the 1960's and 1970's of the supposed right of individuals to sexual fulfilment.[38] Whether or not rates are rising, the fundamental problem, Finkelhor[39] argues, remains the power and dominance which men still exercise in sexual relationships. The new sexual "freedoms" have, as Florence Rush points out,[40] operated to the advantage of males rather than females, and they have led some to believe that all kinds of sexual fulfilment, including sex with children, are legitimate. If sexual abuse of children is to diminish, profound value changes must take place in the whole area of relationships between men and women.

THE SHORT-TERM AND LONG-TERM PSYCHOLOGICAL EFFECTS
OF CHILD SEXUAL ABUSE

There is now reasonably good evidence on the short and long-term physical, psychological, and behavioural sequels of earlier child sexual abuse in adolescents and young adults.[41] The estimates from non-random adult populations suggest that at least a minority of victims carry profound problems into adulthood. Studies of clinical populations also suggest that sexual abuse has many profoundly adverse sequels. Especially in the immediate aftermath of the assault, children suffer a wide range of psychological and physical trauma. These short- and long-run sequels have major implications for the whole of the child care and child welfare system. For at least a minority of the victims, profound personality damage results, which can only be reversed by skilled, intensive, and prolonged individual and group therapy.[42]

In a review of literature on sequels up to 1980, Hill lists the following immediate trauma to child victims: physical trauma, including vaginal and anal lacerations; infections and venereal disease; associated physical abuse, including bruises and burns; pregnancy and menstrual disorders; sleeping and eating problems, bedwetting, thumb-sucking, night terrors; depression, loss of self-esteem, and withdrawal from peers; learning disabilities or developmental delays; running away, drug and alcohol use, subsequent juvenile prostitution; pervasive sense of anxiety, fear, and terror; confusion and guilt over secrecy; anger and aggression at siblings and the non-violating parents.[43]

Our own review of the monograph and journal literature on child sexual abuse in the period 1978 to 1982 has identified the following sequels of earlier sexual abuse in adolescents and adults:[44] suicidal gestures and attempts

(probably in about 5 per cent of all sexually abused girls); long-term personality problems, including guilt, anxiety, fears, depression, and permanent
impairment of self-image (probably in a majority of female victims); more
serious personality sequels, including chronic psychosis, self-mutilation, in-
duced obesity, anorexia, hysterical seizures, and a chronically self-punitive
lifestyle, a reaction to acute feelings of guilt and self-disgust (probably in
about 5 per cent of sexually abused girls); running away from home; or
removal by judicial and child welfare authorities unaware of or indifferent
to the sexual abuse (probably in about 20 per cent of female victims where
the abuse is known to authorities); prostitution or a sexually dominated or
exploited lifestyle (probably in about 5 per cent of female victims); withdrawal, coldness, frigidity, or lack of trust in psychosexual relationships
(probably in about 5 to 10 per cent of female victims); aggression, aggres-
sive personality disorder, and chronic delinquency (in about 5 per cent of
victims); drug and alcohol abuse leading to chronic addiction and health
impairment (in about 5 per cent of victims).

Many of these adverse sequels are linked or overlapping, but I estimate
from these research reports that at least 25 per cent of girls who are sexually
abused within their families have serious long-term problems of adjustment, while a further 25 per cent have chronic personality problems. The
first, most seriously disturbed group feature prominently in disturbed,
drifting, runaway adolescents: but this fact is not well understood by workers in this field, who continue to treat only the symptoms of the abuse
syndrome, often in a superficial, or indeed punitive, way. As Badgley has
shown, adolescent runaways, victims of emotional, physical, and sexual
abuse, are subject to yet further sexual abuse on the streets.[45]

Recent surveys of college populations have indicated the long-term psychological harm which can result from earlier sexual abuse. Finkelhor's
pioneering study of 796 college students in New Hampshire showed that
sexually victimized children of both sexes had, as young adults, lower levels
of sexual self-esteem.[46] Victimized boys also appear to be more likely to be
currently engaged in homosexual activity.

Sedney and Brooks surveyed the earlier sexual abuse of 301 college students in Rhode Island.[47] Sixteen per cent reported some kind of sexual
experience with another person while they were growing up; 78 per cent of
these sexual experiences took place within the family context. The 51
women with "early sexual experience" were compared with a similar number of controls from the main sample. Both groups were then given a detailed psychological investigation. "The pattern that evolved was of a
greater likelihood of symptoms in the early sexual experience group than the
control group, with the negative effects more apparent for the incest group
than for the nonfamilial sexual experience group. In other words, early
sexual experience with a family member seemed to have negative consequences over and above those resulting from just the early sexual experience

itself'' (pp. 216-17). Depression, sleep problems, emotional problems, suicidal feelings, and problems with study were significantly more common in the subjects experiencing prior sexual abuse. Over half of the sexually abused group reported serious and often chronic clinical problems in these areas, while 20 per cent had made a suicide attempt or taken a drug overdose. A quarter of the abused group compared with 8 per cent in the controls had been victims of an ''accident,'' often involving serious injury. The implication of these findings, the authors suggest, are that in any consultation about women's mental health problems, the possibility of earlier sexual abuse should always be investigated and addressed as a major issue in treatment programmes.

In our work in Calgary with young adult students (464 women and 164 men),[48] we found that both males (11 per cent of the total) and females (19 per cent of the total) who had been sexually abused up to age sixteen had significantly poorer self-concept on the Tennessee (TSCS) and Coopersmith Scales as young adults. This poorer self-concept was not confined to any particular subscale on the TSCS (although dissatisfaction with physical self was most marked), but represented a global depression of self-concept and self-esteem among over one-fifth of both previously abused males and females.

Sexually abused males in this sample were much more likely than others to have mainly or exclusively homosexual contact as adults, reflecting perhaps the nature of their earlier abuse. The possibility that homosexual abuse of young boys represents a form of recruitment to the adult sexual role should be seriously considered. A further disturbing possibility is that having been homosexually abused as a child motivates some individuals to become homosexual pedophiles themselves. Certainly the picture given by Badgley of the nationwide prevalence of male homosexual assaults on children[49] and the large clientele for young male prostitutes is consistent with the view that homosexual pedophiles are a self-recruiting, probably permanent, minority in any culture.[50]

THE RIGHTS OF CHILDREN, VIOLATION OF TRUST,
AND DEVASTATION OF SELF-ESTEEM

Finkelhor argues that sexual relations between adults and children are wrong because children cannot give informed consent to such relationships, and he suggests that arguments against such sexual relationships on empirical grounds have the inherent weakness that if no harmful outcome can be identified, then the relationships are, *ipso facto*, permissible.[51] However, there are difficulties with Finkelhor's arguments. There is a considerable and persuasive literature on children's rights which establishes that children do have a legal and moral right to give informed consent at an early age in relation to, say, medical and surgical intervention. By the same token, children have the right to refuse interventions and acts which they regard as unpleasant or demeaning.[52] Given the possibility of informed choice, the vast majority of children will, I believe, refuse the sexual advances of adults.

The ultimate argument against the sexual exploitation of children by adults *is* that in up to half of the cases, long-term and perhaps permanent impairment of mental health results. There is no way of telling with any certainty in advance which children will be most damaged: age, type of assault, and length of time over which the assaults take place do not seem to be good predictors of adult psychosocial outcome. However, the degree of force and coercion used with threats to ensure silence and continued compliance, especially by a previously trusted authority figure such as a father, do appear to be particularly related to long-term harm. The long-term harm upon female victims by sexual abuse wrought by a father figure in combination with force, threat, and physical violence is illustrated in our follow-up study over a twelve year period of forty-seven girls who were the subject of social service intervention following abuse of various kinds. Combinations of physical and sexual abuse were shown to have a particularly devastating influence on self-esteem and led to poor emotional and sexual adjustment, including suicide attempts and prolonged hospitalization for depression and to physical abuse which occurred in later relationships, including prostitution.[53]

Sexual assault within a family context violates a child's *safety* needs, which, in Maslow's important developmental model,[54] are fundamental needs for a child. The violation of these safety needs in the family, hithertofore the context of total safety for most children, imposes on the child a situation of lonely terror in which she is forced to deceive her mother and engage in sexual practices which she may find stimulating but simultaneously disgusting. The long-term effect of this self-disgust is a continued self-hatred and an acute difficulty in many aspects of human relationships. The type of reaction for any individual will of course vary with pre-existing personality, and other factors which influence final outcome include the temperament and vulnerability of the child. All too often, however, the victimized child is one who has poor self-esteem to begin with and who accepts the abuse as just one more demeaning burden which adults impose on children. Such a child tells herself, according to Linda Sandford,[55] "'I don't like this but what do I know? I'm never right about anything. . . .I know if I tell anyone about this, they'll get mad at me for making trouble. . . .Nobody else likes me, not in the whole world, except for this person, so I'll do what he says."

Children with poor-ego strength and impaired self-concept are probably most likely to be victims and are easier to coerce into silence. Children in psychologically open families are likely to have a close relationship with their mother, the ego-strength to resist seductive approaches from an adult male, and the ability to reveal such abuse immediately.[56]

TREATMENT MODELS

The sexual abuse of children often causes long-lasting damage, so clearly treatment has to be intensive and prolonged if profound trauma is to be reversed. Two major treatment programmes, led by Suzanne Sgroi[57] and Hank Giarretto,[58] have recently published clinical handbooks giving detailed accounts for innovative practitioners.[59]

Practitioners need to be mature, skilled, well-educated people who have come to terms with their own sexuality and feelings towards the sexual exploitation of children. Former victims of abuse who have been through extensive healing programmes are particularly valuable as resource people in self-help groups, since they understand the meaning of abuse and empathize with victims. In Giarretto's programme for victims, "Sons and Daughters United," and the parents' group (including offenders), "Parents United," form an important part of an integrated treatment model. The overall approach to treatment has a number of fundamental tasks.

1. To understand and try to change the values of the community, of individuals, and of professionals concerning the sexual abuse of children.
2. To work towards the integration of interested parties — child protection workers, sex crimes detectives, crown prosecutors, specialized therapists — and the wishes of the child herself once abuse has been revealed, in action which serves the fundamental welfare interests of the child and adolescent victim.
3. To engage in a prolonged and intensive treatment programme involving the victim, her siblings, and her mother and father with associated self-help groups.
4. To undertake the treatment of adult former victims still suffering long-term effects of earlier sexual abuse.
5. To undertake preventive education with young children to enable them to understand the sexually abusive approaches of others; to give them a healthy self-concept which will enable them to resist these approaches; and to assure them that responsible adults will listen and take appropriate protective action when they complain of abuse.

The need for community education to achieve value change is clear when we understand the traditional reaction to sexual abuse of a child. Children should be aware that such adult behaviour is wrong and should be resisted. A child who has experienced sexual abuse should complain to a parent, teacher, minister, relative, or counsellor who would first of all believe her, then listen sympathetically, and finally take effective action to end the abuse in a way which did not further damage the child's self-esteem. These expectations were in the past unlikely to be fulfilled; even when she was believed, a girl was unlikely to achieve effective help. Usually the abuse could only be stopped when she was removed from the house to a children's shelter. Here, along with juvenile delinquents and runaways, the victim's concept of herself as a bad or wicked person was likely to be further reinforced.

Value change is crucially necessary if child victims are to receive active, integrated, effective help. In this changed model, it is the offender who should be removed from the home, not the victim. Sometimes a teenage girl will ask to spend a period with a relative or in a foster home: this wish should be respected. All of the action taken at the point of disclosure should involve the fullest integration of different services. In most jurisdictions, reporting child abuse to the director of child welfare is, in theory at least, mandatory, and at that point police should also be informed. However, in all of the actions taken by workers of various kinds, there should be one underlying principle or goal: all actions should serve the best interests of a damaged, unhappy, and traumatized young person, and the goal of all of the actions should be to enable the girl to recover her sense of dignity, self-respect, and self-esteem.

In most Canadian cities, there is not yet any adequate co-ordination of services for sexually abused children. Child welfare or protection workers, unprepared and untrained for such work, can still react with panic, embarrassment, or even denial, remove the child from her home, and leave things at that — the child is "punished," but she receives no therapy related to the sexual abuse at all. Judith Herman reports such a case of a girl removed from home after reporting sexual assault:

> The director of the institution where I was placed had been trained as a counsellor. What I resent about her now is that I lived there for four years, and even though she knew what had happened, she never once took me aside and said, "Would you like to talk about it?" From age fourteen to eighteen I had nobody to help me work out my feelings. I cried myself to sleep every night."[60]

Herman's case is an example drawn from the 1970's. The following case, from a large Western Canadian city in mid-1983 illustrates how far attitudes and treatment have to go:

> Margaret, living in a one-parent family was a lonely, isolated child. She had few friends, and wasn't close to her mother. When she was eleven a neighbour and family friend sexually assaulted and finally raped her over a period of months. This precipitated a crisis of withdrawal, moodiness, crying and wandering from home, but she was not able at that time to reveal the sexual abuse. Her exasperated mother sent her to stay with her father in another Province for a time. In this man's house she was further sexually abused. On return to her mother's house she

was again in conflict with her mother, and finally took off at the age of 13. She was soon recruited on the streets by a leading pimp, and for two years was a very high-priced juvenile prostitute. She gained nothing from this experience except grief and further self-disgust. She was admitted to hospital after a drug overdose, and then went to a group home as a temporary ward of the Province. In the group home she was able to reveal for the first time the earlier sexual assaults on her by her father and the family friend. The only person she felt able to talk to was a sympathetic but untrained aide in the group home. The so-called professionals in the home, as well as her social worker, agreed to "let sleeping dogs lie" hoping that she had blanked out her traumatic past. She entered a very withdrawn phase, and her reluctance to talk about things again was taken as an acquiescence in this denial. As one of her workers put it, "Even if we wanted to refer her for therapy, there's nowhere in this city we could send her." Margaret was returned to her mother, since the Province no longer held any legal responsibility for her, now she was 16. It is not clear what happened between her and her mother, but after two months she was admitted to hospital after a serious suicide attempt. She has been diagnosed as borderline psychotic, and in her acutely withdrawn and depressed state has been, at the age of 16, in a mental hospital for the past two months. She is being treated by psychotropic drugs, and still no one has offered her any therapeutic programme which might exorcise this terrible ghost from her past. She remains in a permanent state of self-disgust. The best she can achieve is a state of numbness, and detachment from herself, "like when I was doing tricks. I used to pretend I was on the wall like a fly or a bird, and then I would fly away into the sky."

How could this disastrous outcome have been prevented? In an ideal community, she would have known about the nature of sexual abuse and would have been able if not to resist the initial threats and coercion, then at least to report the abuse rapidly with the confidence that speedy and effective action would be taken. That action would remove the source of the abuse but would not require her to endure gruelling cross-examination in court. The best judicial systems are those in which a social worker, having interviewed the child, can give evidence in court as a proxy.

But suppose Margaret had been able to reveal the second incident of abuse, when she was thirteen, to someone like a teacher. In an integrated treatment system, a protection worker would be informed immediately and would ensure the girl's safety by removing the offender from the house. In a community model such as the one developed by Giarretto in San Jose, prosecutors would build on community sentiment supporting an integrated treatment programme, and in the face of such pressure, the offender would likely plead guilty in return for a suspended sentence. An intensive programme of therapy would then begin, involving first of all individual treatment of the victim aimed at:

1. Validating her experience and resulting feelings as important and not atypical. Confused feelings of hatred towards those whom we are supposed to love are normal in such a situation.
2. Alleviating her guilt feelings: victims frequently hold themselves responsible for the abuse, and their guilt is intensified upon disclosure, and the ensuing family disruption.
3. Exploration of the child's feelings toward individual family members, particularly ambiguous feelings towards mother and siblings.
4. Exploration of the child's perception of feelings of other family members towards her. The initial goal is to concentrate on increasing self-awareness and self-esteem in the victim, before joining groups of victims, and beginning joint sessions with her mother.

The mother, the most forgotten person in the treatment process, needs counselling too: she needs to know the course treatment will take and its implications; she needs to ventilate and explore her feelings; and she needs to be relieved of her feelings of guilt and shame. Her own childhood history and feelings about sexuality need to be explored too before she can play an active part in treatment and self-help groups.

The adult male must be helped to accept responsibility for the sexual abuse, not only in a legal sense, but in an emotional and moral sense as well. To achieve this, the focus has to be on the personality, feelings, and childhood of the offender rather than on the offence itself. This is an essential prerequisite for dyadic counselling in which adult and victim will eventually talk to one another frankly; the offender tells the victim why he abused her and accepts that responsibility is entirely his. In being able to forgive the adult family member, the child reaches an important stage in recovering self-respect and divesting herself of hatred, both external and internal. Other important dyads include mother-victim and mother-father. Family therapy in a group is not an integral part of this process, and traditional family therapy which includes both offender and victim from the outset has been singularly unsuccessful in meeting the victim's needs.[61]

Finally, an important long-term component in treatment is the self-help groups. Parents United and Sons and Daughters United, which provide an important point of community contact and community education as well as continued peer support for victims.[62]

A single case of sexual abuse will obviously occupy many hours of the time of several therapists, whose work must be co-ordinated with the activities of the protection workers and police who will also be involved. All of this poses a dilemma for child welfare agencies. Adequately treating victims is complex and expensive and requires considerable reorientation of roles, values, resources, and practice. Social service delivery systems have been extremely reluctant to countenance such changes. The argument that expenditure of time, energy, and resources now will save a great deal in the long run, both in the cost of services saved (in reduced need to institutionalize victims) and restored mental health to victims, has failed to convince child welfare authorities of the need for or possibilities of change. Welfare bureaucracies are, unfortunately, rarely open to appeals or arguments on grounds of cost benefits, efficiency, rationality or humanity.

To bring about value change which will not only reorder services and expenditures for the treatment of victims in the short run but will also prevent the sexual abuse of children in the long run requires a major thrust. One way of encouraging change is educational programmes which tell children what sexual abuse is, how to resist it, and how to report it.

Our advocacy of a publicized crisis line in a Western Canadian city caused almost universal panic amongst conventional service deliverers. It was argued (correctly) that offering such a help line would call forth a flood of currently abused children. It was argued further that existing services could not cope and did not have the expertise or the manpower to treat so many abused children adequately. Assuming that it is better to allow continued abuse, rather than to offer inadequate service is simply a modern kind of denial of the realities.

An immediate practical concern in the adequate referral and treatment is for all those who have contact with young people in a professional or volunteer capacity to be aware of the possibility that sexual abuse underlies current distress or disturbed behaviour. In every case the question should be asked, "Are you currently being abused by anyone?" For most young people the question will be meaningless, but for a critical minority the answer will be crucially important.

THE BADGLEY COMMITTEE PROPOSALS

The Badgley Committee made a number of crucial proposals for treating and preventing child sexual abuse. The report's survey of some 10,000 cases of child sexual abuse in Canada shows that the protection afforded these victims by existing law and public services (medical and social) is deeply inadequate. Standards of practice and the type and co-ordination of investigation and treatment vary widely between centres and are particularly poor in rural areas.[63]

The committee proposes the establishment of the Office of Commissioner as a key and fundamental office in order to initiate and marshal the efforts of all levels of government and non-government agencies. Accordingly, the report calls for:

The establishment of a responsibility centre (Office of the Commissioner) reporting directly to the Office of the Prime Minister with the mandate to implement the Committee's proposals for reform, and to establishing a mechanism for coordinating and integrating the efforts of the federal government, the provinces and non-government agencies toward this end. (Recommendation 1)

The prevalence of child sexual abuse and the tragedy it inflicts led the committee to recommend that only the Prime Minister's Office possesses the prestige and influence required to address the problem.

Many of the committee's recommendations elaborate on and detail specific areas in which the Office of the Commissioner would participate:

The development and implementation of a national program of public education focussing on the needs of young children and youth in relation to the prevention of sexual offences and protection for children and youth. (Recommendation 2)

The convening of national conferences in conjunction with the Departments of Justice and of Health and Welfare and including Special Youth Programs of Police Forces, Special Medical and Hospital Programs, Special Child Protection Programs, Special Community and Voluntary Association Programs, pertaining to child sexual abuse, the reports of which are widely circulated. (Recommendation 28)

The development of standards of service for each of the main public services (police, medical and child protection services) in relation to the investigation, assessment and care of sexually abused children. (Recommendation 29)

The review of the funding for the Criminal Injuries Compensation Boards to ensure an adequate level of support for compensation to victims of sexual offences and the informing of Canadians of the existence and purpose of these Boards. (Recommendation 33)

The establishment of an interagency body for the purposes of developing a uniform system of classification of crime statistics and a standard core of information which includes, with respect to sexual offences: a) the age and sex of the victim, b) the association between the victim and offender, c) the injuries sustained, d) the specific offence committed and the specific acts involved, e) the age and sex of the offender, and f) the offender's prior criminal record. This interagency body will develop and review on a biennial basis a National Reporting System with respect to the Standard Core of Information. (Recommendation 35)

The appointment of an expert advisory committee to review the Codes of the International Classification of Diseases (Ninth Revision) to determine the extent to which these permit the identification of diagnosis relating to persons who have been sexually abused; to develop a revised classification with respect to the identification of the physical injuries and emotional harms associated with sexual assault, and the enlarging of this system in relation to the types of acts committed, their circumstances, and the association between the offender and patient; and to review and recommend means of identifying sexual abuse within the framework of medical services. (Recommendation 36)

The implementation of recommended revisions to the classification by Statistics Canada of hospital morbidity and death statistics; the review of means whereby the classification of medical services provided on an ambulatory basis can be revised to statistically identify persons who have been sexually assaulted and injured; and the making of representation to effect amendments to the Tenth Revision of the International Classification of Diseases to reflect these revisions. (Recommendation 37)

The review of the classification of child sexual offences against children and youth used by child protection services to establish a common core of information concerning a) the age and sex of the victim, b) the sexual acts committed, c) the injuries sustained by the victim, d) the association between the victim and offender and e) the disposition of the case. (Recommendation 38)

The assessment and review of general designs of studies plus recommendation for research dealing with sexual abuse, including the review of all research funded by the Government of Canada. (Recommendation 39)

The funding of national research studies focussing on a) injuries to sexually abused children, b) sexually transmitted diseases contracted by children, c) the long-term effects of exposure to children of pornography, acts of exposure, d) the treatment of convicted child sexual offenders, and e) recidivism of convicted child sexual offenders. (Recommendation 40)

The development of special educational programs documenting the conditions and risks associated with juvenile prostitution. (Recommendation 41)

The establishment of support programs for special multi-disciplinary demonstration projects to reach and to serve the needs of young persons involved in juvenile prostitution focussing on the means of affording immediate protection, counselling, and education and job training. (Recommendation 43)

The support to municipalities to enable the establishment of special police force units for the investigation and laying of charges against the clients of young prostitutes and the investigation and charging of pimps working with young prostitutes. (Recommendation 44)

The mounting of a program giving prominent publicity to the names of persons convicted of soliciting juvenile prostitutes under the age of 18. (Recommendation 47)

The review of the operation of the central registry of customs seizures to assure its efficient operation as a means of identifying the importation of child pornography. (Recommendation 50)

The public announcement of active R.C.M.P. cooperation with foreign enforcement agencies to obtain information concerning the producers and distributors of child pornography and the rigorous investigation of any suspected case of importation of child pornography; the seeking out of the mailing lists of all major commercial producers and distributors of child pornography and thorough investigations on the basis of the information so provided. (Recommendation 51)

It is important to note that the Badgley Committee does not single out any particular programme as being better than any other, and a variety of local initiatives are mentioned with approval. The thrust of the proposals are for the funding, through demonstration projects, of a variety of different approaches. All of these initiatives should be carefully evaluated, however. What is required, in the committee's view, is a fundamental recognition by all levels of Canadian society of the widespread nature of child sexual abuse and a willingness to support a variety of approaches at all levels.

NOTES

1. B. Morse, "Native and Métis children in Canada: Victims of the Child Welfare system," in G. Verma and C. Bagley, eds., *Race Relations and Cultural Differences: Educational and Cultural Perspectives* (London: Croom-Helm, 1983).
2. C. Bagley and R. Ramsay, "Research Problems and Priorities in Research on Suicidal Behaviours: An Overview with Canadian Implications," *Canadian Journal of Community Mental Health,* in press.
3. C. Bagley, "Child Abuse and Neglect: Basic Dilemmas of Theory, Research and Practice," in C. Bagley, *Child Welfare and Adoption: International Perspectives* (Aldershot: Gower, 1985).
4. C. Bagley, "Incest Behaviour and Incest Taboo," *Social Problems* 16 (1969): 505-19; P. Van Den Berghe, "Human Inbreeding Avoidance: Culture in Nature," *Behavioural and Brain Sciences* 6 (1983): 91-123; and J. Shepher, *Incest: A Biosocial View* (New York: Academic Press, 1983). The Criminal Code of Canada specifies that "incest" must involve consummated vaginal intercourse between close biological relatives (siblings, parent and child, or child and grandparent). Sexual abuse of children rarely fits this legal definition of incest.
5. K. Meiselman, *Incest* (San Francisco: Jossey-Bass, 1978); B. Schlesinger, *Sexual Abuse of Children* (Toronto: University of Toronto Press, 1982); and the *Committee on Sexual Offences against Children* (Ottawa, 1984).
6. J. Herman and L. Hirschman, *Father-Daughter Incest* (Cambridge: Harvard University Press, 1981).
7. F. Rush, *The Best Kept Secret* (New York: McGraw-Hill, 1980).

8. B. Taylor, ed., *Perspectives on Paedophilia* (London: Batsford Academic, 1981).

9. Herman and Hirschman, *Father-Daughter Incest.*

10. N. Frude, "The Sexual Nature of Sexual Abuse: A Review of the Literature," *Child Abuse and Neglect* 6 (1982): 211-23.

11. J. Peters, "Children Who Are Victims of Sexual Assault and the Psychology of Offenders," *American Journal of Psychotherapy* 30, no. 1 (January 1976): 398-421.

12. S. Butler, *Conspiracy of Silence: The Trauma of Incest* (San Francisco: New Glide Publications, 1978).

13. E. Sarafino, "An Estimate of Nationwide Incidence of Sexual Offences against Children," *Child Welfare* 58 (1979): 127-34.

14. L. Schultz, *The Sexual Victimology of Youth* (Springfield, Ill.: Thomas, 1980).

15. D. Finkelhor, *Sexually Victimized Children* (New York: Free Press, 1979).

16. L. Sorrenti-Little, C. Bagley, and S. Robertson, "An Operational Definition of the Long-term Harmfulness of Sexual Relations with Peers and Adults by Young Children," *Canadian Children: Journal of the Canadian Association for Young Children* 9 (1984): 1. Note the incidence figure of 16 per cent for child sexual abuse in another recent study of female college students in the U.S. — M. Sedney and B. Brooks, "Factors Associated with a History of Childhood Sexual Experience in a Nonclinical Female Population," *Journal of the American Academy of Child Psychiatry* 23 (1984): 215-18.

17. L. Wolfe, *The Cosmo Report* (New York: Arbor House, 1981).

18. C. Bagley, G. Verma, K. Mallick, and L. Young, *Personality, Self-Esteem and Prejudice* (Farnborough: Saxon House, 1979).

19. D. Russell, "The Incidence and Prevalence of Intrafamilia and Extrafamilia Sexual Abuse of Female Children," *Child Abuse and Neglect* 7 (1983): 133-46.

20. C. Bagley and R. Ramsay, "The Meanings and Experience of Suicidal Behaviours in an Urban Population," Paper presented to the Annual Meeting of the American Suicidology Association, Anchorage Alaska, May, 1984.

21. R. Badgley, Chairman, *Report of the Committee on Sexual Offences against Children* (Ottawa: Government of Canada, 1984).

22. C. Bagley, "Mental Health and the In-family Sexual Abuse of Children and Adolescents," *Canada's Mental Health* 32 (1984): 17-23.

23. Badgley Report.

24. E. Ward, *Father-Daughter Rape* (London: Women's Press, 1984).

25. Meiselman, *Incest;* J. Renvoize, *Incest: A Family Pattern* (London: Routledge, 1982); S. Forward and C. Buck, *Betrayal of Innocence: Incest and Its Devastations* (London: Penguin, 1981); and M. Tsai, S. Felman-Summers, and M. Edgar, "Childhood Molestation: Variables Related to Differential Impacts on Psychosexual Functioning in Adult Women," *Journal of Abnormal Psychology* 88 (1979): 407-17.

26. Schultz, *Sexual Victimology;* and K. Hughes, "The Reported Incidence of Incest among Runaway Female Adolescents," *Dissertation Abstracts International* 41 (1981): 4638B.

27. J. Denward and J. Densen-Gerber, "Incest as a Causative Factor in Antisocial Behaviour: An Exploratory Study," *Contemporary Drug Problems* 4 (1975): 323-40.

28. J. James and J. Meyerding, "Early Sexual Experience and Prostitution," *American Journal of Psychiatry* 134 (1977): 1381-85; and M. Silbert and A. Pines, "Sexual Child Abuse as an Antecedent to Prostitution," *Child Abuse and Neglect* 5 (1981): 407-11.

29. L. Anderson, "Notes on the Linkage between the Sexually Abused Child and the Suicidal Adolescent," *Journal of Adolescence,* 5 (1982); and J. Goodwin, "Suicide Attempts in Sexual Abuse Victims and Their Mothers," *Child Abuse and Neglect* 5 (1981): 217-21.

30. C. Bagley and M. McDonald, "Adult Mental Health Sequels of Child Sexual Abuse, Physical Abuse and Neglect in Maternally Separated Children," *Canadian Journal of Community Mental Health* 3 (1984): 15-26.

31. Silbert and Pines, "Sexual Abuse."

32. Badgley Report.

33. C. Bagley, "Child Sexual Abuse and Childhood Sexuality: A Review of the Monograph Literature 1978 to 1982," *Journal of Child Care* 2 (1982): 100-121.

34. D. Finkelhor, "Sexual Abuse: A Sociological Perspective," Paper given to 3rd International Congress of Child Abuse and Neglect, April, 1981.

35. D. Finkelhor, "Risk Factors in the Sexual Victimization of Children," *Child Abuse and Neglect* 4 (1980): 265-73.

36. D. Russell, "The Prevalence and Seriousness of Incestuous Abuse: Stepfathers vs. Biological Fathers," *Child Abuse and Neglect* 8 (1984): 15-22. See too L. Perlmutter, T. Engel, and C. Sagar, "The Incest Taboo: Loosened Sexual Boundaries in Remarried Families," *Journal of Sex and Marital Therapy* 8 (1982): 83-96.
37. Badgley Report.
38. Germaine Greer argues persuasively that this "sexual revolution" has operated to the advantage of men alone and simply made women more sexually available. An increase in the sexual abuse of children may be seen as another outcome of this sexual liberation of men. (G. Greer, *Sex and Destiny: The Politics of Human Fertility,* [Toronto: Stoddart, 1979]).
39. Finkelhor, "Risk Factors."
40. Rush, *Best Kept Secret.*
41. C. Bagley, *Child Sexual Abuse: Annotated Bibliography of Studies, 1978-1980* (Calgary: Rehabilitation and Health Monographs No. 3, University of Calgary Press, 1984).
42. For example, the case of Ethel, aged 55: "had been molested when she was six by her uncle — a priest who was a great source of pride for her religious, French-Catholic family. She had been terrified, bewildered. She told her parents about the molestation, but they reacted in disbelief. They called her a little whore and unknowingly reinforced the guilt that would plague her for the next fifty years." (S. Forward and C. Buck, *Betrayal of Innocence: Incest and Its Devastations* [Toronto: Macmillan, 1978]). Note too the comment of the syndicated columnist Dear Abby: "Whenever I publish a letter from someone who has been sexually abused as a child, I am inundated with letters from readers saying that this has happened to them. Many confide that they had lived with that ugly secret for as long as 40 and 50 years," *Calgary Sun,* 10 June 1983. For an excellent review of literature on long-term effects, see D. Gelinas, "The Persisting Negative Effects of Incest," *Psychiatry* 46 (1983): 312-32.
43. S. Hill, "Child sexual abuse: Selected Issues," M.S.W. thesis, University of Calgary, 1982.
44. C. Bagley, "Child sexual abuse and childhood sexuality;" and C. Bagley, "Child Sexual Abuse: Annotated Bibliography."
45. Badgley Report.
46. Finkelhor, *Sexually Victimized Children.*
47. M. Sedney and B. Brooks, "Factors Associated with a History of Childhood Sexual Experience in a Non-clinical Female Population," *Journal of the American Academy of Child Psychiatry* 23 (1984): 215-18.
48. Sorrenti-Little, Bagley, and Robertson, "Operational Definition," p.1.
49. Badgley Report.
50. Schultz, *Sexual Victimology* and C. Linedecker, *Children in Chains* (New York: Everest House, 1981).
51. D. Finkelhor, "What's Wrong with Sex between Adults and Children? Ethics and the Problem of Sexual Abuse," *American Journal of Orthopsychiatry* 49 (1979): 692-97.
52. H. Cohen, *Equal Rights for Children* (New York: Little Field Adams).
53. C. Bagley and M. MacDonald, "Adult Mental Health Sequels."
54. A. Maslow, *Dominance, Self-Esteem and Self-Actualization* (California: Brooks-Cole, 1973).
55. L. Sandford, *The Silent Children: A Parent's Guide to the Prevention of Child Sexual Abuse* (New York: Anchor, 1980).
56. C. Adams and J. Fay, *No More Secrets: Protecting Your Child From Sexual Assault* (San Luis Obispo: Impact, 1981); and B. and R. Justice, *The Broken Taboo: Sex in the Family* (New York: Human Science Press, 1979).
57. S. Sgroi, ed., *Handbook of Clinical Intervention in Child Sexual Abuse* (Lexington: Lexington Books, 1982).
58. H. Giarretto, *Integrated Treatment of Child Sexual Abuse: A Treatment and Training Manual* (Palo Alto: Science and Behavior Books, 1982). On the adaptation of this approach to meet the needs of a Canadian community, see C. Anderson and P. Mayes, "Treating Family Sexual Abuse: The Humanistic Approach," *Journal of Child Care* 2 (1982): 31-47.
59. I have concentrated in this chapter on the problems of female victims. On intervention and therapy with male victims, see Schultz, *Sexual Victimology,* and Linedecker, *Children in Chains.*

60. Herman, *Father-Daughter Incest.*
61. H. Giarretto, "A Comprehensive Child Sexual Abuse Treatment Program," *Child Abuse and Neglect* 6 (1982): 263-78. Group treatment of victims alone can, however, be highly effective. See Forward and Buck, *Betrayal of Innocence.*
62. C. Bagley, "The Gentle Revolution," in *Starting Over: Newsletter of Sons and Daughters United, Calgary Chapter* [P.O. Box 1161, Station J., Calgary, Alberta, (403) 242-8529], April, 1982. In Calgary, Giarretto's approach has been adapted by Anderson and Mayes to suit local needs; see note 58.
63. Badgley Committee, note 21.

5

THE SPECIAL NEEDS OF ADOLESCENTS: OBSERVATIONS OF A PHYSICIAN

Roger Tonkin

A recent headline in Vancouver's *Province* newspaper reads "Kids All Rotten Now."[1] The front-page headline is accompanied by a colour photograph of a woeful seventy-nine year old woman who is quoted as saying, "after 15 years of taking in troubled youth sent to her by the government agencies, she's closing the door." The reason: she was attacked in her home by three club-wielding thugs and robbed. This sorry tale encapsulates the many dimensions of contemporary adolescent welfare issues. Socrates, Aristotle, and Plato make reference to "youth." Their ancient words have a familiar ring — "they have bad manners and contempt for authority."[2]

The discipline of psychology emerged in the late 1800's, and as part of this new scientific endeavour, studies were begun on adolescent populations. The major work to emerge out of that era was that of G. Stanley Hall, published in 1904.[3] It was not until many years later that Hall's stereotypic view of adolescence as a period of "storm and stress" was effectively challenged by Daniel Offer. He showed that not all adolescents were in turmoil and that for many adolescents the "storm and stress" characterization was inappropriate.[4]

More contemporary thinking and writing reflects a changing view of adolescents. In essence, the second decade of life is being rediscovered. This rediscovery involves the dual process of identifying commonalities or constants within adolescent growth and development and the recognition of changing needs within the adolescent population, their families and social support systems, and the community or environment.

Adolescence is marked by the onset of puberty and the achievement of five developmental milestones. Briefly stated the milestones are: accepting one's physique, developing appropriate sex roles, becoming independent, relating to peers, making vocational and lifestyle choices. The adolescent needs to be supported throughout the pubertal changes and developmental challenges that normally occur. The family and school support systems play a primary role in this regard while peer-related activities provide the necessary channels for experimentation and competitiveness. The environment in which the adolescent experiences change and within which the adolescent's support systems must function contains institutions of commerce, education, regulation or law, and human services. These institutions antedate Socrates and serve much the same functions now as then. However, they, like adolescence itself, undergo cycles of change and experience shifts in emphasis.

Today's adolescents differ from their predecessors in a number of significant ways. They mature earlier and are larger than youth of a century ago. The mean age of the onset of puberty is 11.2 in girls and 11.9 years in boys.[5] Reproductive capability has advanced into the junior high school years and is reflected in broad concerns about teenage pregnancy. The lowering of prohibitions on "adult" behaviours has been associated with issues of teenage sexuality, use of contraceptives, misuse of alcohol and drugs, and the exploitation of the "youth vote," the "youth market," and so forth. Advances in the management of many diseases of childhood have also had an important impact on the adolescent population. These advances are particularly significant in the area of chronic medical and surgical conditions such as diabetes mellitus, cystic fibrosis, spina bifida, and certain causes of mental retardation. There is a small but growing population of handicapped adolescents and young adults who would not normally have survived into or beyond their teen years. Indeed, this small population of special needs adolescents is disproportionately represented in the case load of many child welfare agencies.

The period of dependency on family or state has been changing. In the early 1970's, the age of majority was lowered from twenty-one to nineteen years. The recently introduced Young Offenders Act increases the maximum age within the juvenile justice system from seventeen to eighteen years. These formal changes in the recognition of adult status have been achieved at a time when the young person's dependency on the family or state has been increasing. High youth unemployment rates, escalating costs of living, and changes in educational requirements have combined to keep young people at home and/or in school longer. These young people are, by and large, better educated, healthier, and technically more skilled than in the past, and yet they continue to be our most underutilized resource.

In recent years adolescence or the "second decade" has become a more accepted area of research. A number of excellent "state of the art" reviews about adolescence have recently been released — for example, Rutter's 1979 Rock Carling Fellowship publication on "Changing Youth in a Changing Society."[6] Rutter states "it is clear that to a considerable extent the youth 'phenomenon' and the current concepts of 'psychosocial adolescence' are products of the prevailing western culture." More recently the prestigious journal *Child Development* devoted a special issue to studies of early adolescence. In his editorial introduction to this issue, Hill explains that earlier psychological research emphasized the first five years of life because "adolescents were already too old to warrant much attention. . .now, on the threshold of 1983, the picture is much different. . .adolescents in short, are less often perceived as either too old or too weird to study."[7]

Our ideas about therapeutic environments for adolescents also seem to be undergoing change. The approach to containment, for example, seems confused. Juvenile corrections facilities have been closed, but the opening of psychiatric in-patient units (open and closed) has been slow and insufficient to meet containment needs. Programmes to de-institutionalize the mentally retarded or emotionally disturbed adolescent have moved forward. Unfortunately, the community-based teams and the regional treatment centres needed to manage these adolescents are either non-existent or merely grafted onto other non-adolescent services. The multidisciplinary assessment and management teams needed to work with these adolescents and their support systems have been slow to appear. The lack of a balanced approach to the provision of therapeutic environments has added to the stress and confusion experienced by all concerned. The responsibility for adolescents who are emotionally disturbed, mentally retarded, or in conflict with the law ends up being thrust back upon the support systems in the community, that is, families and schools.

Implications for Human Services. Contemporary thinking and writing reflect a growing interest in adolescents and an emerging consensus that their needs are not well met. While the nature of these needs is changing, there is little to suggest that the resilience of youth is in any way diminished. It is a common observation that despite the difficulties they encounter, most adolescents turn out "O.K." Why, then, should we worry? After all, we have child protection legislation, services for the abused, group homes, child care workers, and so forth.

TABLE 1

DIFFERENTIATION OF ADOLESCENT POPULATION OF B.C.

by stage and coping style

	Stage of Adolescence		
Coping Style	*Early*	*Middle*	*Late*
Tumult	40,000 (a)	41,000 (b)	27,000 (c)
Surges	60,000 (d)	61,000 (e)	41,000 (f)
Continuous	42,000 (g)	43,000 (h)	30,000 (i)
Total number	142,000	145,000	98,000
Age group	12-14	15-17	18-19

Source: "Manual on Adolescence," (Vancouver, 1981).

If we examine the situation from the perspective of the matrix in Table 1, we might begin to see things differently. The matrix has been created by matching the adolescent population of B.C. according to their developmental phase (early, middle, or late) and their coping style (as described by Offer).[4] This matrix consists of nine different cells covering the various categories of adolescents within the total population.

Adolescents in the "continuous cells' (g,h,i) are life's smooth sailors. They have little or no need for special services since they have few problems en route to achieving their developmental milestones. Those that they do encounter will generally be adjusted to with the help of their immediate support systems. Adolescents in the "surges cells" (d,e,f) may not experience any developmental difficulties, or if they do have problems, they tend to be restricted to one stage of adolescence. For example, an adolescent male who engages in minor delinquencies and is caught at it may end up in conflict with the law in early adolescence (cell d), or a middle adolescent female may become pregnant in the course of normal sexual experimentation (cell e). Most of these difficulties will be short-lived. The adolescent will learn from the experience. The human services will be called upon to intervene in a limited or short-term fashion. Adolescents in the "tumult" cells (a,b,c) often present a quite different challenge. This is the group that Hall studied and characterized as experiencing the "storm and stress" of the adolescent period. The tumult group, especially early adolescent (cell a) and middle or late adolescents (cells b,c) from situations where the family is dysfunctional or the school-community support system is inadequate are disproportionately represented in the human services network's lists of problem clients.

TABLE 2

ADOLESCENTS AND HUMAN SERVICES IN B.C. — 12 MONTH PERIOD 1980/81

Agency	Numbers
Education/Employment	
Dropouts/suspended	17,900
Unemployed	32,000
Health	
Admitted to Hospital	25,500
Adolescents Pregnant	7,700
Human Resources	
Placed in Care	5,530
Reported Abused	630
Attorney General	
Admission to Juvenile Jail	1,150
Diverted to MHR	3,000
On Probation	3,020
Juveniles Charged with Offence	13,600
Delinquencies	21,900
Driving Convictions	9,000

Source: "Child Health Profile," (Vancouver, 1983).

When one looks at the numbers of adolescents in each cell within the matrix and compares these estimates with the approximate case loads in the various sectors of the human services network (Table 2), one must ask questions about the effectiveness and efficacy of our programmes. Considering the size of the tumult group and assuming that most of the significant adolescent problems occur within this population, it would appear from the numbers in Table 2 that we are not even batting .500.

Some would argue that the batting average is low because these adolescents have long-standing, demonstrable developmental difficulties that are merely exacerbated in the course of adolescent growth and development. Perhaps Hall would have been comfortable with this argument, but more recent research does not allow the same privilege. For example, Rutter examined the available measures of outcome and concluded that in some areas adolescent behaviour or development had shown improvement, for example, better achieved standards of education but that in others, things seem to have deteriorated, for example, delinquent behaviour, suicide, and other self-destructive behaviours.[6] Data for B.C. (Table 3) tend to support Rutter's findings and demonstrate that B.C.'s position is worse than the national average in either Canada or the U.S.A.[7] An increasing number of adolescents in the province are caught up in the pattern of risk taking and self-destructive behaviour, and as a consequence, the number of violent deaths in adolescence (15-19) rose from 100 in 1961 to 327 in 1981.[8]

TABLE 3

SOCIAL CAUSES OF DEATH — B.C. vs CANADA AND U.S.A.

Mortality Rate* by Cause — 1976

		10-14 yrs.	15-19 yrs.
Suicide	U.S.A.	1.0	7.6
	Canada	1.0	10.7
	B.C.	2.2	13.0
Homicide	U.S.A.	1.2	9.6
	Canada	0.4	2.3
	B.C.	1.8	5.9
Motor Vehicle	U.S.A.	8.4	38.4
	Canada	9.1	45.3
	B.C.	9.2	59.7

*NOTE: Rate per 100,000 age specific.

Source: "Child Health Profile: Violence in Adolescence" (Vancouver, 1981).

The ultimate question is, of course, how should the human service system respond to the needs of adolescents, especially those in the "tumult" group. Do we need specialized programmes for adolescents? Should the rationale be one of comprehensive community-based services for all adolescents or a more restrictive model geared to containing and/or punishing the adolescent who offends, challenges, or transgresses family or community rules? Should our approach thrust the responsibility back on the family, or should it support or even supplant the family? Where should we draw the line between the responsibility of schools, the courts, and the welfare system?

The health care system in North America provides a model for answering some of these questions. For example, a majority of centres now offer adolescent-oriented services. The developing specialty of adolescent medicine has coincided with the emergence of in-patient and out-patient programmes specifically for adolescents. Workers and clients exposed to these settings are generally enthusiastic about them, whereas scepticism and resistance is a more common response among those who must treat adolescent health problems in generalist or adult-oriented models. Adolescent medicine has emerged as a multidisciplinary effort grounded in a common recognition of the developmental issues of adolescence. The Society for Adolescent Medicine states, "The major focus of the Society for Adolescent Medicine is to promote the development, synthesis, and dissemination of scientific and scholarly knowledge unique to the development and health care needs of adolescents."

Within the framework of adolescent medicine programmes many more specific problems or treatment needs can be met. For example, the continuing work of Kempe and others on issues of child abuse has highlighted the problems of sexual abuse and its impact on adolescent development.[9] Progress in the field of chronic handicapping conditions in childhood has now begun to have an impact on the handicapped adolescent, and programmes to assist them with issues of sexuality, vocational planning, and independence are being developed. Topics such as violence in adolescence, adoption and parent search, teenage mothers, adolescent school phobia, and eating disorders are now the subject of active research and service programmes within adolescent medical programmes. While these developments have largely occurred within the traditional medical model, the experience of the last decade does offer some perspective on the questions originally posed about adolescents in the child welfare system.

Adolescent-oriented services are not easy to initiate. There are many attitudinal, financial, and professional training issues to overcome. However, once established, these services seem to make it easier to meet the needs of adolescents and to nurture the professionals who must develop and maintain the much needed teaching, research, and service teams. While it is possible to accomplish these same general objectives in a non-adolescent or generalist programme, it has proven to require much more energy and time and to be accompanied by a tendency to force square pegs into round holes.

Adolescent medicine emphasizes a developmental approach and attempts to introduce it at the community level. It also tries to foster a preventive element in designated areas such as substance abuse, eating disorders, pregnancy, and venereal disease. In general, the emphasis in adolescent medicine is the need for adolescents to develop understanding of and responsibility for their own health. Parents, parent substitutes, and the school system are seen as supportive to the adolescent but not central to the client-provider relationship. This approach is reflected in the style of most adolescent-oriented programmes and in the ways in which they recognize the adolescent's rights with respect to confidentiality and consent. At the same time, most programmes in adolescent medicine recognize the central role that family and school play and attempt to support these systems (especially when their energy, confidence, or patience wanes).

Adolescent medicine considers its mandate to be a concern for the health of all adolescents. The juvenile offender and child welfare systems have more restrictive mandates, that is, youth as a victim or as a problem. In some ways a restricted mandate should make it easier to design and implement adolescent-oriented services. The client population is smaller, and it can be divided in to two major groups; the first and largest will be drawn from the continuous and/or surges portions of the matrix (cells d to i); the second group will most likely represent the tumult portion (cells a to c). The first group's needs are for protection, nurturance, and authority provided in family-like settings whereas the second group's needs may only be met in more specialized resources. Since two-thirds of the children in care today are adolescents, that is, twelve years of age or more and since most are there because of one or other form of family breakdown, it is reasonable to suppose that these young people's needs can be simply and adequately met in a developmentally appropriate or normative model. Some adolescents (15 per cent of cases) are in short-term care and a few (less than 5 per cent) are in care after committing an offence under the Juvenile Delinquents Act. It is reasonable to assume that most of the latter two groups are in care because of their behaviour and the inability of families to cope with them. At any one time the Ministry of Human Resources in B.C. is legally responsible for about fourteen hundred children and youth in special resources. Youngsters with behavioural difficulties account for two-thirds of this caseload, and most are adolescents. This collection of clients, though small, consumes much of the child welfare system's energy and resources.

What are the more general needs of adolescents within the child welfare system? Again let us look to the health care model for some answers. I have already tried to make a case for the development of specialized, adolescent-oriented services. These services would have an important role to play in improving the training opportunities for workers in the child welfare system. Many years of working with social workers, child care workers, agency administrators, and child welfare advocacy groups have left me with the impression that their basic knowledge of adolescent growth and development is deficient, their attitudes towards adolescents usually negative, and the value they place on working with adolescents is low. Why? Is it a function of having to deal with a small but highly problematic client group? Is it a funciton of resource availability and service priorities? Or does it reflect society's value system and the merits of non-adolescent-oriented career choices?

In part the answer to all the above questions is "yes." However, I have come to believe that the training of child welfare workers at both the pre-licensing and in-service level is not adequate to prepare them to meet the challenges of working with today's adolescents effectively. Workers and trainees in the human services field may be given a few courses in adolescence and may, in the course of their practicums, meet a few adolescents. However, their exposure is infrequent and often based on the more deviant portions of the adolescent population. Once into the field, workers have much more contact with adolescents, begin to sense their inadequate preparation, and, as a consequence, often limit or try to avoid the kind of involvement that adolescent clients seek. Workers frequently express a sense of frustration and inadequacy after dealing with adolescents, especially those from the tumult group.

Workers need to be shown how to differentiate between the tumult and surges types of clients. They need to develop an understanding of continuity of care, patience, and firmness for the tumult group and to be trained to negotiate and renegotiate incentive type contracts. There is a need for a more contemporary data base on adolescent fads and fashions and the creation of a vehicle for feeding this information back to line workers. Such an information feedback loop would help workers connect their individual client experience with that of the broader community. Better training and on-going in-service support would help translate the almost universal negativism of adolescent child welfare workers into the sort of positive enthusiasm that workers in adolescent medicine usually demonstrate.

It is often stated that the dilemma for the adolescent in the child care system is that he is neither a child nor an adult. The dilemma is that we have not developed an adolescent-oriented welfare system and have created barriers that keep the adolescent out of the child and the adult systems. It seems reasonable to advocate the development of adolescent-oriented services *and* the elimination of barriers within the existing systems. Certainly there would not be much point in improving the training of workers within the broader system if the clients are denied access to them.

Populations do not always use the resources available to them. For example, community mental health programmes only reach about one-third of adolescents with known long-term mental health problems.[10] Clients do not always use resources in the most appropriate way. For example, hospital emergency departments are frequently misused. Certainly adolescents have gained a degree of notoriety for their non-compliance and/or non-attendance in a variety of clinical settings. However, barriers to service do exist and several affect adolescents. These barriers may involve the legal requirements of the service agency, the style of service delivery, or the costs of providing the services.

LEGAL ISSUES

Society is inconsistent in the way that it applies its rules to adolescents. Token parental consent is required before an adolescent can obtain a driver's licence while even with parental consent an adolescent cannot obtain a credit card. The adolescent can drink and drive with relative impunity, but once he is eighteen, the same offence may result in a jail sentence. Adolescents can become sexually active at a time of their choosing, but parental consent is required before they can terminate an unwanted pregnancy. The adolescent may be considered mature enough to go to adult court or jail at eighteen years but not mature enough to drink or vote. An adolescent who is ill and requires hospital treatment will be required to obtain parental consent (until nineteen years of age) even if the patient has been living away from home for some time. We have provided our adolescent population with a confusing set of ill-conceived and inconsistently applied rules and regulations which have had the effect of disenfranchising them.

The issue of consent is central to many of the problems involved in providing human services to adolescents. It is often confused with issues of confidentiality.[11] Adolescents should always be guaranteed confidentiality. The one exception to this rule is a situation where life is threatened.

Consent is an issue in many child care situations. Two situations illustrate the point. A fifteen-year-old girl is apprehended and placed in short-term care because she has been running away from home and is acting out sexually. Her home is abusive and filled with conflict on sexual issues. The girl has been placed on oral contraceptives by her physician prior to apprehension without parental consent or advisement. In care, child care workers cannot give her contraceptives (or any other medication for that matter) without parental consent. Consider the choices open to this girl and try to justify why the girl should not be able to continue with the course of action which she and her physician had previously agreed upon.

As a second example, consider the situation of an adopted adolescent who is acting out and having identity problems. Some of these problems relate to important questions about his biological roots. He has experienced a delay in the onset of puberty, and in association with his late maturation, he has rage attacks and violent fantasies. He and the workers trying to help him need to know about his biological parents and what they were like during their adolescence. Was their behaviour the reason for his being placed in adoption? How can he or his attending physician find out about these things? Can he see what his parents look like? Why do some societies deny adolescents the opportunity to explore their biological roots during the critical identity formation years and force them to wait until they are legally adult? If adoption is a humane practice for newborn infants, why cannot we make it equally humane for them when they reach puberty?

ISSUES OF STYLE

It is strange to observe a society that prides itself on freedom of choice and the need to respect the rights and sensitivities of various groups as it responds to the demands of adolescents. Institutions that strive to create environments that children will feel comfortable in often seem oblivious to the negative effect of chairs that are too small or piped-in nursery school music upon the adolescents who must use these same facilities. Adults behave in strange ways when adolescents play music too loud or fail to tidy up, but they are often unperturbed by the lack of recreational and employment opportunities for these same young people.

Is it not possible to offer human services in a style that is suitable to adolescents and that offers an environment conducive to safe disclosure and compliance with any treatment required? Professionals working in such an environment need not act like adolescents but rather as confident and mature adults who are interested in the individual's needs and wants. The workers must feel comfortable with their own values and be able to distance themselves from the values clarification or conflict that adolescents must undergo as they mature. The worker's role is to facilitate values clarification, but not direct it. A more important role for workers is to help the adolescent to understand human behaviour and to acquire the necessary information and skills to function in the various adult environments.

The adolescent remains one of the most exploited of our human service consumers. We take advantage of their naivety and inexperience. Given the way many agencies and professionals interact with adolescents, it should cause no surprise when adolescent clients find ways to subvert the system. The adolescent client is notorious for failing to show up on time, lying or withholding information, or simply refusing to do what he is asked. Gentle amusement is generally a better response than anger. Adjustment of the approach is a better reaction than ultimatums. This is not to say that we should not present a clear idea of what we think is important or what our limits are. Quite the reverse! Many of the problems involved in dealing with adolescents stem from our failure to take the time to explain and to ensure that the adolescent client understands the advice offered or our expectations for future behaviour. In essence, we forget that adolescents are just beginning to learn how to use adult-oriented human services and that heretofore their parents or legal guardians have made most of their decisions. This type of experiential learning is often a mixture of positive and negative episodes. It takes many interactions and much time to set the stage for a continuing and positive client/provider relationship.

ISSUES OF COST

In providing services for adolescents we often exact a price. Sometimes it appears as if they are being punished for needing or seeking help. The simplest of these costs are time and money. Many services are only available during school hours. This may require adolescent clients to miss important classes or part-time jobs or, alternately, force them to engage in subterfuge so that their parents will not know that they are coming for help. For some adolescents even the most basic of expenses such as bus fare, taxi money, or parking fees may present a problem. For others the cost of a counselling session, a medication, or a test procedure may prove prohibitive. A more important cost may be the loss of control and a lowered sense of self-worth. This is particularly true in situations where parental involvement is required by the service agency. Inappropriate parental participation often reinforces the adolescent's feeling of powerlessness and results in the rebellious, non-compliant type of response commonly seen.

Adolescent services need to ensure that full information, consistent practices, and proper consent processes are presented to each client on each visit. Adolescents need to be sure of seeing the same person from episode to episode. Proper principles of primary care need to be practised with adolescents. Services must be age appropriate *and* developmentally appropriate if they are to succeed. The late adolescent who is emancipated is not going to accept a child-oriented milieu and may even reject an adolescent-oriented one. The standards of care applied to adolescent patients should be comparable to those for children or adults.

As adolescents make the transition between parent advocacy and self-advocacy the human services system often fails to serve an integrative role; that is, it fails to help the adolescent learn how to enunciate the problem, give a history, make choices about what to do, or follow-up on the chosen course of action. The adolescent client is at the mercy of a fragmented and incomplete range of services. The services usually reflect agency or provider priorities rather than those of the adolescent. Integrating all these services is a daunting task to most adults. Imagine how overwhelmed the adolescent must feel. Some adolescents carry a wallet full of business cards thoughtfully provided by the many professionals they must deal with in the course of seeking proper care. The resultant partitioning of the adolescent is developmentally inappropriate and compromises the adolescent in his or her struggle to develop an identity and a sense of mastery of the environment.

RECOMMENDATIONS

Changes For All. Within the child welfare system there are a number of avenues which should be explored as part of our response in this era of restraint.

The Infants Act should be revised to provide more realistic consent guidelines for minors. Apprehensions under the Family and Child Service Act of British Columbia might be avoided if the Infants Act were revised and better understood by workers involved in administering it.

The Adoption Act should be revised to provide better answers to the medical and identity issues that arise in adolescence and to provide for a disclosure registry which the adolescent could have access to at the age of majority.

"Office for Youth" should be created with the express purpose of developing a network of services for adolescents. These services would include the range of disciplines currently operating under a number of separate ministries including Human Resources, Health, Education, and Attorney-General. The focus of the "office" would be preventive for all adolescents and their families and integrative for those adolescents with complex developmental issues or problems.

Worker Preparation. Training programmes should provide better curricula in adolescent growth and development, offer a conceptual framework for working with adolescent problems, and serve to increase the professional's sense of competence in and satisfaction with working with adolescents and their families.

Supports for Supporters. Families and schools need to be helped to acquire the information and resources for them to fulfil their supporting roles. School consultative groups and local religious or service clubs are useful vehicles in this process. Provision of respite programmes for exhausted families or schools would offer important opportunities for re-education.

Regional Youth Study Centres. A national network of study centres should be established. These university based or affiliated centres should serve two functions. The first would be the development of new knowledge, and the second would involve the dissemination of knowledge. Much is already known about adolescence, but little of it has been applied. We need a vehicle that will promote the rediscovery of this knowledge and will enable us to build upon it. Behavioural research and the study of developmental psychopathology is underdeveloped. At least two subject areas need special attention. The first is the continuing problem of self-destructive behaviour in the adolescent population. Much of it stems from the dynamics of the risk-taking which most adolescents engage in. The second subject area is the monitoring or evaluation of the status of our adolescent population. In particular, we need better information on the impact of shifts in education, employment, and families upon adolescents.

Primary Care Service Models. These community-based interdisciplinary primary care service models should interact with established community resources and serve as a focal point for the development of a range of adolescent-oriented services in each community. These community-based primary care units should also be supported by a network of regional and tertiary care services. The latter group of specialized services should be interdisciplinary and interagency in nature. The service network should emphasize diagnosis and assessment at the local and regional level, and wherever possible, management should be community-based.

CHANGES FOR SOME

Earlier in this chapter reference was made to the tumult group of adolescents. This group warrants special attention from the child welfare and human services system. They and their families have been the special target of the negative attitude that adolescents seem to generate. Clearly we need to create more effective approaches to them. Professionals working with the tumult group tend to vacillate between rigid and laissez-faire postures. Families often respond in similar fashion.

The matrix developed earlier would suggest that the early tumult group (cell a) and the late continuous group (cell i) are very different. A laissez-faire approach could do no harm with the latter but might prove disastrous with the former. The early adolescent needs firm limits. The difficulty is deciding which limits to set and how to enforce them. The same set of limits will be received differently by the tumult group (cell a) than by the continuous group (cell g). Parents, schools, and the adolescents themselves often need help with the process of limit-setting and enforcement.

The conceptual model for the process of limit-setting in adolescence can be likened to a six-sided box. The dimensions of the box delineate the extent to which adolescents experience a sense of restriction and influence the degree of rebellion encountered. Too tight a box is difficult for cell 'a' adolescents and engenders vigorous, random efforts to break out. Too loose a box leaves the cell 'a' adolescents with a sense of insecurity and promotes attempts to see just how far they can go. The sides of the box consist of the elements of space, time, and energy within the family and/or school setting (see Table 4).

TABLE 4
ELEMENTS IN TONKIN'S BEHAVIOUR BOX

	Family	*School*
Space	Tidiness	Grades
Time	Curfews	Attendance
Energy	Considerateness	Motivation

Each element within the model needs to be defined, and the weight and importance to each side must be negotiated. A clear set of "bottom lines" should be established. Once the elements have been defined, they will provide a set of external controls which, when combined with appropriate incentives for adhering to them, will be the most effective way of controlling behaviour and reducing the self-destructive effects of adolescent risk-taking. The child welfare system has a number of clear roles in this regard. The first is to help families and schools set and enforce realistic limits. A second is to define appropriate responses when the model breaks down. These responses may range from simple respite services for a worn-out parent to more restrictive and legalistic approaches to chronic offenders. An "Office for Youth" could assist in this process and might replace the present Interministerial Children's Committee, which has been set up to handle the more serious problems within the system.

Shifts in emphasis that have occurred as a result of the Young Offenders Act and the Family and Child Service Act have placed more responsibility on the individual and the family. Getting the tumult group of adolescents and their parents to accept responsibility is often difficult. The proposed primary care models could interface between child welfare and young offender systems and might enable the desired shift of responsibilities to occur. The tumult group are acknowledged masters of manipulation and evasion. A locally based, integrated, youth-oriented service model would reduce the likelihood of this happening. Such a unit could help delineate the "box" and devise effective ways of keeping the adolescent in it until the critical early and middle adolescent years are over. Such a unit could also co-ordinate the court-ordered assessments and/or treatments for young offenders; monitor the status of youth in care, and provide behaviourally oriented treatment programmes. Such models could be cost-effective, have a preventive focus, and offer youth an alternative to frustration they now experience in seeking help.

CONCLUSION

The nature of adolescence and the social fabric within which it must evolve have undergone important changes. The context in which these changes have occurred has changed from that of the apparently ever-escalating excess of the last two decades to the more conservative and less tolerant restraint of the early 1980's. These changes have been rapid and stressful, but we have done little to recognize or adjust to the unmet needs of adolescents that follow in their wake. Fortunately, most adolescents have the personal strength and the support systems to enable them to withstand the buffeting of rapid social change. About one-third of adolescents are less fortunate, and because of their developmental difficulties, they become highly vulnerable and often fall victim to the inadequacies of our child welfare, health care, and education systems. They are the casualties of restraint just as the adolescents of the late 1960's became the casualties of dissent.

REFERENCES

1. *The Province.* 21 August 1984, p. 1.
2. R.S. Tonkin, *Adolescent Manual.* (Vancouver, 1982): 10.
3. G. Stanley Hall, *Adolescence: Its Psychology.* 2 vols. (New York: Appleton, 1904).
4. D. Offer, *The Psychological World of the Teenager.* (New York: Basic Books, 1969).
5. P.A. Lee, "Normal Ages of Pubertal Events among American Males and Females." *Journal of Adolescent Health Care* 1 (1980): 26-29.
6. M. Rutter, *Changing Youth in a Changing Society.* London: Nuffield Provincial Hosp. Trust., 1979.
7. R.S. Tonkin, *Child Health Profile: Mini-Series No. 2. Violence in Adolescence.* (Vancouver: 1980).
8. ———, *Child Health Profile. — 1981.* (Vancouver: 1982).
9. C.H. Kempe, et al, "The Battered Child Syndrome." *Journal of the American Medical Association* 181 (1962): 17.
10. E.E. Werner and R.S. Smith, *Kauai's Children Come of Age.* (Honolulu: University Press of Hawaii, 1977).
11. A.D. Hoffman, "A Rational Policy toward Consent and Confidentiality in Adolescent Health Care," *Journal of Adolescent Health Care* 1 (1980): 9-19.

6

THE LEGAL PROCESS OF BRINGING CHILDREN INTO CARE IN BRITISH COLUMBIA

David Turner and Brian Shields

The idealistic goals of child protection laws must not obscure the fact that government intervention in family life infringes fundamental personal liberties of both parents and children, and may not fulfill its idealistic and benevolent promise. The personal freedom of parents to have children in their care and custody and to raise them as they see fit and the correlative rights of children to live with their parents unfettered by government interference must be protected and must be set aside only under carefully defined circumstances.[1]

In Canada, child welfare law and process is a provincial responsibility. However, while this article is grounded in B.C. law and process, the procedures are similar across the country. The following review serves to highlight the key procedures and steps required for a social worker to bring a child into care in Victoria courts. Variations in practice occur around the province, which are dependent upon personnel in the court process, primarily the judge and counsel, and the degree of formality of the local court system. At present, there is a trend towards more formality and adherence to legality.

Child welfare and child protection law is contained primarily in one B.C. statute enacted in 1980, the Family and Child Service Act (F.C.S.A.). It was intended to replace some of the archaic aspects of the previous Protection of Children Act of 1908.

Preventive social service powers are contained primarily in the Guaranteed Available Income for Need Act. "Social services" means "services. . . provided to or on behalf of individuals or families. . .that are necessary for the purpose of facilitating access to the necessities of life, maintaining or improving employability or improving social functions of individuals and families and includes. . .social services having as their object the lessening, removal or prevention or the cause and effects of poverty, child neglect and suffering."[2] The Family and Child Service Act contains only twenty-four sections, and it has been criticized for leaving too many issues to the area of regulation, ministry policy, and case law. There are no regulations at the present time.

The Superintendent of Family and Child Services is responsible for the administration of child welfare legislation. The superintendent or his delegate has the power and obligation to act under the statute (Sec. 3). In fact, the superintendency role is covered by one or more deputy ministers,[3] and the superintendent's delegates are social workers, with letters of authority to apprehend, employed by the Ministry of Human Resources (M.H.R.). There are no longer Children's Aid Societies in B.C.

PHILOSOPHY

The goal of the Ministry of Human Resources in child welfare is contained in policy: "Within the mandate of the Family and Child Service Act, to provide a range of services to the child and his family and/or to take such legal action as is required, to ensure a child's safety and well-being, and where possible to preserve the integrity of the family."[4]

The key philosophical premise of this legislation is contained in Section 2, "that the safety and wellbeing of the child shall be the paramount considerations."[5] This gives direct emphasis to the interests of the child as opposed to the rights of parents. Procedurally, parents' rights are protected under the Family and Child Service Act, but they have no right to demand services which will assist them to keep their children from being apprehended. The G.A.I.N. Act section allowing for appeals of refusals of social services has never been proclaimed (S. 25(4)). Hence, the ministry has the mandate to provide preventive services, but not a challengeable obligation. Although many social workers do not want to think of themselves as agents for social control, that is what they are in fact. In protecting children, they are controlling the way parents choose to deal with their children. However, it is clear from the policy of the Ministry of Human Resources that the focus is on keeping child and parent together and reuniting children with their natural parents when at all possible. However, it is not protected in law, and wardship invests total legal powers over the child in the superintendent. Only the act and policy modify these powers — for instance, the public trustee becomes guardian of the child's estate (finances) under permanent care.[6]

A social worker as agent of the superintendent is an enforcer of community standards of child care and this involves difficult value judgments. While a family court judge is the final arbiter of whether minimum community standards have been violated, the social worker makes the front-line judgment call. As the policy manual states:

When a complaint is received that the care of any child is below an acceptable standard so that he may be exposed to danger or lacking basic requirements for healthy development, it is the responsibility of the social worker to investigate, to assess the circumstances and to offer such services as will assist the parents to bring the standard of care up to an acceptable level.[7]

If the social worker decides there is too much risk to the child to leave him at home or if parents are unable or unwilling to change their standards of care, then the social worker becomes the initiator of the legal process of apprehension.

It will be noted that while the mandated duties of the superintendent cover only legal areas, social workers often first encounter families in a supportive counselling role. Thus, they are often forced to switch from concerned counsellor to law-backed apprehender when protection conditions cannot be remedied. For instance, a financial assistance worker may refer a single mother to a social worker because of alcohol abuse which appears to affect her capacity to budget and to give economic and emotional stability to her children. The social worker responds by providing support in arranging a homemaker to teach domestic skills or a contract childcare worker to teach child-raising skills and perhaps to relieve her temporarily of the responsibility of looking after her children. Short-term agreements to care for children are used so that the mother has an opportunity to improve her own situation. However, if the rehabilitation plan falters and serious relapses occur and if the children become seriously affected in their treatment, then the social worker is required to intervene and apprehend. Obviously, a skilled worker would have informed parents as to mutual expectations and possible outcomes.

LEGAL METHODS OF BRINGING CHILDREN INTO CARE

The four major methods are: through agreement with parents or guardian; through the provincial court process under a court order, either under the Family and Child Service Act. Under the Young Offenders' Act,[8] which replaces the Juvenile Delinquents Act, wardship is no longer a disposition available to judges in such youth criminal procedures; automatically on the death of both parents or guardians under the Family Relations Act,[9] if no guardian has been named; through an order of the Supreme Court (under the Family Relations Act) as *parens patriae*.

Agreements

One author estimates that as many as 90 per cent of all children in care in

Victoria are in care at parents' request, consent, or permission. The hotly contested cases are not the run-of-the-mill situations, though they may be increasing. This seeming willingness of many parents to rely on a government ministry to care for their children in non-emergency situations can create unusual tension for social workers. Sections 4, 5, and 6 give the superintendent power to enter into a short-term or special care agreement with a parent requiring temporary assistance in caring for a child. It is intended to cover situations where a parent is temporarily incapacitated or requires special help for a needy child for a short period of time. It is meant to be specific and time-limited with the maximum period of three months. Legally, it is a private agreement with parents retaining guardianship, and they can cancel the agreement at any time. The superintendent can also cancel the agreement but is required to give seven days notice.

If a parent refuses or is unable to resume custody at the end of the agreement term, then, after a period of thirty days, the child is viewed as abandoned and having been apprehended by the superintendent. This initiates the court process.

In B.C., for the purposes of this Act, including agreements and apprehension leading to court process, children are defined as those under nineteen years of age. The B.C. Family Relations Act provides that where both parents die or the single parent dies without naming a guardian in a will, the superintendent becomes the guardian of the person of the child immediately and the public trustee the guardian of the child's estate. This provision is most applicable where parents are killed in accidents, leaving dependent children. The lack of a court process here, except by application, is the source of some criticism.

Apprehension and the Court Process

Procedures for apprehension in court are outlined in the Family and Child Service Act, but details are contained in the Child Welfare Policy Manual of the Ministry of Human Resources and in case law. A very useful handbook is the Child Abuse/Neglect Policy Handbook published by the Ministry of Human Resources in 1979 which provides information on the process of investigation, child welfare complaint, and relationships with other key ministries such as Education, Health, and the Attorney-General. This handbook is part of the ministry's response to the investigation into the death of an abused infant, Charlene Harder. Interdepartmental procedures were strongly recommended at the coroner's inquest.

Steps in Apprehension Process

Step 1: A Complaint
There is an obligation on every person who has reasonable grounds to

believe that a child is in need of protection to report to the Ministry of Human Resources.[10] The statute says that no action lies against a person making a report under the section unless it is made maliciously or without reasonable grounds. Interestingly enough, B.C.'s Supreme Court recently ruled that social workers do not have to divulge the identity of informants,[11] so it could prove very difficult for parents falsely accused to establish maliciousness. The provincial Ombudsman recently investigated complaints of administrative unfairness concerning keeping records of unsubstantiated complaints without providing parents the right to challenge them. This procedure has now been amended by the ministry to allow effective challenge after a period of time with subsequent removal of the record.

Also in 1979, partly as a response to the Harder case, the Minister of Human Resources, Grace McCarthy, established a twenty-four-hour telephone help line, known as the Zenith Line for children, for families and citizens to report situations of abuse and neglect. The process is initiated by a complaint, usually by telephone, to a social work district office (on evenings and weekends to a duty worker or an emergency services section) that a particular child or children is believed to be in need of protection. These calls originate from neighbours, police, hospital staff, and children themselves. The social worker receiving the complaint has to judge whether it is a "crank call" or not. However, policy and practice is to err on the side of caution and to follow through on all complaints by investigation except those which are blatantly disturbed, mischievous, or malicious.

As noted earlier, many apprehensions do not originate from a specific complaint. Those common situations of parent request and "planned" apprehension after failure of support services often lead to special stress on the social worker.

Step 2: The Investigation

It is incumbent on the social worker to react immediately to a complaint—by checking it out as soon as possible and intervening if necessary. A check is made immediately of the Child Abuse Registry located centrally in Victoria where any previous complaint, substantiated or not, has been recorded.

The Child Abuse Manual provides procedures for consultation with other agencies such as school, police, and probation, depending on the case. While communication with other agencies certainly enhances the gaining of information, it raises the serious issue of professional confidentiality. Resolving this dilemma is left basically to the discretion of the individual social worker. Since the subsequent actions of the social worker and the court response are dependent upon what is learned through the investigative process, the investigatory skills of social workers are crucial. The purpose is to determine whether the alleged abuse or neglect is in fact occurring and whether the child is at risk sufficient to warrant immediate apprehension to guarantee the child's safety. The Child Abuse/Neglect Handbook gives some very useful guidelines in assessing risk,[12] including such factors as age or injury, relationship to parents, parent's support, and methods of parental discipline.

One dilemma faced by all investigating social workers is how to interpret a hostile or guarded reaction from parents. It is difficult to determine whether it arises from righteous indignation at an unfair complaint or an attempt to cover up guilt. Obviously, therefore, the total situation, not simply the parental reaction, needs to be carefully examined.

Step 3: Decision to Apprehend

Since the safety and well-being of the child is the paramount consideration, the social worker has to consider some of the following questions in deciding whether to apprehend or provide remedial and preventive services without resorting to the court process.

a. How serious is the alleged neglect or abuse?

b. Is it an isolated incident, or are there likely to be future occurrences?

c. Are parents capable of and amenable to altering their pattern of dealing with their children with assistance of child care workers, parent-training groups, short-term agreements, or financial help, and so forth?

In making the decision to apprehend, the social worker needs to "reasonably believe the child is in need of protection" — which is not the same as the child actually being adjudged in Family Court to be in need of protection; that decision is "on the balance of probabilities." Example: A teenage girl told a school counsellor that her father was beating her and showed serious bruises. A social worker was summoned, the girl repeated the same story, and the social worker decided to apprehend the girl for her protection pending further investigation. Two police detectives examined the circumstances and interrogated the girl and family members. The girl admitted she had made up the story so that she could get out of the home as her older sister had done and that she was feeling vengeful towards her father for some of his past behaviour. When the matter came to court within seven days, the court decided there were no grounds for protection. However, the social worker had acted within the law because he had reasonable grounds to suspect physical abuse at the time of the initial complaint.

The social worker's judgment has to be based on the child's best interests—hence, sometimes children will be apprehended and left at home if risk is minimal, for example, where a sexually abusive parent has left. If done in good faith, a social worker's actions are protected from liability.[13]

Many social workers work in close concert with the lawyer for the superintendent who is available on a regional basis at the local family courts. The descriptive circumstances that indicate a child is in need of protection must be well-known to the social worker and are contained in Section 1, as follows: That the child is (a) abused or neglected so that his safety or well-being is endangered; (b) abandoned; (c) deprived of the necessary care through the death, absence or disability of his parents; (d) deprived of necessary medical attention; or (e) absent from home in circumstances that endanger his safety or well-being. The phrase "disability of parent" under (c) is the one most commonly used and naturally disturbs many parents. The term "emotional neglect" is covered by these sections, but evidence (such as disturbed behaviour in school) that a child's safety or well-being is or may be endangered needs to be presented to the court.

Also, the courts have recently ruled that a fetus can be in need of protection at birth if it is reasonable that the child will be neglected. This decision by Madame Justice Proudfoot in supporting the social worker's apprehension of a baby born addicted to methadone from his mother's habit confirms that "anticipated neglect" is also encompassed by the grounds of Section 1.[14] The Appeal Court has recently upheld this decision and affirmed the permanent order to the superintendent.

Ministry policy also mentions special circumstances in dealing with status Indian children, children of Jehovah's Witnesses, and children ages seventeen and eighteen. Social workers are encouraged to work with Indian bands in developing resources as alternatives to apprehension. The Spallumcheen Band has entered into a separate agreement with the Ministry of Human Resources to operate its own child welfare system and resources.[15] Refusal to allow emergency blood transfusions can constitute need for protection under the act. Social workers are requested to encourage Jehovah's Witness parents to seek advice from their own elders. Children aged seventeen and eighteen can sometimes be viewed as independent from their parents. With such teenagers, the issue often depends on the social worker's judgment whether the criterion "absence from home in circumstances that endanger his safety or well being"[16] justifies apprehension.

The actual grounds and the risk factors are important in forming the decision to apprehend, to offer preventive services, or to find the complaint unsubstantiated. Workers will probably need to consult on these issues or even to apprehend temporarily pending further investigation. However, any apprehension whatsoever has to result in a report to the court within seven days, even if the child has been returned to the parent apparently entitled to custody.

Step 4: Apprehension and Collating of Evidence

If the decision is that the child must be removed from the parental home to preserve his safety, the apprehension process can be the actual physical taking of the child or, at a legal minimum, the deliberate touching of a child with the statement, "I apprehend this child as being in need of protection."

Since this procedure initiates a legal, formal, and a serious process, the social worker needs to begin the collation of evidence as soon as possible so that it may be presented to the court. In particular, documentation of circumstances and observations should be begun for the formal presentation of the case. If serious injury has taken place, a child might need immediate medical attention with an examination and photographs for evidence purposes. All children are examined medically upon admission to care, according to M.H.R. policy.

Where a parent refuses access to a child under investigation, a social worker can apply to a judge for a warrant to enter premises and search them[17] or to enter and apprehend.[18] If the child is in immediate physical danger, the superintendent or police officer can, without a warrant, enter premises forcibly to apprehend the child or remove him to a place of safety.[19] Pending the court appearance, the superintendent retains custody and control over the child.

Step 5: Report to Court

Wherever a child has been apprehended, the social worker must, within seven days, present a written report of the circumstances to the judge in Family Court. In practice this takes place in a courtroom, and the social worker speaks to the report. Some judges require the physical presence of the child during such a report process. The option belongs to the court. The social worker will have briefed the counsel for the superintendent about the circumstances. Parents can and certainly do challenge the circumstances in the report to court hearing; for example, they may say the social worker did not have reasonable grounds to believe the child was in need of protection.

The parents' rights to legal counsel is not mentioned in the Family and Child Service Act, though it appears on the notice of hearing form. As a matter of ministry practice, social workers are instructed to inform parents from the outset about their legal rights and the process that they can expect. Where the custody of the child is hotly disputed (perhaps between parents and superintendent or between parents and the child as to where the child should reside), the court can recommend that a family advocate be appointed to represent the child's best interests alone.[20] Such a recommendation does not guarantee that the attorney-general will actually appoint an advocate.

While the law requires a written report, some judges insist that the social worker give verbal testimony in addition. In this case, the parents' counsel is able to challenge the testimony. It is the expectation of most judges and M.H.R. policy that a copy of the report be given to parents whenever possible prior to this interim hearing.

One key issue of the report to court hearing often challenged by parents' counsel is whether the superintendent will retain interim care pending a protection hearing or whether the child should be returned to the parent. The contest around these issues of residence and access can escalate the report to court process into a mini protection hearing. Another option open for the court is for the child to be returned on the interim supervision of a social worker.

Step 6: Protection Hearing

While the statute directs the court to fix a date for hearing no later than forty-five days, in practice, if contested, this hearing may not be completed on this schedule owing to the volume of trials. In uncontested situations, the hearing may take place immediately after the report to court when all parties are present and willing to proceed. On the other hand, in more complex cases, a number of adjournments of several months duration may occur before the actual hearing takes place.

A pivotal question for the social worker at this stage is *whether the issue is going to be contested or not by parents*. For a trial, evidence must be assembled with the utmost care and attention to detail, with emphasis placed on the preparation of witnesses, affidavits from key individuals, case file documentation, medical reports, and so forth. During the period prior to the hearing, the focus has to be on *case preparation* — every social worker fears the situation where an apparently clear-cut neglect situation is not established in court because of defects in documentation and in the statements of witnesses. However, court decisions are dynamic in the sense that the skill of counsel, the values of the judge, and the demeanour of the witnesses all influence the outcome as well as the factual evidence. The social worker's responsibility is to provide counsel for the superintendent with all the evidence possible.

A second responsibility clearly on the shoulders of the social worker is that of giving *notice* to all parties to the proceedings, within the definition of "parent" under Section 1 of the Family and Child Service Act. Section 12(2) states "Notice of hearing shall be in writing and served at least 7 clear days before the hearing on the parents of the child and on any person who has custody of the child when the child was apprehended." Moreover, if the child is or is entitled to be a registered Native Indian, then the band has to be notified.

Notice has to be served personally. The tracing of natural and step-parents can be onerous, particularly in interprovincial situations. The court can order various forms of sutstituted notice (notice in newspapers, for example, or, in exceptional circumstances, the court may dispense with service of notice). Again, the social worker is subject to directions of the judge in this important function. In order to obtain a court order for substituted service, the social worker has to convince the judge that every effort had been made to find the person, including searches of telephone directories, motor vehicle branch lists, M.H.R. records, and checks with relatives and last known address.

To summarize: the contested hearing represents the classic adversarial process. Hearings might last for several days with the social worker's other witnesses undergoing lengthy examination. Preparation and familiarity with the evidence giving process including rules of hearsay are essential.

In an uncontested (or consent) hearing, the social worker presents only an outline of the circumstances of the apprehension to the judge through the brief to legal counsel for the superintendent. Accompanying it is a statement of the problems, the expectations of parents, and the presentation of a plan for the child. The worker is likely the sole witness, and the parent, if attending, might be asked, "if anything is to be added" by the judge. The judge would normally follow the order requested by the social worker's application.

Format for Hearing

Hearings under this act take place in the Provincial Court, Family Division. Sometimes, they can happen at the Supreme Court level as well in conjunction with a parent's custody application. According to Section 12(3), the hearings shall be (a) summary and civil in nature, and (b) at a different place and time than criminal. Civil indicates that in these proceedings parents or caretaker will not be held criminally responsible for their behaviour, although this in no way precludes the criminal justice system from responding. Also, it suggests that the civil standard of proof "on the balance of probabilities" that the child is in need of protection is the criterion for the judicial decision. Some judges and courts in these situations have argued that the onus should be stronger than the civil balance of probabilities, something between civil and criminal, partly because of the serious consequences to families of apprehension of their children. Some judges have suggested it should be "a strong and clear case" as the standard of proof, but this tends to be minority opinion in British Columbia and has been recently overruled by the B.C. Supreme Court (Re Archibald).

The civil law doctrine of *res ipsa loquitur* applied in the area of the tort of negligence applies also in child welfare. Meaning literally, "The matter speaks for itself," this principle allows circumstances to be taken into account in assessing causation. Where no person witnessed the child being beaten by a parent, if the bruising and other circumstances indicate that a reasonable person could assume that the injury was non-accidental, then the court would presume such.

The normal process for the hearing is as follows: legal counsel for the superintendent presents evidence to the court with an opening statement outlining why the superintendent feels the child is in need of protection. Usually the primary evidence is that of the apprehending social worker along with the testimony of other witnesses, neighbours, and professionals. Each person testifying can then be crossexamined by counsel for the parents and by any family advocate present. This process having been completed, counsel for the parents is then entitled to present his own evidence, for example, testimony by parents or other witnesses who are subject to crossexamination by counsel for the superintendent or advocate. There are, of course, variations in the flexibility of the judge and in the admission of types of evidence. Most judges require first-hand testimony, and since counsel for parents are continuing to challenge more and more in the family courts, the procedure is becoming increasingly rigid, legalistic, and technically correct.

Family Court in B.C. is public and open, but the publications of names or identifying particulars of the child, subject of these hearings, is prohibited. The Supreme Court retains its own common law power and *parens patriae* in child welfare and can intervene in proceedings without waiting for the operation of the F.C.S.A. through an apprehension.

Figure 1

CHART OF COURTROOM LAYOUT

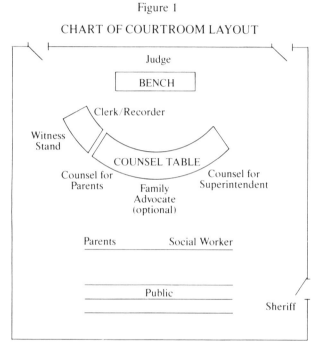

Family court is set up like other provincial courts with a judge, counsel for the superintendent, counsel for parents, family advocate, court reporter, clerk and sheriff. All family courts are courts of record, and transcripts are available to the parties.

Court Orders

The judge makes the decision about whether the child is in need of protection or not within the meaning of the act. If there is insufficient evidence, the case must be dismissed and the child returned to the parents entitled to custody. On finding that the child is in need of protection, the following court options are possible: Section 13, 14, and 15 (F.C.S.A.):

a. *Return the child* to parents or the parent entitled to custody;
b. *Return under supervision* of a social worker for a period not exceeding six months;
c. *Temporary custody order* not exceeding twelve months;
d. *Permanent order.*

Under a temporary order, custody is given to the superintendent for a specified limited period. Parents will be required to pay a sum of money for maintenance, however nominal. The circumstances can be varied upon request of superintendent and/or parent before the court. Extensions of the temporary order for six months can be made where the judge "considers it likely that the conditions that led to the taking of the child into custody will be remedied."[21] The court can make a permanent order directly at the first hearing, but frequently, it will be subsequent to a temporary order.

A supervision order is meant to allow the ministry to monitor the care of a child returned home. However, it does not bestow guardianship on the superintendent. Hence, if parents refuse to allow access, the social worker does not have powers of automatic removal (as prior to the F.C.S.A., 1981). The social worker will have to seek a warrant to investigate.

Not sooner than thirty days before the expiry of temporary order, the superintendent can apply for permanent order where the child's parents cannot or refuse to resume custody, where their whereabouts is unknown, or where the negative conditions still exist and are not likely to be remedied. What is interesting about this section is that the statute directs the judge to consider several factors in making a permanent order,[22] including parents' emotional and mental condition and ability to care for the child; the abuse or neglect by the parent of any child in the family; the child's feelings; the emotional ties of the family; and the efforts made by the parents to ameliorate their home conditions and any other factors considered relevant.

A recent example involved a single mother, mentally retarded, who was unable to benefit from and raise her parental skills through specialized resources offered over time. The child was apprehended when the mother planned to return to her abusing spouse. Upon considering the above factors, the court made a permanent order.

A permanent order is the most serious action the court can take, and so such an application is not considered lightly. On the other hand, the statute is intended to prevent children remaining in limbo for indefinite periods of time under temporary wardship status. A permanent custody order invests total legal powers over the person of the child permanently in the superintendent. He has the power to apply for recision, which is not frequently used. The superintendent can place any permanent ward for adoption acting as the consenting parent, though under the Adoption Act, children over twelve must also consent.

Appeals

Similar to criminal law, against a Family Court order, parents can seek an appeal within 30 days. The appeal is to the County Court on a point of law, of law and fact, or excess jurisdiction to the B.C. Supreme Court, and then to the B.C. Court of Appeal. Likewise, the superintendent may also appeal after consultation with counsel, the social worker and the ministry's Family and Child Service Division.

The Social Worker and the Court

There are three aspects to consider: the power and obligations of the social worker under the act; the social worker as evidence-giver; and the social worker and the total court process.

Social Worker's Authority and Responsibilities. As mentioned, the social worker has the duty to investigate, authority to enter into agreements, to apprehend, to instruct counsel on the position of the superintendent, to arrange for notice, and to make application for the variation of court orders. He does this in consultation with the district supervisor and/or regional manager in the ministry.

Responsibilities include the social worker's monitoring of agreements, meeting with parents regularly to make sure expectations and standards are maintained, ensuring that cases are ready for the report to court and protection hearings, and completing plans for return of a child to parent prior to the termination orders. These legal powers and responsibilities must be clearly understood and judiciously exercised by the social worker to maximize the effectiveness of his child welfare role.

It is worth mentioning that the superintendent is not a "parent" under this act. Thus, he cannot be held responsible *under this act* for failure to provide a reasonable standard of care. Obviously, however, the ministry will act internally to ensure the standards of its own care are acceptable.

Social Workers and Evidence-Giving Skills.[23] In most child welfare cases, the social worker is the key witness providing the major evidence for the superintendent's position. Therefore, social workers need to be very clear about the court process and their function and to be prepared to present their testimony on court in the witness stand skilfully.

The Skills of Giving Evidence

a. *Preparation.* The social worker's preparation of himself and his evidence is an essential component of effective evidence-giving. He must be aware of the expectations of his particular court, both the protocol required, and the form and procedures in court, so that he can present his evidence in the manner required. The preparation of his evidence should be concise yet comprehensive in a clear written document, either the report to court or brief to legal counsel. Written documentation is essential, presenting the letter of authority or affidavits or even being prepared to inform the court of his credentials and experience to avoid challenges to his credibility. The social worker should also enter the courtroom familiar with the data. The case file should be complete and up-to-date and should be available since the court may require it. The social worker may be expected to give information first of all from memory and to refer to written notes or the file on direction of the judge only with consent of counsel.

b. *Demeanour.* In presenting evidence, any witness should strive to inspire confidence. His credibility can be directly influenced by his manner and demeanour in actually giving evidence in the witness stand. Confident, open, yet non-arrogant or threatening posture is important, and conduct should reflect the measure of respect and decorum that is expected in serious proceedings of this nature. It is important to speak clearly, slowly, and loud enough so that everyone in the courtroom will be able to hear and understand the statements made. Ask for clarification or the repeating of the question if necessary.

c. *Content of Testimony.* There are two important questions to which the evidence-giver should address to himself: (i) "How will the judge interpret the statements I am going to make?" and (ii) "Will he understand them in the same context and meaning as I intend?" Therefore, it is most important that the social worker use plain and simple language and avoid professional jargon or ambiguous terms which cloud the specific meaning of the evidence. He must adhere to the professional standards of objectivity in his testimony. Evidence submitted must be derived from a thorough investigation of all potential sources of information. He must try to avoid value judgments and generalizations and be able to distinguish actual observations and facts from opinion. Most judges do rely upon the expression of assessment and professional opinions from social workers. The social worker must make a conscious effort to think answers through in advance and to present them slowly and deliberately so that the court receives the full impact of these responses. Answers should be directed, as far as possible, to the judge, and reasonable eye contact with the judge can enhance credibility. The words of Falconer and Swift summarize this part well.

In the courtroom, you are generally considered to be a witness with some expertise. This gives you the right to give evidence and state opinions *(in certain situations).* It is necessary to establish this expertise by citing your credentials — degrees, diplomas, experience, publications — which give weight to your evidence.

If you are young, inexperienced and your degrees are few, counsel for the parents may try to discredit your testimony by pointing this out to the court. In this event, you must focus on your direct experience with this family:

> I have met with the family many times. I have observed their behaviour over the past six months. I have interviewed both parents and children and have documented their responses. I have discussed their situation with my supervisor, and as a result I have made recommendations to the court. I do have opinions which I believe are valid.[24]

Important Tips

1. Try to be aware of your personal biases when presenting evidence. Distinguish facts from opinion.
2. Use simple non-jargon language.
3. Simply answer the questions as accurately and in as full a way as possible.
4. Do not challenge the lawyers.
5. Try to remember facts and details as much as possible. This can maintain credibility.
6. Be aware of weak spots in your evidence which may lead to confusing or conflicting testimony.
7. Try to remain poised.
8. Above all, prepare *yourself and your case.* If you have not had sufficient time, inform the counsel for the superintendent. Keep counsel advised and fully apprised of the quality and content of your evidence.
9. Know the rules of evidence, especially hearsay, as it applies in child welfare trials.
10. Finally, be very clear on the expectations of your particular court to formality, process, and so forth.

The Social Worker and the Total Court Process. From the comments in this article, the reader will recognize that the social worker's role, as the initiator, central witness, and stage manager of the evidence, is key to the court process. Legal knowledge in the area of child welfare is complex and ever-changing (since all case law is dynamic), but mastery of legal principles and statutes and a working familiarity with protocol and process is essential to be an effective, credible, and professional social worker in child welfare.

Conclusion

Although the authors have a bias toward preventive and supportive activities which keep families together, this does not mean that apprehension per se is a negative action. If the social worker thinks that apprehension is justified, he should not shrink from exercising that mandate. The intent of this chapter has been to encourage all social workers to become fully aware of their role and legal mandate and of the total process of child welfare in which they play such a fundamental part.

The interests of children and the rights of parents demand no less.

Appendix to Chapter 6

CHILD WELFARE PROCESS CHART

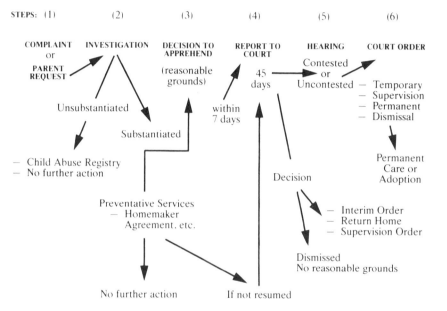

NOTES

The authors are indebted to social workers Donna Mae McCargar (the Vancouver court system) and Ray Ferris (Victoria) for their constructive comments.

1.　D.N. Duquette, "The Legal Aspects of Child Abuse and Neglect," in *Social Work with Abused and Neglected Children,* ed. K.C. Faller (New York: Free Press, 1981), p. 115.
2.　R.S.B.C., 1979, ch. 158, s. 1.
3.　The superintendency has traditionally been a position separate from a government ministry level. It has been suggested that this blending into the deputy minister position could blunt the independent advocacy function superintendents have been able to exercise.
4.　Vol. 2, *Family and Children's Services, Policy and Procedure Manual,* 2.9.2., Ministry of Human Resources, Victoria, B.C.
5.　Family and Child Service Act, R.S.B.C. 1980, ch. 11, s.2.

6. Ibid., s. 14(5).
7. Vol. 2, Family and Children's Services, *Policy and Procedure Manual.*
8. Young Offenders Act, R.S.C., 1982, ch. 110. Proclaimed April 1984.
9. Family Relations Act, R.S.B.C., 1978, ch. 121, s. 29. This involves no court process.
10. Family and Child Service Act, s. 7. Failure to report constitutes an offence.
11. Re Infant, B.C.S.C. 1981, 32, B.C.L.R. 20.
12. *Child Abuse/Neglect Policy Handbook,* pages 4 and 5 of the Ministry of Human Resources section, Province of British Columbia, Victoria, B.C., 1979.
13. Family and Child Service Act, s. 23.
14. Re D.J.: Superintendent of Family and Child Service, McDonald and O'Brian, B.C.S.C. 1982, 37, B.C.L.R. 32
15. See J. MacDonald. "The Spallumcheen Indian Band and Its Impact on Child Welfare Policy in British Columbia," unpublished paper, April 1981, Vancouver, B.C.
16. Family and Child Service Act, s. 1(e).
17. Ibid., s. 8.
18. Ibid., s. 9.
19. Ibid., s. 9(3).
20 Family Relations Act, s. 2.
21. Family and Child Service Act, s. 13(7).
22. Ibid., s. 14(3).
23. The authors were assisted in this part by social work students, J. Crawford, E. Ip, and L. Tulloch.
24. N.E. Falconer with K. Swift, *Preparing for Practice, The Fundamentals of Child Protection* (Toronto: Children's Aid Society of Metro Toronto, 1983), p. 154. Chapter 14 of this handbook contains very useful information on the legal and court process in Ontario. Note: words in italics are this author's amendment to reflect situation in British Columbia.

7

NATIVE CHILDREN, CHILD WELFARE, AND THE COLONIZATION OF NATIVE PEOPLE

Brad McKenzie and Pete Hudson

INTRODUCTION

A 1974 band council meeting in northwestern Ontario links the disappearance of family surnames from the band lists to the actions of the child welfare system. The chief of the Spallumcheen Band, a small Indian reserve of three hundred people in British Columbia, reports that from 1951 to 1977 one hundred and fifty children were removed from his reserve by child welfare authorities.[1] In another case, an infant native girl is beaten to death by her white foster father. These and other similar reports indicate why the issue of child welfare services to native people has emerged as one of the most controversial social policy issues involving governments and native people in the 1980's. Such examples characterize a social service system that has not always acted in the best interests of native clients, and they dramatize the need to re-evaluate the relationship of the child welfare system to native people and their communities.[2] The intent of this chapter, then, is to examine the role of the child welfare system and its interaction with native people from a theoretical perspective that recognizes the historical significance of colonialism to the situation affecting native people today. The chapter concludes with a discussion of some of the policy and practice implications that emerge from this analysis.

CURRENT RECOGNITION OF THE PROBLEM

The 1980 report of the Canadian Council on Social Development indicated that native children comprised more than 20 per cent of the total number of children in substitute care, while people of native background accounted for only about 6 per cent of the Canadian population.[3] Figures from Western Canada were even more dramatic. A 1972 review of children in care in the province of British Columbia found that status Indian children were eight times as likely as non-Indian children to be in some form of substitute care, and a 1980-81 review indicated a similar ratio.[4] In 1977 native children represented 44 per cent of the children in care in Alberta, and 51 per cent of the Saskatchewan total. In Manitoba, where native people accounted for approximately 12 per cent of the provincial population, native children represented approximately 60 per cent of the total number of children in care.[5]

The problem of native children in care is not limited simply to concerns about overrepresentation. Most native children taken into care are removed from their culture and communities and placed in non-native temporary or long-term substitute care arrangements. The impact of this development on native communities and culture is predictable. Native children removed from their community are often lost as future members of that community. They are also socialized into the dominant non-native culture, and as a result, they often lose contact with and come to devalue their own cultural background. Because these practices contribute directly to the destruction of native culture and community, they have been correctly labelled by native leadership as examples of "cultural genocide." The extent of this problem and the response of the traditional child welfare system is illustrated by data released on adoption placements for the province of Manitoba for 1981. In that year, 45 per cent of the native children placed for adoption were placed outside of Manitoba, and only one of these children was placed in a native home. In addition, more than half of the children were sent to adoptive parents living in the United States.[6]

The conflict and concern related to the issue of native child welfare does not end here, however, because there is beginning evidence that suggests that the child welfare system's objective of providing secure and stable care for children is not being fulfilled for native children. One American study has indicated that the psycho-social development of children in foster care is not substantially different from that of other children.[7] For native children, however, there is much in the way of case study information that tells a different story.

In a highly publicized case during the spring of 1984, an Indian adolescent, adopted in the United States several years ago, was convicted of killing his adoptive father. It was subsequently learned that he had been subjected to homosexual assaults. He is now serving a life sentence "far from the reservation." While this example and others may be regarded as extreme, child welfare workers cite a body of case evidence to indicate that native children often experience frequent movement culminating in conflict with the law and institutionalization. One very recent informal review of native adults incarcerated in a Manitoba correctional institution determined that a majority of them had earlier been under the care and supervision of the non-Indian child welfare system.

Furthermore, the experience of native children while in care is generally different from that of non-native children. Native children who are placed primarily in white substitute care homes or institutions are less likely to be visited by parents once in care, and they are less likely to be returned home than their non-native counterparts. There is also evidence that native children raised in non-native homes are more likely to experience an identity crisis in adolescence, leading to acute social and psychological problems when they find they no longer fit in the society to which they have been socialized.[8] If this is true, there can be little argument with the general observation that placement practices and the related actions of the child welfare system have reduced the opportunities for cultural reinforcement of the native child's identity and have, therefore, directly contributed to the negative outcomes which are too often associated with native children who graduate from the child welfare system.

TRADITIONAL INTERPRETATIONS OF NATIVE CHILD NEGLECT: A CRITIQUE

There are three predominant groups of explanations on the topic of native child welfare. The first group draws heavily on psychosocial theories of human development, and interprets child neglect as the result of individual deviation. No attempt is made to differentiate between the native and non-native condition, and family breakdown and child neglect in native communities are correlated with the inadequate extension of a range of social services and good social work practices to such communities. Such explanations have represented the dominant pre-occupation of the traditional child welfare system, and the solutions advanced have included increased service provision and more attention to generalized tools for assessment and follow-up.[9] Despite the popularity of these generalized responses, there has been little concern expressed about the fact that the very extension of such traditionally oriented services to native communities has resulted in dramatic increases in the numbers of native children coming into care.

The second group acknowledges that cultural differences between native and non-native people do exist. These explanations attempt to demonstrate how value differences lead to cultural conflict.[10] Native parents and children, caught between the new and the old, often end up rejecting both and react with either passivity or hostility to their surroundings. Increased family breakdown and child neglect among native people are seen as a consequence of the clash between two cultures. Too often, this analysis has led to the ethnocentric conclusion that interventions must be designed primarily to assist native people to adopt the values and practices of the dominant society.[11]

The third group attributes a cause and effect relationship between socio-economic status and the ability of parents to extend adequate child care. The widespread incidence of poverty, substandard housing, poor education, and poor nutrition is linked to native powerlessness, despair, alcoholism, and family violence. The consequences, these adherents argue, are quite naturally increased neglect and child welfare problems.[12]

It has been well documented by the National Council of Welfare that the majority of people serviced by the child welfare system are poor,[13] and because the incidence of poverty among native people is disproportionately high, support for these explanations is not misplaced. However, while these explanations accurately reflect the class bias of social problems that contribute to dependency and child neglect, there is little recognition of other differences between the native and non-native condition and how these interrelate with problems of poverty in native communities. Accordingly, these and other traditional explanations of native child neglect fail to account for the poorer outcomes achieved by native children once they are taken into care. In addition, proposed solutions designed to modify the chronic and widespread poverty of native people usually involve training and relocation programmes designed to promote native participation within industrial capitalism. Such responses typically misrepresent the causes of underdevelopment in native communities and, therefore, ignore solutions involving the resolution of land claims and the transfer of control over the nature and scope of economic development to native communities.

While there are obvious differences among the theoretical explanations for native child neglect that have been presented, all share an ideological commitment to an assimilationist ideal of native-white relations. Approaches based on this common interpretation of social reality have focused on members of the minority group, requiring them to become adapted to, and thus assimilated within, the dominant group. Such a consensus view of society ignores three fundamental aspects of native reality.

One factor concerns the differing historical realities facing native children who have been exposed to the child welfare system in this country. It is well illustrated by reference to a study that describes the identical realities faced by aboriginal children in Australia:

Aboriginal history since the invasion of their land in 1788 by Europeans has been one of conquest, dispossession, institutionalization, exploitation and discrimination. . .the root cause of the socio-economic deprivations and disadvantages suffered by Aborigines was the loss of their land and the denial to them of any alternative economic base. Their institutionalization and almost two centuries of discriminatory administration and legislation reinforced their powerlessness. And this very powerlessness was used by white authorities as a *justification* for, and a means of removing Aboriginal children from their families. . . . Aboriginal children caught up in the [child] welfare system, therefore, are most often going to be there for different reasons than are non-aboriginal children. . .they are going to have had a significantly different history, and will return, be it sooner or later, to a significantly different future. This difference is not only quantitative, but also qualitative.[14]

A second factor is the widespread racism in our society. The prevalence of prejudice and discrimination against native people is illustrated by the 1982 survey of 662 junior high school students in the city of Winnipeg.[15] In this survey, one-third of the respondents indicated they would prohibit native Indians from living in Canada. The extent to which all non-native people have been socialized to respond to native people in stereotypical ways that fail to see sources of strength in the individual, the family, and the community is not addressed by any of the traditional explanations for native child neglect. This results, then, in failure to acknowledge evidence supporting overzealousness on the part of child welfare workers in the removal of native children from their communities.

Finally, each group of explanations and the solutions suggested focus attention almost exclusively on the behaviour of the client population. No causal explanation of child neglect is complete without directing considerable attention to the behaviours and practices of the institutions that provide child welfare services and the dynamics of the interaction that occurs between the service provider and the consumer. None of the prevailing theories concerning native child neglect critically examine the institutions responsible for extending child welfare services to native people.

Recognition of the legitimacy of these factors to any study of native-white relations supports a conflict model of society rather than one that is based on consensus and the assimilation of minority groups.[16] Here attention is given to the struggle between an intruding society with its own culture and an indigenous society with markedly different values and objectives. Using this analytical framework, consideration of the dominant society's access to power and resources which can be utilized in overcoming resistance and subjugating an indigenous society becomes important. A conflict perspective of race relations leads to an examination of colonialism, and the next section of this chapter develops the argument that the child welfare system has been, and continues to be, involved as an agent in the colonization of native people. This view provides a more complete understanding of the current failures in the native child welfare field and leads to an examination of needed changes in institutional policies and practices in the development of responses oriented to the objective of decolonization.

COLONIALISM AND THE CHILD WELFARE SYSTEM

Colonialism involves creating dependency among a nation or group, the objective of which includes the extraction of benefits by the dominant nation or group. Kellough distinguishes between structural and cultural colonialism.[17] Structural colonialism involves the explicit control of power and decision-making by the dominant group for the purpose of extracting benefits. Governments, through treaties and the actions of Parliament, have removed native rights to land and implemented policies leading to the depletion of traditional native resources such as the buffalo and fur-bearing animals. The historical benefits of land, fur, and buffalo which accrued from the colonization of native people are well known. Less well accepted is the fact that modern society continues to benefit from the dependency and underdevelopment of native people. Such benefits today include resource extraction from lands occupied by native people and the utilization of native people as reserve labour and as consumers of goods and services, including social services. Current efforts by the dominant society to develop hydro projects and pipelines unilaterally with little recognition of the rights of native people represent an extension of structural efforts to achieve colonial objectives.

Cultural colonialism involves efforts to achieve normative control of a minority group or culture. These efforts are designed to explain and legitimize actual control, and historical efforts designed to "civilize the savage" reflect this tradition. The missionaries, the educational system, and the health system have all been oriented to objectives associated with cultural colonialism.[18] While the child welfare system can be seen primarily in this light, it is clear that both types of colonialism interact in contributing to native subordination within Canadian society.

There are obvious parallels between the child welfare system and the traditional practices of the health and education systems. In particular, all three have been involved in the separation of native children from their families, communities, and culture. The health system developed an early pattern of removing native children to foster homes or medical facilities in urban centres for long periods of time. Many children were never returned home, even when medical problems failed to justify such a separation, and those who did return after prolonged absences found themselves alienated from their families and cultural environment. The early educational system consisted of residential schools which removed native children from their parents and home communities for most of each year. Native languages and practices associated with native culture were systematically discouraged and held up to ridicule. Many argue that this practice of separating children from parents and the parenting role model is singularly responsible for many of the problems related to child care now found among native parents. The role of the child welfare system in the separation of children from family and culture has already been established by the statistical evidence presented earlier. In fact, it is the child welfare system that is now primarily engaged in the process of separating children from their parents, community, and culture.

A major attribute of the colonial relationship involves the location of power and decision-making structures within the dominant society. In the health services system, the widespread practice of removing native children for medical treatment has usually been carried out not by legal authority, but in keeping with arbitrary policies created by white administrators and medical institutions. Social and cultural impacts were simply not considered in the decision-making process, and most parental consents, if obtained at all, were obtained without full information and mutual understanding.

The residential school system was established unilaterally by the dominant society in an effort to perpetuate the definitions and perspectives of the colonizer. Similarly, in the child welfare system, policies and procedures have been established in law and executed by courts and agencies with no input from native people. The child welfare system is geographically removed from native communities, and services have been provided primarily by non-native workers who live outside those communities. Decisions related to apprehension and custody, then, have been made primarily outside native communities, and these processes have generally continued to deny the existence of formal or informal political and social structures within the local community. This reality is illustrated by the 1982 appeal hearing (Children's Aid Society of Winnipeg vs. Big Grassy Indian Band), where the Children's Aid Society argued successfully that the Big Grassy Indian Band in northwestern Ontario could not have jurisdiction or be entrusted to select an appropriate substitute care resource for a child apprehended by that agency even though an Ontario child welfare agency supported the band's application.[19]

Devaluation of an indigenous people is a particularly significant characteristic of the colonial relationship. This process depends on acceptance of the belief that the colonizer is the sole carrier of a valid culture. Its manifestation in the health system was in ignoring traditional native skill and knowledge in preventive and curative medicine. In the education system, content which reflected native customs, lifestyle, and language was denied. During the residential school period, administrators are known to have stated that the isolation of native children from the "prejudicial influences of home and community" was an essential prerequisite to "proper" training.[20]

Similarly, the child welfare system has paid little attention to the ways in which native communities have traditionally handled parental neglect or child care problems through communal and serial patterns of parenting. The outcome of this omission is significant. As in the case of traditional native medicine, the transmission of knowledge and patterns of child care have been so severely interrupted that many native communities have had great difficulty in re-establishing patterns of community care or in creating local substitute care resources. This has contributed to a culturally biased perception of native families and communities as impoverished, primitive, socially disorganized, and as generally unsuitable environments for children. Little recognition is given to the validity of both positive and negative aspects of culture and lifestyle in these communities or to the fact that struggles for self-determination over despair and violence in this context are not unlike the struggles that occur in other cultures and communities. This devaluation has enabled the dominant society and child welfare authorities to justify the control and maintenance of universally applied definitions of standards, both in relation to the existence of neglect and for substitute care resources. Such definitions, especially in their attention to material standards and their failure to acknowledge the existence of cultural and communal norms, have contributed to a further bias against native people.

It is more commonly accepted now that differences in child-rearing practices and standards do exist in some native homes which may represent past cultural practices or specific responses to white society. Permissiveness in a native family or the independence and autonomy afforded a young child in self-care or school attendance may create certain problems, but they do not necessarily imply a lack of parental caring which justifies removal. It follows, then, that the universal application of objective standards including specification of physical facilities, material possessions, opportunities, and lifestyles consistent with patterns of the dominant society guarantees discriminatory judgments that are identical to those of the early colonizers. This misplaced need of the child welfare system to objectify standards applies equally to decisions made about substitute care arrangements. The development of native substitute care resources has been severely inhibited by the rigidity of physical standards and issues of income and lifestyle considered by child welfare officials in the licensing of such resources.[21]

The impact of cultural devaluation is important to consider in evaluating cross-cultural placements, and here the evidence of unsatisfactory outcomes for native children in care can be directly related to the overuse of non-native resources for native children. In this regard, it is important to recognize that what is happening to a total group has a much more focused impact on an individual child who is taken into care and placed in a white environment. In this situation, the cultural stripping is complete. The child is isolated from the environment of his people where there was some support and encouragement to insulate himself from the opinions and judgments of white people and institutions. It is difficult enough for any child to build a new identity when taken into care. But when that child is native and placement means physical uprooting and either implicitly or explicitly expressed cultural devaluation, the struggle for an identity is compounded. Even if cultural reinforcement is successfully denied and the young child becomes assimilated with his non-native milieu, he frequently confronts his nativeness in adolescence when he can no longer be sheltered from the negative and racist stereotypes of the dominant society.[22]

A final characteristic of colonialism is its interactive quality because, as Puxley suggests, "colonialism must be seen as an experience, and not simply as structured relationships."[23] One of the manifestations of this interaction is the way in which many of the responses of the colonized to the colonizer serve only to reinforce the low status of the subordinate group. In the health system, native people have frequently declined to use proferred services.[24] High absentee rates and the passive withdrawal of native children in school are frequent complaints of the school system. Such behaviours tend to confirm views of native people as ignorant or unmotivated, and they evoke counterresponses from white administrators, ranging from despair to invocation of legal authority.

In the child welfare system, the interactive quality of the colonial relationship was first illustrated by the practice of the early settlers on the eastern seaboard, who, scandalized by "pagan" and "primitive" child-rearing practices, forcibly removed a number of native children and shipped them to England to be "christianized." Retaliation by the Indian band took the form of what is now known as the "Jamestown Massacre," which provoked a systematic policy of extermination directed against the offending band. Current examples of the interactive nature of dominant-subordinate relationships include the not uncommon response of retreat into alcoholism by the mother of an apprehended child. This despairing response is ultimately self-defeating, since it confirms original perceptions of inadequacy, often resulting in application for permanent wardship and perhaps the removal of other children. A recent case example in Winnipeg is illustrative of this pattern:

A native mother of three children is encouraged by her child welfare worker to enter hospital and obtain a tubal ligation as a method of birth control. While the woman and her husband have had problems with alcohol in the past, the woman has not had a drink for five months. Following her return from the hospital, she is confronted by her husband, who, angry at her actions, physically assaults her. A drinking party ensues, and after voluntarily placing the children with a local child welfare agency, the husband leaves. The woman, left without her children and her husband, makes several attempts to regain custody of her children. Despite efforts, she can obtain no clear indication from the child welfare agency about the conditions she must fulfill before her children are returned. In desperation, she returns to an earlier pattern of excessive alcohol consumption. At the child welfare hearing, she is surprised to learn that earlier indications of agency support have turned into an application for permanent guardianship.[25]

The internalization of negative perceptions of inferiority also manifests itself in other ways. It has not been uncommon to receive requests from native parents for placement of their child in a white, middle-class home in order to give the child a better opportunity for success. Here, the ongoing process of removing children from community and culture has systematically contributed to the internalization of perceptions among the colonized which emphasize the inferiority and inadequacy of their own community and culture.

In this section, past and present examples have been cited to demonstrate that the interests of the dominant child welfare system have resulted in unilateral actions to remove large numbers of children from circumstances which are regarded by the dominant group as being inferior. While the present child welfare system may not acknowledge the overt pursuit of colonial objectives, to many native people there is a striking similarity in the pattern which resulted in the removal of children by the early settlers, the placement of children in the residential school system in the early twentieth century, and the patterns associated with the apprehension and placement of native children by child welfare authorities that continue to this day.

TOWARDS DECOLONIZATION

It has been argued that the nature of the interaction between the child welfare system and native people has been dominated by characteristics associated with the process of colonialism. Changes designed to further the objective of decolonization will, of necessity, involve efforts to develop the strengths of the minority culture. Decolonization requires, then, the transfer of autonomy and control of mandated child welfare services for native people to native people. Movement towards native-controlled child welfare systems is apparent in various regions of the country, and there are three general models of service delivery that are emerging.

The first has involved attempts by existing agencies to hire and train decentralized native workers to deliver more culturally relevant services to native people. The legal mandate for child welfare services is retained by the child-caring agency, although in some cases a considerable amount of decision-making authority and actual control may be vested in the local community worker. One example of this type of service is the Preventive Services Project operating in the Rainy River District of northwestern

Ontario.[26] In the pilot phase of this project, the Indian worker on one reserve was successful in halting the removal of children. Moreover, he extended his mandate and became involved in repatriating several children who had been previously apprehended and placed in off-reserve foster care arrangements.

A second model has involved movement towards community-based delivery of non-statutory services, primarily at the band level. Child welfare services related to foster home finding, supervision, homemaker services, and supportive counselling are provided by a community-based agency, but statutory authority is retained by a child welfare agency external to the native community. In some instances, structures such as child welfare committees have been used at the local community level to oversee programmes and provide advice. There are several examples of the successful application of this model including programmes at Fort Alexander Reserve in Manitoba, Sandy Bay in Saskatchewan, and at Vanderhoof in British Columbia. In Vanderhoof, the Stoney Creek Band effectively utilized a child welfare committee in reinforcing community responsibility for child care and reducing the necessity of the apprehension of Indian children.[27]

A third model that has developed only very recently involves full community control of all child welfare services. One example of this response is the action initiated by the Spallumcheen Band in British Columbia. This band enacted a by-law through which they assumed total jurisdiction over child welfare services on their reserve.[28] While the by-law has been respected by both the federal and provincial governments, it is probable that the declared authority of the band for child welfare services under Section 81 of the Indian Act could be successfully challenged in the courts. An alternative example of community control of child welfare services has evolved from the landmark agreement signed by the Dakota-Ojibway Tribal Council (DOTC), the Department of Indian Affairs, and the Province of Manitoba. This agreement, which became effective in July 1981, provided for the development of the Dakota-Ojibway Child and Family Service agency (DOCFS) with full responsibility for the provision of child welfare services to the eight reserves within the tribal council.

This Indian agency provides services mandated by the Manitoba Child Welfare Act and utilizes a service delivery model that includes sixteen social service workers living in the local communities and a child welfare committee on each reserve. The service delivery model pioneered by DOTC has been extended to other Indian reserves in Manitoba as a result of the signing of the master agreement on Indian Child Welfare,[29] and by the fall of 1983, all but two of the reserves in the province had a system of community-controlled child welfare services in place. While developments in urban centres and Métis communities in Manitoba have been less dramatic, the Manitoba Métis Federation has endorsed a strongly worded policy statement asserting their intent to acquire local control over child welfare services,[30] and they have hired staff to begin to develop this capability.

These developments have not been uncontroversial, and one constraint has involved objections to the development of parallel services by traditional child welfare agencies and government planners. One objection involves the fear that the fragmentation of social services will be further exacerbated by the development of independent native child welfare agencies with their own approaches to service delivery. Service gaps and jurisdictional disputes are expected by human service professionals, who are philosophically committed to comprehensive planning and the orderly development of unified social service delivery systems.

A second objection has been that some agencies perceive a native-controlled child welfare system as a direct political threat to their continued existence since financial resources will be redirected to native agencies as they assume responsibility for services previously provided by the traditional system. Finally, the traditional child welfare system has expressed misgivings about the possibility that the ideals of professional practice and competence may be sacrificed by an overzealous commitment to the principle of self-help. Here professional adherence to a body of knowledge and skills that enables effective social work practice has been threatened by a movement that claims that social services for native people must be native-controlled and provided by native people. Moreover, the profession can argue beyond self-interest in demonstrating the limitations of the self-help position when it is taken to its logical conclusion.

Native people and other proponents of a parallel system have perceived these objections as evidence of the inability of the dominant society to acknowledge the colonial history of native-white relations and the right of native people to transform that relationship. Essential to that transformation is an affirmation by the dominant society of the claim by native people to some form of sovereignty and control over the services provided to its membership. That recognition is essential to facilitate honest dialogue between native and non-native service providers in ways that enable non-native representatives to nurture and support an emerging community-controlled native child welfare system. Once recognition is achieved, attention must be given to the development of procedures to govern service responsibilities and relationships between agencies, and models of service delivery must be developed for both urban centres and Métis communities. For most native people, control over child welfare services is still too often subject to the goodwill and uncertain funding of governments and the traditional child welfare system. Extension of the right to native-controlled child welfare services, as demonstrated by the Manitoba experience, can evolve into a generally collaborative working relationship between the Indian system and the provincial child welfare system. Moreover, a recently completed evaluation of the Dakota-Ojibway Child and

Family Service system indicates the success of this programme in building community competence for the return and maintenance of Indian children in Indian communities.[31]

Another major constraint facing native child welfare agencies involves the legislative mandate. Even in Manitoba, where native agencies have responsibility for the provision of a full range of child welfare services, they must operate within the Manitoba Child Welfare Act and the policies that have evolved from it. Native child-caring agencies, then, have administrative control over child welfare services, but they do not have legislative control. A legal framework that enables native and non-native child-caring agencies to respond with culturally appropriate child welfare services is required. It is not the intention here to comment on the jurisdictional issues that confront consideration of legislative change, but it is important to recognize the essential intent of required adaptations.

At the present time, when a native child is apprehended under the authority of the Child Welfare Act, the band or community of origin which claims the child as a member has no right to notification or input into the future planning for that child. While this may be practised in some jurisdictions, legislative changes are required to uphold the rights of the native group or community in the decision-making processes. Such provisions should also include the right to community notification of any pending child welfare proceeding involving a community member, the right of the community to examine documentation and have status before the court, and the right of the community to have input into planning for a child's future.

Child welfare legislation should also be altered to give priority to the preservation of the cultural heritage of the native child. Consideration of culture and community must be included in determining the "best interests of the child," and proposed child welfare legislation in Manitoba now includes this provision. Legislative requirement should also oblige the child welfare authority to seek out substitute care placements in order of preference with the extended family, other members of the community, and other native families before seeking out non-native placements. In the event that non-native resources are to be utilized, particularly in long-term substitute care arrangements, the child welfare agency should be obliged to show cause why cultural heritage was unable to be accommodated or unimportant in any specific situation. The American Indian Child Welfare Act mandates such measures,[32] and in the Canadian context, the province of Nova Scotia has articulated a policy designed to preclude the indiscriminate adoption of Indian children by non-Indian parents. This province has stated

that because of the understanding of the importance of cultural heritage to the Indian child in the developmental years, approval for the adoption of the Indian child with non-Indian parents will not be given unless it can be demonstrated that such a placement is in the child's best interests.[33]

A major area of concern relates to the issue of standards, and here again provisions within the American Indian Child Welfare Act are instructive. This act espouses the principle of relativity of standards by referring to "the prevailing social and cultural standards of the Indian community in which the present or extended family resides or with which the parent or extended family members maintain social and cultural ties"[34] when judgments are to be made about the adequacy of substitute care arrangements. Not unrelated to this issue is the need for the provision of subsidized adoption designed to ensure that potential native adoptive parents are not ineligible simply because of material circumstances.

Central to the debate concerning the issue of heritage for the child is the relative priority that should be given to the principle of cultural bonding and early pairing with a permanent, primary parent figure. While there is a rhetorical commitment to the principle of "native homes for native children" within the child welfare system, there is an obvious bias, based on research supporting the principle of early bonding,[35] to move to a permanent placement plan for the child as soon as possible in order to ensure effective pairing between parent and child. Predominant patterns of service delivery, then, have often reinforced the need to remove the child at risk and expeditiously develop a permanent placement plan for the child. In adoptive placements and permanent foster care arrangements, ties with the birth parent and extended family are most often severed, and there are limited provisions to facilitate natural family contact or cultural reinforcement with the community of origin even in later years. In situations where a native substitute care resource is not readily available or such a resource is likely to be temporary in nature, placement decisions have reflected a bias towards permanency for the child rather than cultural bonding.

This practice of permanent removal of the child from family and community coupled with provisions designed to prevent and limit subsequent contact is antithetical to the way in which many native people view substitute care. Multiple care-giving has been a traditional means of providing substitute care in many native communities. In these situations, care of the child was regarded as a trust arrangement, and return of the child to the natural parent or a member of the extended family was always regarded as a possibility. In most circumstances, there was frequent contact between the child and parents, and competition between natural and substitute parents was unusual. These traditions challenge the principle of permanent placement planning, which is a major attribute of current child welfare practice. They suggest the need to re-examine adoption policy and the practice of pursuing permanent orders resulting in separation of the child from the natural family and community.

Finally, recognition of the importance of colonialism to the study of native child welfare implies a need to re-define the client-worker relationship in native communities. Neglect investigations and subsequent interventions are usually carried out in the context of private and confidential transactions between agency worker and family. The focal point is the immediate family context, and the local community is not generally regarded as having responsibilities or resources that should be considered in determining intervention. This pattern of service provision is entirely inappropriate in most native communities, and in the Manitoba Indian child welfare system the community and not the family is seen as the primary client. This shift has resulted in case management which promotes a partnership relationship in assessment and intervention with band leadership and community networks as well as extended and immediate family. One consequence of this approach has been that the native community has begun to renew its tradition of seeing all children as "communal resources" rather than as the "private property" of parents. Both formal and informal provision of help, ranging from assistance in improving a housing problem to the occasional provision of substitute care have occurred, and the DOCFS experience indicates that this approach has been successful, not only in halting the removal of children, but also in repatriating children who had been previously removed to non-native substitute care. This emphasis on collective responses of issues of child care has been encouraged by the creation of community child welfare committees, which are a major component of the Indian child welfare system in the province of Manitoba.

CONCLUSION

Traditional explanations of child neglect in native communities provide incomplete guides to the development of an effective native child welfare system. As this chapter suggests, a theoretical perspective that examines child welfare services to native people within a colonial context is required. This recognition should lead to policy and practice responses that emphasize principles of cultural autonomy and local control. Non-native child welfare agencies must identify those aspects of service provision that are transferable to the native context, and they must be prepared to offer enabling assistance to emerging native child welfare agencies.

Native agencies and organizations must recognize that the movement to "native-controlled" services is no panacea for the problems related to child care that exist in many native communities. The real test of service effectiveness will be whether more responsive child welfare services are developed and whether community concern and support for children as their most important resource occurs as a result of this change. To achieve these objectives, native communities will require an adequate funding base, and native organizations must avoid being placed in the position of having a mandate to provide child welfare services without adequate resources to respond systematically to the needs in their communities. It is also apparent that any fundamental change in the colonial nature of native-white relations will depend on concomitant efforts to resolve native land claims and achieve economic self-sufficiency. Without these efforts, native control over child welfare services will remain only a limited achievement.

NOTES

1. Wayne Christian, Speech to Native Child Apprehensions Conference, Saskatoon, September 1981, as reported by Richard Thatcher, "Stop Stealing Our Children," *Canadian Dimension* 16, no.6 (1982): 3.
2. The term "native" in this article is intended to refer to all indigenous people in Canada, whereas the term "Indian" refers more specifically to status Indians as defined by the Indian Act. The authors argue that while specific historical events and the present circumstances of sub-groups may differ, the general analytical perspective and conclusions suggested in this article apply across sub-groups.
3. H. Philip Hepworth, *Foster Care and Adoption in Canada* (Ottawa: Canadian Council on Social Development, 1980), p. 111.
4. John A. MacDonald, "The Spallumcheen Band," see chapter 15 of this publication.
5. National Council on Welfare, *In the Best Interests of the Child* (Ottawa: The Council, 1979). An estimate obtained from the child welfare director for the province of Manitoba in 1982 indicated that the relative percentage of native children in care may have increased somewhat since 1977 in that province.
6. Department of Community Services and Corrections, Program Review and Evaluation Branch, "Data on Adoption Placements" (Winnipeg: Government of Manitoba, 1982).
7. Henry Maas, *Research in the Social Sciences: A Five Year Review* (New York: National Association of Social Workers, 1979).
8. Joseph Westermeyer, "Ethnic Identity Problems among Ten Indian Psychiatric Patients," *International Journal of Social Psychiatry* 25 (1979): 194.
9. Henry Maas, "Assessing Family and Child Welfare Practice," *Social Work* 24, no. 5 (1979): 365-72, and Mary Ann Jones, Stephen Magure, and Ann W. Shyne, "Effective Practice with Families in Protective Services: What Works?" *Child Welfare* 60, no. 2 (1981): 67-80.
10. Rosalie Wax and Robert Thomas, "American Indians and White People," *Phylon* 2, no. 4 (1961): 305-17; and Bruce Sealey and Verna Kirkness, eds., *Indians without Tipis* (Winnipeg: William Clare, 1973).
11. Henry Zenter, ed., *The Indian Identity Crisis* (Calgary: Strayer Publications, 1973); and Grafton H. Hull, Jr., "Child Welfare Services to Native Americans," *Social Casework* (June 1982): 340-47.
12. Joseph Ryant et al., *A Review of Child Welfare Policies, Programs and Services in Manitoba* (Winnipeg: Government of Manitoba, 1975); and Canadian Council on Children and Youth, *Admittance Restricted: The Child as Citizen in Canada* (Ottawa: The Council, 1978).
13. National Council of Welfare, *Poor Kids* (Ottawa: The Council, 1975).

14. "Assimilation and Aboriginal Child Welfare — The New South Wales Community Welfare Bill, 1981 — Discussion Paper 3." Aboriginal Children's Research Project, September 1981.
15. Rodney A. Clifton, Stella Hrynuik, and Raymond P. Perry, "Research Indicates Ethnic Prejudice," *Winnipeg Free Press,* 9 September 1982, p. 8.
16. See Peter Leonard, "The Function of Social Work in Society," in N. Timms and D. Watson, eds., *Talking about Welfare* (London: Routledge and Kegan Paul, 1976), for a more complete discussion of conflict and consensus theories of society.
17. Gail Kellough, "From Colonialism to Economic Imperialism: The Experience of the Canadian Indian," in John Harp and John R. Hofley, eds., *Structured Inequality in Canada* (Scarborough: Prentice-Hall, 1980), p. 343-77.
18. See for example, Harold Cardinal, *The Unjust Society.* (Edmonton: M.G. Hurtig, Ltd., 1969), and Howard Adams, *Prison of Grass,* (Toronto: General Publishing, 1975).
19. Manitoba Court of Appeal, "The Children's Aid Society and the Big Grassy Indian Band," 28 January 1982.
20. Edgar Dosman, *Indians, The Urban Dilemma.* (Toronto: McClelland and Stewart, 1972), p. 20.
21. Evidence for the continued existence of such practices is demonstrated in the article "Native Foster Children Denied Cultural Links by Aid Society: Worker," *Toronto Globe and Mail,* 29 November 1982, p. 4.
22. Clifton, Hrynuik, and Perry, "Research."
23. Peter Puxley, "The Colonial Experience," in Mel Watkins, ed., *Dene Nations. The Colony Within* (Toronto: University of Toronto Press, 1977), p. 104.
24. The medical ship *C.D. Howe* would often dock at native settlements only to find that many residents had disappeared, unwilling to avail themselves of its medical services. In many settlements today, there is resistance to the use of medical personnel, except in cases of emergency or crisis. See "Decline Noted in Natives' Trust of M.D.'s," *Winnipeg Free Press,* 29 June 1981.
25. Case record, *Native Family Services,* Winnipeg, Manitoba.
26. Peter Hudson, *Report on the Preventive Services Project of the Family and Children's Services of the District of Rainy River* (Winnipeg: University of Manitoba School of Social Work, 1980).
27. Brian Wharf, "Preventive Approaches to Child Welfare," Chapter 12 of this publication.
28. *A By-Law for the Care of Indian Children.* By-law #3, 1980, passed 3 June 1980.
29. *Canada—Manitoba—Indian Child Welfare Agreement* signed 28 February 1982.
30. Manitoba Métis Federation Inc., *Position Paper on Child Care and Family Services.* Winnipeg, 15 May 1982.
31. Pete Hudson and Brad McKenzie, *Evaluation of Dakota Ojibway Child and Family Services,* prepared for Dakota Ojibway Child and Family Services and Evaluation Branch, Department of Indian Affairs and Northern Development, June 1984.
32. Public Law 95-608, "Indian Child Welfare Act," 92 Statute 3069-3077, 8 November 1978.
33. Correspondence from John Angus MacKenzie, deputy minister, Nova Scotia Department of Social Services, as quoted in Patrick Johnston and Stephen Novosedlik, "Child Welfare and the Native Peoples of Canada," Paper presented to the Canadian Association of Schools of Social Work Annual Conference, Ottawa, 1-4 June 1982.
34. Public Law 95-608, section 105.
35. A summary of some of the literature on bonding is found in Community Task Force on Maternal and Child Health, "Adoption: The Issue of Bonding in the Adoption of Newborn Infants," in *Child-bearing Families and the Law* (Winnipeg: 1981). Also see John Bowlby, *Maternal Care and Mental Health* (Geneva: World Health Organization Monograph Series #2, 1951).

8

SUBSTITUTE CARE: THE RANGE OF RESPONSES

H. Philip Hepworth

This chapter reviews the array of resources used by the child welfare services when they seek to assist children and their families in their homes and in substitute care facilities. The question of what happens to children in care is briefly considered in the light of the available data. That there is a need for longitudinal research to find out what truly happens to children over a period of years is the main conclusion.

PROTECTION AND PREVENTION SERVICES: SERVING CHILDREN AT HOME

In the chapter on apprehension and reasons for children being admitted to care, I discussed the protection and prevention services provided in Ontario to children in their own homes, including cases where children were subsequently admitted to care and also cases where children were being supervised in their own homes after being in care. Within a given period of time, most children receiving such services do not enter care, though the large proportion of reopened cases suggests the persistence or recurrence of problems in children's own homes. Only a case-by-case longitudinal study could properly verify the extent to which children receiving protective/preventive services are ultimately admitted to care. The other major feature of these services is the extent to which they have grown in recent years.

The Ontario protection/prevention figures are useful for showing the linkage with the in-care services. What in effect protection and prevention services do is to act as a buffer so that the direct demands on in-care services are regulated, deferred or even diverted. The protection services are defined in Nova Scotia as follows:

Protection services are the backbone of the Family and Children's Services. The overall priority and philosophy of this service is to keep families together, if at all possible. The better the protection services provided in the community, the fewer children will be taken into care. (Nova Scotia, Annual Report 1981, p. 32)

The Nova Scotia report mentions various types of services which can be drawn on to help families cope with their problems: homemakers, day care, mental health units, public health units, and family counselling services. Where such help does not suffice, Nova Scotia uses voluntary care agreements quite extensively as a kind of respite service whereby children are placed outside their own homes for a period of time. Such an arrangement is not greatly different from Ontario where such children are recorded as non-wards within the in-care services. As in other provinces, protection cases have increased in Nova Scotia from 2,640 in 1969 to 3,576 in 1980. During the same period unmarried mother cases have declined from 830 to 430 (see Table 1).

British Columbia apparently attempted to enshrine the same type of family support strategy in its 1980 Family and Child Service Act, though the comments of David Cruickshank in this volume should be noted:

Prevention, rather than apprehension, is the goal. Nearly 42 per cent of the ministry's 1980 budget for Family and Children's Services was earmarked for family support and preventive services. In 1980, 1000 fewer children were in the care of the superintendent of Child Welfare than in 1975; an encouraging measure of the success of these programs. (British Columbia, Annual Report 1981, p. 24).

Such developments should be seen against a background of an overall fall in the child population in British Columbia aged 0 - 14 years between 1975 and 1980 from 619,000 to 576,000 (Statistics Canada, 1982). At the same time the number of family service cases (including unmarried mother cases) rose from about 16,000 in 1976 to 24,000 in 1979 (see Table 2).

The same goals were reaffirmed by British Columbia in the 1982-83 Annual Report of the Ministry of Human Resources, "to preserve the integrity of the family unit, to enable children to remain within their own families and communities, and to encourage independent functioning" (British Columbia, Annual Report 1984, p. 30). This programme was terminated in the round of cuts conducted by the Government of British Columbia in 1983.

At various points in this chapter warning notes are sounded about the need for caution before the assumption is made that child welfare interventions are always beneficial to children and families. The above quotation ascribed the fall in the number of children in care to the success of the family support programme, but appeared to leave out of account the fall in the total child population. At the same time the number of family cases had increased by as much as 50 per cent in a three-year period. There are obviously many different ways in which the statistics can be interpreted. It is possible to take an optimistic, a pessimistic, or even a cynical view. The historical growth in the staff of the child welfare services was associated first of all with the growth of the total child population, which ended in 1969 at a time when the highest number of children were in care. In addition, after 1970, not only did the number of illegitimate births decrease, but with it the number of babies relinquished for adoption, but increasingly mothers of these children chose to raise them themselves. In some ways, therefore, the pressures on the child welfare services were reduced at a time when the number of child welfare staff continued to increase. The opportunity thus arose to deploy staff in areas of work perhaps previously neglected, particularly direct preventive work with families. The tendency for native mothers to retain their babies when born outside marriage, but then for disproportionately higher numbers of native children to be admitted to care at somewhat older ages than from the comparable non-native population was noted in *Foster Care and Adoption in Canada* (Hepworth, 1980, p. 115). We know also that the number of one-parent families has increased substantially in recent years, that they are usually led by women, and that the majority of them are poor.

We begin to see in this set of circumstances some of the factors justifying the growth of family support services with families, many of them poor and vulnerable, who have traditionally been clients of the child welfare services. It is perhaps worth restating here that many family support programmes do appear to be successful at least in the short term. However, they do point to the need to look for real prevention beyond the boundaries of child welfare services as they have traditionally been understood. If vulnerable families are to be expected to cope in society, they obviously cannot do so without adequate help and resources. The price of their failure to cope is very high, both for them and for society.

Family support services represent a logical extension of protection/prevention services into related areas of a child's functioning and involve other relevant social services such as education and health. Along with the basic income assistance programmes, it is possible to glimpse the beginning of a coherent preventive strategy in those provinces with such support programmes. But there is still a long way to go. At the same time promising developments in preventive programmes must be set against the continued existence of the traditional child welfare services. Over a period of twenty years British Columbia has ranked third highest in the proportion of its child population in care (Hepworth, 1982, p. 24). In 1980, for example, it had proportionately twice as many children in care as did Ontario, in part owing to the high proportion of native children entering care in the western provinces.

CHILDREN IN CARE

What happens to children in care? There is surprisingly little direct evidence. Again, case-by-case analysis is required, and few research studies have attempted such an approach. There have been some attempts to single out the effects of particular modes of supervision (Shulman, 1981). However, what is probably required is a clinical approach in which the quality of the in-care experience is assessed on a day-to-day basis along with a charting of the major events such as kinds of placement, visits from parents, periodic reviews, long-term planning sessions, and ultimate relocation either at home or in an independent living situation, as well as what happens subsequently.

Periodically we hear of former foster children suing the act for their "stolen childhood," of multiple foster home placements, of unhappy experiences in residential institutions (MacVeigh, 1982; Harris, 1982; Davis, 1982; Pragnell, 1982). It may be the nature of substitute care to hear only the negative stories. But it is not surprising that the results of radical interventions in children's lives and families are mixed. Substitute care means what it says, second best, the best that can be hoped for in the circumstances. Similarly, the adoption experience is increasingly being recognized as different from natural parenthood; it is one of the best replacements for the care of biological parents, but different (Seglow, Pringle, and Wedge, 1972). Care-givers of children who have experienced neglect and deprivation and who have suffered the loss of family and home must therefore have realistic expectations of the children in their care. Such an approach or attitude is difficult to acquire and hard to practice in the rough and tumble, the give and take, of daily care giving. What is being sought in the care-givers is an informed sort of caring, not a professional or clinical detachment, but an ability to understand not only the children in their care, but also themselves and their own motivations for providing care. This ideal is hard to achieve. Moreover, it is not really surprising that placements break down. The trial and error approach to child placement may in fact be the method most likely to arrive at the desired result. At the same time, too many breakdowns in placement create further havoc in the lives of children already badly damaged and disturbed (Parker, 1966).

TYPES OF PLACEMENT

Many factors influence the type of placement arrangements made for children in care. The characteristics of the children and their legal status are relevant as are the type of placement resources available. Moreover, it may often be the characteristics of the available placement resources rather than the needs of the children involved which determine the types of placement made. In other words, placement resources are not in such an elastic state of supply that ideal placements can always be made. Some types of placement may be more inelastic than others; this is obviously true of residential institutions, but it may also apply to foster homes and group homes. It is quite likely that the better homes will be in high demand with the turnover of places in them being slow. In fact, a degree of permanency and security will often be sought for children in care. The management of placement resources is therefore not easy.

There is little doubt that foster care is the backbone of the in-care, child welfare services in Canada. Despite the current talk of deinstitutionalization, institutional care has been reserved primarily in the past for children with special needs, especially those who are mentally retarded or who have physical handicaps. Moreover, modified forms of institutional, or what may preferably be called residential, care are always likely to be needed for severely handicapped children. Families caring for such children will need respite care, and where parents are unable to cope or are not present, small residential homes are probably the best type of alternative placement.

It is nonetheless reassuring that at least three-quarters of children in care live in family type homes (see Table 3). The bulk of such homes are foster homes. Developments in recent years have tended to blur the distinctions between foster care and residential (or institutional) care. Group homes and special foster homes care are often indistinguishable in official records. For example, the smallest category of homes for special care designated for cost-sharing under the Canada Assistance Plan is homes of one to nine beds.

If, as is argued above, substitute care is "different" from care provided by natural parents, so the experience of living in a large group situation is different from that of a smaller group home. To pretend otherwise is misleading and does not reflect the type of experience a child in care is actually receiving. At the same time, there are some, especially older children, for whom group forms of living are more appropriate than smaller, nuclear family type foster homes. The emotional and psychological demands are likely to be less intense in the more impersonal setting of the larger group. Older children are likely to retain strong links with, or memories of, their families; at the same time they may already, or soon, be adolescents, and they need to resolve their feelings about themselves and their families and about growing up; the last thing they need is a whole new set of emotional demands made by adults acting as surrogate parents.

As already indicated, the distinction between types of placement is not always obvious. In 1977-78, the latest year for which an accurate distribution of children can be made nationally 77.6 per cent of all children in care were living in a family type placement. Some 15.9 per cent were actually living with family or relatives; 4.1 per cent were living in adoption homes, and 56.2 per cent were in foster homes. Some 17.4 per cent were in institutional care, and 3.6 per cent were in designated group homes.

This distribution does not completely reflect the child care picture in Canada. Children in adoption homes in Newfoundland, Prince Edward Island, Quebec, and to a large extent in British Columbia are not included. Similarly non-wards in Nova Scotia are not shown, nor are children living in their own homes in Manitoba. However, the overall in-care picture is reasonably accurate.

FOSTER HOMES

The striking feature of the placement statistics is the dependence on foster homes. The proportion of children in this type of care has never fallen below 54.9 per cent in the period 1959/60-1977/78 (Hepworth, 1980, p. 89). Moreover, during the peak years for total number of children in care from the mid 1960's to the early 1970's, the proportion rose above the 60 per cent level, and as high as 70.1 per cent in 1966-67. During this period the number of children in foster care has fluctuated between 28,605 in 1959-60, 65,139 in 1969-70 and 42,499 in 1977-78. On 31 March 1979 there were 34,165 approved foster homes (Hepworth, 1980, pp. 223-38).

A few studies have been conducted of foster care in Canada, but as yet a definitive picture is lacking (Rosenblum, 1977; Poulos, 1972). It should not be supposed that foster parents are a homogeneous group of people; rather, there are indications that they are a cross-section of society with a corresponding spread of attitudes, beliefs, values, and prejudices (Rosenblum, 1977). On a controversial subject like corporal punishment, for example, foster parents reflect a wide range of views. Child welfare services may well prohibit corporal punishment, but this is no guarantee that all foster parents will follow such a rule. Moreover, except in exceptional circumstances, the child welfare services are unlikely to enforce such a rule very strictly. Foster homes are a valued resource and not readily relinquished. Maintenance payments for foster children are more realistic than they were twenty years ago, but there is no real element of remuneration in them, except where the foster home services being provided are clearly recognized and designated as special. Accordingly, there is no basis for supposing that the motivation for fostering is monetary; instead, it is much more likely to be a love of children, but a love given on the foster parents' terms, rather than on lines prescribed by the child welfare services (Rosenblum, 1977).

ADOPTION PLACEMENTS

As already indicated children relinquished for adoption are not always admitted to care or shown in the in-care statistics. In addition, in recent years fewer babies have been relinquished for adoption, so that the proportion of adoptions, in which the child welfare services are directly involved in placement, has fallen to below 40 per cent in recent years. Manitoba and Saskatchewan are exceptions, and here the high proportion of native children in care and available for adoption has swelled the number of placements. In fact, most provinces have switched their attention to placing for adoption children with special needs, whether related to mental or physical disabilities, age, or ethnic status. The proportion of native children placed for adoption in Saskatchewan in recent years has risen as high as 40 per cent of all placements, but even so this is not sufficient to offset the disproportionate number of native children entering and remaining in care (Table 4).

As indicated earlier, demographic trends appear to influence the child welfare services quite strongly. The total number of adoptions peaked in the years 1969, 1979, and 1971 when the number of illegitimate births was highest (Hepworth, 1980, p. 135). However, some provinces went on to show higher proportions of the child population being adopted in the mid-1970's. Another feature worthy of some comment is the spread in the proportion of children adopted between provinces. Quebec has tended to have the lowest proportion of children adopted, 0.19 per cent of the population aged 0-14 years in the period 1961-62 to 1979-80. Manitoba has had the highest proportion adopted, 0.41 per cent of the 0-14 year population in the period 1961-62 to 1979-80. The persistence of the spread between provinces is not easy to explain given the increasing proportion of relative adoptions, except, of course, that variations between provinces in divorce rates and other related indices will also have an influence. Be this as it may, Quebec has the lowest proportion of completed adoptions resulting from child welfare agency placements, and Manitoba has the highest in recent years, respectively 21.7 per cent and 69.3 per cent of completions in 1979-80 (Hepworth, 1982, pp. 25-28).

The increasing tendency in recent years for unmarried mothers to keep their babies rather than relinquish them for adoption has been remarked in all provinces. This trend combined with the increasing number of remarriages in which children from previous marriages are involved accounts for some of the increased popularity of parental or relative adoptions. The many legal, social, and moral issues involved in such adoptions cannot be discussed here, but they warrant careful scrutiny (Bissett-Johnson, 1978). The child welfare services are usually involved in supervising relative adoptions, but their involvement is usually nominal. The need to protect the welfare of children in relative adoptions remains a paramount social concern, but it is not clear how this can best be done. Sometimes legal arrangements falling short of full legal adoption may be desirable, as already implemented in England and Wales and as currently contemplated in Ontario (Bromley, 1978; Bissett-Johnson, 1978; Ontario, 1982). Generally child welfare services have not played an intrusive role once adoption placements of any kind have been made. The pressure for disclosure of adoption information, along with other social trends already noted, may bring further changes in the definition of adoption and in the types of substitute or replacement care legally sanctioned in future years.

RESIDENTIAL CARE

The residential care of children in institutions is proportionately less than it was twenty years ago, but in absolute numbers is about the same — 14,958 in 1959-60 and 13,166 in 1977-78 (15,920 if clearly designated group homes are added (Hepworth, 1980, p. 136) (see Table 4). But the distinction between foster care and group homes is not always apparent. In 1982, for example, there were 5,616 beds in homes of 1-9 beds listed in the Homes for Special Care statistics of Health and Welfare Canada (see Table 5). For cost-sharing purposes, homes for special care are treated separately by the federal government, but they are not always distinguished from foster homes by the provincial governments.

Furthermore, the Homes for Special Care statistics indicate many more homes and beds than appear to be occupied by children at any one time, and these numbers have grown absolutely and as a proportion of the child population since the 1966 Canada Assistance Plan came into operation. There have been some changes in the types and size of homes. In the seven years 1976-82, the number of homes has grown from 1,056 to 1,358, with the average number of beds in each home falling from 27.5 to 22.3 (Hepworth, 1980, p. 92). These figures are somewhat skewed by the inclusion of the Quebec statistics; when they are excluded the overall bed size falls to 12.6 in 1982. Some 45.3 per cent of beds are in homes over 100 beds, but this involves only 5.7 per cent of homes. Homes with 1-9 beds represent 66.6 per cent of homes with an average size of 6.2 beds (see Table 5.)

The type of regime prevailing in homes of such widely differing sizes obviously varies. To some extent there is a persistence of some traditional types of institutional care for children with mental and physical disabilities, as well as the continued operation of some very large sets of buildings.

Given the mixed picture presented by the available statistics, it seems necessary to draw a distinction between large and small homes. Deinstitutionalization as a concept primarily relates to the larger homes, and we may expect to see continued reduction in their use. But the growth in the number of small homes suggests an area of development which warrants careful monitoring. It has been implied above that foster parents are likely to reflect the values and opinions of the general population. Despite the introduction of training and orientation courses for foster parents, it is not usually suggested that foster-parenting should be a professional activity. The same cannot be said of residential care. Staffing arrangements, therapeutic programmes, and codes of conduct clearly tip the balance towards a professional orientation for residential care. Certainly there may be a blurring between the types of care, but the expectations made of foster parents and residential care workers are different.

CHILDREN "IN CARE" IN THEIR OWN HOMES

We come back finally to children being cared for in their own homes. It may seem a contradiction in terms that some children living in their own homes or with relatives are still technically speaking "in care." In this case, special supervisory arrangements or agreements are in operation, as in Alberta with the Handicapped Children's agreements. In Quebec, there were 5,648 children living in their own homes or those of relatives (en milieu naturel), and of these 4,023 were receiving support services for themselves or for their families in 1978 (Quebec, 1979). For most of the other children, individual casework or marriage or family therapy are involved. Clearly, the lines between "in care" services and protective/preventive services are blurred, and given the dynamics of the human situations and the procedures of the child welfare services, it is not altogether surprising that a snapshot view of services at any one time will not capture all the essential elements of a complex reality in which children are often moving in and out of their own homes.

Given the fluidity of the child welfare services, some attempt should be made to follow children through care until their return to the community. Elsewhere I have suggested the need for longitudinal studies of children; this remains a desirable goal (Hepworth, 1980). In the meantime, that the child welfare services have contact with so many children in their own homes, that so many children in care are in their own homes, that so many children move from an in-care situation to a supervised placement in their own homes, and finally that so many children return to their own homes after leaving care, all raise the fundamental question about the original justification for apprehending and removing children from their families.

DISCHARGES FROM CARE

Available statistics on admissions and discharges suggest a higher rate of activity in the child welfare services than was the case twenty years ago

(Hepworth, 1980, p. 124). Even so, some provinces show a much higher level of activity than others. In Ontario admissions and discharges during the year as a percentage of children in care at the end of 1980 were 189.2 (see Table 6). In Nova Scotia, on the other hand, where the figures are only available for wards, the percentage was only 35.0 (see Table 7). To some extent these figures on the rate of turnover of children in care reflect differences in the characteristics of the in-care populations involved as well as the degree of activity of the relevant provincial child welfare services.

Some differences show up with respect to discharges from care resulting from adoption placements. In 1977-78 41.3 per cent (170) of discharges resulted from adoption placements in Nova Scotia, and 36.3 per cent (246) in Newfoundland. By contrast 15.0 per cent (1,741) in Ontario, 19.0 per cent (436) in Saskatchewan, and 9.9 per cent (487) in British Columbia were the result of adoption placements (see Table 8). In the case of British Columbia, a large proportion of children relinquished for adoption are never formally admitted to care.

In Newfoundland, Ontario, Saskatchewan, and British Columbia, the bulk of discharges is designated as children returned to their parents, respectively 53.4 per cent, (362), 68.7 per cent (7,974), 69.6 per cent (1,597) and 49.5 per cent (2,426) (see Table 8). There are other designations, such as commitment terminated, which also imply return to parents' custody. Relatively small proportions of discharges involve children reaching the age of majority, getting married, or taking employment — 5 per cent (34) in Newfoundland, 5.6 per cent (654) in Ontario, 9.5 per cent (219) in Saskatchewan, and 15.2 per cent (744) in British Columbia. The exception here is Nova Scotia with 42.1 per cent (174) of permanent wards being discharged under this type of designation, again perhaps a reflection of their permanence of status, with no indication being given that most of these children or young people reaching the age of majority are not also returning to their own parents. Finally, a small proportion (between 0.4 and 1.9 per cent) of discharges reflect deaths of children in care (see Table 8).

The available statistics suggest that the vast majority of children return to their own parents, and the increased levels of activity in most provinces suggest that the turnover of most children in care is fairly rapid. Of course, some children stay in care for long periods of time. The available figures for protection and adoption in Saskatchewan show that proportionately fewer native children than white children are adopted, and one consequence is that native children stay in care longer. Permanence of ward status also permits and implies two outcomes, either placement for adoption or a long stay in care, but both also depend on the age of the children.

LONG-TERM EFFECTS OF CARE

Little is known about the long-term effects of periods in care. But apprehension and care are disruptive of family and social ties no matter how warranted such intervention is. Though adoption is one of the better forms of substitute care, the effects of the original disruption in the child's life is often manifested sooner or later in some form of disturbed behaviour (Seglow, Pringle, and Wedge, 1972).

In the case of other children discharged from care, most return to their parents, and only a small proportion strike out on their own. In many cases the personal and social situations of parents may not have improved (Fanshel and Shinn, 1978; Jenkins and Norman, 1972; Jenkins and Norman, 1975), and there is no guarantee that family reunions will be successful. It is known, for example, that a high proportion of native children who have been in care later appear in correctional facilities. A period in care is also often part of the history of white persons in prison.

FUNDAMENTAL QUESTIONS

A review and analysis of the available statistics on the child welfare services therefore prompt some fundamental questions about the rationale for the child welfare services. Are radical intrusions in children's and families' lives really justified? Obviously, in extreme situations the grounds for intervention are sound. But the available information suggests that child welfare services detect many cases of neglect and abuse and that help is often already being tendered before apprehension is considered or undertaken and that admission may result from a sudden crisis. Even so, should situations have to become so desperate that surveillance and drastic preventive measures have to be undertaken? Which is the greater intrusion in a family's life: the provision of good supportive social services, health care, income support, education, and employment help or the temporary or permanent removal of a child?

When so many children are at risk, it is not really wishful thinking to look for alternatives to traditional apprehension procedures, nor to think that the fault lies more in the social system than in the child caring abilities of parents. As it is, the child welfare services have to intervene at a stage when the odds are already tipped against the children they seek to help. It is not surprising that the results are sometimes problematic.

REFERENCES

Bissett-Johnson, A. "Step-Parent Adoptions in English and Canadian Law." In I.F.G. Baxter and M.A. Eberts, eds., *The Child and the Courts* (Toronto: Carswell, 1978), pp. 335-58.

British Columbia, Ministry of Human Resources. *Annual Report, 1980* (Victoria, 1981).

British Columbia. *The New Family and Child Service Act, Explanatory Notes.*

Bromley, P.M. "The New English Law of Adoption." In Baxter and Eberts, pp. 359-90.

Canada. Statistics Canada. *Population Estimates.* Catalogue No. 91-001 (1982).

Davis, L. "Whose Life?" *Social Work Today* 14 no. 11,(1982): 10.

Fanshel, D., and Shinn, E.B. *Children in Foster Care: A Longitudinal Study* (New York: Columbia University Press, 1978).

Harris, D. "The Sadness, the Guilt and the Anger." *Social Work Today* 14 no. 11, (1982): 8-9.

Hepworth, H.P. "Child Welfare Services in Longitudinal Perspective." *Canadian Journal of Social Work Education* 6 (1980).

———*Foster Care and Adoption in Canada* (Ottawa: Canadian Council on Social Development, 1980).

———"Trends and Comparisons in Canadian Child Welfare Services" Paper prepared for presentation at the First Conference on Provincial Social Welfare Policy, University of Calgary, Calgary, Alberta, 5-7 May 1982.

Jenkins, S., and Norman, E. *Beyond Placement: Mothers View Foster Care* (New York: Columbia University Press, 1975).

———*Filial Deprivation and Foster Care* (New York: Columbia University Press, 1972).

MacVeigh, J. *Gaskin* (London: Cape, 1982).

Nova Scotia. Department of Social Services. *Annual Report, 1981.*

Ontario. Ministry of Community and Social Services. *The Children's Act: A Consultation Paper* (Toronto: the Ministry, 1982).

Parker, R.A. *Decision in Child Care* (London: Allen and Unwin, 1966).

Poulos, S. *Foster Care Study: Factors Associated with Placement Stability* (Vancouver: Children's Aid Society of Vancouver, 1972).

Pragnell, C. "Dickens and Worse." *Social Work Today* 14 no. 11, (1982): 1.

Québec. Ministère des Affaires sociales. *Opération 30000, Annexe Statistique* (1979).

Rosenblum, B. *Foster Homes and Adolescents: A Research Report* (1977).

Seglow, J., Pringle, M.K., and Wedge, P. *Growing Up Adopted: A Long-Term National Study of Adopted Children and Their Families* (Slough: Children's Bureau, National Foundation for Educational Research in England and Wales, 1972).

Shulman, L., Robinson, E., and Luckji, A. *A Study of the Content, Context and Skills of Supervision* (Vancouver: University of British Columbia, B.C., 1981).

TABLE 1

VOLUME OF SELECTED CHILD WELFARE SERVICES ACTIVITIES IN NOVA SCOTIA IN 1969/70, 1971/72, 1976/77-1980/81

	1969/70	1971/72	1976/77	1977/78	1978/79	1979/80	1980/81
(a) Adoption studies:							
(1) First reports	728	878	855	634	726	733	461
(2) Second reports	619	720	730	590	706	574	524
(3) Supplement reports	23	99	60	21	24	38	66
(b) Protection cases	2,640	2,724	3,023	3,306	2,848	3,150	3,576
(c) Unmarried mother cases	830	715	680	622	636	536	430
(d) Foster home studies	829	744	464	404	350	311	258
(e) Court appearance (delinquents)	1,244	1,867	331	344	325	336	336
(f) Probation cases	941	680	135	129	97	86	82
(g) After care cases	282	258	20	36	15	9	9
(h) Nova Scotia Youth Centre cases	97	75	22	1	18	24	21
(i) Investigation for divorce court	49	99	89	46	46	73	66
(j) Family allowance cases	14	4	4	2	2	6	10
(k) Transient poor cases	24	16	7	10	11	60	63
(l) Investigations for Department of Education	84	29	16	8	65	121	109
(m) Investigations for hospitals—social service	59	39	41	43	124	69	88
(n) Other cases	324	246	509	681	700	611	664

Source: Nova Scotia, Department of Social Services, *Annual Reports,* 1969/70, 1971/72, and 1976/77-1980/81.

TABLE 2

NUMBER OF FAMILY SERVICE CASES INCLUDING UNMARRIED MOTHERS (NOT IN RECEIPT OF FINANCIAL ASSISTANCE FROM THE MINISTRY OF HUMAN RESOURCES) SERVED BY THE BRITISH COLUMBIA MINISTRY OF HUMAN RESOURCES, 1976-1980

Year	Total at Beginning of Year	No. of Cases Opened	Total No. of Cases Served During Year	No. of Cases Closed	Total at End of Year
1976/77	6,883	9,372	16,255	8,042	8,213
1977/78	8,213	—	—	—	10,165
1978/79	10,165	14,383	24,548	12,966	11,582
1979/80	11,582	12,308	23,890	11,585	12,312[1]

Source: British Columbia, Ministry of Human Resources, *Annual Reports, Statistical Tables, 1976-1979.*

1. As shown in text.

TABLE 3

THE LOCATION OF CHILDREN IN CARE IN 1977/78

Province		Foster Homes	Boarding Homes	Free Homes Relatives	Adoption Homes	Sub-total	Residential Institutions	Group Homes	Sub-total	Other Locations	Total
Newfoundland	No.	839	22	64		925	295	10	305	44	1,274
	Percentage	65.9	1.7	5.0		72.6	23.2	0.7	23.9	3.5	100.0
P.E.I.	No.	253[a]				253	8	16[a]	24		277
	Percentage	91.3				91.3	2.9	5.8	8.7		100.0
Nova Scotia	No.	1,556	93	155	152	1,956	179		179	36[b]	2,171[c]
	Percentage	71.7	4.3	7.1	7.0	90.1	8.2		8.2	1.7	100.0
New Brunswick	No.	1,900[d]		300[a]	277[a]	2,477	169[e]		169		2,646[f]
	Percentage	71.8		11.3	10.5	93.6	6.4		6.4		100.0
Québec	No.	16,824	560	5,648		23,032	6,428	779	7,207	110	30,349
	Percentage	55.4	1.8	18.6		75.9	21.2	2.6	23.8	0.3	100.0
Ontario	No.	7,286		1,116	1,034	9,436	2,094	1,126	3,220	469[g]	13,125[h]
	Percentage	55.5		8.5	7.9	71.9	16.0	8.6	24.6	3.5	100.0
Manitoba	No.	1,886			304	2,190	772	567	1,339	109	3,638[h,i]
	Percentage	51.8			8.4	60.2	21.2	15.6	36.8	3.0	100.0
Saskatchewan	No.	1,794[j]		290	224	2,308	154		154		2,462[k]
	Percentage	72.9		11.7	9.1	93.7	6.3		6.3		100.0
Alberta	No.	4,237	151	3,560	721	8,669	1,510	256	1,766	39[l]	10,474
	Percentage	40.5	1.4	34.0	6.9	82.8	14.4	2.4	16.8	0.4	100.0
British Columbia	No.	5,924	203	838	381	7,346	1,557		1,557	178[l]	9,081
	Percentage	65.2	2.2	9.2	4.2	80.9	17.1		17.1	2.0	100.0
Total	No.	42,499	1,029	11,971	3,093	58,592	13,166	2,754	15,920	985	75,497
	Percentage	56.2	1.4	15.9	4.1	77.6	17.4	3.6	21.0	1.3	100.0

Source: Provincial departments of Social Services, Annual Reports and unpublished statistics, and Québec, Ministère des Affaires sociales, Opération 30000, rapport final, and annexe statistique, octobre 1979.

a. estimate
b. includes 13 at university or educational establishment
c. wards only
d. includes group homes
e. Dr. William Robert's Hospital School
f. See N.S., Department of S.S., Annual Report 1977-78

g. reduced by 6 to balance
h. as at 31 December 1977
i. excludes children with parents or relatives
j. includes group homes and special foster homes
k. excludes 176 children in care of Department of Northern Sask.
l. children away without leave

TABLE 4

CHILDREN PLACED FOR ADOPTION BY AGE AND ETHNIC ORIGIN IN SASKATCHEWAN, 1977/78-1980/81

Year	Age Group 0-6			6-10 Years			Over 10 years			Total			
	Indian	Métis	Other	Indian	Métis	Other	Indian	Métis	Other	Indian	Métis	Other	Total
1977/78	66	45	274	19	5	11	4	3	6	89	53	291	433
1978/79	87	42	247	11	3	11	5	5	15	103	50	273	426
1979/80	39	37	231	22	10	7	4	3	2	65	50	240	355
1980/81	66	50	223	15	13	7	6	4	4	87	67	234	388

Source: Saskatchewan, Department of Social Services, unpublished statistics.

TABLE 5

THE NUMBER AND SIZE OF CHILD CARE INSTITUTIONS IN EACH PROVINCE AND TERRITORY, MARCH 1982

Province/Territory		1-9 Beds	10-24 Beds	25-49 Beds	50-99 Beds	100-199 Beds	200-299 Beds	300-499 Beds	500 Beds and Over	Total Institutions	Total Beds
Newfoundland	Number		2	4	2	2				10	
	Beds		38	139	136	310					623
Prince Edward Island	Number	5		1						6	
	Beds	26		25							51
Nova Scotia	Number	11	9	8	2	1	1			32	
	Beds	63	159	306	125	150	230				1,033
New Brunswick	Number	6	1		1	1	1			10	
	Beds	48	20		80	173	227				548
Québec	Number	16	22	21	44	49	6	7		165	
	Beds	140	387	736	3,264	6,549	1,379	2,888			15,343
Ontario	Number	447	131	16	12	4		1		611	
	Beds	2,698	1,839	520	791	487		350			6,685
Manitoba	Number	106	6	8	3	2	1	1		127	
	Beds	729	78	273	192	208	265	350			2,095
Saskatchewan	Number	16	8	3						27	
	Beds	108	119	95							322
Alberta	Number	91	21	9	6	1				128	
	Beds	586	301	298	429	160					1,774
British Columbia	Number	196	20	8						224	
	Beds	1,132	277	252							1,661
Northwest Territories	Number	7	4	1						12	
	Beds	54	70	26							150
Yukon	Number	4	2							6	
	Beds	32	26								58
Canada	Number	905	226	79	70	60	9	9		1,358	
	Beds	5,616	3,314	2,670	5,017	8,037	2,101	3,588			30,343
% distribution of homes		66.6	16.6	5.8	5.2	4.4	0.7	0.7		100.0	
% distribution of beds		18.5	10.9	8.8	16.5	26.6	6.9	11.8			100.0

Source: Health and Welfare Canada, Homes for Special Care, March 31, 1982.

TABLE 6

ONTARIO ADMISSIONS, DISCHARGES, AND CHILDEN IN CARE

Year	A Admissions	B Discharges	A + B	C Children in care	A + B as % of C
1976	—	—	—	12,962	—
1977	11,771	11,602	23,373	13,131	178.0
1978	12,397	11,708	24,105	13,814	174.5
1979	12,297	12,103	24,400	14,008	174.2
1980	11,840	12,815	24,655	13,033	189.2

Source: Ontario, Ministry of Community and Social Services, unpublished annual statistics.

TABLE 7

ADMISSIONS AND DISCHARGES COMBINED AS PERCENTAGE
OF NUMBER OF WARDS IN CARE IN NOVA SCOTIA, 1976/77-1980/81

Year	A Admissions of Wards	B Discharges of Wards	A + B	C Children in Care	D A + B as % of C
1976/77	353	500	853	2,294	37.2
1977/78	290	413	703	2,171	32.4
1978/79	245	457	702	1,959	35.8
1979/80	277	396	673	1,840	36.6
1980/81	267	348	615	1,759	35.0

Source: Nova Scotia, Department of Social Services, *Annual Reports, 1976/77-1980/81,* Halifax.

TABLE 8

DISCHARGES FROM CARE BY TYPE OF DISPOSITION IN FIVE PROVINCES, 1977/78

	Newfoundland		Nova Scotia		Ontario		Saskatchewan		British Columbia	
	No.	%	No.	%	No.	%	No.	%	No.	%
Adopted	246	36.3	170	41.3	1,741	15.0	436	19.0	487	9.9
Reached age limit, marriage, employment	34	5.0	174	42.1	654	5.6	219	9.5	744	15.2
Discharges died	13	1.9	5	1.2	48	0.4	14	0.6	45	0.9
Returned to other province										
Transfers of supervision	23	3.4	4	1.0	20	0.2	29	1.3	85	1.7
Supervision order* return to parents									172	3.5
Commitment terminated			60	14.5	621	5.4			547	11.2
Other					544	4.7			396	8.1
Returned to parents	362[1]	53.4			7,974	68.7	1,597	69.6	2,426	49.5
Total	678	100.0	413	100.0	11,602	100.0	2,295	100.0	4,902	100.0

Source: Provincial annual reports and unpublished statistics.
1. Parents 315, relatives 47.
* Juvenile Delinquents Act.

9

PERMANENT PLANNING FOR CHILDREN IN CARE

Elizabeth M. Robinson

INTRODUCTION

This chapter and the next on subsidized adoption deal with the importance of ensuring permanency in children's lives. When children are separated voluntarily or involuntarily from their parents, the primary task of the agency is to restore or create a sense of permanency. Not only must the planning be systematically developed but reasonable possible outcomes must be achievable.

Well-validated research in social work and psychiatry over the last thirty years has yielded generalizations which give direction to policy development, to programme planning, and to direct practice in child welfare. Some of this research has led inductively to the construct of "permanent planning for children in care," which is an effort to address the needs of any child coming into care. It is an active decision-making process of examining alternatives and making plans. Victor Pike, one of the pioneers of permanent planning, has said,

> Permanent planning means clarifying the intent of the placement, and, during temporary care, keeping alive a plan for permanency. When a temporary placement is prolonged, foster care may have the appearance of permanency but it lacks the element of intent that is critical to permanency.[1]

This chapter will examine some specific conceptual issues or principles which form the basis of a permanent planning framework for child welfare practice in a Canadian context.

LITERATURE REVIEW

The construct of permanent planning developed over a period of years when enquiries into the nature of foster care revealed deficiencies in the child welfare system. Several key findings are vital to our understanding.

Time in Care. It has been a consistent finding that children remain unnecessarily in care for long periods of time and that the longer a child is in care, the less likelihood there is of the child returning home or being adopted (both options are seen as preferable to foster care). Maas and Engler reported in their pioneer study of four thousand children in care in nine communities throughout the United States that the majority of foster children remained in care from two to five years.[2] Plans were indefinite, and there was little sense of permanence. Fanshel's study of foster children in New York City found that after three and one-half years, 46 per cent of children were still in care, and at the end of five years, almost 40 per cent continued in care.[3] In more recent studies, Stein and Gambrill showed that probabilities for return to parents are greatest during the first year and that movement out of care is reduced substantially after a child has been in care more than three years.[4] British researchers Rowe and Lambert, in their study of children-in-care, reported that once a child has been in care for more than six months, there was 75 per cent chance of his remaining in care throughout childhood.[5]

Parental Visiting. Maas and Engler found that unvisited children are the least likely to return home.[6] Subsequent studies confirmed the relationship between parental visiting and discharge from care. In a five-year longitudinal study, Fanshel and Shinn reported that children whose parents visited them frequently were almost twice as likely to be discharged compared with those children who were visited minimally or not at all.[7] Fanshel concluded that, with few exceptions, parental visiting and return of the child from care were highly correlated. Sherman, Newman and Shyne showed the frequency of contact between the biological mother and the child had a statistically significant relationship to the child's return to the natural home.[8] Parents who visited the child regularly were able to effect the child's discharge in 73 per cent of the cases during the first year and 64 per cent of the cases during the second year. Gruber's Massachusetts study revealed that 70 per cent of children in care were visited infrequently or never.[9]

Agency Involvement. The effects of placement are discouraging when one examines agency involvement. Maas noted that most parents of long-term children had little, if any, agency involvement.[10] The frequency of case-worker contact with the natural parent while a child is in foster care leads to increased parental visiting, and both factors together increase the probability of discharge.[11] In her study of foster care and agencies, Shapiro noted that worker-family relationships deteriorated over time, both with respect to frequency of contact and to the evaluation of the parents.[12] Continuity and worker-family relationships were critical factors associated with return. As well, Shapiro found that experience and training of case-workers were important to discharge during the first year of placement. Sherman, Newman and Shyne reported that between 62 percent and 77 per cent of children had no plans made for their future,[13] a finding also reflected in other studies.[14, 15]

Other Fields. Concurrently, conceptual issues were being addressed in other fields which could be reformulated in the child welfare context. For example, the studies on maternal deprivation[16] and separation[17] showed that children removed prematurely and suddenly from their mother's care suffered developmental consequences. For optimal development, it was shown a child needs continuity of relationships, stability of environment, and mutuality of interactions.[18] Basing his arguments on Erik Erikson's concept of identity development on a gradual basis, Hoffman noted that separation from natural parents and placement in long-term foster care interfere with the development of the child's sense of identity.[19] Thus, the duality of the separation/attachment phenomena that is inherent in all foster placements by its very nature is contrary to the needs for optimal development.

Deprivation applies to the parents too. "Filial deprivation" was identified by Jenkins and Norman,[20] that is, the various feelings of parents at placement and its effects. The response to filial deprivation was shown to have predictive value in regards to the eventual return of the child. For example, the parents' feelings of guilt could lead to apathy, depression, or projection, which hindered attempts to return children to the care of their parents. Less urgency for discharge was expressed by parents the longer the child was in care. Finally, Jenkins and Sauber examined pre-conditions to placement and found that,

> Although it is usually a specific family crisis that brings children into. . .foster care, during the year prior to placement these families, by and large, were functioning marginally and had experienced difficulties so severe that it might have been anticipated that further stress could not be tolerated.[21]

The Guiding Principles. In summary, some specific principles derived from the construct of permanent planning are:

1. Early planning for children is necessary, especially in the first year in care and prior to apprehension if possible.
2. Natural parents must be involved with their children, in a highly structured way, from the time of placement until final decisions are made.
3. Social workers must be in frequent contact with the natural parents.
4. Social workers must make decisions.
5. Cases must be monitored or "tracked" through the system until completion.

These principles must be addressed not only on a practice level, but on a policy and legislative basis. They are, in fact, the principles to which any child welfare agency must be committed.

REACTION TO THE PRINCIPLES: EVIDENCE OF SUCCESS

Two key projects undertook to address these principles. The Alameda Project was a two-year experimentally designed project which focused on the delivery of services at the time a child came into care.[22] Three specially trained workers were assigned a limited workload. Using systematic case management procedures, they offered intensive service to the natural parents. In the control group, county child welfare workers provided the usual services to the child in the foster home. At the end of the two years, a significantly greater percentage of the experimental group were returned home or were headed for adoption. The researchers attribute their success to early systematic planning by the demonstration workers, facilitating early decision-making on the part of the parents.

The Oregon Project,[23] a multi-faceted three-year demonstration and research project, had as its goal bringing about permanent plans for children already in care, thus reducing the backlog of children in the system. It developed a framework for decision-making, for case management methods, and for identification of barriers to planning. At the end of the project, 27 per cent of the children returned to their parents (even though these children had been identified as adoptable initially), 52 per cent were freed for adoption, and in total, 72 per cent were in permanent placements. Four factors were identified as essential to the success of the project: administrative resources (supervisory and management support); institutional framework (statutes and policy); goal-oriented methods used by workers; and staff resources and consultation.

Since that time, demonstration projects similar to the one in Oregon but with necessary adaptations to meet individual needs have been launched in various states. They have been sponsored and financially supported by the federal government. In 1980, the federal act, Adoption Assistance and Child Welfare Act (P.L. 96 - 272) was passed, making it possible to implement a comprehensive service delivery system at state and local levels. As well, the act mandated the use of case plans and a case review system. Essentially, then the concept of permanence was incorporated into federal law.

THE CANADIAN EXPERIENCE: BARRIERS TO IMPLEMENTING
A PROVINCE-WIDE PERMANENT PLANNING PROGRAMME

The New Westminster Project in British Columbia was conceptually based on the Oregon Study on a minor scale.[24] In 1977, forty-nine children not already in permanently approved placements were the targets for intense review and planning. At the end of the year, 59 per cent had permanent plans and 22 per cent had plans in process. This small pilot project grew into a region-wide approach to planning, and it was later replicated in several parts of the province. However, neither permanent planning as a concept nor the use of it to influence legislation, policy, programme, and practice has been a fact either in British Columbia or Canada generally. Why? What are the factors that have caused an irrefutable concept not to take hold?

Legislation. In Canada, child welfare laws are among provincial powers. Generally, each province has facilitating legislation; that is, laws that do not prevent the implementation of a permanent planning programme. Neither, however, do those statutes clearly address the principles outlined above. For example, in British Columbia, the recent Family and Child Service Act (1981) makes provisions for time-limited planning and involvement of parents with children through financial maintenance payments. It does not, however, address a comprehensive service delivery system in which permanence for children is made clearly explicit.

Standard Definition. A standard definition for permanent planning does not exist. In some areas, it is defined as planning for wards who are permanently committed to the province; in others, it is for all children at risk who come to the attention of the child welfare authorities either as temporary provincial wards or in their own homes. The following definition is proposed by Anthony Maluccio:

> Permanency planning is the systematic carrying out, within a brief time-limited period, a set of goal-directed activities designed to help children live in families that offer continuity of relationships with nurturing parents or caretakers, and the opportunity to establish lifetime relationships.[25]

The all-inclusiveness of this definition has impact on policy and procedures with all types of families; that is, case-workers can permanently plan for a child in his own home, or out of it, as long as the key goals of continuity of relationships, nurturance, and stability are met. The objectives of the agency and the tasks which follow can all be focused to this end.

Practice. The practice principles described previously must be put into operation by field staff. Methods in caseload management, and goal-directed casework and decision-making as ways to address the principles have been shown to be effective. Schools of Social Work as well as provincial or local staff training departments need to focus both beginning and on-going professional training in these methods.

Commitment from the Top Administration Levels of Bureaucracy. The success of the Oregon Project and other states' projects demonstrated very clearly that without top level administrative agreement, endorsement, and active participation, the implementation of a planning programme was doomed. British Columbia's programme did not follow in the footsteps of its American predecessors. It began on an ad hoc basis in New Westminster and continued in pockets through the province. It has never become a full-scale provincial programme, although lip service is paid to the concept. During those beginning years, government (in British Columbia the only deliverer of child welfare services) did not give endorsement to the principle in theory, even though it was demonstrated a programme could be implemented without increasing current staff complements. Rather than becoming a provincial policy, permanent planning programmes became a more "soft," regional policy where local managers had discretion whether to implement or not.

A philosophical and political commitment is the first step, and planning must be clearly defined as the child welfare agency's objective. Following from the political commitment comes the resources to help achieve the objective: a range of placements to meet individual needs; enough staff to plan adequately for children on a direct service as well as supervisory and consultative levels; and ancillary services such as homemakers, day care, and family counselling.

One of the weaknesses in a structure that provides for child welfare services solely through government agencies is that in times of restraint government makes choices based on money issues not on programme issues. The government's philosophical and political objectives can change, and services to family and children may become expendable. Nevertheless, statutory services must be provided, and children at risk must be afforded safe homes and long-range plans. The corollary to protecting children is ensuring a placement that is intended to be permanent. We cannot afford to complete only one-half of the statutory obligation.

CONCLUSION

While there have been spasmodic attempts, permanent planning is not a matter of provincial or national policy in Canada. There has not been an organized, well-orchestrated move to make it an overall objective. But there is a recognized problem, and there are well-demonstrated solutions.

Permanent planning is not a passing phase. It is sound child welfare practice based on proven research. The time has come for child welfare agencies to have permanent planning for children as an explicit objective.

NOTES

1. Victor Pike et al., *Permanent Planning for Children in Foster Care: A Handbook for Social Workers* (Washington, D.C.: Department of Health and Welfare, 1977), p. 1.
2. Henry S. Maas and Richard E. Engler, Jr., *Children in Need of Parents* (New York: Columbia University Press, 1959).
3. David Fanshel, "The Exit of Children from Foster Care: An Interim Research Report," *Child Welfare* 50 (1971): 65-80.
4. T.J. Stein and Eileen Gambrill, "The Alemeda Project: Two Year Report," *Social Service Review* 51 (1977): 502-13.
5. J. Rowe and L. Lambert, *Children Who Wait* (ABAFA, 1973).
6. Maas and Engler.
7. David Fanshel and Eugene Shinn, *Children in Foster Care: A Longitudinal Investigation* (New York: Columbia University Press, 1978).
8. E.A. Sherman, R. Newman, and A. W. Shyne, *Children Adrift in Foster Care: A Study of Alternative Approaches* (New York: Child Welfare League of America, 1974).
9. Alex Gruber, *Children in Foster Care: Destitute, Neglected. . .Betrayed* (New York: Human Sciences Press, 1978).
10. Henry Maas, "Children in Long-Term Foster Care," *Child Welfare* 48 (1969): 321-33, 347.
11. David Fanshel and J.F. Grundy, *CWIS Report* (New York: Child Welfare Information Services, 1975).
12. Deborah Shapiro, *Agencies and Foster Children* (New York: Columbia University Press, 1976).
13. Sherman, Newman, and Shyne.
14. Fanshel and Grundy.
15. K.T. Wiltse and Eileen Gambrill, "Foster Care, 1973: A Reappraisal," *Public Welfare* 32 (1974): 7-15.
16. Michael Rutter, *Maternal Deprivation Reassessed* (Harmondsworth: Penguin, 1973).
17. John Bowlby, *Maternal Care and Mental Health* (Geneva: World Health Organization, 1952).
18. Peg Hess, "Parent-Child Attachment Concept: Crucial for Permancy Planning, *Social Casework* (January 1982): 46-53.
19. M. Hoffman, "Problems of Identity in Foster Children," *Child Welfare* 42 (1983): 10-18.
20. Shirley Jenkins and Elaine Norman, *Filial Deprivation and Foster Care* (New York: Columbia University Press, 1972).
21. Shirley Jenkins and Mignon Sauber, *Paths to Child Placement Family Situations Prior to Foster Care* (New York: Community Council of Greater New York, 1966).
22. Gambrill and Stein, "Behavioural Techniques in Foster Care," *Social Work* 21 (1976): 34-39.
23. Arthur Emlen et al., *Barriers to Planning for Children in Foster Care and Overcoming Barriers to Planning for Children in Foster Care* (Portland, Ore.: Regional Research Institute for Human Services, 1976), p. 77.
24. Brian McParland, *Forty-Nine Children: A Project to Free Children for Permanent Placement* (Victoria, B.C.: Ministry of Human Resources, 1979).
25. Anthony Maluccio and Edith Finn, *Child Welfare League of America* 62 (1983): 197.

ADDITIONAL REFERENCES

Bowlby, John. *Maternal Care and Mental Health.* Geneva: World Health Organization, 1952.

Emlen, Arthur, et al. *Barriers to Planning for Children in Foster Care.* Portland, Ore.: Regional Research Institute for Human Services, 1976.

———. *Overcoming Barriers to Planning for Children in Foster Care.* Portland, Ore.: Regional Research Institute for Human Services, 1977.

Fanshel, David. "The Exit of Children from Foster Care: An Interim Research Report." *Child Welfare* 50 (1971): 65-80.

———. "Parental Visiting of Children in Foster Care: Key to Discharge." *Social Services Review* 49 (1975): 493-514.

———. "Status Changes of Children in Foster Care: Final Results of the Columbia University Longitudinal Study." *Child Welfare* 55 (1976): 143-71.

Fanshel, David, and Henry Maas. "Factorial Dimensions of the Characteristics of Children in Placement and Their Families." *Child Development* 33 (1962): 123-44.

Fanshel, David, and J.F. Grundy. *CWIS Report.* New York: Child Welfare Information Services, 1975.

Fanshel, David, and Eugene Shinn. *Children in Foster Care: A Longitudinal Investigation.* New York: Columbia University Press, 1978.

Freud, Clarice. "The Meaning of Separation to Parents and Children in Child Placement." *Public Welfare* 13 (1955): 13-17, 25.

Gambrill, E.D., and K.T. Wiltse. "Foster Care: Plans and Actualities." and "Foster Care: Prescriptions for Change." *Public Welfare* 32 (1974): 12-21, 39-47.

Gruber, A.R. *Children in Foster Care: Destitute, Neglected. . .Betrayed.* New York: Human Sciences Press, 1978.

Goldstein, Joseph, Anna Freud and Albert Solnit. *Beyond the Best Interests of the Child.* New York: Free Press, 1973.

Hess, Peg. "Parent-Child Attachment Concept: Crucial for Permanency Planning." *Social Casework* (1982): 46-53.

Hoffman, M. "Problems of Identity in Foster Children." *Child Welfare* 42 (1983): 10-18.

Jenkins, Shirley, and Mignon Sauber. *Paths to Child Placement: Family Situations Prior to Foster Care.* New York: Community Council of Greater New York, 1966.

Jenkins, Shirley, and Elaine Norman. *Filial Deprivation and Foster Care.* New York: Columbia University Press, 1972.

———. *Beyond Placement. Mothers View Foster Care.* New York: Columbia University Press, 1975.

Kadushin, Alfred. *Child Welfare Services.* New York: Macmillan, 1974.

Lahti, Janet, et al. *A Follow-up Study of the Oregon Project.* Portland, Ore.: Regional Research Institute for Human Services, 1978.

Lindsey, Duncan. "Achievements for Children in Foster Care." *Social Work* 27 (1982): 491-96.

Littner, Ner. "The Importance of the Natural Parents to the Child in Placement." Paper presented at the First National Conference of Foster Parents, Chicago, 1971.

———. "The Challenge to Make Fuller Use of our Knowledge about Children." *Child Welfare* 53 (1974): 287-95.

Maas, Henry S. and Richard E. Engler Jr. *Children in Need of Parents.* New York: Columbia University Press, 1959.

Maas, Henry S. "Children in Long-Term Foster Care." *Child Welfare* 48 (1969): 321-33, 347.

Maluccio, Anthony N., et al, "Beyond Permanency Planning." *Child Welfare* 59 (1980): 515-30.

McParland, Brian. *Forty-nine Children. A Project to Free Children for Permanent Placement.* Victoria: Ministry of Human Resources, 1979. (M.S.W. Thesis, University of British Columbia, 1977).

———. *Forty-nine Children: One Year Later.* Victoria: Ministry of Human Resources, 1979.

Pike, Victor, et al. *Permanent Planning for Children in Foster Care: A Handbook for Social Workers.* Portland Ore.: Regional Institute for Human Services, 1977.

Rapp, Charles A., and John Poertner. "Reducing Foster Care: Critical Factors and Administrative Strategies." *Administration in Social Work* 2 (1978): 335-46.

Rooney, Ronald H. 'Permanency Planning: Boon for all Children?" *Social Work* (1982): 152-58.

Rutter, Michael. *Maternal Deprivation Reassessed.* Harmondsworth: Penguin, 1973.

Shapiro, Deborah. *Agencies and Foster Children.* New York: Columbia University Press, 1976.

Sherman, E.A., R. Newman, and A.W. Shyne. *Children Adrift in Foster Care: A Study of Alternative Approaches.* New York: Child Welfare League of America, 1974.

Sisto, Grace W. "An Agency Design for Permanency Planning in Foster Care." *Child Welfare* 59 (1980): 103-11.

Stein, T.J., and E.D. Gambrill. "Behavioural Techniques in Foster Care." *Social Worker* 21 (1976): 34-39.

———. "The Alameda Project: Two-Year Report." *Social Service Review* 51 (1977): 502-13.

Stein, T.J., E.D. Gambrill, and K.T. Wiltse. "Foster Care: The Use of Contracts." *Public Welfare* 32 (1974): 20-25.

Wiltse, K.T., and E.D. Gambrill. "Foster Care 1973: A Reappraisal." *Public Welfare* 32 (1974): 7-15.

Zischka, Pauline C. "The Effects of Burnout on Permanency Planning and the Middle Management Supervisor in Child Welfare Agencies." *Child Welfare* 60 (1981): 611-16.

10

SUBSIDIZED ADOPTION

Kenneth L. Levitt

Comprehensive child welfare planning must include a subsidized adoption programme. In Canada, Ontario, Quebec, New Brunswick, and the Yukon have implemented such programmes. In the remaining seven provinces and the Northwest Territories no programmes exist. While there is a growing awareness and acceptance of subsidized adoption in Canada, there are a variety of reasons why many provinces are reluctant to establish it. A better understanding of what it means may pave the way for greater acceptance and implementation.

SUBSIDIZED ADOPTION: A DEFINITION[1]

For the purpose of this chapter subsidized adoption is defined as a situation in which the family receives some form of monetary support or support in kind (medical, drugs, and so forth) on an on-going basis. The adoption authority provides this support to the family's adopted child.

It is similar to other types of income support programmes for children-in-care, such as Special Care Home Contract[2] and long- or short-term foster care. However, these payments cease when the child is adopted, whereas they continue in subsidized adoption.

Major Components of a Subsidized Adoption Programme

There are a number of essential components to any subsidized adoption programme. Planners must address the following: eligibility, type of subsidy, duration of subsidy, amount of subsidy, and contractual agreement. In order to be eligible for adoption subsidy,[3] children must be considered hard-to-place for a variety of reasons:

a. a medically diagnosed physical and/or emotional handicap that required on-going care and/or treatment;
b. a potential problem by virtue of hereditary background or a congenital or birth problem leading to a substantial high risk of future disability;
c. a child over the age of six years;
d. a child under the age of six years if placed in the same foster home for one or more years and whose best interests are to remain in the present foster home:
e. a sibling group who should not be separated;
f. a child who has a strong potential to become a long-term ward of the state;
g. any combination of the above.

It is generally accepted that the subsidy would only apply where the child is legally free for adoption. In addition, all efforts must have been exhausted to find placement in a non-subsidy home or with a relative.

Types of Subsidy[4]

Once eligibility for the subsidy has been established for the child, such subsidy may proceed in one or a combination of three classifications. In a maintenance subsidy, payment is made for the support of a child as a continuance following adoption completion. This payment may be an amount equal to the appropriate foster care rate. In some jurisdictions, the rate may be related to the adoptive family's financial circumstance. A second type of subsidy is medical. This allowance is paid in situations where medical insurance does not provide for special needs. A non-exhaustive list of special needs might include orthodontia, orthopaedic surgery, high-risk medical treatment, prosthetic devices, home renovations to accommodate a child's disability, or psychiatric treatment. The third type of subsidy is special services. By this type of subsidy is meant any non-medical payment for needed services. It may include special education and training needs, transportation, speech and/or occupational therapy, and court-related adoption costs.

Duration of Subsidy[5]

Once the type of subsidy has been determined, its duration must be considered. The duration may be time-limited or long-term. A time-limited subsidy is an amount calculated to assure a child's or family's financial needs are met for critical, short-term expenses. Medical or special service subsidies might be included here. The amount and duration of the subsidy is negotiated between the adoptive parents and the administering authority.

Under a long-term subsidy, a family would receive an allowance for an indefinite period, perhaps until the child reaches the age of majority. Adoptive parents receiving the long-term subsidy would have limited financial means. It would enable the family as a whole to continue an acceptable standard of living and at the same time make them able to meet any special needs.

Calculating the Amount of Subsidy[6]

Once a child becomes eligible for a subsidy, an amount is calculated based on a variety of factors. These factors may include the actual or expected cost of medical payments, the actual or expected cost of special services, and the current foster care rate in pay at the time legal adoption was finalized.

An adoptive family applying for a subsidy may be required to undergo an income test, and the family's net income will determine its ability to meet the child's financial needs. Different subsidy amounts are then related to the family's income. The adoptive family may be expected to assure that all potential sources of financial assistance have been exhausted or are being used.

In a number of jurisdictions there is no income test. Family income is not a prime consideration since the subsidy is based on the needs of the child. There are a variety of opinions regarding the establishment of subsidy rates. Should they be related to the child's needs exclusive of the family's income? The question will, undoubtedly, have to be addressed in each jurisdiction.

Contractual Agreement[7]

Immediately prior to the commencement of the subsidy payment, a contract is completed. The contract between the adoptive parents and the administrative authority outlines the obligations of the adoptive parents; the obligations of the agency, in particular, financial and service; and the conditions under which the contract may be terminated. Agreements are usually reviewed annually when either party to the agreement may request specific changes.

SUBSIDIZED ADOPTION IN CANADA[8]

The provinces of Ontario, Quebec, and New Brunswick have active and well-defined subsidized adoption programmes. The status of this program in these active provinces is as follows:

Ontario. Section 88 of the Ontario Child Welfare Act allows the minister to grant adoption subsidies. The act was proclaimed on 15 July 1979. It enables many children waiting for adoption to be adopted by families whose financial status might otherwise prevent them from adopting.

As of 29 February 1984, there were approximately 336 children in adoption subsidy.[9] Of this number, about 270 were direct adoptions from short- and long-term foster care placements. The remaining 66 were applicants from low- and middle-income families. Most children in adoption subsidy placements were not considered as adoption candidates without a continued financial support. This group is representative of children whose needs are significantly greater than most children in foster care placement.

Subsidized adoption policy and procedures in Ontario are set by the Ministry of Community and Social Services. They are administered through local Children's Aid Societies (C.A.S.) The details of this programme closely parallel those described above. There is no limit to the number of children who may be placed for subsidized adoption. Financial planning, management, and accountability are the responsibility of the C.A.S. However, the C.A.S. must remain within ministerial guidelines.

It was recently determined that the Ontario subsidized adoption programme was not cost-sharable under the Canada Assistance Plan (C.A.P.).[10] It has been concluded by C.A.P. officials that because the adoption subsidy is not means-tested for adoptive parents, there can be no cost-sharing. Until the legal adoption order is completed it is cost-sharable. The result of this determination means that Ontario must return some funds to the federal government. Despite this ruling, Ontario intends to continue its subsidized adoption programme.

Quebec. Within Quebec the by-law with regard to financial support in adoption came into effect during 1980.[11] Current legislation and policy provides for children in the same foster home for at least two consecutive years where regular adoption may be detrimental or the child has a special need. The adopting parents receive a subsidy based on the current foster rate. Each subsequent year the rate is decreased by 20 per cent until at the end of five years there is no longer any subsidy. At the end of October 1982, approximately two hundred children had been placed in adoption subsidy. Children with special needs who require considerable extra personal and financial support have not yet been included in the adoption subsidy group for special attention. However, there is a review underway, and it is possible that modifications to the legislation and policy could result.

New Brunswick.[12] In May 1982, New Brunswick implemented subsidized adoption under a programme called Special Services for Adopted Children. To qualify a family must submit to a means test by completing a special services determination form. Depending on the family's net income, they could qualify for up to $250 per month support. In addition, if the child has a special need — emotional disturbance, learning disability, physical handicap or mental handicap — an additional sum of money will be made available. Following the determination of the subsidy, a special services agreement for adopted children is signed. At least once each year the agreement is reviewed.

At the end of March 1984, seventy children had been approved for adoption subsidy. However, since only thirty-five are in receipt of a subsidy, the remaining thirty-five must await adoption completion. The programme is not cost-shared under C.A.P.

Yukon. On 22 January 1970, the Yukon Territory became the first Canadian jurisdiction to permit subsidized adoption. The legislation provides payment for any person who incurs an expense in the maintenance of an adopted child. According to information available from the director of child welfare in Whitehorse, the subsidy is used very infrequently. On those few occasions when it was used, it enabled long-term adoptive foster parents to receive a needed subsidy.

Status of other Provinces and Territories. No legislation exists in British Columbia, Alberta, Manitoba, Prince Edward Island, Newfoundland, or the Northwest Territories. The majority of the provinces report that the establishment of a subsidized adoption programme is under review. However, the priority of these reviews is not known.

In its review Manitoba looked at children with special needs as the target group. More specifically, a subsidy programme would include: foster parents who are adopting a child in their care for two or more years; new adoptive parents when the child has special needs — learning disability, emotional disturbance, physical or mental handicap, part of a sibling group, a high-risk child (physical or mental), aged ten to eighteen, or for whom no adoption placement has been found.

Although there is no provision for subsidized adoption in Prince Edward Island, Bill 57 (Child Welfare Act) was introduced to the legislative assembly in 1980.[13] In Section 118 provision is made for a subsidy as follows:

(1) Where the Director or the Director of an agency has reason to believe the interest of a child may best be served by the granting of a subsidy to an adoptive parent of the child, he may authorize payment in accordance with the regulations.

Enabling legislation exists in Saskatchewan. Enacted in 1981, it is contained under section 50 of the Family Services Act.[14] Financial assistance may be provided to adopting parents as follows:

50-(1) When reasonable efforts have been made to secure a suitable person to adopt a child who has been committed to the Minister and a suitable person to adopt the child cannot be found because of special needs of the child the Minister may:

(a) provide to any person who is desirous of adopting the child such financial assistance as may be necessary to meet the initial and continuing expense of rearing the child; or

(b) facilitate the adoption of the child by providing financial assistance to any person desirous of adopting the child to help defray the initial and continuing expense of adopting more than one child simultaneously.

Despite the legislation, there is no operational programme of subsidized adoption in Saskatchewan. However, a Saskatchewan Social Services Discussion Paper published in 1983 points out the need to implement such a programme.[15] The paper notes there are many children who because of age, handicap, being part of a sibling group, or racial background, are less attractive for traditional adoption. Revised legislation is being proposed to enable financial assistance to an adopting parent.[16]

Although no legislation or formal subsidy programme exists in Nova Scotia, a pilot project began in 1982. Ten children have been selected who are physically and/or mentally handicapped. However, once the adoptions are finalized, Nova Scotia will lose the cost-sharing from the federal government. It is hoped that a successful pilot project could lead to legislative amendment.

THE UNITED STATES EXPERIENCE

It is important to reflect on the United States experience in the development and administration of the subsidized adoption programme. Canadian social service practitioners, administrators, policy-makers and politicians should "beg, borrow and steal" from programmes that have experienced success. This experience can only serve to strengthen the initiatives and development of subsidized adoption in Canada.

In 1968, New York became the first state to enact subsidy legislation. It was followed shortly by Illinois. Other states followed, with the vast majority passing legislation in the 1970's. With the one exception of Hawaii, which has an administrative rule, all states and the District of Columbia have legislated subsidized adoption programmes.

There are 50 separate sets of rules, regulations, and administrative procedures. Although there are common objectives in policy and procedures, there are vast differences based on traditional funding relationships between the states and the federal government. Some states have been more active than others in promoting the subsidy programme. Few have undertaken evaluative studies, but one notable exception is Washington State.[17]

A demonstration project, which began in 1971, concluded that "Children for whom adoption subsidy was available experienced a higher rate of adoption than similar children for whom support was not available."[18] The pilot project investigators found that there was an administrative savings of 9.2 per cent.[19] There was also a savings of 18.7 per cent in the subsidy payments on the assumption that foster care support and adoption subsidy were equal.[20] Following the success of the demonstration project, the programme was expanded. By the fall of 1978, 592 children had been adopted within the programme. A second evaluative study had more conclusive findings than the first:

1. By comparing actual adoption support expenditure with equivalent foster care costs, there is a 28.9 per cent savings with adoption support.
2. 584 (97 per cent) of children in receipt of adoption support were foster parent adoptions.
3. Over one-half (52.3 per cent) of the children had been in foster care five years or over; approximately one-quarter (26 per cent) had been in care less than two years.
4. Slightly more than one-half (52.6 per cent) of the children were hard-to-place as a result of physical or emotional problems, mental retardation, or a combination of these categories.
5. At the time they were available for adoption, 86.5 per cent were four years of age or older.
6. 83 per cent of the children were in homes where the annual income was less than $20,000.[21]

The Washington State programme continues to thrive. By late fall 1982, nearly eight hundred children in over five hundred adoption homes were receiving the subsidy.

Shaffer studied the progress of 348 children in adoption subsidy in Illinois.[22] This number represented 21.5 per cent of those in the state's programme. He found that many children previously considered unadoptable ended up in permanent adoptive homes. Foster parents proved to be an excellent source of adoptive parents for children with special needs, and single parents tended to emerge as an important resource for these children. As in Washington State, the subsidy programme in Illinois led to significant savings in child welfare.

Recent federal legislation in the United States, the Adoption Assistance and Child Welfare Act of 1980, allows federal funding for state subsidy programmes. These funds are administered through the foster care and medicaid programmes in each state. Without a doubt, the federal government's commitment to cost-sharing makes it very attractive for a state to implement the subsidy.

Approximately nine thousand U.S. children were reported to be in receipt of an adoption subsidy in 1982.[23] It is estimated that 20 per cent

(100,000) of the nearly half million children residing in foster homes, group homes, or institutions could benefit from this programme.[24] However, these children are not healthy white infants. They are special needs children who present the least attraction to potential adoptive parents. They can be said to be "at risk."

ARGUMENTS AGAINST THE DEVELOPMENT OF SUBSIDIZED ADOPTION IN CANADA

As a subject, subsidized adoption is not mentioned extensively in Canadian social welfare literature. Canadians have had to look to the United States for leadership in both a philosophical and practical sense. Despite the apparent success of this programme in the United States, the attitude towards it in Canada, for the most part, is cautious, and it is given low priority within child welfare programmes. The hesitancy to implement adoption subsidy is surprising considering that of the estimated 80,000 children in care,[25] at least 10 per cent could benefit.[26]

Some Canadian policy-makers believe the adopting family should be prepared to assume the full responsibility, including the financial, for all the child's needs.[27] The adopting family must accept that adoption is absolute. By accepting a payment, it is no more than a foster home. Subsidized adoption therefore waters down the concept of adoption and causes the emotional pledge to be suspect.

Low-income families, it is argued, do not receive special income supports. It would, therefore, be grossly unfair to create a privileged class of parents. Some opponents to the subsidy believe that by providing a fee to adoptive parents the state diminishes parental ability, commitment, and independence.[28] Financial support cannot be separated from legal responsibility. The best interests of the child may not be served by retaining the former and giving up the latter.[29]

One prominent advocate of subsidized adoption has stated that child welfare personnel may have negative feelings about a foster parent adoption. They may feel annoyance if a foster parent continues to receive payment upon legal adoption.[30] Another writer has suggested that child welfare staff may be reluctant to undertake the considerable effort necessary in altering the child's situation from stable long-term foster care to adoption subsidy.[31]

Provincial ministries today face the monumental task of trying to operate child welfare programmes on decreased budgets. It is small wonder that controversial programmes are put "on hold" or dropped. Little effort is being made to evaluate the quality of child welfare programmes by provincial governments. For example, an evaluation of the effectiveness of programmes serving children in long-term care in Canada has seldom been undertaken.[32] Such research could result in major changes in the child welfare service delivery system. As it stands, this lack of research results in the maintenance of what is.

BENEFITS OF AN ADOPTION STUDY PROGRAMME

Despite the criticisms, there is strong evidence that a subsidized adoption programme is both essential and practical. As stated above, many adoptive parents are from the ranks of foster parents. The financial burden of a hard-to-place or special needs child prevents low- and middle-income earners from adopting. Thus, a subsidy programme affords every couple or individual, regardless of income, the opportunity to adopt.

There is a growing body of evidence that subsidized adoption is more cost-effective than foster care.[33] While the cost of the care is reduced, it also enables the agency to undertake more qualitative work with fewer families. The actual savings could be directed to the development of new child welfare programmes and the evaluation of on-going ones.

In permanent planning for children, it is often learned that the only barrier to adoption is financial, and thus an adoption subsidy frequently provides a viable alternative to permanent or long-term care. The act of legal adoption bestows the status of a real son or daughter of the family.

A main objective of permanent planning is to free children for adoption. Current child welfare practice tends to focus earlier on creating permanency in a child's life. Where children are freed for adoption in less time and the need for prolonged foster care decreases, more children become available for adoption. A subsidized adoption programme will help to prevent multiple placements and foster care drift.

RECOMMENDATIONS

Several ingredients are needed to assure the development of a subsidized adoption programme:
1. The Canada Assistance Plan should broaden its definition of "children who are in need" to include children placed in a subsidized adoption home. (C.A.P. could become the driving force to encourage all the provinces to develop a subsidized adoption programme.)
2. An active dialogue among provincial ministries, service users, and interested agencies should take place. Through mutual consultation, the strengths as well as the shortcomings of subsidized adoption could be shared. Policy decisions are rarely carved in stone. Full information-sharing could result in greatly altered views of subsidized adoption.
3. Child welfare staff, through well-documented case illustrations, can

support the case for subsidized adoption. Professional associations and community groups can contact political and ministerial officials to lend support to a subsidy.
4. The development of demonstration projects should be considered. Minimal risk-taking would be involved since there are a number of successful programmes that may be duplicated. The Ontario and Washington State experiences are two examples.

CONCLUSION

Section 68 of the Ontario Child Welfare Act, proclaimed on 15 June 1979, states: "Every Children's Aid Society shall endeavour to secure the adoption of Crown Wards, having regard to the best interest of each Crown Ward."

Adoption must not be limited only to those families with sufficient income. Undoubtedly, income and adoption approval are closely related in most agency adoption standards. It is highly desirable that a child whose parents cannot rear him be adopted.[34] It is the community's responsibility through its agencies to assure adoptive homes are available for each child who is in need. If adoption is desirable for every child for whom it is appropriate, then an adoption subsidy must be a viable planning alternative.

In 1974, a Royal Commission on Family and Children's Law was convened in British Columbia. The commission's Fifth Report made two important recommendations regarding subsidized adoption. It states:

> Where the best interests of the child will be served by being adopted by a particular adoptor and the adoption would not be possible without subsidization, the Superintendent should be able to enter into an agreement with the prospective adoptors to provide financial assistance as needed to the adoptive family.

It also suggested that "Subsidies should be available as needed, both in adoption and guardianship proceedings to enable Native families, both status and non-status, to adopt children of Native origin."[35] These two recommendations, made a decade ago, provide strong evidence of the recognized need for an adoption subsidy programme.

This chapter has indicated the beginnings of a subsidized adoption programme in Canada. It noted the positive benefits that can result from the availability of such a programme, including broadening the source of adoptive parents, decreasing the cost of foster care, and increasing the number of children available for adoption. Failure to address this issue will result in the continued disruption of children's lives.

Can we afford to ignore the constant replacement of children throughout the country when sound planning could have such a positive impact? Subsidized adoption is certainly not a cure-all for children permanently separated from their families. However, until subsidized adoption becomes one of the options open to children not returning to their families, the present child welfare system in Canada will be inadequate and incomplete.

NOTES

1. See "Subsidized Adoption: A Call to Action," (Moline, Ill.: Child Care Association of Illinois, 1968) p. 5; and G.L. Shaffer, "Subsidized Adoption: An Alternative to Long Term Foster Care," Ph.D. diss. University of Illinois, 1977, p.7.

2. Special Care Home Contracts are part of British Columbia's child welfare programme. A fee-for-service in addition to the foster home rate is paid to persons who provide care for special needs children. The fee is computed by a number of factors including the child's needs and the care giver's abilities.

3. There are a variety of eligibility definitions. The following offer reasonable clarity: G.L. Shaffer, "Subsidized Adoption in Illinois," *Child and Youth Services Review* 3 (1981): 56-57; "Subsidized Adoptions," *Adoptions Manual* No. 6 (State of Oregon: Children's Services Division, January 1980), p.1; "Adoption Manual Adoption Subsidy — Eligibility" (Government of Ontario: Queen's Printer, 1979), p. 1; "State Fund for Adoptive Children with Special Needs," State of North Carolina Division of Social Services, *Family Services Manual,* vol. 1, Children's Services, ch. 6, "Adoption Services," January 1980, pp. 5-6; "Guidelines for Subsidized Adoption Programs," *Social Service Instruction Memorandum* No. 63 (Columbus, Ohio: Department of Public Welfare, Bureau of Children's Services, 1980) pp. 1-2; *Model State Subsidized Adoption Act and Regulations* (Washington, D.C.: U.S. Department of Health, Education and Welfare, 1976) pp. 1-6.

4. For further information, see the references in note 3. Depending on the particular situation, more than one type of subsidy may be paid in combination with another.

5. For more detailed discussion and information, see references in note 3.

6. For explicit detail, see *State Fund for Adoptive Children With Special Needs,* pp. 3-5; *Adoption Support Manual G,* ch. 38, in Department of Social and Health Services, State of Washington, Olympia, Washington, 1 September 1978, pp. 5-9.

7. For good examples of contractual agreements, see "Subsidy Agreement for Subsidized Adoption," in *Guidelines for Subsidized Adoption Programs,* Ohio Department of Public Welfare, form 1615.

8. This author has corresponded with and/or been in contact with all provincial and territorial child welfare administrative authorities. (Not all correspondence received a reply.)

9. Personal communication with the Ontario Ministry of Community and Social Services, March 1984.

10. "Canada Assistance Plan" (Ottawa: Queen's Printer, 1977).

11. "Adoption Act," L.R.Q., ch. A-7, art. 41, para. f, Province of Quebec; 1979. "Loi Modifiant la loi de l'adoption," ch. 17, Province of Quebec, 1979.

12. Personal communication with Department of Social Services, New Brunswick, March 1984.

13. "Bill Number 57, Child Welfare Act" (Charlottetown: Queen's Printer, 1980).

14. "Family Services Act" (Regina: Queen's Printer, 1972).

15. *Review of The Family Services Act: A Discussion Paper,* Part Two: Adoption/Foster Care Issues and Proposals, Saskatchewan Social Services, Regina, November, 1983.

16. "The Child and Family Services Act: Legislative Proposals" (Regina: Queen's Printer, 1985).
17. J. Merrick and S. Sanders, "Descriptive Analysis of Subsidized Adoption in Washington State" (Olympia: Department of Social and Health Services, 1979).
18. "The Adoption Support Demonstration Act of 1971" (final report of the legislature) (Olympia: Washington State Department of Social and Health Services, 1975), p. 11.
19. Ibid., p. 15.
20. Ibid.
21. Merrick and Sanders, pp. 15-18.
22. G.L. Shaffer, *Subsidized Adoption,* also G.L. Shaffer, "Subsidized Adoption."
23. Gloria Waldinger, "Subsidized Adoption: How Paid Parents View It," *Social Work* 27 no. 6 (1982): 517.
24. Ibid.
25. *In the Best Interests of the Child.* A report by the National Council of Welfare on the Child Welfare System in Canada (Ottawa: The Council, 1979).
26. Alfred Kadushin, "Children in Adoptive Homes," in Henry Maas, ed. *Social Service Research: Reviews of Studies* (Washington, D.C.: National Association of Social Workers, 1978), pp. 52-56.
27. J. McEwan MacIntyre, "Subsidized Adoption—Love Plus Money," *Perception* (December 1977), p. 32.
28. Ibid., p. 34.
29. Ibid.
30. Communication from Elizabeth Cole, Director, Permanent Families for Children Unit, Child Welfare League of America, New York.
31. Alfred Kadushin, *Child Welfare Services,* (New York: Macmillan, 1974).
32. Brian McParland, "Forty-Nine Children"; "Forty-Nine Children One Year Later" (Victoria: Ministry of Human Resources, 1977, 1979).
33. G.G. Seeling, "The Implementation of Subsidized Adoption Programs: A Preliminary Survey," *Journal of Family Law* 15 (1976-77): 732-69.
34. Kenneth W. Watson, "Subsidized Adoption: A Crucial Investment," *Child Welfare* 51 (1972): 221.
35. Royal Commission on Family and Children's Law. *Fifth Report* (Vancouver, March, 1975).

ADDITIONAL REFERENCES

British Columbia Federation of Foster Parents Association, "A Brief on Subsidized Adoption." Vancouver, B.C. January 1977.
Canadian Council on Children and Youth. *Admittance Restricted: The Child as Citizen in Canada.* Ottawa, The Council, 1978.
Byrne, Kathleen O., and Matilda T. Belucci. "Subsidized Adoption: One County's Program" *Child Welfare* 61 (1982).
Cole, Elizabeth S. "A Closer Look at Subsidized Adoption," Paper delivered at the American Bar Association National Institute, San Francisco, California, June 1981.
Doehler, Ruth. "Can a Case Be Made for Subsidized Adoption?" *Journal of Ontario Association of Children's Aid Societies* (May 1970).
Child Welfare League of America Standards for Adoption Service, 1978 (Revision).
Gentile, Angela. "Subsidized Adoption in New York: How Law Works — and Some Problems." *Child Welfare* 49 (1970).
Goldberg, Harriet L., and Llewellyn H. Linde. "The Case for Subsidized Adoption." *Child Welfare* 48 (1969).
Graham, Betty. "The Director of Child Welfare, Ontario Comments on Subsidized Adoption." *Journal of Ontario Association of Children's Aid Societies* (May, 1970).

Hepworth, H. Philip. *Foster Care and Adoption in Canada*. Ottawa: Canadian Council on Social Development, 1980.

Keniston, Kenneth, and Carnegie Council on Children. *All Our Children: The American Family Under Pressure*. New York: Harcourt Brace Jovanovich, 1978.

Levitt, K.L. "A Canadian Approach to Permanent Planning." *Child Welfare* 60 (1981).

Meezan, W. "Adoption Services in the States," U.S. Department of Health and Human Services, Office of Human Development Services, Administration for Children, Youth and Families, Children's Bureau, October, 1980.

Polk, Mary. "Maryland's Program of Subsidized Adoption" *Child Welfare* 9 (1970).

Robinson, Elizabeth. "The Case for Subsidized Adoption: The Concept and A Model for Implementation." Master of Social Work term paper, University of British Columbia, 1980.

"Subsidized Adoption in America." U.S. Department of Health, Education and Welfare, Children's Bureau, Washington, D.C., 1976.

11

THE BERGER COMMISSION REPORT ON THE PROTECTION OF CHILDREN: THE IMPACT ON PREVENTION OF CHILD ABUSE AND NEGLECT

David A. Cruickshank

INTRODUCTION

From 1973 to 1975, the most comprehensive inquiry into family and children's law anywhere in Canada was conducted in British Columbia. The Royal Commission on Family and Children's Law (better known as the Berger Commission) in a period of nineteen months produced thirteen reports, a draft children's statute, and a working Unified Family Court project. As research director to the commission, I had the opportunity to take a subject of special interest to me — child welfare — and bring together an interdisciplinary team to examine existing child welfare law and policy. This paper reflects on the results of that work, seen in the Royal Commission's *Fifth Report, Part V—The Protection of Children,* and singles out the recommendations that touch on the prevention of child abuse and neglect. What was the rationale for the report's strong emphasis on prevention? Where have the recommendations been implemented — in British Columbia and beyond? What is the future for preventive child welfare law and policy?

The reflections and analysis in this paper have a bittersweet flavour. On the one hand, the Berger Commission Report has received national attention, and its recommendations have been implemented from New Brunswick to Victoria, Australia; on the other hand, the British Columbia government has recently eradicated the entire front line of child abuse and neglect prevention programmes in the name of restraint. There was so much hope in 1975 and following years, as family support social work and child abuse teams were developed; there is now despair among those concerned with prevention because the Social Credit government has dismantled the

Family Support programme and the child abuse teams. It is difficult to see how any commentator could miss the irony of discussing a report that is in one sense history, because its recommendations on prevention were slowly coming to pass; but which also is now again contemporary because the clock has been rolled back more than ten years by a government decision that makes those recommendations more applicable than ever.

To put this paper in a broader perspective, the case study of Marilyn Callahan and Brian Wharf is recommended reading.[1] It traces the policy process that led to the passage of the current Family and Child Service Act (S.B.C., 1980, ch. 11), and details the work of the Berger Commission and subsequent government studies and initiatives in the child welfare field. For further detail on the recommendations dealing with post-apprehension law and policy, the reader is referred to the Fifth Report[2] and to my earlier article on keeping protection cases out of court.[3]

THE PREVENTION RECOMMENDATIONS:
THEIR RATIONALE, IMPLEMENTATION AND IMPACT

It is difficult to point out direct cause-and-effect relationships between the recommendations and their implementation. Sometimes other provinces reached the same result by a different route; sometimes, the recommendations have merely influenced change, rather than been wholly adopted. As Callahan and Wharf have pointed out, the metamorphosis of the Berger recommendations involved a complex policy process to which few outsiders had access.[4] At best, the recommendations were the collective progressive wisdom of the time refashioned in British Columbia and adopted elsewhere by design or accident.

Family Support Services

The Problem. The Berger Commission attempted to convert a child welfare practice philosophy into legislative and practical reality through two recommendations on family support services. For years, social workers had urged that families be kept together unless imminent danger to the child required his removal from the home. In order to do this, short-term practical services are required to get a family unit to function well or to become educated on effective parenting. In the past, there were no legislative or policy sanctions in British Columbia for this kind of activity, although other jurisdictions were introducing homemaker services, family support social workers, and the like. The commission believed that family support was such an important first step that it should not only be encouraged, but required in most cases.

The Recommendations.

> The government and its child care agencies should be obligated by legislation to offer child care services to families who cannot meet the needs and rights of their children. This offer of services should be accompanied by legislative protections for the persons who are carrying out the services. (p. 13)
>
> Parents or guardians who are offered child care services on a voluntary basis should have the absolute right to refuse the services offered. (p. 13)

Rationale. When government exercises its "state as parent" role (*parens patriae*), it may do so in a voluntary or compulsory manner. Voluntary methods usually fall into the "preventive" category and include education, direct service in the home, indirect services (for example, food vouchers), and other services offered, but not compelled by any court or other agency. The new "family support" theory of state intervention that supports these recommendations has been stated as follows:

> The practising doctrine of "the state as parent" centres around the need to substitute legally the state as a parent. The rationale for intervention is to protect the child because of the state's interest in future generations. Wherever compulsory intervention seems necessary, the courts are relied upon to give a fair hearing and attendant legal rights for those objecting to the state's interference. Yet, at an earlier stage, before courts even become entitled to hear a case for intervention, there should be statutory protections which reflect a new doctrine of parens patriae.
>
> The developing doctrine could be termed the "family support" theory of state intervention. It holds that no compulsory intervention by the courts should be permitted unless the family has first been offered supportive services in the home. Furthermore, in the event that services are refused or would clearly be late and inadequate, the neglect finding of the court should always be tested against the available dispositions and resources. If the child cannot get a proper placement through the child care agency, the finding of neglect should be vacated and the child returned to the parents. It has also been suggested that the judicial finding should be one of "family intervention," not "neglect," in order to remind child care workers of the family reunification goal.
>
> This "family support" theory cannot be found in Canadian legal literature. Social workers and other child care professionals have been negligent in their failure to educate lawyers, judges and legislators about the trends in their practice which keeps families together and away from courtrooms. Lawyers are unlikely to learn from their col-

leagues about child abuse programmes involving lay therapists, parents' anonymous groups, crisis nurseries and homemakers. Law schools which take a multidisciplinary approach to their family law courses are beginning to remedy this situation for future lawyers. In the meantime, it is submitted that an evolutionary doctrine of parens patriae could be founded by new legislation that requires attempts at supportive services to precede judicial intervention.

In the United States, the "family support" doctrine has received attention as a "right to remedial services," which in turn can be traced to the "right to treatment" cases. The emerging right is derived in part from the intention clauses of the state child care statutes; in terms of federal policy, there is increased financial backing for those agencies which can demonstrate better community prevention services and well-organized service delivery.[5]

Furthermore, the parental right to refuse an offer of services represents the balancing interest of family privacy. Without that right, made clear to parents from the beginning, family support services could be a form of unwanted coercion by child welfare workers. A government interested in "keeping government out of the lives of families" would find such a right easy to embrace, particularly since it places ultimate responsibility on the parents.

Prevention has two facets. It means the prevention of child abuse and neglect. But it also means preventing children being brought into care. Prevention in the latter sense recognizes that there are significant risks to the child who is brought into care. While his immediate physical needs may be met, there is loss of continuity with the family and the potential that his childhood will be shaped by a series of substitute parents. Family support services can address both of these facets of prevention.

Implementation and Impact. The current British Columbia legislation wholly ignores terms like "family support" and "prevention." It deals almost exclusively with the compulsory side of state intervention (apprehension, court hearings, and so forth). The superintendent of child and family services has no broad duties specified in the area of family support. Despite the absence of legislative commitment, the B.C. Ministry of Human Resources had family support social workers in most major service areas. Until late 1983, when these workers were fired, there was no indication that their work was ineffective or, indeed, unproductive in preventing the costly step of apprehending children.

The former British Columbia policy of using family support workers for a distinct social work function contrasted to the child welfare worker function (that is, to investigate, apprehend, process through a hearing, and place a child in care) has been implemented in several other provinces. Alberta, Ontario, and Manitoba have all used this approach. However, the degree to which other jurisdictions have been willing to *legislate* this commitment varies.

In Ontario, the children's aid societies are required to provide preventive services as one of their basic purposes:

> 6(2) Every society shall be operated for the purposes of . . . . .
>
> (c) providing guidance, counselling and other services to families for protecting children or for the prevention of circumstances requiring the protection of children.[6]

Ontario also provides for homemaker services and the material needs of a child.[7]

New Brunswick legislation give the minister the power to provide "community social services" directly or by contract and those services are fully defined as:

> "community social services" or "social services" means services that are protective, preventive, developmental or rehabilitative in nature and which
>
> (a) facilitate access to the necessities of life;
>
> (b) assist disabled or disadvantaged persons to live as normally and independently as possible or support them in doing so;
>
> (c) prevent the need for institutional care as well as provide alternatives to it;
>
> (d) support or assist the aged, children or families;
>
> (e) facilitate or support the involvement and participation of people in their communities;
>
> (f) enhance or maintain employment skills and capabilities of persons;
>
> (g) provide protection to children and adults;
>
> (h) provide information and refer people to available services;
>
> and includes
>
> (i) homemaker services;
>
> (j) day care services;
>
> (k) family services;
>
> (l) children's services;
>
> (m) adoption services;
>
> (n) employment-related services;
>
> (o) sheltered workshops;
>
> (p) rehabilitation services;
>
> (q) community services for seniors;
>
> (r) services for the disabled;
>
> (s) social development services;
>
> (t) protection services for children and adults;

(u) headstart services; and

(v) any other services prescribed in the regulations.[8]

The emphasis on preventive services is clear, but the minister is not compelled to use support services before moving to apprehend a child. However, New Brunswick legislation encourages requests by child care agencies for preventive social services and provides a review of a minister's decision if he refuses any request.[9]

British Columbia does not require preventive services as part of its social services mandate, but it does provide for them in an oblique, discretionary manner. Section 3 of the Family and Child Service Act allows the superintendent of child and family services to enter into contracts for "services to children," while making it clear that such contractors are independent contractors, not government employees. This means that any discretionary preventive service would be delivered by persons other than statutory child welfare workers. This makes sense for homemaker services and similar programmes, but it gives no encouragement to front-line workers to develop preventive programmes and ideas. Furthermore, as recent cutbacks have demonstrated, the discretion to provide preventive services also means the discretion to eliminate them.

Within the statutory service of the Ministry of Human Resources, there is some budget flexibility in each region to provide preventive child welfare services. Regional managers can re-direct money from direct service to prevention. This is often done by the purchase of outside services for family support. However, this is not new money replacing the lost services of family support workers and child abuse teams. It is often "robbing Peter to pay Paul." Furthermore, without a provincewide policy, any region can decline to channel flexible money into prevention.

The jurisdiction that seems to have gone the farthest with the Berger Commission recommendation on mandatory support services is the State of Victoria, Australia. Following a 1976 inquiry, known as the Norgard Enquiry, the Victoria government acted in 1978 and 1979 to pass an act that is impressive for its attention to prevention.[10] One key section reads:

35(2) A child shall not be admitted to the care of the Department under the provisions of this section unless the Court is first satisfied that all reasonable steps have been taken by the Director-General or an authorized children's protection agency to provide such services as are necessary to enable the child to remain in the care of his family and that admission to the care of the Department is in the best interests of the child or young person in the circumstances.

Besides illustrating the wide-ranging impact of the Berger Commission Report, this section brings the legal process together with the social service process in a unique way. The judge must be "satisfied" that services have been attempted before he can move to the wardship decision. This is handled in practice by the presentation of a written and verbal report to the court, outlining all the "reasonable steps" that have been taken by child welfare workers.[11] This prevents a hasty decision to bring a child into care and puts an additional, but necessary, burden on governmental child care services. In short, it makes "non-intervention" a legislative reality, not just a philosophical guideline.

While no jurisdiction has yet implemented the two key "family support" recommendations of the Berger Report, many have used them to write in legislative provisions with the same spirit. Ontario, for example, took into account the Berger Commission proposals when it revised its Child Welfare Act in 1978 to add a new duty when the judge makes a disposition:

> 30(5) In determining which order to make under sub-section (1), the court shall inquire of the parties whether any efforts have been made by a society or any other agency or person to assist the child while the child was in the care of his or her parent or other person and before the child came into the care of the society.[12]

This section does not impose the burden of being "satisfied" as the Victoria legislation does, but it does make agencies accountable for efforts in the direction of family support services. Ontario, like many other jurisdictions, has accepted prevention as a legitimate, essential, and cost-effective tool in the delivery of children's services.

Custody by Agreement

The Problem. Prior to 1980, the only legal method for bringing children into care in British Columbia was by apprehension, court hearing, and an order for temporary or permanent wardship. However, as the Berger Report documented, children were being placed in care under so-called "non-ward care agreements" or temporary care by agreement without any legislative authority or guidance.[13] That questionable administrative practice meant that there was no limit on the length of these agreements and no clear statement of the rights of the superintendent, the parents and the child with respect to the powers exercised under the agreement.[14] Despite the commission's concern about the potential abuse of these well-intentioned agreements, no legislative action was taken until 1980, in the Family and Child Service Act.

The Recommendation.

> New legislation should provide for custody by agreement between parents and the Superintendent of Child and Family Services. The max-

imum period for custody by agreement should be fifteen months. (p. 15)

Rationale. The commission went on to explain the safeguards that should accompany "custody by agreement":

> The essential features of custody by agreement are:
> (i) It is for a short term — three months, plus a maximum of two six-month renewals.
> (ii) Planning aims at return of the child to the parents at the earliest possible date.
> (iii) The parent must be involved in planning and visits to the child.
> (iv) Termination of the agreement is based on the mutual expectations of the parents and the Superintendent of Child and Family Services representatives.
> (v) The parents are in a geographical location accessible to the child.
> (vi) The parents may terminate the agreement unilaterally. (p. 14)

The agreements were not meant to provide a back door to avoid a court hearing. A clear case of abuse or neglect would still go to court. Instead, they were aimed at preserving a working relationship with parents who had not neglected or abused their children, but who need help over a difficult time. For example, if a single mother without extended family support was hospitalized, she would have to abandon her child to the court hearing process unless a short-term, specific agreement was reached. The recommendation also contemplated the two parties, the parents and the superintendent, coming to the agreement on an equal footing. Equal rights to direct the child's future and to extend or terminate the agreements would be minimum requirements. For these reasons, custody by agreement represented a primary instrument for prevention of harm to a child and for mutually acceptable restoration of family unity.

Implementation and Impact. The 1980 Family and Child Service Act provides for short-term custody by agreement and agreements for children requiring special care in the following sections:

Short term custody agreements

4. Where a parent requires temporary assistance in caring for his child, the superintendent may enter into a short term care agreement with the parent providing for
   (a) care and custody or intermittent care and custody of the child during a period that does not exceed 3 months,
   (b) emergency medical treatment of the child in the absence of the parent,
   (c) resumption of care and custody of the child by the parent, and

(d) other matters agreed between the parent and superintendent.

Special care agreements

5. Where the superintendent and a parent agree that the parent's child is in need of special care, the superintendent may enter into a special care and custody agreement with the parent providing for
(a) care and custody or intermittent care and custody of the child during a period that does not exceed 6 months,
(b) the nature of the care to be provided to the child,
(c) emergency medical treatment of the child in the absence of the parent,
(d) renewal of the agreement for further periods of not more than 12 months each, and
(e) other matters agreed between the parent and superintendent.

General provisions respecting agreements

6. (1) Where a short term care or special care agreement has been made,
(a) the parent may on notice to the superintendent terminate the agreement and retake custody of his child at any time during the term of the agreement,
(b) the parent is not relieved of his obligation to maintain the child,
(c) the agreement does not limit the power of a court to hear an application or make an order respecting the child, and
(d) the superintendent may terminate the agreement by giving the parent 7 days' notice of termination.

(2) Where a short term care or special care agreement expires or is terminated and the parent neglects, refuses or is unable to resume custody of the child, the term of the agreement is extended for a period of 30 days.

(3) If within the 30 days referred to in subsection (2) the parent does not resume custody of the child, the child shall be deemed to be abandoned, and the superintendent may proceed under this Act as though he had apprehended the child.

These sections have implemented the Berger Commission recommendation and gone beyond it to take account of mentally or physically disabled children who need special full-time care for periods of time, but who are in no way abused or neglected.

Both types of agreement have the kind of balance called for in the Berger Report. Both sides can terminate the agreement. The parental responsibilities to pay maintenance and make decisions on health care and education remain. Renewal is limited to periods of twelve months (with no upper limit) for special care agreements; therefore, court review is assured, but court-ordered wardship is sensibly avoided. With short-term care agreements, only a thirty-day extension is permitted, bringing the maximum period to four months (significantly lower than the fifteen months suggested in the report).

The only concern raised by the new legislation surrounds the "deemed apprehension" in section 6(3). Parental neglect or abandonment does not have to be proved — it is assumed. This alone raises questions of legal fairness. Furthermore, the short fuse on the short-term agreements may force some unnecessary wardship orders. As Professor John MacDonald has pointed out, the government's policy manual appears to recognize this problem because it advises workers that extensions for up to six months are permitted — apparently in contravention of the legislation![15]

The agreements fulfil the aim of dealing with short term or special care problems without forcing the parents to artificially confess to "neglect" or "inability to care" in a court of law.[16] When that kind of limited intervention is balanced with parental rights, as it is here, the social worker has an excellent alternative that may prevent family breakdown.

Emotional Neglect

The Problem. Although some Canadian child welfare statutes have developed definitions of "emotional neglect" as a ground for removing a child, British Columbia has not recognized, in legislation, the need for some form of support or intervention for children whose needs are primarily emotional. The dilemma for a government considering "emotional neglect" is whether legislation might authorize excessive intervention in the family. Should a child who is physically healthy and not abused be removed in order to provide him with emotional stimulation? What are the reliable symptoms of emotional neglect? What form of intervention will prevent future neglect?

Pediatricians, child psychiatrists, and social workers have been able to document clear indicators of emotional neglect or deprivation over the years, but the courts have been reluctant to accept those indicators unless physical deprivation results from the neglect.[17] In recent years, Manitoba has taken the lead nationally in the study of emotional neglect, but there is still substantial disagreement among experts on the best methods of legislating emotional neglect or, for that matter, treating it.[18] The Berger Commission relied on several American definitions in developing its own recommendation.

The Recommendations.

New legislation should contain a definition of "emotional neglect" as a basis for finding that a child is "in need of care." (p. 27)

The commission's recommended definition was:

A child whose emotional or mental health and development is endangered, or is likely to be endangered, by the lack of adequate affection, emotional stimulation, guidance and discipline, or continuity in the child's surroundings and relationships, and who is in need of care or control which the child is unlikely to receive unless the court makes an order. (p. 27)

A further recommendation advocated restricted intervention in these cases:

Cases of "emotional neglect" should only be brought into court by way of a summons, after all previous remedies have been exhausted. New legislation should also restrict the types of dispositions available to the court in these cases (p. 29).

Rationale. The aim of the recommendations was to steer a course between unwarranted intervention in the family and complete omission of emotional neglect in legislation. Because the state of knowledge concerning the problem is so uncertain, the commission believed that three main restraints were necessary. First, the definition itself requires that other avenues (for example, family support services) be explored before a court order is made. This is seen in the phrase "who is in need of care or control which the child is unlikely to receive unless the court makes an order." Second, children could not be apprehended; a court appearance would be by summons, thus assuring that the child remains in the home until a court order is made. Finally, the commission recommended that a court should rarely order permanent wardship or lengthy temporary wardship.

The prevention aspect of these recommendations was twofold. If emotional neglect could be detected and treated at once, it was thought that resultant physical neglect and further emotional neglect could be prevented. Furthermore, the aim was to prevent removal of a child from his family for a lengthy period. The risk of added emotional harm resulting from separation could be avoided.

Implementation and Impact. The Family and Child Service Act pares down the definitions of a child "in need of protection" to five sparsely worded statements. Emotional neglect is not included. One might be able to argue a case of emotional neglect on the basis of these words in the definition:

s. 1 "in need of protection" means, in relation to a child, that he is

(a) abused or *neglected* so that his safety or *well being* is *endangered* (emphasis added).

However, it is submitted that the concept of endangerment would lead most courts to hold that endangering physical effects of neglect must be proven.

It is worthwhile noting that the brief definition section and the concept of endangerment follow the commission's recommendation concerning the breadth of the "in need of protection" definition.[19] However, the legislators apparently did not accept that emotional neglect could be separately defined and limited on its potential for state intervention.

Most other Canadian provinces have opted for the inclusion of emotional neglect, defined broadly, but few have imposed the limits recommended by the commission. New Brunswick's revised definition, for example, is very broad:

s. 31(1)   The security of development of a child may be in danger when . . . .
(d) the child is in the care of a person whose conduct endangers the life, health or emotional well-being of the child;
(e) the child is physically or sexually abused, physically or emotionally neglected,[20] sexually exploited or in danger of such treatment.

The Ontario definition is fairly representative of other Canadian jurisdictions:

19(1)(b)   "child in need of protection" means. . . .
(x) a child whose emotional or mental development is endangered because of emotional rejection or deprivation of affection by the person in whose charge the child is.[21]

Under the Ontario statute, two restraints on intervention are available, but not mandatory. Instead of apprehension, a children's aid society can seek an "order to produce" a child, somewhat like a summons.[22] When the child comes before the court, the society must then "show cause" why the child should remain in its custody pending a full hearing.[23] The court has the power to return the child home if it is satisfied that cause for interim removal has not been shown.[24]

The main impact of British Columbia's failure to specify emotional neglect in legislation is difficult to judge. On the one hand, there will be little unwarranted judicial intervention in families. On the other hand, the recent restraint policy has eliminated most of the Human Resources Ministry's ability to deliver preventive services for children who may be emotionally neglected. This means that even a non-legislated policy on emotional neglect could hardly be implemented. This significant gap in child welfare policy seems to imply a retreat to a "pick up the pieces" philosophy. If a child is so emotionally deprived that workers can measure physical results and justify a court application, the Ministry will act. Before that, neither legislation nor policy encourages involvement in the problems of the emotionally neglected child.

Child Abuse Teams and Community Volunteers

The Problem. It is now a professional cliché to say that child abuse is a multidisciplinary problem that requires the skills of many individuals for successful treatment of the family. This fact presents a challenge for the organization of services to deal with the detection and treatment of neglect and abuse. Where is the best entry for service delivery — the social worker's office? — the family doctor? — the emergency ward? Who will provide follow-up after the identification of a family with difficulties?

These issues have always troubled child welfare workers, who have a statutory duty to "protect children" but who must rely on doctors to prove abuse, on family therapists to provide effective counselling, and on self-help groups to enhance rehabilitation. The worker has to rely on someone to co-ordinate the professional services and the voluntary efforts of community groups in order to prevent duplicated individual work and service delivery. The worker alone has neither the time nor the expertise to do this. In short, everyone deals with a small slice of the pie, but no one is responsible for the whole. The problem is not a legal question, but a management issue.

The Recommendation.

> The government should develop team approaches for the prevention and treatment of child abuse. In addition, the government should be prepared to finance and support volunteer community efforts aimed at the prevention of child abuse. (p. 76)

Rationale. As the Berger Report points out, there is no single expert who can handle all varieties of child abuse. The commission supported the idea of a hospital-based team, working with community resources, in order to further the dual aims of treatment and the prevention of recurrent child abuse. Connected to the hospital, such a team would involve pediatricians, radiologists, surgeons, neurologists, psychologists, psychiatrists, and social workers. In the community, liaison and education efforts must take place with teachers, the police, day-care supervisors, public health nurses, family doctors and volunteer organizations. A child abuse team, whether based at a hospital or in a community, has a staff that can pull together these resources. Unlike statutory government services, they can act as a bridge between the legally mandated role of the child welfare worker and the array of private services that could promote rehabilitation of a family.

In the team approach, the theory is that detection will take place early and be done by trained observers. The teacher or public health nurse is trained to identify particular signs of abuse. Upon intake at a hospital, emergency room doctors call in a social worker, a pediatrician, and other specialists. If necessary, apprehension and investigation can begin at once. On the other hand, the team could carry on its own approach while a child is hospitalized, deferring compulsory intervention until there is clear evidence of abuse and there is a breakdown in a "family support" approach to the case. The team also connects parents with self-help groups such as Parents' Anonymous and gets them plugged back into the community with less reliance on the expensive services of the professionals.

In 1975, there were very few child abuse teams operating in Canada. Dr. Sydney Segal, a commission member and pediatrician, provided the commission with vital information on the fledgling Vancouver General Hospital team (founded in 1975) and other Canadian and U.S. teams. The commission supported that direction and its recommendation was picked up to a significant degree across Canada between 1975 and 1981.

Implementation and Impact. A federal study completed in 1981 revealed that twenty-five hospital-based child abuse teams were operating in Canada.[25] Most were founded after 1973; in British Columbia, teams were founded in Vancouver, New Westminster, and Victoria.[26] All British Columbia teams began with the initiative of the hospitals and the funding of the hospitals and the universities. However, the provincial Ministry of Health began to pick up programme (that is, non-medical) staff salaries in 1977 after a successful demonstration period (1975-76) by the team at the Vancouver General Hospital. With more secure funding, the teams became established as the most cohesive network for handling child abuse problems in the major cities. In addition, they devoted considerable time to public education, research of their cases, and medical education for new doctors.

In July 1983, those efforts came to a halt when the provincial government eliminated funding. Fortunately, the province does not have the jurisdiction to tell hospitals to disband the teams altogether. However, with programme staff eliminated, the handful of remaining hospital or university staff on the teams will have to curtail most activities. The deep cuts in hospital budgets will also make the remaining team skeletons candidates for internment.

Once more, a proven children's service with a team approach that prevented recurring abuse and neglect has been dismantled by the government. It will not only result in a direct loss of service to the public, but also in a later increase in the number of children coming into care as victims of abuse. Because child welfare workers will have no resource base against which to check their opinions, they will tend to apprehend children first and leave it to someone else to ask the questions later.[27] Line workers will continue to identify children in need of protection. However, because the workers will have less liaison with the community volunteers known to the teams, the solutions to child abuse problems will become increasingly legalistic and interventionist. This government decision, coupled with the decision to fire family support workers, will destroy ten years of planning, development, and implementation of the child abuse management approaches recommended by the Berger Commission. The impact will be felt not just by professionals and volunteers, but by a generation of children.

Elsewhere, the development and funding of child abuse teams is growing. In Ontario, there are twelve teams.[28] At the Alberta Children's Hospital, new facilities and an increased staff have permitted the team to make advances in research. The Winnipeg Children's Hospital team is the national leader in the field of emotional neglect.[29] Newfoundland, a perennial "have-not" province, began a team in St. John's in 1981. British Columbia, on the other hand, seems determined to unravel the most progressive treatment approach to child abuse developed in Canada in recent years.

CONCLUSION

The progress of implementation of the Berger Report in British Columbia has been like a train going up a steep grade; as it approaches the crest, the power fails and it slips backward. With regard to prevention, the main achievements have been the introduction of legislated custody by agreement and the development of more narrow grounds for apprehension that may limit state intervention. At the same time, the significant advances with family support services and child abuse teams have been rolled back. Other recommendations of the commission addressing prevention have not been implemented at all.

In retrospect, one could make a strong case for the use of the "big lie" by government. It began with the very title of the Family and Child Service Act in 1980. The act does not mandate any services to families and children; at best, it provides discretionary contract services through nongovernmental bodies.[30] Professor MacDonald forecast the next step in the process — the 1983 cutbacks — when he wrote in 1982:

> Undoubtedly there are reasons why the present government chose not to include a range of preventive family and children's services in the new legislation. This permits it to avoid a commitment to providing such services on an on-going basis. It also affords the Ministry of

Human Resources complete discretion as to the nature and scope of services to be developed and delivered. In the writer's opinion this fails to recognize members of the general public as partners in efforts to strengthen family life and relieve family distress. It also has the effect of reducing public visibility of social services and rendering such services as are provided vulnerable to cut-backs in government funding. One is forced to conclude, therefore, that notwithstanding its title, the new Family and Child Service Act fails to break new ground in the provision of services to families and children.[31]

Having created the illusion of legislatively mandated services and followed with the reality of cutting virtually all child welfare primary preventive services, the government's most recent tack has been to throw the torch to the voluntary sector. Presumably thriving volunteer organizations are expected to pick up vital functions such as family support work or the diagnosis of child abuse. These expectations are as false as the statute title or the promises of support to families because the government has eliminated funds for volunteer co-ordinators and other voluntary sector initiatives.[32]

Who will be deceived by the message delivered in legislation and policy by the B.C. Ministry of Human Resources? In the end, it may be government itself. Financially, it will be forced to deal with more children in care, at greater cost, because the preventive "front end" of the child care system has been removed. The costs and organizational upheaval of losing experienced child welfare workers will be the next reality. Loaded with added burdens, and no accompanying benefits, workers will quit.[33] Morally, the government may have to face repeated instances of preventable death or injury to children who are no longer reached by services or legislation. The final irony is that the government probably is not interested in researching the future impact of its measures to find the financial and social costs — because that would cost money.

At the national level, the outlook is more optimistic. Since 1975 virtually every province has been revising or reviewing its child welfare law and policy. The Berger Commission Report has provoked thinking and reform in many jurisdictions, particularly Ontario, Manitoba, and New Brunswick. It continues to be a relevant message in British Columbia, but one that goes largely unheeded by the decision-makers.

NOTES

1. M. Callahan and B. Wharf, *Demystifying the Policy Process: A Case Study of the Development of Child Welfare Legislation in B.C.* (Victoria, University of Victoria School of Social Work, 1982).
2. *Fifth Report of the Royal Commission on Family and Children's Law,* Part V, "The Protection of Children (Child Care)." (Victoria: Queen's Printer, 1975). Other separate titles within the Fifth Report Series include Part I, "The Legislative Framework"; Part II, "The Status of Children Born outside of Marriage"; Part III, "Children's Rights," Part IV, "The Special Needs of Special Children; Part VI, "Custody, Access, and Guardianship"; Part VII, "Adoption."
3. David Cruickshank, "Court Avoidance in Child Neglect Cases," in Baxter and Eberts, eds., *The Child and the Courts* (Toronto: Carswell, 1978; reprinted in *U.B.C. Law Rev.* 12 (1978) and in Irving, *Family Law: An Interdisciplinary Perspective* (Toronto: Carswell, 1981).
4. Callahan and Wharf, pp. 84-88.
5. Cruickshank, p. 209.
6. *Child Welfare Act,* R.S.O., 1980, c.66, s. 6(2).
7. Ibid., s. 23.
8. *Child and Family Services and Family Relations Act,* S.N.B., 1980, C. C-2.1, s. 1.
9. Ibid., s. 20.
10. Community Welfare Services Act, 1978, No. 9248, amended by 1979 Act No. 9266, s. 2(b) (Victoria, Australia). The connection between the Berger Commission Report and this legislation was confirmed by interviews in 1980 by this writer with T. Carney, a law professor at Monash University. Mr. Carney was a consultant to the Norgard Enquiry and a committee member of the legislative review sub-committee of the central implementation committee that implemented the Norgard Report. Mr. Carney advised that the Berger reports were influential in regard to support services and provisions for "unmanageable children."
11. This practice was described to the author by judges of the children's court in Melbourne, Australia, in January 1980.
12. R.S.O. 1980, c. 66, s. 30(5). See also n. 23.
13. *Fifth Report,* Appendix IV.
14. *Fifth Report,* Appendix III. In a study titled "Length of Stay of Children Taken into Care", the commission noted that 14 per cent of children in non-ward care remained there for over two years.
15. J. MacDonald, "An Analysis of the Family and Child Service Act", in Callahan and Wharf, p. 53, n10.
16. Other judisdictions have had custody by agreement for years, and the British Columbia version is most likely patterned after Alberta (Child Welfare Act, R.S.A., 1980 c. C-8, s. 28).
17. For example, Per Wallace, Prov. J. in *Re: Golka* (1974), 13 R.F.L. 167, pp. 169-70 (Ont. Prov. Ct.):

    The submission is made to the Court that this evidence should satisfy the requirement of s. 20(1)(b)(xi), and that the child is:

    "(xi) a child whose emotional or mental development is endangered because of emotional rejection or deprivation of affection by the person in whose charge he is. . ."

    I have considerable difficulty in finding any sufficient acceptable evidence to meet the requirements of this section. First, the section refers to an existing situation, and the child has never been in the custody of the mother and has never thus been endangered because of her emotional rejection. Further, it is my opinion, that such evidence could not in such a case be given by one without special training or experience justifying the acceptance of such opinion. It is noted that there was no attempt to bring out any evidence of special qualifications of the social worker in the area in which she sought to give opinion evidence and upon which it is urged that the decision should rest. . . .

    Evidence of deprivation may be physical, a loss of weight, and general decrease in activity, or it may be emotionally a failure to achieve academically or in interpersonal relationships. Emotional neglect may occur because a parent is unwilling or unable to provide the warmth and encouragement necessary for normal development. (Anna Freud, "Safeguarding the Emotional Health of Our Children," Child Welfare League of America [1955]).

I am not of the opinion that the indication by a mother that the possession of a child that she has never seen before court proceedings provides such evidence, although it may indicate a situation of potential neglect.

18. *Proceedings: Think Tank on The Emotional Abuse of Children,* Manitoba Working Group on the Emotional Abuse of Children, Winnipeg Health Sciences Centre, 1981. The Manitoba Working Group has sponsored provincewide seminars on this issue. See also, S. Stephenson, "Emotional Neglect and Abuse," in *Fifth Report.* Part V, Appendix VI.

19. *Fifth Report,* p. 32, n2:

    The basis for apprehension of a child and for a judicial finding that a child is "in need of protection" should be re-written. The new grounds for apprehension should be characterized as "emergency" situations within one of these categories:
    (1) parental responsibility for the child;
    (2) child dangerous to self or family;
    (3) breakdown of custody by agreement or child care agreement. (p. 32)

20. S.N.B., 1980 c. C 2.1. See also n. 16 in *Re: Golka* the court noted that the former N.B. definition required emotional neglect to be supported by the evidence of a registered psychiatrist.

21. Child Welfare Act, R.S.O., 1980, c. 66, s. 19(1)(b)(x).

22. Ibid., s. 21(1).

23. Ibid., s. 28(12).

24. Ibid., s. 28(12).

25. C. Robertshaw, *Child Protection in Canada* (Ottawa: Health and Welfare, 1981), p. 152:

    Formal Hospital Based Teams in Canada by Province/Territory

    | B.C. | — 3 | — Located in Vancouver, New Westminster and Victoria |
    | Alberta | — 1 | — Calgary |
    | Saskatchewan | — 0 | |
    | Manitoba | — 2 | — Winnipeg |
    | Ontario | — 12 | — Located in Toronto, Hamilton, St. Catharines, Brampton, Ottawa, Sudbury, Belleville and Cornwall. |
    | Quebec | — 5 | — Located in Montreal, Quebec City, and St. Jean |
    | Nova Scotia | — 1 | — Halifax |
    | New Brunswick | — 0 | |
    | P.E.I. | — 0 | |
    | Newfoundland | — 1 | — Located in St. John's (unfortunately, information on the Newfoundland team was obtained too late to be incorporated in this paper). |
    | Yukon | — 0 | |
    | N.W.T. | — 0 | |
    | TOTAL | — 25 | |

26. Ibid., p. 148.

27. R. Oberlyn, "The Children Being Sacrificed to Government Restraint," Vancouver *Sun,* 5 August 1983, p. A5.

28. Robertshaw, *Child Protection in Canada.*

29. *Proceedings: Think Tank on the Emotional Abuse of Children.*

30. Ibid. p. 1000.

31. MacDonald, p. 38.

32. Oberlyn.

33. In the current period of recession, there has been less turnover of workers because fewer alternative careers are available.

12

PREVENTIVE APPROACHES TO CHILD WELFARE

Brian Wharf

INTRODUCTION

Toward a Definition of Prevention and Child Welfare

Prevention is most often defined by distinguishing three levels. Primary prevention seeks to eradicate causes of particular problems to prevent them from arising. Secondary prevention efforts are concerned with early identification of problems and with extending appropriate assistance before they are fully formed. Finally, tertiary prevention consists of effective treatment of an established problem in order to prevent recurrence. Although this classification is not without limitations and critics, it is frequently used and widely understood. For these reasons it will be used in this chapter as the organizing framework.

"Child welfare" commonly refers to the full range of services provided by public and private organizations to prevent and to respond to problems experienced by families in caring for their children. Child welfare is therefore a subset of social welfare with connections to other fields such as income security, health, and corrections, but it is distinguished by its primary concern with the welfare of children. Programmes and services included within this definition are day care; homemaker services; family counselling; infant development programmes and other services to children in their own homes; the investigation of complaints of child neglect and abuse; substitute care of children in a variety of arrangements, and adoption.

Perspectives of Social Welfare

The perspectives of social welfare that have been developed diverge markedly regarding the division of responsibility which does and should exist between the individual and the state. These perspectives have been described in Chapter 1, and it is necessary here only to connect them with prevention because they influence the determination of the desirable level of prevention. In turn this leads to differences in the target selected for change (the child, the family, or the environment), and in the choice of intervention strategies.

According to the residual view of social welfare, prevention constitutes an unwarranted interference into the lives of individuals and families. In this view, individuals are quite capable of managing their own affairs, and intervention by the state is warranted only as a last resort.

The diametrically opposing position from residualism is social development, which holds that prevention at all levels is a legitimate and appropriate responsibility of the state. Thus, the Berger Commission on Family and Children's Law in B.C. argued that the state should make a commitment in law to provide services to families and to develop a charter of children's rights. David Cruickshank argues for this view in the preceding chapter in the following terms. ''This developing doctrine holds that no compulsory intervention by the courts should be permitted unless the family has first been offered supportive services in the home.''[1] In other words, the social development position requires the state to provide preventive services in order to develop the potential of children and families.

The institutional position is similar but less demanding in its requirements of the state. It holds that all families require social services as a right and in the same way as education and health. Social services are seen as social utilities to be used by all families. However, the initiative for using services, either in order to avert crises or to enhance development, rests with the individual and the family, not the state.

It can be argued with some historical evidence that until very recently the field of child welfare has been dominated by a condemnatory attitude, ''blame the parents.'' This view held that parents who neglected or abused their children were evil or, at best, completely inadequate people, who could not be trusted to give proper care. Hence, the only appropriate response was to remove the children and provide acceptable substitute care arrangements. Despite the committed attempts to provide a range of alternative care arrangements from orphanages to foster homes, experience from practice gradually illuminated the barrenness of both the explanation and the response. The field has now developed more effective responses, anchored on one essential piece of practice wisdom — it makes sense for all concerned to keep children in their own homes whenever possible. This gradual change in policy and practice is referred to again in a later section of this chapter.

The typical response in Canada toward prevention in the field of child welfare has been to develop residual, tertiary-level programmes aimed at individuals and families. However, there have been occasional efforts to move into secondary level programmes, and some of them are described in this chapter. And in other fields such as health and income security, Canada has developed universal programmes which can be seen as primary prevention.

The following table summarizes the discussion to this point.

Level of Prevention	Target of Change	Change Strategy	Conception of Child Welfare	Examples
Crisis Intervention	Child	Apprehension of children	Blame the parent	Placement of children in foster care or institutions
Tertiary	Child & Family	Self-help supports and professional therapy	Residual	Provision of both self-help and professional assistance to fully formed problems
Secondary	Family and Community	Education, Training	Residual	Enhancing the competence of families and communities to deal with problems at an early state of development
Primary	Societies and environment	Social and political reform	Social Development and institutional	Modifying environments, universal health care, education and income provision

It should be emphasized that the above classification of levels of prevention should not be interpreted as exclusive categories. Pragmatic considerations require a mixing and blending between the levels. The classification should be viewed as indicating emphases and preferences. Thus policies and programmes developed according to a social development or universal perspective must contain provision for crisis intervention. Similarly, a residual conception of child welfare will often allow for some local level initiatives in secondary prevention.

Barriers to Prevention

Programme brochures of the B.C. Council on the Family proclaim in bold letters that "An ounce of prevention is worth a ton of cure." This statement of faith epitomizes the attractiveness of the concept of prevention. But for all of its appeal on the grounds of reducing costs and damage to families, for many reasons the concept is exceedingly difficult to put into practice.

Prevention requires that the cause of the problem be defined in precise and exact terms and that an effective remedy can be applied. Neither of these two essential requirements obtain in child welfare. With respect to causation, we know that "children of poverty are at risk nutritionally, educationally, and psychologically."[2] For example, the National Council on Welfare estimates that "by the age of eleven more than 10 per cent of disadvantaged children have been placed in alternate care situations, compared to less than 1 per cent of non-poor families."[3] The full implications of poverty on children and family life are covered in Chapter 3 of this book.

Yet poverty is not a sufficient explanation. Most poor parents do not neglect or abuse their children, and some parents in middle- and upper-income classes do. However, psychological explanations also lack clarity. Parents who were themselves neglected as children and who have low feelings of self-esteem, a limited capacity to share and care, and a slight tolerance for stress are most likely to neglect and abuse their children. But terms such as "self-esteem" and a "low tolerance for stress" are vague and imprecise and invite differing judgments from professionals.

In fact, a host of intervening variables combine to make a complete and sufficient explanation of child neglect elusive. Research undertaken by Gray and his associates over a period of years has resulted in a screening device which, at least in one study, identified 79 per cent of child abusers.[4] But even such a reasonably effective instrument raises some troublesome questions. What might be the reaction of families incorrectly identified as being in the high-risk group? Is there a danger of the self-fulfilling prophecy coming into play, and perhaps most importantly, is an effective remedy available? In the confines of this chapter there is space to address these issues in only a very cursory fashion, but the following comments seem pertinent.

Incorrect Identification. There is a distinct difference between respectable and disreputable problems. As individuals and as members of families we are quite prepared to accept information about our predisposition to and capacity to cope with problems such as sickness, retirement, and death of relatives. We are far less willing and may indeed actively resist information which indicates that we are prone to problems such as delinquency and child abuse. Given the degree of stigma and blame attached to problems in the child welfare field, those who are incorrectly identified as likely to engage in such behaviour may well be resentful and may seek legal action. In an age of litigation, this constitutes no small barrier to primary prevention.

The Self-Fulfilling Prophecy. Perhaps the most instructive example of the self-fulfilling prophecy comes from the field of delinquency where children identified as being prone to delinquent behaviour proceed to confirm the label. While it is not suggested here that parents identified as belonging to a high-risk group of potential abusers would immediately inflict harm on their children, the argument is persuasive with respect to child neglect. Thus, parents attempting to cope with a limited income, inadequate housing, and other problems might, on learning that they were classified as being potentially neglectful, simply give up the struggle and request that the appropriate child welfare agency assume the responsibility for the care of their children.

SECTION II

Child welfare is a provincial responsibility, and Chapters 1 and 2 contain a comprehensive description of child welfare legislation in most provinces. It should be emphasized that five provincial acts do not even mention prevention, five provide for preventive activities at the discretion of the ministry, while only two (the Yukon and New Brunswick) require their ministries to provide preventive services.

Following a review of child welfare practice in Ontario, Sally Palmer concludes with a judgment which can be applied with equal force to other provinces: "After nearly ninety years of public responsibility for child welfare in Ontario we are still providing a residual service responding only to particular situations."[5]

While acts and regulations provide a mandate to undertake certain activities, the annual reports of provincial ministries are the vehicle through which activities are described and reported. The annual reports of all ministries except two were reviewed in preparation for this chapter, and only one, Prince Edward Island, makes any reference to prevention.

It seems reasonable to conclude that the prevention of problems in child welfare is not a high priority of provincial governments. However, provinces have accepted the responsibility of responding to established problems, and these responses can be viewed as tertiary prevention.

The Present Scene and Tertiary Prevention

Two criteria are used in this discussion to assess effective practice. The first refers to efforts to keep children in their own homes, and the second is the concept of permanent planning, which has been dealt with in Chapter 9. As noted in Chapter 1, the number of children in care as a percentage of the total number of children in each province, except Quebec, declined between 1977 and 1981. And the decline in some provinces was dramatic. Thus Newfoundland reduced the number of children in care from 4,803 to 2,717 — a difference of 2,086, and a similar record was compiled by ministries in the Yukon and the Northwest Territories. In these jurisdictions the number declined from 1,030 to 503.

Provincial ministries in Canada have developed an array of programmes ranging from day care, homemaker services, voluntary agreements between parents and the ministry for short periods of care in times of stress, family counselling, and intensive child care programmes for children in their own homes. These programmes gradually evolved in child welfare agencies following years of experience with well-meaning attempts to provide substitute care for neglected and abused children. This shift from substitute care to providing support to enable parents to care for children in their own home occurred gradually over a long period of time.

Thus, B.C. introduced a Family Support programme in 1978 with the objective of providing intensive counselling services and other support services to fragile and at-risk families. The programme was considered to be successful—so much so that in the 1980 *Annual Report* the Ministry stated, "in 1980, 1000 fewer children were in care than in 1975—an encouraging measure of the success of these programs."[6] While the number of children in care had been declining prior to the introduction of the Family Support and Special Services programmes, they achieved a much more dramatic decline. During the period 1972-77, the number of children in care was reduced by 264—an average of 53 per year. However, during the following three years, the numbers fell by 603 or 300 per year.

Supporting evidence for the effectiveness of such programmes comes from the State of California which introduced a Family Protection Act. This act requires the provision of support services such as "in-home caretakers, housekeepers, homemakers, emergency housing, respite and shelter care." Its effectiveness has already been demonstrated. After three years of operation in a demonstrator county, the number of children placed in foster care declined by 33 per cent, and the number in residential care by 44 per cent. Another project conducted under the auspices of the Child Welfare League of America identified 220 families where the children were judged to be in jeopardy of placement and provided an intensive array of services. The project achieved a number of positive changes in child care and training by the family in the following areas: (1) supervision and guidance; (2) protection from physical abuse, exploitation or exposure to dangerous situations; (3) sleeping arrangements and supervision, and (4) dress, including sufficiency, cleanliness and appropriateness.[7]

The above projects do not satisfy the rigours of experimental research which demands that families or individuals be divided into control and treatment groups and only the latter receive assistance. And it is indisputable that without an experimental design, the outcomes cannot be unequivocally and conclusively attributed to the treatment programme. Nevertheless, the results of these projects reinforce each other and taken together correspond to common sense—the majority of parents want to care for their children, and with resources and support can do so in an adequate fashion.

In the writer's view family support programmes should be an integral part of services to families and children in Canada. A number of provincial governments have developed and are continuing to develop such programmes, although only two require that preventive services be offered to families prior to consideration of apprehension. However, six provinces recommend that more practical supportive programmes be provided, and, regrettably, B.C. eliminated its Family Support Program in the name of restraint in 1983. Critics of this decision argued that cancelling the programme was penny wise and pound foolish.

Using the criterion of reducing the number of children in care may yield the judgment that child welfare is increasing its effectiveness. However, the same cannot be said using the criterion of permanent planning. At present, despite the impressive evidence from practice and research reported in Chapter 9, no provincial government or child welfare agency in Canada has made a commitment to this concept. The time and attention of staff are disproportionately directed to the front end of the system: to investigating complaints of child neglect and abuse; to determining whether children should be supported in their own home or apprehended; and to arranging the initial foster home placement. And this is precisely the consequence of the absence of a permanent plan for each child in care. A permanent plan ensures that attention and resources are given to children continuing in care, and without this commitment, child welfare practice cannot be judged effective at the tertiary level.

The Present Scene and Secondary Prevention

Despite the achievements which have been made at the tertiary level, there is little to indicate that provincial ministries have been able to make any appreciable advances at the secondary and primary levels. As noted above, the annual report of only one ministry referred to prevention, and an inventory compiled by the Tree Foundation on Canadian Research and Demonstration Projects on Child Abuse and Neglect identified only 36 of the 372 projects as being concerned with prevention.[8] Significantly, while most of these were funded by grants from federal or provincial governments, only three of the preventive projects were actually carried out by child welfare agencies. The majority were sponsored by private organizations or by associations specifically established to initiate and implement the project.

This information hints at one other very important barrier to prevention. Child welfare agencies were established to cope with casualties, not to reform family structure or society. And coping with casualties is a demanding and stressful occupation which leaves little time for reflection or developing new programmes. Coping behaviour is, in fact, notoriously inimical to innovation, and moving into secondary and primary prevention requires the capacity to break away from established modes of practice dominated by interventions with individuals and families in crisis.

The following discussion of secondary prevention outlines three strategies: environmental modification, enhancing competence,[9] and the more familiar approach of early identification of high-risk parents. Julian Rappaport attacks this approach to prevention in the following caustic terms:

> This underlies much of what is called prevention: find so-called high risk people and save them from themselves, if they like it or not, by giving them, or better still their children, programs which we develop, package, sell, operate or to otherwise control. Teach them how to fit it in and be less of a nuisance."[10]

For Rappaport the barriers cited earlier are of such significance that they warrant rejection of the strategy. And it is very likely that band councils in Indian communities in Canada would give strong support to Rappaport's indictment because the approach rarely gives adequate attention to cultural variables and standards.

But the approach cannot be dismissed so lightly. The research conducted by Gray and his associates demonstrated that assigning a physician and lay health visitor or public health nurse to fifty high-risk mothers for two years following the birth of their first or second child prevented any injuries being inflicted on the children. However, five children in a control group of another fifty high risk mothers required hospitalization for serious injuries.[11] Parenthetically, it should be noted that this was one of only three studies identified by Ray Helfer in a comprehensive review of research into the prevention of child abuse and neglect over a twelve-year period.[12]

On the basis of this study, it can be argued that the "targeting" strategy works. Even more importantly, the findings can be applied to all families; namely, careful and systematic follow-up of young mothers, combining as it does the monitoring of behaviour and the clear evidence of concern, attention, and support with deliberate instruction in parenting skills does provide effective assistance. The findings corroborate common sense: raising children is a demanding job and one which is made even more difficult by the absence of one parent, an adequate income, and the supports usually provided by an extended family. Thus, while all young parents can use help, particularly following the birth of the first child, assistance offered in a way that does not label or stigmatize is likely to be extremely helpful to fragile families. Thus, the targeting strategy has much to commend it, particularly if it is also used to identify the harmful effects of environmental conditions on family life.

Environmental Modification

Modifying environments can take place at a variety of levels from major social change to local arrangements for the care of children. As asserted earlier, the child welfare field does not have the capacity to bring about fundamental and large scale changes directly, but it can make an important contribution to social reform.

One promising avenue for exploration lies in extending the kind of programme already available to families where the children are deemed to be in need of protection to families where neglect has not yet occurred. To explore this path staff must be given time to devote to other than crisis situations so that they can develop the capacity to recognize environmental factors which produce stress for families and create programmes which will assist families without labelling them.

An example will illustrate the differences between the services of the community health and social service centres and traditional medical practice. In one centre a number of young married women reported being in a depressed state, and requested medication. The physician, noting that the living situations of these women included isolation, and no transportation into town, referred them to the centre's social worker. After further investigation the social worker arranged transportation on the school bus into town, and planned discussion groups and other programmes for the mothers at the centre. This action resolved the problem of depression without the need to resort to the customary solution of medication.

Other examples of changing the environment of families include the following:

1. promoting the involvement of fathers in child care. Few fathers attend the Parents in Crisis groups in B.C., which is probably typical in all the self-help groups in the country. However, securing the active participation of fathers in such groups and in the on-going care of children would constitute a welcome change in the environment of some families. Capital Families in Victoria, for example, is attempting to promote and enhance the relationship between fathers and their children by arranging Dads and Kids Drop-In evenings. This event has the added benefit of providing some free time for mothers.

2. developing emergency child care centres where parents can take their children at times of acute stress without risking the fear of "establishing a record" with the child welfare authorities. The Queen Alexandra Hospital for Children in Victoria provides such a resource, albeit only in times of crisis.

3. promoting informal day care networks on a neighbourhood basis and the development of day care arrangements in the work place. In addition, a number of communities have established Family Places which provide a setting both for self-help groups and for the temporary care of children.

With his intimate and extensive involvement in the field of child neglect and abuse, Ray Helfer advocated the development of a "community con-sortium committed to the dictum that family violence in this community is unacceptable." The consortium would undertake a "mass media and never ending campaign to educate the public about this dictum."[13]

Enhancing Competence

Another promising approach to secondary prevention is to enhance the competence of individuals, families, and community groups. Pursuing this thrust should not be interpreted as adopting the simplistic notion that man is the captain of his ship and master of his soul — that the individual can control societal events such as depressions and regional disparities and can overcome the effects of lack of opportunities for education and employ-ment. Nevertheless, it seems reasonable to support the notion that compe-tent, confident families can deal more adequately with difficulties than the helpless and inept.

Two types of strategies are discussed here: those directed at the develop-ment of community competence and those which enhance the capacity of families. The first is a redefinition of the old term "community organiza-tion" as described by Murray Ross.[14] More recently, Jack Rothman coined the term "locality development" in order to distinguish it from other and different strategies of community organization.[15] The essence of locality development consists of enhancing the capacity of neighbourhoods or small communities to deal with locality relevant problems — delinquency, specific threats to the neighbourhood, housing, school conditions and standards, and so forth. It is exemplified in the development of the Brit-annia Service Centre in Vancouver. Across the country another example of locality development occurred in Regent Park in Toronto and accounts of both these developments are contained in *Community Work in Canada*.[16]

Other examples can be found in recent B.C. practice. David Turner, a former probation officer in Victoria, transformed the typical probation officer role into one of locality development in Blanshard Court, a low-rental housing unit in the city.[17] A similar transformation of the child wel-fare role has been achieved by Randy Diehl and Terry Clark of the Minis-try of Human Resources in Vanderhoof, together with members of the Stoney Creek Band and the Department of Indian Affairs.[18]

Despite the fact that the Regent Park experience occurred in Toronto, the Blanshard Court project in Victoria, and the Stoney Creek achieve-ment in rural B.C., some similarities can be identified:

1. A well-bounded and identified community with a relatively homogene-ous population;
2. A reputation of being different from the larger community and, in some instances, a definite stigma attached to residence in the com-munity;

3. The recognition on the part of professional staff that traditional strategies had simply not worked — to continue dealing with child neglect on a one-to-one basis was an exercise in futility;
4. The existence of professional staff who were prepared to risk and try something different.

Whether rooted in theory or in expediency, the "something different" in each case can be described as locality development — the deliberate recasting of problems as not a Ministry of Human Resources or Attorney-General responsibility, but as a community problem which can only be resolved by community action. In each case, a community structure was formed which developed resources such as temporary foster homes so that children were not removed from the community because of parental illness or absences, recreation resources for teenagers, day care centres, and Mothers Time Out programmes. In Vanderhoof, the Child Welfare Committee resembles citizens committees in Europe which perform the judicial function in delinquency hearings. The Child Welfare Committee hears complaints about child abuse, interviews parents, attempts to locate resources, and follows up progress. It has begun to establish policies for child care within the reserve that may well have the kind of sanction that no outside group could achieve.

These ventures could be discussed at length, but the critical points are the following:

1. In all instances the power of the professional and of the outside agency has been shared with representatives of the community;
2. In all instances the incidence of problems has declined dramatically; in Blanshard Court, the number of police complaints totalled 70 in 1972. The programme discussed here began in 1973, and in that year the complaints dropped to 51, to 31 in 1974, 22 in 1975, and 17 in 1976.[19] In Vanderhoof, 8 children were apprehended in 1974 and 1975 and 9 in 1976 from the Stoney Creek Reserve. In 1977, following initiation of the locality development programme that number was reduced to 4, and since October 1978 the rate has been stabilized at three per year. In the three years following initiation of the Community Services Unit in Regent Park, the Metro CAS applied for guardianship of only one child.
3. In all instances there has been a return to the kind of community surveillance of behaviour that once was typical of life in small communities — which was effective but for some oppressive.
4. In all instances the competence of the community to take care of its own problems has been increased.

A concluding point is worth mention. Although the evidence of success is impressive, these projects have not been replicated in either Ontario or B.C., and they remain isolated ventures. Since they depart substantially from traditional practice, they demand staff who are forceful, independent, imaginative, and prepared to engage in community work practice. If the child welfare field is to move in a committed fashion into secondary prevention, it will have to develop conscious policies for recruiting and training personnel.

Enhancing the Competence of Families

In her book, *Helping Ourselves,* Mary Howell, a pediatrician and psychologist, advocated building into the role of human service professionals the functions of information-giving, consultation, and training. Rather than being restricted to the role of the expert in pathology — diagnosing sickness and prescribing remedies — human service professionals should increasingly become "coaches," and not only to current clients but to all families. Howell demands that "experts and professionals give us information and teach us skills that we can use to become joyous parents."[20]

The following discussion identifies three strategies for enhancing competence — providing information, organizing self-help groups, and developing training programmes. All of these can be useful for families whether problems have arisen or not.

Providing Information. Families require information about available services in health, education, and social welfare, and about child development. The authors of a recent article on "Developing Consumer Information" contend that "comprehensive and comprehensible information to consumers about the social services is rarely published, and if published is not readily accessible."[21] And this lack of information "has extensive negative consequences, particularly for consumers and front line workers. It hampers their ability to make decisions, to engage in planning, or to participate actively in the broader service system."[22] In the opinion of these researchers, pamphlets and brochures which describe available services and benefits in clear and simple terms are needed. While some beginnings have been made in this direction in the field of income security, little has occurred in child welfare. Thus, most citizens are neither aware of the provisions of child welfare legislation, particularly sections referring to child neglect, nor familiar with the legislation surrounding custody in divorce and separation proceedings.

A development of considerable promise in Ontario has been the establishment of privately organized and operated information centres which provide information over the telephone and through print material about all community services. But information centres have not been developed in other provinces despite their modest cost and potential for being significant additions to the human services.

A third strategy for providing information is afforded by the example of a child development series organized by Capital Families. This series consists of a three-part course on child development covering conception to three years, the years three to twelve, and adolescence. The intent is to offer basic information about the normal path of child development, focusing on well-accepted notions of physical and psychological development.

Organizing Self-Help Groups. In an age when all forms of the media are bursting with information about the care and raising of children, it may seem unnecessary to advocate the above strategy. One frequently heard complaint is that there is too much information, that it is unconnected and often contradictory, and that it results in confused rather than informed parents. The validity of this argument is acknowledged. One way of making sense of this welter of information is to provide opportunities for parents to discuss things together, to absorb what makes sense to them and to reject that which appears bizarre or irrelevant.

One promising example of this approach is again provided by Capital Families. This agency has organized New Parent Discussion Groups, which allows parents to exchange information about the problems and joys of parenthood. They provide a way to sift through the deluge of information, and on occasion, human service professionals are invited to address particular points of interest or concern.

Perhaps the most significant examples of self-help groups in child welfare are Parents in Crisis and Parents Anonymous for abusers and potential abusers of children. The experience with these self-help groups is that they can restore and build feelings of competence. While few formal evaluations have been conducted, the continuous growth of groups across the country and the positive view of them accorded by human service professionals attest to their usefulness. The evaluation of one Parents Anonymous Group in London, Ontario, concluded that "participation in the program had significant effects on verbal abuse and a reduction in physical abuse."[23]

Training Programmes. The Tree Foundation Inventory is replete with examples of training programmes for parents. The following list is by no means exhaustive, but does give some indication of the variety and extent of programmes developed across the country:

— the Teaching Home Makers Services Demonstration Project in Saint John, N.B.;
— Program for Parent Enrichment, Montreal;
— the Caring Centre, Montreal. (This project is one of the most comprehensive enhancement programmes contained in the inventory. The outline of the purposes of the Caring Centre provides an excellent introduction to objectives and the programmes provided by all the projects listed here. It is attached as Appendix I);
— Parenting for Teens and Children, Sudbury;
— the Family Education Centre or School for Parents in Niagara Falls;
— Preventive Marriage Counselling, Toronto; and

— the Native Family Life Counselling Program, Winnipeg.

Based on his research and experience, Ray Helfer is particularly forceful in advocating the enhancement of competence as an effective strategy. He recommends:

> — a major change in health services to include training for all new parents in the act of communicating with one's baby;
>
> — a home health visitor for all parents for the 1-2 year period after the birth of the first baby;
>
> — an early childhood education programme for all pre-school children;
>
> — an interpersonal skills program in how to get along in the public schools, built on simple skills in grade school and advancing to courses in sexuality and parenting in high school;
>
> — an adult education program for two levels of adults — those who had a positive rearing and want a refresher course in childhood before they become parents, and those whose childhood was minimal and need a crash course in childhood before parenting is undertaken.[24]

Not mentioned in the Inventory, but a fairly common programme in B.C., is the effective parenting training programme built upon the work of Dr. Theodore Dreikurs. Agencies such as the Pearkes Centre for Children in Victoria and a number of mental health centres and community colleges have found programmes to be well received.

Again a common difficulty is evaluation. Typically, direct service agencies have the resources, the expertise, and the inclination to develop training programmes, but none of the resources necessary to evaluate their ventures. Hence, we still lack even beginning responses to such questions as, Who comes to these sessions? What difference does it make? Over what period of time?

The Present Scene and Primary Prevention

Child welfare agencies are not and cannot be solely responsible for primary prevention. But in Canada child welfare is a component within comprehensive provincial ministries responsible for income security and a variety of social services programmes which have close connections with other ministries charged with functions in health, education, and housing. In all provinces the task of connecting social policies for the benefit of citizens rests with the provincial cabinet. Child welfare agencies are thus in a unique position to bring to the attention of senior civil servants and politicians the reasons why children come into care. For example, Martin argues in a convincing fashion that children in poverty are at risk, and this in turn raises some crucial policy questions for consideration. If children of poor families require extensive and intensive home-based services in order to ensure that they remain at home, would other and earlier approaches eliminate the need for the intervention of child welfare agencies? What does this argument mean in terms of other social provisions: income for single-parent families? social assistance rates for families? the child tax credit schemes? All of the above and perhaps provision in the housing and employment fields?

The point here is that child welfare officials are in a unique position to document the effects of current policies and provisions. If this documentation occurs on a continuous basis and if it is communicated to policy makers and, indeed, to the public in what Rainwater describes as forceful communication "breaking the conspiracy of silence that maintains the status quo by exposing as publicly and as repetitively as possible what actually goes on,"[25] it will help ensure that debates on social policy occur on the basis of detailed and precise information about the circumstances in family life.

The most significant Canadian provisions at the level of primary prevention are family allowances, universal health care, and public health programmes such as pre- and neonatal care, and public education. All of these seek to provide basic supports to all families in order to promote positive family life. However, we have not ventured far enough in the direction of primary prevention, and the concluding section charts some promising directions.

SECTION III

Not for the Poor Alone

> The issue is not whether the government will intervene. It will. The question is whether it will intervene for enhancement and prevention or whether it will respond to breakdown, problems and deviance alone. Will we seek to create a sufficient supply of social utilities as we seek to provide a supply of other public utilities?[26]

The argument of the authors is that certain features of Canadian and U.S. societies require that social programmes be made available as social utilities to be used by all citizens who require them in a way that ensures accessibility. The societal features include the disappearance of the extended family and of the small community, both of which provided support for families and functioned very effectively to deter deviant behaviour; the emergence of the two-income family; the increasing incidence of divorce; and the growing number of single-parent families. In addition, a number of writers on the social policy scene have pointed out that many people experience adjustment problems and that these are most likely to occur at times when a dramatic change in roles occurs. Thus, we all recognize the "normalcy" of adjustment problems experienced by teenagers, by new parents, and by workers when they first retire.

Taken together these arguments constitute a persuasive case for the transformation of the social services, including day care, homemaker services, counselling, and information and referral services from their present residual status into social utilities to assist all families who need and wish to avail themselves of these aids and supplements to family life. As Kahn and Kammerman comment:

> We believe in public education yet we somehow cannot give public support to high quality community living and care arrangements for the aged. We apparently consider it legitimate, whether in the interests of economy or of equality of the sexes, to open broader opportunities for women in the labor force, yet we do not face rapidly and thoughtfully the need for a parallel child care policy, fearing that its outcome will be to "federalize" the children.[27]

The transformation envisaged here includes relocating the social services to places and under auspices which do not stigmatize the users. If we know anything from practice wisdom, it is that services which stigmatize people, which identify them as rejects and failures, have not worked and will not work. In Richard Titmuss's phrase "services for the poor end up being poor services."[28]

To be precise, the relocation would mean using sites such as the workplace for day care programmes; libraries for information and referral services; recreation centres and schools for counselling, self-help groups, and training programmes; and health facilities for education in health lifestyles and parent education. Such locations would enhance the accessibility of services and the potential for early use.

This transformation may not be achieved as long as stigmatized programmes such as social assistance, services to delinquents and drug addicts, and child protection services are provided as part of the same structures which offer support services to all families. The issue is a difficult and contentious one. A review of the Community Resource Board experience in B.C. concluded that despite all the efforts that have been undertaken to integrate services, there is still no compelling formula to indicate which of the human services are compatible and should be provided together under the same structure and which are incompatible and should be offered under distinctly different auspices. The review took the position that income programmes are, however, part and parcel of the labour and employment sectors since they provide income usually gained through employment. Hence, income should be integrated with employment and not with social or health services, and in Canada it should be the responsibility of the federal government.[29]

The CRB review is useful for two other reasons. The study develops the case that provincial ministries should be responsible only for policy, setting and monitoring standards, and operating a few specialized services. Social services such as child welfare should be provided through community agencies governed by locally elected boards. These boards would be responsible for developing "community coherence" plans which would determine which of the non-statutory services were required in the community and how these would be meshed with the statutory services. Communites would, therefore, decide what supplemental services and preventive services would be required to support and enrich the core programme in child protection and adoption, where these services would be located, and what provisions were needed for ensuring the participation of citizens. Communities would not, however, have the option of whether or not to provide services mandated by provincial legislation.

A second important point arising from the review is that the local control of services is important both to staff and to citizens. It has the potential for ensuring that services are seen as belonging to the community rather than as the outpost of a provincial ministry and for accepting, if not overcoming, the negative images usually assigned to child protection.

CONCLUSION

To conclude, this chapter has argued that child welfare agencies in Canada provide effective services in the difficult task of responding to the increasing number of complaints of child neglect and child abuse. They have developed an impressive array of programmes to assist families in caring for their children and avoiding the necessity of apprehension and substitute care. However, agencies have not adopted the policy of permanent planning for children in care, and they have yet to move into secondary and primary prevention. A beginning can be made by providing core services to families by community-governed structures in a variety of nonstigmatized locations, such as health centres, schools, and libraries.

In addition, child welfare staff must increasingly reorder their service perspectives and skills to enhance the capacity of families and communities to care for children and to alter negative aspects of the environment. A singular contribution to primary prevention can be achieved through documentation of environmental factors which interfere with family life.

NOTES

1. David Cruickshank, "The Berger Commission Report on the Protection of Children: The Impact on Prevention of Child Abuse and Neglect," Chapter 11 in this volume.
2. Emory Cowen, "Social and Community Interventions," *Annual Review of Psychology* 24 (1973): 453.
3. National Council of Welfare, *Poor Kids* (Ottawa: The Council, 1975), p. 25.
4. Gray, Cutler, Dean, and Kempe, "Predictions and Prevention of Child Abuse and Neglect," in *Child Abuse: The International Journal* 1 (1977).
5. Sally Palmer, "Government Commitment to Child Welfare as Shown by the Monitoring of Services," *Social Worker* 50, no. 1 (Spring 1982): 6-9.
6. British Columbia Ministry of Human Resources, *Annual Report 1980-1981* (Victoria: Queen's Printer, 1981), p. 34.
7. E. Sherman, M. Phillips, B. Harvey, and A. Shyne, *Service to Children in Their Own Homes* (Child Welfare League of America, 1974), p. 123.
8. *Inventory of Canadian Research,* a research report prepared by the Tree Foundation, Solicitor-General of Canada, and Minister of National Health and Welfare, 1981.
9. Emory Cowen, "Baby Steps Toward Prevention," *American Journal of Community Psychology* 5, no. 1 (March 1977): 1-22.
10. Julian Rappaport, "In Praise of Paradox: A Social Policy of Empowerment Over Prevention," *American Journal of Community Psychology* 9 (1981): 13.
11. Gray et al.
12. Ray Helfer, "A Review of the Literature on the Prevention of Child Abuse and Neglect," *The International Journal* 6 (1982): 259.
13. Ibid., p. 259.
14. Murray Ross, *Community Organizations: Theory, Principles and Practice* (New York: Harper and Row, 1955).
15. Jack Rothman, "Three Models of Community Organization Practice," in *Strategies of Community Organization: A Book of Readings,* eds. Cox, Erlich, Rothman, and Tropman (Itasca: Peacock Publishing, 1970).
16. Brian Wharf, *Community Work in Canada* (Toronto, McClelland and Stewart, 1979).
17. David Turner, "Community and Prevention: The Case of Rose Blanshard Court," Corrections Branch Newsletter, Victoria, Fall 1976.
18. A. Farquharson, "Self-Help in the Provision of Child Welfare Services: The Stoney Creek Indian Band," a paper presented to the Conference on Self-Help and Mutual Aid in Contemporary Society, Dubrovnik, Yugoslavia, September 1979.
19. Turner.
20. Mary Howell, *Helping Ourselves* (Toronto: Fitzhenry and Whiteside, 1977).
21. M. Callahan and M. Martin, "Developing Consumer Information — A Strategy for Service and Policy Change," *Social Worker* 49 (1981): 170.
22. Ibid.
23. Inventory of Canadian Research, p. 113.
24. Helfer, p. 259.
25. Lee Rainwater, "Neighborhood Action and Lower Class Life Styles," in *Neighborhood Organization for Social Action,* ed. John Turner (New York, National Association of Social Workers, 1968), p. 37.
26. A. Kahn and Sheila Kamerman, *Not For the Poor Alone* (Philadelphia: Temple University Press, 1975), p. 172.
27. Ibid., p. 171.
28. Richard Titmuss, *Commitment to Welfare* (New York, Pantheon Books, 1968), p. 145.
29. M. Clague, R. Dill, R. Seebaran, and B. Wharf, *Reforming Human Services: The Community Resource Board Experience in B.C.* (Vancouver: U.B.C. Press, 1984).

13

APPROACHES TO FAMILY TREATMENT

Barbara Whittington

Family problems encountered in public agencies are complex and demanding. Few families are self-referred or well-motivated to begin counselling. More often, families arrive on an involuntary basis; they may have been persuaded or coerced to seek professional help by any number of people or systems — the court, the school, the community. These families pose additional dilemmas which will be explored. The primary purpose here is to examine the theoretical perspectives for family therapy and from them to derive practice principles for engagement and ongoing work. Engagement is stressed because it is more than a prerequisite for counselling or therapy; it is often tantamount to a successful outcome.

The Family and Child Welfare — Definitions

The Family. The family will be defined here not solely in biological terms and not necessarily in legal ones. "A family consists of a minimum of two people with a shared network of relationships including a past history, a present reality and a future expectation of interconnected relationships."[1] There are thus many ways a family can be composed. The nuclear family has given way to a variety of alternatives: families based on common-law relationships or on communal living, those with the intermittent presence of sexual partners of single parents or with joint parenting by homosexual unmarried parents, as well as those that include foster or adopted children.

A family may be a blended or stepfamily. This is a reconstituted family formed by the marriage (common-law or legal) of divorced or separated persons, establishing stepparent relationships as children from previous families merge into a new family unit. Some 40 per cent of Canadian marriages end in divorce, and over half a million children have been involved in this reality over the last two years.[2] Now economic factors are making more families familiar with the stresses caused by economic factors as more and more join the frustrated ranks of the unemployed or under-employed: do we now have the unemployed family?

Child Welfare. Child welfare commonly refers to the full range of services provided by public and private organizations to respond to and prevent problems experienced by families in caring for their children. In Chapter 12 two aspects of child welfare work are discussed, first, the modification of the environment and, second, the enhancement of individual family competence. Day care, homemaker service, substitute care for children in foster homes and group homes are all attempts by society to respond to familial problems. Have these responses enhanced competence or truly modified the environment? For some families solutions have increased problems since family services have been deemed privileges and those who need them judged failures. Those who believe in that major piece of practice wisdom mentioned in Chapter 12, "keep children in their own homes" must look seriously at the effect our child welfare "solutions" have on the families they are meant to serve.

> Social workers, in spite of their historical focus on human beings in relation to their social environments, have also often been slow to reccognize the far-reaching destructive effects that policies, programmes and service delivery approaches may have on delicate but vital human systems. A case in point is the undermining effect some kinds of practice have had on that most important natural human system, the family. Perhaps nowhere has resistance to change, resistance to take account of, support and protect natural systems been more troublesome or more paradoxical than in the field of family and children's services, that area of practice known, interestingly enough, as "child welfare."[3]

Years later, I am amazed at the naivete of a residential treatment centre where I worked. Children ages seven to fifteen came to live there after having been determined to be "emotionally disturbed." The majority of them lived far away from their families and only had a minimum of contact. After a period of treatment, they were returned home to families who not only had had little part in the treatment, but who had also often been labelled as the problem. We somehow expected the child to maintain his new-found emotional "nondisturbance" in a family system that had been ignored by the professionals. As Laird asks, "How long will it be before the child has been recast into his or her traditional role, whether it be scapegoat, delinquent or some other type of family symptom-bearer?"[4] She concludes that such practices are both un-ecological and anti-family in their effects.

Key Issues for Families in Child Welfare. Many clients are identified and served according to statute, not because they voluntarily request social service. For child welfare workers interested in families, this has tremendous significance. The legislation under which they act has emerged from conflicting ideologies focused on the role of the state and the role of the parent. For the worker, the following emerge as key issues:

1. How to balance the needs of the family, the child, and the community? Child welfare workers must be able to investigate community complaints of child abuse, explain the province's right to intervene, and yet give the often conflicting message that they are there to assist the family and work with them, not against them. Workers must try to inspire trust, and yet they know that if the family intervention is unsuccessful, they may use that same information, that same trust, to prove the government's case — to remove the child. Is it possible to be both an authority figure and a helper-counsellor-therapist? With agency support and clear contracting with the family, I believe it is. The family must know from the beginning that the focus under the law is the protection of the child. If the worker sincerely believes that a child's family is the best source of nurturance and support, the family will get the message and engage in a meaningful therapeutic relationship. Many times when children are subjected to lengthy and emotionally damaging court battles, the social worker sees in hindsight that more effort could have been made at the family level.

In some cases, the authority of the social worker and the community concern he represents can serve to mobilize a family's network of relatives and friends. In isolated families where members feel overwhelmed by the caretaking demands of the children, the social worker's intervention may be welcomed. In child protection cases, the family will sometimes say they are relieved that finally "something has happened." Generally, this relief goes hand in hand with a fear that something worse could have happened; their child could have died; they might have killed her.

2. The question can be revised, how many truly "voluntary" families does one encounter in professional social work practice? Voluntary here means families requesting counselling of their own free choice. Involuntary means families where promise or threat has coerced them into the counselling relationship. Some family workers argue that *no* family is in fact "involuntary." Families may choose between their present "pain" and the unknown of therapy. Is it a free choice? Therapists see themselves as helpers of those who want to be helped. "However, it is characteristic of involuntary clients that although they desperately wish to be helped, they react with fear, hostility and avoidance to conventional [voluntary] methods to help them."[5] Are these clients then involuntary or merely appropriately sceptical and wary?

Berstein looks at the voluntary/involuntary dilemma from a values perspective and concludes, "Social work and other professionals may enable, stimulate, impose and even use force, but what the client feels, thinks and values is ultimately his private affair and more within his controls than that of the professional."[6]

These two points address the reality that voluntarism is not a linear notion. There are degrees to which families may present themselves as voluntary or involuntary. Clients who come for counselling may feel somewhat coerced even at the voluntary end of the scale, and in the final analysis clients and client families have the ultimate choice to feel and think and be as they choose.

OVERVIEW OF FAMILY FRAMEWORKS

A framework is a basic structure of ideas to assist in the process of working with families. Frameworks are inventions which are important only if they are useful.

Conceptual Frameworks; An Ecological Framework. A conceptual framework looks at ways of thinking about families while practice frameworks refer to ideas about assessing and working with families. Both types order experience and, if useful, serve to improve family practice. The ecological framework is an umbrella which covers many practice frameworks useful in child welfare work. It is not new, but here it is being emphasized as a useful knowledge base for work with families.

An ecological approach to child welfare and family work in particular leads to a focus on improving the transactions between people and their environments in order to enhance adaptive capacities and also to improve the environments for all who function within them. The major factors are the coping patterns of families, the qualities of the environments in which they live, and the interaction between the families and the environment.

To understand the problems of the children and families, it is necessary to look at the family structure and how it functions *and* at the systems external to the family. Since this external environment impinges upon the family, it is part of the concern, and the child welfare system itself, both public and private, forms part of the external system that families interact with. In their article, "An Alternative to Placing Children: Intensive and Extensive Therapy with 'Disengaged' Families,"[7] Tomlinson and Peters comment on the usefulness of an ecological approach in dealing with families who have often been seen as multi-problem and hard to reach. They state that to be effective the therapists must be ready and able to become involved in the many external systems affecting the family. Just as there is a growing recognition of the need to see the whole family as the "patient" in medicine, so too in the field of child welfare it is becoming clear that to attend to the child's welfare, the family's welfare must be considered. This holistic view includes the network of school, neighbourhood, work, and extended family.

In the residential treatment centre there existed a division between child welfare and family social work that was counterproductive. This split is often still evident in the manner in which children as victims of child neglect or sexual abuse are treated separately from their families. Despite the gloomy predictions of the fall of the family, this last decade has seen the creative flexibility and durability of the family in its many forms. It is an enduring institution and the primary provider of love, help, and care to individuals. Nurturance, growth, and development take place in a family, just as neglect, abuse, and failure can thrive.

The family is therefore the most crucial unit of treatment. In her article, "An Ecological Approach to Child Welfare: Issues of Family Identity and Continuity,"[8] Laird directs attention to the life and death issues of separation, loss, abuse, and neglect in reference to parents and families as well as children. Society's neglect of the natural parent and the consequences to families and children when they are torn apart or fall apart are examined later on. The important point here is to suggest that child welfare practices need to be family welfare practices.

The family focus is a generic part of all social services which must be addressed philosophically and practically. It appears that many accept this conceptually but fail to practice it. As Salvador Minuchin bluntly states it:

> Our armamentarium of interventions has failed to change in response to our broadening conceptualizations. . . . [The] response of social agencies in general is still to break up the family. The records of improvement in foster care and residential treatment are not encouraging, and the costs of these approaches is discouraging, but there still has not been an organized, overall conceptualization of the delivery of services to families in this country. The family is studied and respected as a viable socialization unit when it is working; when trouble arises, the response is to split it.[9]

Practice Frameworks. The ecological perspective is useful because it directs the worker to consider primary areas.
1. Knowledge of family — life-cycle tasks in relation to the environment.
2. Knowledge of resources available to and needed by families and the factors influencing the linkages between families and larger systems (educational, economic, health care).
3. Knowledge of the family as a system of communication that differs from other systems in its shared history and intimate ties.
4. Knowledge of family structures and relationships.

How can the gap between *knowing* (the conceptual component) and *doing* (the skill or practice component) be bridged? There have been many terms used to describe this territory between conceptual frameworks and practice skills. For the purposes of this discussion, four frameworks will be examined and specific practice principles of engagement discussed.

Any selection of theories is somewhat arbitrary. This selection emphasizes the particular dilemmas and key practice problems in working with families in child welfare. Basically, family approaches with an active role for the worker and a brief-problem-focused orientation appear to fit with the types of families presenting problems and agency demands in the child welfare field.

There has been a great deal written on how to classify family therapy frameworks. Some authors looked at the "focus" of the treatment.[10] Thinking of the practitioner, we will ask the two questions, "How does this theory help us make sense of the complexity of family life?" And "Is the theory suitable for the field of child welfare?"

The four basic directions mentioned under the ecological systems framework lead directly to four practice frameworks:

1.	Knowledge of family life-cycles	Family stages and development theory
2.	Knowledge of resources available to and needed by the family	Network theory
3.	Knowledge of family as a system of communication	Communication theory
4.	Knowledge of family structures and relationships	Structural family therapy theory.

The Family Life-Cycle and Family Development as a Framework

Individuals and families proceed through developmental cycles in which certain life tasks become critical turning points, moments where a family might proceed over the bump or around the corner or bog down. Families, like individuals, face challenges, and both sometimes need encouragement or assistance. A functional family is one with problems and challenges, but one that has been able to respond to demands for change (external and internal) with new patterns and interactive strategies.

The stages of the family life-cycle are presented in the chart below; it addresses the tasks all family systems face as well as the key emotional/attitudinal issues with which they must grapple. (See Table 1.) The purpose in presenting this view of the life-cycle is to provide a positive, healthy view of families where "problems" are seen as normal and as opportunities for families to respond to challenge. The important events noted often correspond to the comings and goings of family members. In order to discuss treatment approaches, it is necessary to take into account the variations resulting from the family's stage of development. In defining the basic assumptions of the model they have been developing over many years, Nathan Epstein and his colleagues state that the primary function of the family is to support the development of its members; and that in carrying this out, all families must deal with basic tasks (food, shelter); developmental tasks related to individual growth and to the stages of the family life-cycle, and hazardous tasks such as illness, death, moving, and loss of income.[11] This perspective is essential in the child welfare/family service field. "With this orientation, many more families who enter therapy would be seen as average families in transitional situations, suffering the pains of accommodating to the new circumstances."[12] "Problems can be seen as derailments from the family life cycle and therapy as getting the family back on the track."[13]

TABLE 1

FAMILY LIFE CYCLE

Family System Stage	Key Systems Tasks	Child Welfare Implications
1. Unattached young adult	—leaving home economically/ physically/emotionally —establishment of strong peer relationship —change in relationship between generations	—often leaving is premature (juvenile runaways) —time of experimentation for young adult, alcohol/drug abuse —often still economically tied —social assistance
2. The joining of families— couples	—development of new system —change in relationship with extended families —often change in relationship with peers	—role issues —issues of separation —patterns of relationships are forming, e.g., family violence —adoption/abortion issues
3. Family with young children	—accepting entrance of new family members —learning parenting roles; emotional and physical endurance	—stress of role change —adoption issues —child abuse; neglect; escalation of family violence —family support skills needed for parenting; day care —system isolated from others
4. Family with adolescents	—flexibility of boundaries for beginning of independence	—runaways; delinquency and court involvement; school issues —foster care; separation from family, role reversal— parent/child
5. Family with young adult children	—new roles for parents and children; adults to adults —a couple again	—economic dependence may continue —often second generation involvement in child welfare
6. Family in later life	—acceptance of shift in roles of children and parents —preparing for retirement —dealing with loss of spouse and peers	—grandparents may become surrogate parents in neglect and abuse situations —issues of loss and loneliness —abuse of the elderly

TABLE 2

DISLOCATIONS AND NEW FAMILY FORMS

Stage	Developmental Issues	Child Welfare Issues

1. Separation
  1. The decision
  2. The move
	—uncertainty
	—marital tensions
	—acceptance of inability to
	  resolve problems
		—family violence
		—custody issues; children in
		  middle
		—temporary child placement
		  family grieving

2. The divorce	—working cooperatively on
	  custody, maintenance, access
	—involvement of extended family
	—emotional issues
		—court involvement—custody
		—geographical movement
		—worker continuity
		—emergence of symptoms—
		  school behaviour, delinquency

3. Single parent
  1. Custodial
  2. Non- "
  3. Joint "
	—making mutually acceptable
	  arrangements
	—rebuilding peer group and
	  contact with family
		—financial support issues
		—parental subsystem still exists
		—spousal subsystem does not
		—court involvement

4. New
  relationships
	—adequate emotional divorce
	—recommitment to marriage or
	  long term relationship
		—child neglect
		—loyalty conflicts
		—often concludes with adolescent
		  issues

5. Planning new marriage	—fears of new relationship —resolution of old relationship	—legal involvement —blended family issues —adolescent independence

6. Remarriage &
  reconstitution
  of family
	—integration of new family
	—complex relationships with
	  extended family
	—often new baby
		—custody issues revisited
		—economic issues revisited
		—new spouse as stepparent
		—stepfamily complexity his/
		  mine/ours

The family worker must make a careful evaluation of families within this larger time frame and develop an ability to assess points of dislocation or derailment. Just as an infant must struggle with the developmental tasks of creeping and crawling prior to walking, so a family must struggle to adjust its marital system to make space for children prior to taking on the flexible parenting roles necessary for dealing with adolescents. The first development task relates to the adjustment of the couple to the entry of a new baby while the second developmental task relates to the impending exit of the adolescent from the family system. Many of the families seen in child welfare have not completed the developmental tasks related to coupling before they encounter the task of parenting.

There is still a great tendency for families to operate in isolation; their public and private faces are very different. Many families are unaware that the stresses and strains of family life are natural. Knowledge of developmental stages allows the worker to see a broader picture, to realize, for example, that it is natural to feel the strains of children passing through adolescence. Having remained relatively stable for twelve or thirteen years, the family is suddenly required to change its entire structure and function. The family must let adolescents go, be prepared to support them financially and emotionally if and when they come back, and to "encompass the barrage of people and ideas they bring into the family from the outside. Their pushing and pulling in family relationships goes through the system with a 'domino effect'."[14] A family developmental perspective puts such struggles in context.

Few families now fit the traditional pattern of two parents, a male breadwinner and a female housewife with one or two children. In fact, fewer than 10 per cent of Canadian families fall into this traditional category. Families where separation or divorce is the reality, couples who have chosen to not have children, single parents, widowed and blended families all bring additional stages to the family life-cycle and additional challenges to the family worker. In child welfare work, many of the families a worker encounters are in chaos. A knowledge of developmental issues directs the worker to assess the developmental stages of the family, and begin to sort through the chaos. (See Table 2.)

Social Network Framework

Where unexpected events and stresses force the family to adapt, the worker must be aware of the environment within which the family develops, its social network. The family's network usually includes the extended family, friends, and neighbours and may include a school or work group. For the worker using a social network strategy in working with families, whole new possibilities arise.

A network is a term used to describe the interconnections between people. These connections often become most visible in times of family crisis. There is a growing literature about the utility of social networks as a unit of intervention.[15] Using this framework, a family worker could involve all the significant family members as well as those service providers involved with the family. The goal of the networking would be to reinforce the supportive capacities of a family's or an individual's personal networks and to promote independence and future coping abilities. For example, prior to removing a neglected child from his home and neighbourhood, a family worker would invite family members, neighbours, and others involved to assist in the assessment of the situation and use the family's natural support system to plan and care for the child. Social work practice has long turned to formal substitute care — foster homes, group homes — rather than informal, natural care. Many cultural groups have their own internal "child welfare system," aunts, uncles, and godparents, who readily assume nurturing and care-giving functions. The use of neighbours as foster parents is another possibility too often ignored; a child's neighbourhood, block, school, and friends all contribute to his/her feelings of connectedness. Carel Germain summarizes the price paid for not thinking of natural networks by stating: "No matter how nurturing the substitute care, the child's ongoing task will always be to reweave the jagged tear in the fabric of his identity, to make himself whole again."[16] To keep families, as well as individuals, whole, one task is to empower families.

In addition to demanding access to information, it can be demanded that experts and professionals instruct us in skills that are needed to provide reasonable care from *within* families. Instead of becoming more dependent upon professional services, impersonally rendered by paid workers who cannot care deeply about members of families not their own, we can ask for instruction, assistance and supervision in nursing our own sick kin, educating our own children and ourselves and coping with our own handicaps and disabilities. Professional services as presently organized tend to replace rather than to supplement family services, to take control rather than to foster self-sufficiency.[17]

Communication Framework

The communication model of family work is identified with the works of Virginia Satir, Paul Watzlawick, John Weakland, and Jay Haley. The treatment goals on which these theorists agree is that to alleviate family members' presenting problems (what or who they see as wrong or bad or mad), the family interaction patterns must change. These theorists say that the communication styles of the family unit will determine the family's success in negotiating the various developmental stages. Obviously, these frameworks overlap with each other.

Communication theory tells us to look at the manner in which family members communicate both verbally and non-verbally, to focus on the current observable interactions within the family system. This theory warns that it is impossible *not* to communicate since even silence or withdrawal indicates something about the relationship between people.

The communication theories say that each communication has a content/report and a relationship/command aspect to it. The latter classifies the former and is therefore a metacommunication. The metacommunication is the nonverbal message about the verbal. It is that aspect that places a demand on the recipient. Many families attempt to resolve a conflict on the content level: "You didn't tell me you were going out." "I did so." "You did not!" The conflict is really on the relationship level — the metacommunication is "Who are you to tell me what I did or didn't do?" The command part of the message can be unclear, and misunderstandings can result when communicators are unaware of the commands they are giving, receiving, and obeying. For family systems communication concepts may be summarized as follows:

1. The primary need of individuals within a relationship is to *form and maintain the relationship itself.*
2. There are two major tasks involved in this process: deciding *what* the *rules* of the relationship are and negotiating *who* actually makes the decisions regarding the rules.
3. The tasks of *setting rules* and *negotiating who has control* over the rules are accomplished through the exchange of *messages.*
4. *Messages* form the substance of the communication between people in the relationship and, as such, are the *basic* element of the *interactional process.*
5. Messages have two major aspects: the *communicational,* dealing with the *content* of the message itself and the *metacommunicational,* dealing with the *message about the message.* The latter seeks to impose behaviour or to define the self and the nature of the relationship.[18]

Structural Family Framework

The final framework is termed structural family therapy. This approach is most closely identified with Salvador Minuchin and Braulio Montalvo. Minuchin and his co-workers developed a therapeutic approach that was founded on the immediacy of the present reality, oriented to solving problems, and *above all* contextual, referring to the social environment that is both a part of and the setting for an event. "Unlike most therapies which had their roots in the middle class and were adapted to work with lower socio-economic patients, structural family therapy was generated from work with the poor and subsequently expanded to other socio-economic strata."[19]

The family is seen as inter-acting within a context; the family life-cycle and developmental stage are important both in assessment and defining therapy strategy. A problem family is often seen as "stuck" at a particular stage in its development. Structural family therapy sees "symptoms" as both system-maintained and system-maintaining (for example, a child's "bad" behaviour may *detour* mom and dad; keep them and the system together). This therapy looks at family members' positions relative to one another, who is aligned with whom, who has too much or too little power, and whether family members are overinvolved with or too distant from each other. Too intrusive involvement is termed enmeshment and too great a distance from each other is defined as disengagement. Structural theorists see the family as a system with rules and structures, such as coalition patterns, that need to be able to adapt and change continuously as the family enters new developmental stages and deals with changing environmental demands. If a family is unable to meet these changing demands, there is resultant emotional distress. A family's response to an adolescent's growing need for independence may be to keep the adolescent enmeshed with the mother; the mother and adolescent may be overinvolved with each other, and the adolescent may develop symptoms. These symptoms could include failure at school, conflict with the law, or emotional withdrawal and depression.

The strategies that evolve from this framework centre on the therapist challenging the family's view of reality by a variety of "restructuring techniques." They might include asking the family to enact or demonstrate their interactions to enhance the therapist's and family members' awareness of these; therapists may reduce enmeshment by having family members speak for themselves or reduce disengagement by seeing non-aligned family members together while excluding others. Therapists using this framework may focus on the interaction between the family system and other environmental systems; the therapists may work together, for example, with the family to intervene in the school system if that is where the difficulty appears. The emphasis is on having family members behave differently and try alternative patterns of interaction. The important structural units or subsystems of the family are the spousal subsystem, the parental subsystem, and the sibling subsystem. The family carries out its functions through these subsystems and provides opportunities for family members to differentiate and develop skills. "The development of skills for negotiating with peers," Minuchin maintains, "is learned among siblings and requires no interference from parents."[20]

PRACTICE APPROACHES EMERGING FROM THE FOUR FRAMEWORKS

How, when, and where can a family approach be used in child welfare and how effective is such an approach? The practice principles discussed operationalize concepts from developmental theory, from networking theory, and from structural and communication theory. In day-to-day practice, a child welfare worker must look to all these conceptual frameworks and more to focus on the relationship between the family and its environment. Germain says that "Child Welfare is considered by many to be the most difficult of all fields of practice. This is not only because of the built-in conflicts of its triangular structure (substitute care-giver; child's natural family; and agency-worker) but because of the unrelenting demands placed on the worker by the life and death issues of separation, loss, abuse, and neglect."[21]

Research

With the realities of child welfare practice in mind, family approaches must be examined for their usefulness in terms of process and outcome.

The state of research reflects the beginning status of family therapy and family therapy outcome research. Firstly, what should be included in the 'measurement'? What is being addressed? Whose perception of the process or the outcome counts? The families', the workers'? Some researchers look at the family's satisfaction with therapy as a measure. Other researchers attempt to compare the "normal" family with the abnormal. But what is the baseline?

The second difficulty addresses the question of what research paradigm is useful for families. How does one measure or assess interactional patterns? How can indicators or symptom change be connected with a specific intervention? There are so many other variables that might influence the outcome that family therapy does not lend itself easily to traditional research methodologies. In 1972 Wells et al published the first review of outcome studies. There were thirteen studies in the family area. In 1978, Germain and Kniskern examined over two hundred studies; an increase of 1500 per cent in just five years.[22]

These authors caution the reader to bear in mind the following consideration:

(a) In general, it is impossible to disentangle treatment effects from therapist effects in the studies done to date.

(b) The treatments that have been studied have almost never followed "pure" applications of given treatment models.

(c) With infrequent exceptions, it is impossible to be certain just what specific treatment interventions have actually been used, since treatment operations have almost never been described in detail.[23]

The question of what percentage of families receiving family therapy improve during treatment is of interest to workers. In summary, the improvement rate is roughly two-thirds. Of specific interest to those in the child welfare field is the finding that there is a trend toward a *better* outcome when the identified patient (the family member that either the community or family sees as the "problem") is a child or adolescent (71 per cent improved).[24]

The all important question of what treatment for what problem with what families and what therapist is even more complicated. Germain and Kniskern conclude:

At the moment, structural family therapy should be considered the family therapy treatment of choice for these childhood psychosomatic conditions and, to our knowledge, it is the most empirically supported psychotherapy approach of *any* sort of these conditions. The studies of structural family therapy with drug addicts are among the very best controlled outcome studies in the entire research literature on family therapy.[25]

Stanton deals with the family therapy of drug abusers and addicts, an extremely complex and discouraging area. He examines the outcomes of standard drug counselling and compares these with other combinations of treatment and found family therapy treatment to be superior to any of the other combinations. Many of the characteristics of these families can be compared with families in child welfare; families are often isolated from other natural networks and are difficult to engage in a counselling relationship, and workers and families have the issues of authority, voluntarism, and court involvement as considerations.[26]

Thus far, there are several trends noted which have direct relevance to the child welfare field:

1. Brief time limited treatments (up to twenty sessions) are in general probably equal in effectiveness to lengthier family therapies. Many child welfare workers hesitate to work with families because they feel a long treatment plan would be necessary. Apparently not. The workload in most child welfare agencies is high, and an approach that is brief and focused is important.

2. The involvement of the father appears to exert a powerful effect, clearly improving the odds of good outcomes in many situations. The tentative finding should encourage workers to involve estranged fathers, foster fathers, and fathers from the family of origin in their work with foster children, troubled adolescents, and adoptive families.

3. The evidence is accumulating to support the relationship between treatment outcome and a therapist's relationship skills. A worker must develop the basics of genuineness, empathy, and positive regard before relying on therapeutic techniques.

This literature suggests that it is generally important for the marital-family therapist to be active and to provide some structure to early interviews, but not to confront tenuous family defenses very early in treatment. Excesses in this direction are among the main contributors to premature termination and to negative therapeutic outcomes.[27]

These trends support the selection of frameworks discussed earlier and encourage the worker to be direct, active, and human with the family, to time-limit the intervention and to encourage involvement by fathers in the therapeutic endeavour.

Engagement

Unless a family comes for treatment, it cannot begin. A disengaged family calls for the therapist/worker to use what might be termed unconventional strategies. The first task is for the worker to "engage this disengaged family." An example might be the less verbal family where the capacity or willingness of the family to "come for counselling" is the question. Minuchin describes such families in the following way: "Abuse and neglectful families typically act out their lives; they do not value talking in problem-solving, are not introspective and expect help to be in the form of advice or concrete goods."[28]

How is it, then, that a family agrees to come? The factors to address are: first, the family, the employing agency, the mandate of the agency, and the authority, commitment, and skill of the worker and, second, the actual "intake" or interaction.

1. Public child welfare family services are primarily offered to those families who are deemed to be "at risk." Philosophically, the bureaucracy may state its commitment to the quality of family life in general as a preventive approach. In practice, the families a public child welfare worker typically sees are those where the family is "at risk of being torn apart" through abuse, neglect, illness, or incarceration. In many cases, family work is deemed a last ditch effort so the child will not be apprehended.

   In private agencies, the content may be different, the issue may be alcohol abuse or drug misuse, but the process remains the same. The family is in trouble and pain, *and* it is at such a desperate point that someone has called in "the professionals." In public child welfare family service, the therapist may be the same person who will be called to court to give evidence in an adversarial situation where the state has apprehended the child and is making application for custody.

   The philosophical *and* practical commitment of the agency to family service are practical indicators of the depth of commitment to serving families that an agency has. For example, is there a room/space large enough to accommodate a family within the agency, and is it furnished in a warm, non-intimidating manner? Most families can be seen in their own homes, but in some instances only certain family members will be involved or a neutral territory is desirable — is there the physical space for this? Are workers' hours flexible enough to allow for evening visits; is there a supervisory/consultation support system available? Family work is challenging and exhausting. Agency stance and support in policy, procedures and education will either encourage or undermine family work and ultimately family functioning. The all-important prerequisites for family approaches working have less to do with the motivation of the family than with the motivation and commitment of the child welfare agency and professionals.

2. The first contact can be *the* determining factor in a family deciding to agree to come. The majority of beginnings happen by telephone. Whoever answers that first call, the receptionist or the intake worker, will

begin the process whereby requests for help are translated into family terms. Does that key person have a knowledge of and a commitment to family work? The intake worker would be realistic to assume some initial resistance to the idea of family involvement by the individual referring. In an interesting article called "The Telephone Intake: Engaging the Family in Treatment,"[29] Steinitz sees resistance as genuine concern expressed by persons introduced to this concept for the first time. The therapist/intake worker is actually beginning the work at this point: answering questions, redefining issues and explaining the family approach. The intake shapes the family's treatment expectations and sets the tone for the ongoing therapeutic relationship.

In addition to the first client contact, two important factors influencing engagement of clients are the framework and the stance of the therapist.

Steps Toward Engagement

Framework
1. Use an action-oriented framework with an emphasis on the present and on the problem as it is at the moment. Families see this as both sensible and hopeful. The approaches discussed in this chapter meet this criterion.
2. Emphasize obtainable practical goals so that families can easily see what they want to work on and can measure their progress in concrete ways.
3. Be completely clear on any conflict of roles. If you are responsible for a report to the court, or to an employer, outline your role and your own personal limits.

The Therapist/Social Worker
1. The therapist must be active and directive, and not a detached "expert." Be human.
2. The therapist should be prepared to go into the families' homes rather than insisting on office visits. Clients will appreciate this as a significant shift in the usual style of counselling and a sign of acceptance of them and of commitment to them.
3. The therapist must indicate a willingness to intervene in the outside systems influencing the family. Many clients will be simultaneously attempting to feed, clothe, house, and educate their families, and they are often the "involuntary" clients of several agencies. The family therapist with a systems framework will be alert to the "ecological perspective." One might be more helpful to the family as a systems advocate than as a therapist with the nuclear family. The family may need you as an advocate.
4. The therapist must show an ability to join with and accommodate to the family; he or she must be willing and able to be themselves and to

use their own feelings and experiences as part of the encounter.

5. The therapist must model her commitment to build a non-critical accepting atmosphere. One of the distinct advantages in using a family approach is that there is less of a focus on individual inadequacies — a sore point for many parents and children.

6. The therapist must be aware of the various cultural or familial injunctions around "family business" and around authority figures, learning from the families their own rules and boundaries.

7. The therapist's sheer perseverance, her consistent nonblaming attitude, and her willingness to meet on the family's ground can be all-important in engaging families.

8. One of the therapist's main tasks is exploring with the family her job of developing and maintaining appropriate family boundaries. While disengaged families need to address themselves to taking back their parenting tasks from agencies and systems external to their family, the enmeshed family must work to relinquish part of the "parenting" and become more clear about lines of responsibility.

Principles of engagement centre on the agency and the workers' commitment to family therapy as a constructive and productive approach to counselling. An ecological system perspective opens the door to new approaches to all too familiar child welfare "cases." A child welfare worker might convene sessions of entire neighbourhoods to assist a family in distress (network approach); he might work with the natural parents and foster parents together so that the foster child can free himself from the triangle (structural and communication approach); or a child welfare worker might undertake counselling a new family where abuse of an infant has involved the authorities (developmental framework) and apprehension is a real possibility.

CONCLUSION

This chapter has reviewed family frameworks which proved useful. There is a dimension to family work that is difficult to comment on. A principle of systems theory is that the whole is different from and greater than the sum of its parts. A chapter on approaches to family treatment is a part; it is not the whole. The whole of family work is much different than looking at this approach or that technique. Approaches and techniques are inadequate attempts to make a science from an art. Certainly there is a portion of the whole that is measurable and teachable; that is a science. The conviction of professionals that child welfare is really part of the whole of family welfare stems from a personal belief that the "art of being a family" is an art we as human beings must nurture and support.

NOTES

1. Allon Bross, ed., *Family Therapy: A Recursive Model of Strategic Practice* (Toronto: Methuen, 1982), p. 221.
2. Statistics Canada, *Divorce: Law and the Family in Canada* (Ottawa: Canadian Government Publishing Centre, 1983), p. 60.
3. Joan Laird, *An Ecological Approach to Child Welfare,* in Germain, Carel, ed., *Social Work Practice: People and Environments* (New York: Columbia University Press, 1979), p. 176.
4. Ibid., p. 80.
5. Suzanne M. Sgroi, *Handbook of Clinical Intervention in Child Sexual Abuse* (Lexington, Mass.: D.C. Heath, 1982), p. 259.
6. S. Bernstein, "Self-Determination, King of Citizen in the Realm of Values?" *Social Work* 5 (1980): 8.
7. R. Tomlinson, and P. Peters, "An Alternative to Placing Children; Intensive and Extensive Therapy with 'Disengaged' Families," *Child Welfare* 60 (1981): 95-103.
8. Laird, *Ecological Approach.*.
9. Salvador Minuchin, "The Plight of the Poverty-Stricken Family in the United States," *Child Welfare* 49 (1970): 125.
10. Barbara F. Okun and Louis J. Rappaport, *Working with Families: An Introduction to Family Therapy* (North Scituate, Mass.: Duxbury Press, 1980), p. 68.
11. N. Epstein, D. Bishop, and S. Levin, "The McMaster Model of Family Functioning," *Journal of Marriage and Family Counselling* 4 (1978).
12. Salvador Minuchin, *Families and Family Therapy* (Cambridge, Mass.: Harvard University Press, 1974), p. 60.
13. E.A. Carter, and M. McGoldrick, *The Family Lifecycle: A Framework for Family Therapy* (New York: Gardner, 1980), 1.
14. Ibid., p. 14.
15. Ross V. Speck, and Carolyn L. Attneave, *Family Networks* (New York: Pantheon Books, 1973).
16. Carel B. Germain, ed., *Social Work Practice: People and Environments* (New York: Columbia University Press, 1979), p. 176.
17. Mary C. Howell, *Helping Ourselves: Families and the Human Network* (Boston: Beacon Press, 1975), p. 23.
18. Okun, and Rappaport, *Working with Families,* p. 79.
19. Alan S. Gurman and D.P. Kniskern, *Handbook of Family Therapy* (New York: Brunnermazel, 1981), p. 311.
20. Minuchin, *Families,* p. 54.
21. Germain, *Social Work Practice,* p. 174.
22. Gurman and Kniskern, *Handbook,* p. 747.
23. Ibid., p. 745.
24. Ibid., p. 748.
25. Ibid., p. 750.
26. M.D. Stanton, "Engaging Resistant Families," *Family Process* 20 (1981): 419.
27. Gurman and Kniskern, *Handbook,* p. 751.
28. Salvador Minuchin, "Conflict Resolution: Family Therapy," in *Changing Families,* edited by J. Holey (New York: Grune and Stretton, 1971).
29. M. Worby and E.M. Steinitz, "Telephone Intake: Engaging the Family in Therapy," *Social Casework* 57 (1976): 334.

14

DAY CARE IN CANADA

Alan R. Pence

INTRODUCTION

If the provision of day care services in Canada were viewed from a geological perspective, the description 'a zone of intense subterranean and surface activity' would be appropriate. Deep beneath the heated surface displays of articles in the popular press, organizational protests, and calls for "a return to. . ." or, conversely, "reform," immense sociological and economic 'plates' grind against one another demolishing old structures while new forms emerge to replace them. Central to this transformation is the extension of the day care issue from its traditional child welfare focus on the need-of-the-few, to the "Well Fare" of the majority of Canadian families with young children. This chapter will explore in overview both the enormous social pressures at work beneath the surface and the more readily observable surface phenomena which together are changing traditional understanding regarding the need for day care while creating a unique and challenging field within child welfare.

The most significant interface of plates underlying contemporary day care discussion is the replacement of one dominant family form with a multiplicity of forms. The relative decline of what has been termed the Victorian family model with its tightly prescribed roles of father — breadwinner, mother — homemaker, and child — angelic/dependent[1] is closely associated with changes in a second set of "plates" consisting of changes in the Canadian economy and labour force.

These two sets of immensely powerful plates—family and labour force—converge beneath and activate surface debates regarding the care of young children. Unfortunately, the bulk of discussion and debate on day care in Canada focuses on surface elements such as regulations, ministerial responsibility, and private versus public sponsorship without examining in sufficient detail the underlying deep-shifts in social structure that activate these and other surface phenomena. In addition, public debate all too often mistakenly identifies the provision of day-care services as a causal rather than as a resultant factor in the "equation":

(Family change) × (Labour force change) = New Societal Needs,
including Day Care

The remainder of this chapter will examine these three components of the day care equation noting how we have arrived at our current policies and practices; in addition, possible future courses of action will be presented.

FAMILY CHANGE

The relative position of the sexes in the social and political world, may certainly be looked upon as the result of organization. The greater physical strength of man enables him to occupy the foreground in the picture. He leaves the domestic scenes; he plunges into the turmoil and bustle of an active, selfish world. . . . Hence courage and boldness are his attributes. . . . Her inferior strength and sedentary habits confine her within the domestic circle; she is kept aloof from the bustle and storm of active life. . . .grace, modesty and loveliness are the charms which constitute her power.[2]

This and similar exhortations from the pulpit and press dominated the commentary on families during the mid to late nineteenth century. These images and expectations are present today in both subtle and subliminal, and as conscious, overt ways. So effective were the nineteenth- and twentieth-century promoters of the Victorian family model that today's society has great difficulty accepting the fact that other models have developed in other parts of the world and that alternative family models exist in growing numbers within our own society.

An example of our Victorian ethnocentrism can be seen in the author's annual survey of students' responses to the question: "Which of the following forms of care for children aged three to five is most common among various societies of the world?"

(a) Care by related adults;
(b) Care by mother;
(c) Care by non-related adults;
(d) Care by an older child;
(e) Institutional (Day Care Centres).

The vast majority of students select (a) and (b), reflective of the Victorian and related "Walton's Mountain" models of the family, popular in our society, while virtually none select the correct answer, (d) "Care by an older child."[3] In North America, where option (d) was common in the period preceding compulsory schooling, that practice could now result in apprehension for child neglect.

In light of the "world view" study noted above and similar historical perspectives, it is clear that there is no one, universal family form that exists across time or geographic space. The Victorian family model has predecessors in western civilization, as it has successors.

Canadian society is presently in a state of transition in family forms—the enormous socio-economic plates beneath us, relatively quiet for an extended period of time, are once again in motion. Some of these key transformations, particularly as they relate to the experiences of children in families, include: an increase in Canadian marriage, remarriage, and divorce rates; a decline in typical family size and a decline in fertility rates; a significant increase in the number of female-headed, single-parent families, and a major increase in the number of married women in the out-of-home, paid labour force.

Each of these areas of change affecting family form, functions, and composition will be briefly examined below. The final item, mothers in the labour force, will lead into a discussion of the second component in the day care question, changes in the economy/labour force.

Marriage and Divorce

Marriage in Canada is presently a popular institution. In the late 1970's approximately 65 per cent of the adult population were married as opposed to 50 per cent in the late 1920's, and 52 per cent at the turn of the century.[4] Divorce, however, has become even more popular. During the "Roaring Twenties" the divorce rate per 100,000 was less than 8 per annum compared to 280 per 100,000 today. A fairly stable divorce plateau was reached in the 1950's and early 1960's when rates stood at between 35 and 40 per 100,000. Subsequent to the new divorce act in 1968, the rate has soared: 148 in 1972; 235 in 1976;[5] and, as noted, almost 280 per 100,000

TABLE 1

MALE HEAD AND FEMALE HEAD OF LONE PARENT FAMILY
AS A PERCENTAGE OF ALL CANADIAN FAMILIES, 1961-1991

	Year	Male head	Female head
	1961	1.9	6.5
	1976	1.7	8.1
	1981	2.0	9.3
(projection)	1991	2.1	9.8

Source:
J. Perreault and M.V. George "Growth of Households and Families in Canada in the 1980's and 1990's." *Canadian Statistical Review,* October 1982, Figure 1.

in 1981.[6] One result of the steep increase in marriage, remarriage, and divorce rates is that a very large and growing percentage of the Canadian population has experienced being reared in more than one family unit. The implications of this change in the socialization experience of children is an area in need of additional research.

Family Size and Fertility Rates

While an increasing number of Canadians are getting married and divorced, the average household size is decreasing. It has declined from 3.7 in 1971 to 3.5 in 1976, and 3.3 in 1981. This decrease is in part reflective of families having a fewer number of children on average: 1.9 in 1961, 1.8 in 1971, and 1.4 in 1981. The number of families having four or more children has decreased from 16.4 per cent in 1961 to 8.7 per cent in 1981.[7]

Chart 1

LABOUR FORCE PARTICIPATION RATE OF MARRIED WOMEN
1951-1981

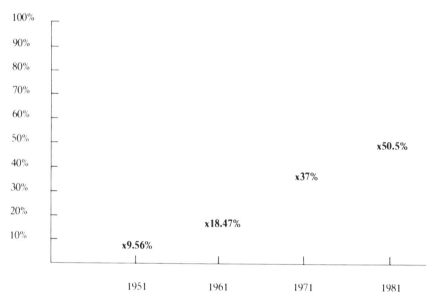

Source: 1951 and 1961: J.D. Allingham and The Australian National University, "The Demographic Background to Change in the Number and Composition of Female Wage-Earners in Canada, 1951 to 1961," Special Labour Force Studies, Series B, No. 1 (Ottawa: Dominion Bureau of Statistics, 1967), Table VI, p. 15. 1971: C. Swan, "Women in the Canadian Labour Force: The Present Reality," in *Women and the Canadian Labour Force,* ed. Naomi Hersom and Dorothy E. Smith (Supply and Services Canada: The Social Sciences and Humanities Research Council of Canada, 1982), Table 2, p. 60. 1981: Statistics Canada, Historical Labour Force Statistics, Cat. 71-201, 1981.

Single-Parent Families

A growing percentage of single-parent families are the result of divorce (as opposed to death of a spouse). The most conspicuous increase in single-parent families have been those that are female-head of household. While the number of male-headed families has remained fairly constant over the last twenty years (so much for Kramer vs. Kramer), the percentage of female-headed families has increased by almost 30 per cent as can be seen in Table 1.

Married Women in the Paid Labour Force

The phenomenon of married Canadian women entering the out-of-home, paid labour force is most dramatically presented graphically (chart 1). Women now account for approximately 41 per cent of the total Canadian labour force.[8] Within the ranks of women engaged in the paid labour force, the fastest growing component has been married women with children, and, more specifically, the younger the age of the child, the more rapid has been that group's increase in the labour force over the last ten years.

TABLE 2

PARTICIPATION RATES OF MARRIED WOMEN IN CANADA (HUSBANDS PRESENT), BY AGE GROUP AND PRESENCE OF CHILDREN IN THE HOME, 1971, 1976, 1981
(Percentage)

	Wives Aged 15-34	Wives Aged 35-44
Wives without Children Present		
1971	73.9	59.4
1976	77.5	65.5
1981	87.3	16.5
Absolute increase (1971-1981)	13.4	16.5
Relative increase	18.0	27.7
Wives with Children, all over six		
1971	46.0	44.2
1976	54.9	53.6
1981	65.2	63.4
Absolute increase (1971-1981)	19.2	19.2
Relative increase	41.7	43.4
Wives with Children, under six		
1971	28.0	25.4
1976	36.9	35.8
1981	47.8	46.3
Absolute increase (1971-1981)	19.8	20.9
Relative increase	70.0	82.2

Source: 1971, 1976: C. Swan. *Women in the Canadian Labour Force, The Present Reality,* Table 3.
1981: Statistics Canada, unpublished data.

The statistics evidence a change not only in family forms, such as the increase in blended and single-parent families, but in family members' functions as well. Women's role as family members has shifted a great deal from Reverend Dew's pronouncement that "she [be] kept aloof from the bustle and storm of active life." Increasingly, women are expected to participate in out-of-home labour force activity in much the same way as men. The implications of this transition extend far beyond the individual and the home to a necessary reconsideration of how society's and governments' obligations to families and children is altered by that transformation within families.

The next factor in the day care equation, changes in the labour force, considers the historical balance that has been struck between familial and governmental obligations to achieve the common good for society and how that balance has now been displaced.

CHANGES IN THE LABOUR FORCE

The creation of, and the ethos supporting, the Victorian family model is inextricably intertwined with the needs of the economy. In fact, the Victorian family can be viewed as the industrial model of the family. Through the creation of a dyadic spheres of influence conception of familial roles, industrial society was able to, in actuality, "[make] its cake and eat it too." That is, the family itself was successfully split into the two functions required by a developing, industrial society: production and consumption. The consumption function also performed an unpaid domestic and human services task of care for children, care for the elderly, and other caregiving tasks. This unpaid service both within and outside the family relieved the state of an expense that it might otherwise have been called on to provide. The cult of domesticity, subsumed within the ethos of the Victorian family model, contained within it a strong admonition to perform charitable and spiritually redeeming acts on behalf of others. This admonishment forms part of the genesis of various human service professions as can be discerned in Catharine Beecher's 1873 advice to every woman to obtain "appropriate scientific and practical training for her distinctive profession as housekeeper, nurse of infants and the sick, educator of childhood, trainer for servants and minister of charities."[9]

Interestingly enough, the assignment of these separate functions on a gender basis, that is male-producer and female-consumer/human service worker, was secondary in importance to the fact of their creation itself. That is, it was more important that the roles were created, than was the determination of who would perform them.

This particular division of responsibility, which is the hallmark of the Victorian family, served Canada efficiently for many decades. It allowed the country to make a transition from a rural, agriculturally oriented society based on a model of family self-sufficiency to an urban, industrial society with an interlocking system of production and consumption. This transition was accomplished at a relatively minimal cost to, and a minor role for, government. The woof of the new social fabric was an industrially based workforce receiving a "family wage,"[10] the warp was the Victorian family and its prescribed familial roles. The origin of many of today's government-supported social services can be found in this period of transition. Uniformly, those services were and are targeted at individuals who slipped through the new fabric of employability and family services; the birthmarks of their origin in a period of limited government can be seen in many social services today, day care included.

Fortunately (for the sake of this Victorian family/industrial economy model), the *man*power needs of the out-of-home, paid labour force have not, until recently, outstripped the supply of native-born and immigrant male labourers available to fill it. However, during times of war when the supply of men available for production was depleted and an alternative market for consumption existed, women's role in society took on a third dimension — becoming members of a reserve and totally fluid, back-up labour force.

The multi-functional role of women in Canadian (and all of North American) society has been greatly restricted by women's recent entry into the more uni-functional sphere of production. One result of this transition has been a greatly increased need for various human services and alternative methods for delivering them, particularly services for the very old and the very young. The reaction in some parts of the country to this transformation in women's responsibilities has been to "slay the messenger" rather than to analyse the message. Using the geological analogy, public and political discussion has focused on the surface issues, with loud protestations that "Women's place is in the home," while a necessary analysis of the "deep structure" shifts, required for the development of an enlightened social policy, have gone largely unperformed and when undertaken have been largely ignored.

There is a cruel irony in the fact that government services are entering a period of restraint and cut-back at the very moment that the need for certain services, such as day care, is expanding. There is further irony, and a basis for cynicism, that those groups calling the loudest for restraint, business and government, are the forces most responsible for the deep shifts in family form and function over the last thirty years. Without a demand for an increase in female labour, there could not have been an increase in the participation rate.

As has been noted earlier, married women's rate of work-force participation has increased an astonishing 500 per cent over the last thirty years. Several theories have been put forward to explain this transformation; they range from Marxist and other structuralist interpretations to more individualized, me-generation and women's lib explanations. Without going into a detailed discussion here of motivational cause and effect, it is apparent from a purely descriptive perspective that the following related events have occurred: one, an expansion of jobs in areas generally held by women; two, a continuation of a lower salary structure for women's work; and three, an increasing need within the family for female employment to *maintain* the family's standard of living. Each of these factors related to women's participation in the out-of-home, paid labour force will be briefly discussed.

The Jobs Women Hold

Although the labour force participation rate of all women has increased fourfold since the turn of the century, from 12 per cent to more than 50 per cent (and more than fifteenfold for married women), the number of occupations in which the majority of women work has not increased. "At the beginning of this century, three occupations — domestic service, teaching, and seamstressing accounted for over 60 per cent of all female employment. In 1979 over 60 per cent of all women worked at three jobs as well — clerical, sales and service."[11] The concept of "separate spheres" has followed women into the labour force creating female job ghettoes. Resistance to integration within the labour force has been difficult to overcome with over "two-thirds of all employed women in occupations where they represent a strong majority."[12] In her book *Last Hired, First Fired* (1978), Patricia Connelly argues that there exist in Canada two labour forces, male and female, and given this division, it can successfully be argued that women constitute an increasingly active reserve army of labour. The structural implications of this thesis would argue against the "free choice" interpretation of women's involvement in the labour force that is epitomized by "women's place is in the home" statements.

Women's Salaries

Job segregation in the labour force is accompanied by pay differentiation. In an analysis by Armstrong and Armstrong, industries ranked by female participation rate show a corresponding decrease in average employee earnings as female participation increases.[13] In 1981 the average salary for a female employee stood at 58 per cent of the average male working salary,[14] demonstrating *virtually no change* over the preceding twenty-year period. This relatively stable Canadian figure compares with the Biblical determination that "a male between 20 and 60 years shall be valued at 50 shekels. . . . If it is a female she shall be valued at 30 shekels," a 60 per cent differential.[15]

Families' Standard of Living

One of the surface debates heard in the press and Parliament is that womens's entry into the labour force has been a matter of free choice or, as some suggest, spiteful rebellion against a century of oppressed and unrecognized labour within the domestic sphere. As noted above, the expansion of certain parts of the labour force in concert with relatively cheaper wages provide a more compelling rationale for women's increasing share of the labour market. Another obvious reason for female employment, in addition to job availability, is economic need. According to the National Council of Welfare (1979), there would be a 51 per cent increase in the number of poor families in Canada if the wife in two-parent working families had no earnings.[16] Economic need as a primary determinate for maternal employment is obvious in the case of single-parent mothers; however, as can be seen below, the same motivation is apparent in the relative decline of female participation rates as family income (exclusive of the wife's earning) increases:

> families with incomes of less than $15,000 — 67 per cent
> families with incomes of $15-20,000   — 57 per cent
> families with incomes of + $25,000   — 46 per cent

The increasing need in Canada for wives and mothers to join the labour force[17] in an effort to maintain the family's economic position raises a concern that the concept of a "family wage" system that facilitated the Victorian family's viability has been significantly eroded. That erosion in a livable family income, operating in concert with the following pressures in our labour force — the creation of a two-army force of reserve labour; an increasing segmentation in the labour force composed of those with and those without upward mobility;[18] the possible reinforcement of that segmentation through the informatics revolution;[19] and the spectre of increasingly reactionary labour legislation such as that introduced by the Social Credit Party in British Columbia in 1983[20] — raises enormous concerns for the future financial security of the family and its ability to meet family members' basic needs for food and shelter. Remembering Maslow's Needs Hierarchy[21] and historical evidence as presented by Lloyd deMause (1974) leads to the question of the quality of family life where an ongoing quest for food and shelter predominates.

FAMILY CHANGE AND LABOUR FORCE CHANGE

It should be highlighted briefly that even though family change and labour force change have been treated separately in this essay, the two are intimately interrelated, and changes in one must affect the other. Shifts and changes in these plates have major implications from the micro-personal through to the macro-societal levels. Unfortunately, public discussion on these issues seldom delves beneath the surface phenomena and has attracted far too little of the research interest it deserves and which the society requires. Given the enormous changes that have taken place in Canadian society, families, and in the labour force over the last thirty years, and their effects on the ability of the family to provide care for their young children, what has been the response to a growing need for day care services? That question will be explored in the final component of the Day Care Equation:

THE PROVISION OF DAY-CARE SERVICES

We are witness to a society in transformation. No longer moored to one family form, no longer divided into separate spheres of influence, what has been our societal-governmental response to the resulting need for child caring services? The answer can be seen in the following figures.

TABLE 3

NUMBER OF CHILDREN NEEDING DAY CARE SERVICES,
NUMBER OF LICENSED SPACES, AND PERCENTAGE IN LICENSED SPACES
1973-1982

Year	Number preschool children (3-5) with working mothers	Number spaces in licensed or registered day care	Percent of preschool enrolled in registered facilities
1973	304,000 (3-5)	21,736 (3-5)	7.15
1976	345,000 (3-5)	63,501 (3-5)	18.38
1979	504,000 (2-6)	77.929 (2-6)	15.46
1982	664,000 (2-6)	95,350 (2-6)	14.36

Source:
National Daycare Information Office. Status of Day Care in Canada, 1973-1982. Ottawa: Canada Health and Welfare.

It can be seen that after an initially promising start in governmental response towards meeting the changing care giving needs, that momentum was lost by 1982 when more than 85 per cent of all Canadian preschool children between the ages of two and six were cared for in unregulated care giving facilities.[22] In short, governmental response (quite uniformly across the provinces) is that *families and not government are responsible* for the care of their preschool-aged children despite changes in family structure and changes in work-force composition. All provincial day care licensing and funding regulations reflect their origins in the Victorian family/limited government milieu. The result has been the enormous expansion of an unregulated, cottage industry of poorly paid child-caregivers about whose service little is known. Only two Canadian studies, both based in Ontario, have attempted to examine this largely invisible phenomenon, and both would concur in the following recommendation from the Guelph study: "That federal, provincial and municipal governments recognize and respond to parents' needs for access to a variety of quality child care arrangements for young children."[23] Dr. Laura Johnson, director of the Toronto study, went further on the subject describing the current situation as "an epidemic of child neglect."[24] A third study hopes to shed additional light on the phenomena from a British Columbia perspective.[25]

The provision of day care services in Canada is predicated on a Victorian family model in a post-Victorian society. The Victorian model restricts state services to those families who slip through the Victorian family/industrial economy social fabric (described earlier and who are thereby at risk to themselves, their children or to society at large). It is in some ways ironic that this welfare-related, preventive role for day care, the efficacy of which has long been held in question and debated, should only now, at the point of its eclipse by day care as a normative service, yield substantial data supporting its long-term effectiveness. In longitudinal studies at the Ypsilanti Perry Preschool Project, research indicates that by the age nineteen individuals "who attended a high quality preschool program made greater gains in education, employment and social responsibility than similar young adults who did not attend preschool."

In Education. Fewer classified as mentally retarded (15 per cent vs. 35 per cent); more completed high school (67 per cent vs. 49 per cent); more attended college or job training (38 per cent vs. 21 per cent).

In Employment. More support themselves by their own or their spouses' earnings (45 per cent vs. 25 per cent).

In Social Responsibility. Fewer were arrested (31 per cent vs. 51 per cent); lower birth rate (64 vs. 117 per 100 women); fewer on public assistance (18 per cent vs. 32 per cent).[26]

Utilizing a meta-analysis approach to findings across many studies similar preliminary results to the Perry Preschool Project emerge: children make immediate gains in basic cognitive competence, school readiness, and achievement; Head Start improves language development, especially for bilingual and handicapped children; the children who appear to benefit the most from Head Start are the most needy (children from mothers who had a grade ten education or less; children of single-parent families; and children with low initial I.Q. at the beginning of Head Start).[27]

These relatively recent findings, demonstrating the effectiveness of early intervention, group care programmes for various types of at risk children, have little import on the existing day care delivery system in Canada. Additional elements of that system will be discussed, as well as recent reactions to the system by newly established advocacy groups, in the following pages.

Funding for day care services in Canada is generated from both private and public courses, generally in the form of user fees. Public revenues are provided on a provincial-federal, 50-50 sharing formula and restricted to

"Canadians who require social services to prevent, overcome or alleviate the causes and effects of poverty or child neglect."[28] This restriction, a vestige of the Victorian family definition of government responsibility, is generally tied to an income eligibility fee scale which biases funding toward single-parent families; for example, in British Columbia single parents constitute approximately 12 per cent of the family population, yet public dollars for day care serve an estimated 70 per cent or more single parents.[29] At a time when over 50 per cent of all Canadian mothers of preschool children are in the labour force (and the percentage increases annually), many question if state support for day care services should continue to be restricted to those families who are economically in need when the vast majority of Canadian children are cared for in governmentally unregulated care-giving sites.

With an increasing number of parents in need of day care services, the growing concern regarding the current *caveat emptor* (buyer beware) approach to regulating the majority of care and the recognition that there are positive alternatives to exclusive maternal care, makes the call for day care reform grow stronger. At the Second National Conference for Day Care, co-sponsored by Health and Welfare Canada and the Canadian Council on Social Development held in Winnipeg, September, 1982, keynote speaker Judy Erola (minister responsible for the Status of Women) called for day care to be reorganized as a public utility, a universal service for all families requesting care.[30]

That same conference saw, for the first time in Canada, broad-based coalitions composed of women's groups, labour organizations, parent advocates, and more traditional early childhood associations come together to discuss current inadequacies in the system. Using the key words "affordability and accessibility," a comprehensive system of publicly subsidized, alternative care was envisioned by Day Care Action Coalitions from across the country. Such a universal system would ensure that any infant, preschooler, or after-school aged child requiring care would be able to receive it.

The cost of such a universal system, as with public education in general, would be very great. A 1981 task force of the British Columbia Day Care Action Coalition projected a figure of $411,158,000.00 required to provide care for 50 per cent of the B.C. population of preschool aged children (0-5 years).[31] This figure is approximately 24 times greater than the 1980-81 B.C. expenditure for day care subsidies ($16,903,220.00).[32] Such an increase would raise the day care budget into the realm of the budget figures for B.C. Transportation and Communication ($581 million) and Courts and Policing ($285 million).[33] The coalition study paper asks: "could anyone argue convincingly that our children are not at least as valuable a resource as highways or the court system?" Indeed, that argument cannot be made, but more to the point, the question of who will bear the primary financial responsibility for the care of young children — the state or parents — is a point of contention, and the decision to date reflects a belief that parents will continue to bear the economic responsibility for their children's care.

The issue of governmental versus parental responsibility for the care of children of working parents remains central to the Canadian day care dilemma. Unfortunately, the polarization of the issue itself contributes to its lack of progress. However, this adversarial all or nothing approach to increased services for day care children appears to have been avoided to some degree in various European countries where a *services and benefits* approach has evolved over the last twenty to thirty years. In many of these countries, the issue of state versus parental versus employer responsibility is diffused and distributed in a way too seldom discussed in Canada. For instance, in Spain "any worker who is directly responsible for the care of a child under the age of six is entitled to a reduction of not less than one-third and not more than one-half of their working day." In France, West Germany, Italy, Spain and Austria, provision for nursing breaks for nursing mothers is found in the legislation.[34] And in Sweden either parent is eligible for nine months of parental leave at 90 per cent of usual salary to care for their newborn.[35] In addition to these and other benefits not currently available in Canada, varying day care services from infant through after-school care have been created. A partial listing of these services and benefits as enumerated in Kahn and Kammerman (1981) is contained in Table 4.

TABLE 4

CHILD CARE BENEFIT-SERVICE PACKAGE (MAJOR COMPONENTS) BY COUNTRY

	Hungary	*France*	*Sweden*
1. Benefits			
A. CASH			
Income replacement	Maternity leave to care for an ill child at home	Maternity leave	Parental leave to care for an ill child at home
Income substitution	Child care allowance	—	—
Income supplementation	Family allowance, housing allowance, child health services	Family allowance, housing allowance, child health services, family allowance supplement, single parent allowance, family-based tax system	Child allowance, housing allowance, child health services, tax allowances for all dependents

TABLE 4 *(continued)*

CHILD CARE BENEFIT-SERVICE PACKAGE (MAJOR COMPONENTS) BY COUNTRY

	Hungary	France	Sweden
B. EMPLOYMENT			
Right to leave	Maternity leave	Maternity leave	Parental (9 months) leave
Work and job security	(20 weeks) Child care up to child's third birthday	(16 weeks) Parental education 2 years	Unpaid 18 months; 6 hour day up to child's 8th birthday
2. *Services* (1975)			
Percentage of children 0-3 in out of home care	12% mainly 1½-3 years old	31%	23%
Major care mode	Centre care (almost completely)	Coequal in policy but family day care predominates	Policy favours centre care but present reality is family day care primarily

Source: Sheila B. Kamerman and Alfred J. Kahn, *Child Care, Family Benefits, and Working Parents* (New York: Columbia University Press, 1981), p. 225.

The benefits and services structures that have evolved in these various western countries demonstrate their governments' awareness of the underlying economic and social realignments that have been discussed in this essay and which have yet to be discovered in Canada. These creative responses, which share the caring among parents, industry, and government and which enhance parents' options as primary caretakers should serve as experimental models that we in Canada can observe and consider as we move from our current stance of inappropriate reaction and indifference to one of pro-active planning for our children and our country's future.

SUMMARY AND A LOOK TO THE FUTURE

This essay has identified change in family forms and change in the economy/labour force requirements as the principal plates that are in motion deep within our social structure and which activate our surface debates and contemporary need for day care services. The current provision of day care in Canada evolved during a period of social services development when the Victorian family was numerically and ethically powerful. This milieu enforced a major role for families in the provision of many human services, including the day care of preschool aged children, and a catchment role for government designed to assist/support those who had slipped through the social fabric of employment and family. Current legislation, funding, and regulations regarding the provision of day care services are uniformly, across the various provinces, based on this model.

This model is the reality of legislation; however, it is not the reality of society. The widening chasm between the existing legislation and social need has brought together an increasingly vocal coalition of parents, day care workers, women's groups and labour organizations. At the second, decadal Conference on Day Care in Canada held in 1982, the major focus of discussion was on a new role for governments in providing accessible, affordable, quality day care for those parents requiring it. Using the provision of public schooling as an example, many of the provincial coalitions are calling for a universally available, publicly funded day care system. The cost of such a system, as with public education in general, would be vers great.

Certain European countries, faced with the need for full female employment at an earlier period in their histories, have evolved various services *and* benefits structure that can either assist parents in the care of their own children or provide alternative care-giving arrangements for children as young as six weeks of age. It would appear that a services and benefits structure would allow the greatest range of options for families, with greater flexibility for the cost of care to be shared by parent, employer, and government.

Despite protestations the forces beneath us will not be reversed to recreate Canada at the turn of the century. Our options at this time appear to be the three discussed in this chapter: (a) continue to provide Victorian services in a post-Victorian era; (b) create a universal preschool care system; (c) reconsider the triangular relationship of Parenting — Labour Force Participation — Government, and utilizing cost and social benefit considerations, create a new services and benefits structure in Canada. Option (a) is our present course of action—its implications appear severe in terms of parental stress and negative effects on child development. Option (b) is presently the most discussed alternative — its implications are primarily financial. We must ask if the tide of public and governmental opinion has now turned against the creation of massive, publicly funded, social service projects and an institutional approach to the care of children. Option (c) has generated little discussion to date — its implications in terms of revealing governmental and business manipulation of the labour force and disregard for child and family welfare is potentially damaging to them both. At the same time, a reconsideration of the importance of parenting, the relationship of parents to the labour force, and the role of government in fostering a just and humane society is long overdue in Canada. This option requires a far-reaching and interdisciplinary examination of the shifting, triangular relationship of family/government/labour force with an emphasis on a creative redefinition of the role(s) each must play in fostering the positive development of Canada's children.

The essence of the day care dilemma in Canada is that as a result of extremely powerful shifts in the ways in which we constitute ourselves in families and in which we perceive our relationship to and participation in the out-of-home labour force, a vacuum has developed where the role of child care giver once existed. The question of who could or should fill this vacuum has yet to be adequately addressed. The question cannot be understood or dealt with on its current surface level, we must become aware of the subsocial dynamics, the plates beneath, that have an impact on our daily lives and on the lives of our children.

NOTES

I would like to acknowledge the assistance of Alvina Harrison in the preparation of certain parts of this manuscript.

1. Charles Strickland, "Day Care and Public Policy: An Historical Perspective," paper, Department of History, Emory University, Atlanta; Jessi Bernard, *The Future of Motherhood* (New York: Penguin, 1974).
2. Thomas R. Dew, "Dissertation," in *Up from the Pedestal,* edited by Aileen S. Kraditor (New York: New York Times Book Co., 1968), pp. 45-46.
3. Thomas S. Weisner and Ronald Gallimore, "My Brother's Keeper: Child and Sibling Caretaking," *Current Anthropology* 13 (1977): p. 170.
4. Statistics Canada, *Canada's Families* (Ottawa: Supply and Services, 1979), p. 3.
5. Statistics Canada, *Divorce: Law and the Family in Canada* (Ottawa: Supply and Services, 1983), pp. 59-61.
6. Statistics Canada, *Marriages and Divorces,* Vol. 2 (Ottawa: Supply and Services, 1981), Cat. no. 84-205, chart 5, p. xii.
7. Statistics Canada, *Canada's Families,* p. 4; 1981 Census of Canada (Ottawa: Supply and Services, 1981), Cat. no. 92-905, Tables 1 and 2.
8. Statistics Canada, *Canada Update from the 1981 Census* (Ottawa: Supply and Services, 1983), vol. 1, no. 5.
9. Sheila M. Rothman, *Woman's Proper Place* (New York: Basic Books, 1978), p. 22, quoting Catharine E. Beecher, "On the Needs and Claims of Women Teachers," First Women's Congress of Association for Advancement of Women, 1873, in *Letters and Papers,* p. 159.
10. Martha MacDonald, "Implications for Understanding Women in the Labour Force of Labour Market Segmentation Analysis," in *Women and the Canadian Labour Force,* edited by Naomi Hersom and Dorothy E. Smith (Ottawa: Supply and Services Canada, Social Sciences and Humanities Research Council of Canada, 1982).
11. Carole Swan, "Women in the Canadian Labour Force: The Present Reality," in *Women and the Canadian Labour Force,* ed. Naomi Hersom and Dorothy E. Smith (Ottawa: Supply and Services Canada, The Social Sciences and Humanities Research Council of Canada, 1982), p. 60.
12. Ibid., p. 60.
13. Pat Armstrong and Hugh Armstrong, *The Double Ghetto: Canadian Women and Their Segregated Work* (Toronto: McClelland and Stewart, 1978), Table 4, p. 28.
14. Swan, pp. 31-103.
15. Swan, p. 84, quoting Ruth Blumrosen, "Wage Discrimination, Job Segregation and Title

VII of the Civil Rights Act of 1964," *University of Michigan Journal of Law Reform* 12 (1979): 425.

16. National Council of Welfare. *Report on Women and Poverty,* (Ottawa: The Council, 1979), p. 20.
17. Swan, p. 54.
18. MacDonald, pp. 165-208.
19. Heather Menzies, *Information Case Studies* (Supplementary Material to "Women and the Chip"), Labour Market Development Task Force Technical Studies Series, no. 23 (Ottawa: Supply and Services, 1981).
20. "A Shock Wave of Change," Victoria *Times Colonist,* 8 July 1983, p. 1.
21. Abraham Maslow, *Motivation and Personality,* 2nd ed. (New York: Harper and Row, 1970), p. 22.
22. The Status of Day Care in Canada report for 1983 performed a more complex differentiation of children in need of care by type of parent occupation (full time/part time, student status, and so forth). This analysis yielded children-in-unregulated-care perce..t-ages ranging from approximately 65 per cent up to 84 per cent depending on parent classification.
23. Donna Lero, *Factors Influencing Parents' Preferences for, and Use of Alternative Child Care Arrangements for Pre-School-Age Children* (Ottawa: Health and Welfare Canada, 1983), p. 175.
24. Laura C. Johnson and Janice Dineen, *The Kin Trade — The Day Care Crisis in Canada* (Toronto: McGraw-Hill Ryerson, 1981).
25. Alan Pence and Hillel Goelman, "Day Care in Canada: Developing an Ecological Perspective," A research proposal, funded by The Social Sciences and Humanities Research Council of Canada, 1983.
26. David P. Weikart, "Basic Findings: The Perry Preschool Project in Support of Early Childhood Education." Ypsilanti: High Scope Educational Research Foundation, 1984.
27. Raymond C. Collins, "Head Start: An Update on Program Effects," *Newsletter of the Society for Research in Child Development,* Summer, 1983.
28. Susan Shaw, *Better Day Care for Canadians: Options for Parents and Children* (Ottawa: Canadian Advisory Council on the Status of Women, 1982), p. 11.
29. Private conversation with a Ministry of Human Resources official, Government of British Columbia, Victoria, B.C., September 1983.
30. "Day Care 'Highly Inadequate,' " *Globe and Mail,* 24 September 1982, p. 10.
31. British Columbia Daycare Action Coalition, *Report of the Ministerial Task Force,* 5 November 1981, p. 7.
32. British Columbia, Ministry of Human Resources *Annual Reports, 1980-81.* p. 27.
33. British Columbia Day Care Action Coalition, *Report,* p. 7.
34. Rosemary Gallagher and Donna Noel, *An International Perspective on Parental Benefits,* Victoria Caucus of the National Association of Women and the Law, 1983, pp. 64, 66.
35. Sheila B. Kamerman and Alfred J. Kahn, *Child Care, Family Benefits, and Working Parents* (New York: Columbia University Press, 1981), p. 225.

15

THE CHILD WELFARE PROGRAMME
OF THE SPALLUMCHEEN INDIAN BAND
IN BRITISH COLUMBIA

John A. MacDonald

INTRODUCTION

The plight of Native Indian children and youth in Canada has been a subject of grave public concern for the past two decades. During this time public attention has been focused on high rates of infant mortality, suicide rates among native teenagers six times the national average, a secondary school drop-out rate of 80 per cent, and widespread family breakdown contributing to disproportionate admissions of Indian children to the care of provincial child protection agencies.[1]

Readers of this volume will probably be familiar with the shocking rates of child separation experienced by Indian families in British Columbia since the early 1960's. Throughout most of this period native children have comprised between 35 and 40 per cent of the children in the care of the B.C. superintendent of child welfare.[2] A smaller but still significant number of Indian children have experienced substitute care in residential schools or with relatives and friends because of family problems.[3]

The causes of the widespread breakdown in Indian family life are complex, but they seem principally rooted in a lengthy Indian experience of poverty, cultural deprivation, and enforced dependency. I believe that the family problems of native Indians have been exacerbated by the failure of provincial child welfare policies and programmes to engage fully the potential capacity of Indian people to address family problems within their own communities.

In recent years federal and provincial authorities have sought by various means to increase participation by native Indians in the resolution of child welfare problems. One model which reflects a high degree of native self-determination is the child welfare programme of the British Columbia Spallumcheen Band. This chapter examines the history of the programme, its principal features, and its future prospects.

THE CHILD WELFARE EXPERIENCE OF THE SPALLUMCHEEN BAND DURING THE 1970'S

The Spallumcheen Indian Band is located on a reserve which straddles both sides of the Shuswap River near Enderby at the northern end of B.C.'s Okanagan Valley. The band is relatively small in numbers, consisting of approximately four hundred members, over a hundred of whom reside off the reserve, principally in adjoining communities.

Most Canadians look back on the decade of the 1970's with some nostalgia as a time of prosperity and promise when young people could look forward to a steady improvement in lifestyle and material attainment. For most B.C. Indian bands, this same period was one of growing awareness of their disadvantaged status in Canadian society and increasing concern to prevent the erosion of their culture amid pervading pressures from the outside society. The Spallumcheen Band shared with other B.C. bands high rates of unemployment and welfare dependency among its members. It also experienced family discord and social disruption occasioned by alcoholism and petty crime. This decade was especially traumatic for the band's families since eighty children were apprehended and admitted to the care of the B.C. Superintendent of Child Welfare.[4]

To appreciate fully the shocked reaction of band leaders and members at the loss of their children, it is important to recognize several features of provincial child welfare policy. First, although provincial child protection services had been extended to Indian reserves since the mid-1950's, they did not include preventive family counselling services as in the case of non-Indian families. The typical pattern was for non-Indian social workers to apprehend children in severe crisis situations and seek court-ordered committals to care, followed by placement in substitute homes off the reserve. Second, given the absence of on-going services for Indians on reserves to facilitate family re-unification, social workers tended to favour adoption or long-term foster care in planning for the children who had been separated from their parents. Thus children apprehended from families of the Spallumcheen band, as in the case of other Indian children, often experienced much longer periods of foster care in comparison to non-Indian children in need of protection.[5]

If the widespread apprehensions of the children of Spallumcheen Band members caused trauma and heartache to the families concerned, they also posed a potential threat to the survival of the band itself. At a time of rising political consciousness among Indians, their rights to a better future in

Canadian society seem jeopardized by the loss of their children to what were perceived as alien outside agents of assimilation. And while many Indian Bands gave priority in their political activities to negotiating improved economic arrangements for their people, the Spallumcheen Band chose to combine such initiatives with a vigorous attempt to reclaim control over the decisions affecting the well-being of their children.

Late in 1978 the band hired Earl Shipmaker, a non-Indian social worker, to assist band members to develop child-care resources on the reserve. This resulted in increased utilization of the homes of band members for voluntary placement of children requiring short- or long-term care. Shipmaker also developed close working relationships with social workers from the district offices of the provincial Ministry of Human Resources in an effort to avoid, where possible, the off-reserve placement of band children. However, these beginning attempts to address child welfare problems at the band level proved insufficient to tap the full caring potential of band members. In the last analysis, the most critical decisions continued to be handled by staff of the Ministry of Human Resources. Moreover, by the beginning of 1980, approximately twenty-five children of the band remained in the care of the ministry in off-reserve foster homes.

1980—A YEAR OF POLITICAL ACTION

In the early spring of 1980, the Spallumcheen Band began a series of decisive steps aimed at achieving band control over child welfare decision-making. Following intensive consultation with the staff and legal advisers of the B.C. Union of Indian Chiefs, the band council enacted a by-law entitled "A By-law for the Care of our Indian Children," which assigned to the band exclusive jurisdiction over any custody proceeding involving a band child, whether located on or off the reserve. When the by-law was forwarded to Ottawa for scrutiny by John Munro, the minister of Indian affairs, he was at first disposed to disallow it, based on legal advice that the by-law was probably unconstitutional. Subsequently, however, following intensive lobbying and minor changes in content, the by-law was again submitted to the minister, who this time chose not to exercise his powers of disallowance. Thus, the by-law came into effect 3 June 1980.

With this level of tacit, although far from enthusiastic support from the federal government, the band proceeded during the early fall of 1980 to mount a political campaign to persuade the provincial Ministry of Human Resources to respect the authority of the band as conferred in the by-law. This culminated in a well-publicized protest march by some six hundred Indian men, women, and children, which ended in a demonstration in front of the minister's home in a fashionable district of Vancouver. The following day, after an extended discussion between Chief Wayne Christian and

Grace McCarthy, Minister of Human Resources, a short hand-written agreement was concluded. The agreement reads as follows:

> The Minister of Human Resources agrees to respect the authority of the Spallumcheen Band Council to assume responsibility and control over their children. The Minister of Human Resources agrees to the desirability of returning Indian children of the Spallumcheen Band presently in the care of the Minister. . .to the authority of the Spallumcheen Band and both parties agree to work out an appropriate plan in the best interests of each child presently in care, assuming that the Spallumcheen Band will develop necessary resources in negotiation with the federal government.

During the next nine months, Chief Christian and other employees of the band moved expeditiously to consolidate a Band Child Welfare Programme within the mandate provided by the new by-law and the accord that had been reached with the Minister of Human Resources. On 1 April 1981, a formal agreement was signed between the band and regional officials of the Indian Affairs Branch, whereby the branch undertook to contribute $263,000 to the band's child welfare programme for the 1981-82 fiscal year.[6] The agreement was for a five-year period terminating in 1986, with the amounts of federal contributions to be negotiated annually. The band agreed to provide regional officials of the Indian Affairs Branch with annual audited financial statements as well as monthly reports on programme activities.

With these agreements in place, the band social worker met in May of 1981 with the Minister of Human Resources and worked out arrangements for transferring the care and supervision of band children then in the care of the Ministry of Human Resources to the Spallumcheen Band. This entailed the formulation of a written care plan for each child signed by the band social worker, the ministry social worker, the foster parents, and in some cases the natural parents and children. These individual care plans were subsequently approved by the band council and incorporated in case records for each child. This process was completed within three months, entailing for the most part no transfer of children from their foster homes but rather the assumption of on-going supervision of existing foster care arrangements by the band social worker. Also significant from a legal perspective was the fact that the written care plans, while transferring supervision of the children to the band, contained a statement that the B.C. superintendent of child welfare would continue to serve as legal guardian of each child. It was therefore evident that the provincial child welfare authorities were not prepared to acknowledge legally the jurisdictional claims of the band's Child Welfare by-law.[7]

THE SPALLUMCHEEN BAND CHILD WELFARE BY-LAW

The preamble to the by-law stresses the right of Native Indians to self-determination and emphasizes the right of the Spallumcheen Band to care for its children, who are considered the band's most vital resource in ensuring its integrity and future. The preamble also voices concern that in the past a high percentage of Indian families experienced breakdown as a result of the often unwarranted removal from the reserve of Indian children by non-band agencies, thereby hurting "our children emotionally," fracturing "the strength of our community," and "contributing to social break-down and disorder within our reserve" (by-law preamble).

The main body of the by-law assigns to the band exclusive jurisdiction over any custody proceeding involving a child (defined as an unmarried person under age twenty-one who is a member of the band, regardless of residence). For purposes of child protection, the chief and band council or any persons authorized by them are empowered to apprehend an Indian child and bring the child before a meeting of the chief and band council within seven days in the following circumstances:

(a) when a parent, extended family member or Indian guardian asks the Band to care for a child;

(b) when the child is in a condition of abuse or neglect endangering his/her health or well-being;

(c) when the child is abandoned;

(d) when the child is deprived of necessary care because of death, imprisonment, or disability of his parents. (Section 7.)

Where a child has been apprehended, the chief and band council are authorized to reach a decision on placement, guided by Indian customs and preferences. In making this decision they are required to consider the wishes of the child whenever he is old enough to appreciate his situation. When the child cannot be immediately returned to his family, placement is to be made according to the following order of preference:

(a) with a parent (presumably a parent not exercising custody at apprehension);

(b) with a member of the extended family living on the reserve;

(c) with a member of the extended family living on another reserve;

(d) with a member of the extended family living off the reserve;

(e) with an Indian living on a reserve;

(f) with an Indian living off a reserve;

(g) as a last resort — with a non-Indian living off the reserve. (Section 10.)

However, in reaching placement decisions, the chief and band council are required to give paramount consideration to the best interests of the individual child.

Further sections of the by-law authorize a general band meeting to review a decision on placement at the request of any band member, including the child's parent. Review decisions are to be made by majority vote of those attending in accordance with Indian customs and the above order of preferences. Upon review, the decision of the general meeting may be to return the child to his parent(s) or to place him in another home (Sections 12, 15, 18, 19, and 23).

The Spallumcheen Child Welfare By-Law Compared to Conventional Child Welfare Legislation

This by-law differs in a number of ways from conventional child protection statutes. Significantly, it assigns apprehending, fact-finding, and disposition powers to the same persons, namely the chief and members of the band council. These persons therefore are given both protective intervention and judicial functions. Moreover, both placement and review decisions are made not in the context of a formal judicial hearing, but rather by discussion at a band council or general band meeting, followed by a vote of those present. An obvious danger exists that decisions affecting the future of children could be made without the safeguards of an impartial judicial hearing. However, Indian leaders tend to discount this potential problem, pointing to the protracted pattern of careful and consensual decision-making that is typical at band council meetings. Moreover, to date this has not surfaced as a problem in the application of the Spallumcheen by-law, since apprehension has been necessary only on four occasions during its first three years of operation, and the parents of the children apprehended have subsequently supported the placement decisions of the band council. In all other cases, children admitted to the care of the band since enactment of the by-law have been admitted at the request of their parent or parents.

The Spallumcheen Child Welfare By-law can also be distinguished from regular child welfare statutes in the priority assigned to Native Indian foster care placements, commencing with those on the home reserve. Here the band is concerned equally with the well-being of its children and its future as a collective Indian community. Whether in these circumstances the welfare of an Indian child could become subordinated to the collective concerns for future band strength and continuity would seem to depend largely on the resources made available for child-care on the reserve. Assuming the availability of such resources, the priority assigned in the by-law to native Indian placements goes a considerable way towards ensuring that most children admitted to care will have their personal needs met while retaining an affinity with the traditions and culture of the Spallumcheen Band.

Finally the Spallumcheen By-law can be contrasted with many provincial child protection statutes in Canada since it requires that the band consider the wishes of the child, whenever he is old enough to appreciate his situation, prior to making a decision as to custodial or living arrangements (Section 10(i)). This may be contrasted with the B.C. Family and Child Service Act, also enacted in 1980, which permits a judge of the Provincial Family Court to make a disposition in a child protection case without seeing the child or being apprised of his wishes.[8]

SOME KEY FEATURES OF THE SPALLUMCHEEN BAND
CHILD WELFARE PROGRAMME

In our society child welfare services have tended to be regarded as residual services which become activated to sustain families in crisis or to provide substitute care for children whose health and well-being would be in jeopardy if they were permitted to remain in their homes. Given this residual mandate, child welfare services have evolved separately from other human services such as education, recreation, and health services. A key feature of the Spallumcheen Band child welfare programme is seen in the degree to which traditional child welfare functions are integrated with other services aimed at promoting the collective well-being of the community, its families, and its children.

Within the mandate of the child welfare by-law and under the general guidance of the chief and band council, the programme employs a director of child and youth services who is responsible for the co-ordination and supervision of the work of direct service staff members. These include a family support worker, who is responsible for protective services and foster care services to the children admitted to the care of the band. The child welfare staff also includes a preventive youth counsellor, who provides individual and group counselling services to school-age children, especially those experiencing difficulty in school or encountering stressful family situations. This counsellor works in close liaison with teachers in the local elementary and secondary schools. Since 1983 the band has also employed a child care worker to provide special therapeutic services to children with severe speech and hearing problems and related learning, behavioural, or emotional problems.

While the foregoing services are both preventive and remedial, the band also employs within its child welfare programme a group recreation worker whose functions include the organization of special cultural and recreational activities for older teenagers designed to foster healthy leisure-time pursuits and identification with the collective activities and traditions of the band.

Since commencement of the programme four years ago the band has been able to provide foster home or group home placements on the reserve for all children admitted to care. A group home capable of serving up to eight children in the age range of ten to fourteen years was opened in August 1982. This resource provides full-time employment for two house parents and part-time employment for one relief worker. Child welfare staff members work closely with a registered nurse who, in addition to providing basic nursing care and referral services for band members, offers guidance to band members in family planning and home-making skills. Child welfare staff also work in close liaison with the band's alcohol counsellor.

Although the Spallumcheen Band child welfare programme has much in common with progressive child welfare programmes in other settings, the observer is struck by the level of commitment and energy displayed by the staff members, most of whom are women. They also have a high degree of pride in the work accomplished over the past few years, especially in the area of preventive programming. In addition, the concern for the families of the band extends beyond the boundaries of the reserve to families in crisis elsewhere in the province. Thus an important service rendered by the band consists of offering placement resources for the temporary or long-term care of band children apprehended in off-reserve communities.

Any discussion of the Spallumcheen programme would be incomplete without acknowledgement of the leadership and organizational skills contributed by Chief Wayne Christian. As a result of his efforts, the band has been able to negotiate annual renewals of the funding arrangements with the federal government which have permitted consolidation and expansion of the programme. Chief Christian has also been responsible for negotiating loans with the Central Mortgage and Housing Corporation to enlarge and modernize the housing stock on the reserve in recent years. This, in turn, has enabled the band to develop necessary on-reserve placement resources for children. In addition, Chief Christian has facilitated an extensive programme of in-service training for staff and band members, focused both on practical service skills and cultural awareness. Finally, he has maintained positive contacts with social work professionals throughout the province, thereby contributing to continuing professional support for the band's programme.

The Spallumcheen child welfare programme is not without problems. Alcohol abuse and unplanned pregnancies among teenage band members continue to place many children at risk. Moreover, young persons returning to reside on the reserve following lengthy periods in foster care often display serious behaviour problems which are predictive of future instability in family relationships. The band has also experienced difficulty in attracting and retaining professionally qualified people to serve as programme director. Perhaps the most serious problem, however, stems from the uncertain future of the programme in light of its vulnerability to legal attack on constitutional grounds and the current orientation of federal policy towards tripartite arrangements in the field of Indian child welfare.

LEGAL VULNERABILITY OF THE SPALLUMCHEEN PROGRAMME
AND THE ALTERNATIVE TRIPARTITE MODEL

The Minister of Indian Affairs chose in 1980 not to exercise his authority to disallow the Spallumcheen Band by-law in spite of advice that it lacked constitutional validity. This advice was probably based on the absence of clear authority in Section 81 of the Indian Act for Indian bands to legislate in the field of child protection. This being the case, any such by-law runs the risk, in the event of a court challenge, of being declared unconstitutional as infringing on the general legislative powers of the province in this field.[9] A clear indication that the federal government has adopted this view of the law is seen in a policy statement issued by the Department of Indian and Northern Affairs on 1 May 1982,[10] part of which reads:

> Indian people living on or apart from reserves are governed by provincial and territorial legislation pertaining to the protection and care of children. (p. 8)
>
> Section 91(24) of the British North America Act empowers Canada to enact legislation in respect of Indians and Indian lands. Canada has not exercised this discretionary power in respect of legislation to govern the protection and care of Indian children and, accordingly, Section 88 of the Indian Act makes Indian people residing on or apart from reserves subject to provincial child welfare laws. (pp. 11-12)

This interpretation of the law was given reinforcement in practice in October 1982 when the Minister of Indian and Northern Affairs disallowed a child welfare by-law of a small Indian band located in the East Kootenay area of B.C. The by-law in question was almost an exact copy of the one establishing the Spallumcheen child welfare programme.[11] Although it is clearly within the powers of the federal government to amend the Indian Act to grant Indian bands legal authority to enact child welfare by-laws, it appears that the federal authorities have decided to pursue a different course of action. Thus, the same policy statement which endorsed provincial legislative jurisdiction in child welfare gave official support for the negotiation of tri-partite agreements between Indian child welfare organizations, the federal Indian affairs ministry, and provincial child welfare authorities for the delivery of child welfare services to native families by Indian child care agencies in designated areas.[12] The first such agreement came into effect on 1 February 1982, when the federal and Manitoba governments and the Four Nations' Confederacy announced the signing of an agreement for the delegation to the confederacy of major responsibilities for the development and delivery of child welfare services on Indian reserves in Western

Manitoba.[13] Since that time agreements have been entered into covering services to all Indians residing on reserves in that province.

The experience to date under the Manitoba arrangements is discussed elsewhere in this volume, and further developments will be of great interest to native peoples and social workers throughout Canada. However, it is useful to comment briefly on the comparative strengths and potential weaknesses of the Manitoba model as compared to that adopted in B.C. by the Spallumcheen band. It seems to be a distinct advantage of the Manitoba model that it permits development and delivery of services to *all* Indians residing on reserves in the geographical area covered by an agreement. Provided adequate funds are made available, services can be deployed equitably according to need rather than on the basis of membership in a small band. The potential impact of the Manitoba programme is thus much greater. The Manitoba model also envisages active support and on-going collaboration between provincial child welfare authorities and native social service personnel. This could be especially important in the co-ordinated delivery of services to status Indians residing off reserves. This may be contrasted with the cautious, "arms-length" relationships between provincial child welfare officials and the Spallumcheen band.

One potential shortcoming of the Manitoba model is that it incorporates the legislative base of the Manitoba Child Welfare Act in defining standards of child protection, the mode of judicial decision-making, and the dispositional options available when a child is found in need of protection. One of the strengths of the Spallumcheen model is that its by-law expresses Indian standards of child care while ensuring decision-making at all levels by band members according to placement preferences that promote in Indian children a strong sense of ethnic and cultural identity. This difficulty could of course be overcome by appropriate amendments to provincial child welfare legislation which would make explicit provision for participation by Indians in the judicial aspects of child protection hearings, define culturally congruent grounds for protective intervention, and provide culturally responsive disposition options.

It is significant, however, that in British Columbia by the end of 1984 there had been no significant initiatives taken by the provincial government or Indian bands to adopt the tripartite system of child welfare service delivery. At the provincial government level this could reflect a reluctance to abandon administrative responsibility for child welfare services to Indians on reserves. It could also reflect the reduced priority attached to child welfare services during a prolonged period of fiscal restraint. The reluctance of B.C. Indian organizations to embrace tripartism is probably based on their belief that this could impede progress towards Indian self-government through bands or tribal councils. In this connection it should be noted that the present tripartite policy favoured by the federal government appears to be at variance with recommendations contained in the 1983 Report of the

House of Commons Special Committee on Indian Self-Government in Canada. This report specifically identifies child welfare as a subject over which a band or group of bands should have the option of exercising full legislative and policy-making powers.[14] From the foregoing, it seems reasonable to conclude that B.C. Indian leaders will await the outcome of negotiations on Indian self-government before adopting a firm position on the future delivery of child welfare services on Indian reserves.

CHILD WELFARE AND URBAN INDIANS

Both the Spallumcheen and Manitoba models of native child welfare programmes focus on the situations of families residing on Indian reserves. Neither is explicitly designed to address the problems of status and non-status Indians residing in urban centres. The present reality, however, is that the majority of families of Indian descent currently reside in towns and large cities and demographic forecasts indicate that the trend towards urban migration is likely to continue in the years ahead.[15] Given the serious problems of unemployment and culture shock experienced by most urban Indians, it seems clear that Native Indian child care problems will become more and more centred in the stresses native families encounter in adapting to urban life. This is not a criticism of either the Manitoba or Spallumcheen child welfare models. However, it emphasizes that urgent attention must be paid in the immediate future to the development and refinement of a range of environmental, economic, and social support services to both status and non-status Indians living off reserves.

CONCLUSION

First, this programme would not have come about were it not for the organizational skills and vigorous activism of the leaders and members of the Spallumcheen band. Moreover, the political activism that helped to shape the Spallumcheen programme was successful in linking child welfare concerns with much broader objectives aimed at promoting the general social, cultural, and economic well-being of the band members. Second, the Spallumcheen experience has demonstrated that even a small band may have within its membership the talent, dedication, energy, and imagination to develop a child welfare programme of potentially excellent quality.

Given the current inclination of the federal government to support tripartite child welfare agreements, it seems unlikely that the Spallumcheen programme will be replicated in the near future. However, in the event that constitutional negotiations result in the assignment to status Indians of jurisdiction over family and child welfare matters, the experience of the Spallumcheen Band could prove to be a valuable guide for other bands and tribal councils in developing programmes to promote the interests of their families and young people.

NOTES

1. Department of Indian and Northern Affairs, *Indian Conditions: A Survey* (Ottawa, D.I.A.N.D., 1980).
2. Statistics provided by the B.C. Ministry of Human Resources reveal that for the fiscal year 1980-81 native children, status and non-status, comprised 36.7 per cent of all children in care in British Columbia, a reduction of 2.5 per cent from fiscal year 1978-79. During 1980-81 native children constituted 42.7 per cent of all children in foster homes in the Province (Patrick Johnston, *Native Children and the Child Welfare System* [Ottawa: Canadian Council on Social Development, 1983], p. 27).
3. During the fiscal year 1980-81 an average of 1,313 children with registered Indian status in B.C. were residing in the homes of relatives or friends because of family problems (*Report of the Child Care Task Force on B.C. Indian Child Care* [Ottawa, Department of Indian and Northern Affairs, May, 1982]).
4. Letter to Hugh Millar, executive director, B.C. Association of Social Workers, from Louise Mandell, legal counsel for the Spallumcheen Band and B.C. Union of Indian Chiefs, 11 June 1980.
5. In a report prepared for the B.C. Royal Commission on Family and Children's Law, W.T. Stanbury found on the basis of 1972 statistics that 53 per cent of the status Indian children in the care of the superintendent of child welfare had been in care for longer than five years, compared to 23 per cent of the non-Indian children in the superintendent's care (W.T. Stanbury, *The Social and Economic Conditions of Indian Families in British Columbia,* Report prepared for the B.C. Royal Commission on Family and Children's Law, Vancouver, 1974).
6. Agreement between the Spallumcheen Band of Indians and Her Majesty The Queen in Right of Canada, 1 April 1981. This agreement has been renewed annually since 1981. The budget for 1984-85 is $404,000.
7. A By-law for the Care of Our Indian Children: Spallumcheen Indian Band By-law no. 3, 1980.
8. Family and Child Service Act, S.B.C., 1980, ch. 11, sec. 11, 12.
9. This view seems to be supported by the Supreme Court of Canada decision in the case of Natural Parents v. Superintendent of Child Welfare 60 D.L.R. (1976): 148 which held that the B.C. Adoption Act, a child welfare statute, had full application to status Indian children. It remains to be seen, however, whether the recognition of "existing aboriginal rights" in the new Canadian Charter of Rights will lead to a modified judicial interpretation of an Indian band's jurisdiction to legislate in the field of child welfare.
10. Programme circular on child welfare policy, Indian and Northern Affairs Canada, Ottawa, 1 May 1982.
11. Declaration of Hon. John C. Munro, 29 October 1982, disallowing by-law No. 3-1982, a by-law for the care of Indian Children enacted by the Tobacco Plains Band of Indians in the Province of British Columbia, at a meeting held 21 September 1982.
12. Programme circular on child welfare policy, pp. 13-19.
13. *Canadian Family Law Guide* (Toronto: C.C.H., 9 March 1982).
14. *Report of the Special Committee of the House of Commons on Indian Self-Government in Canada* (Ottawa: Queen's Printer, 1983), pp. 63-64.

15. In 1980 researchers from the Department of Indian and Northern Affairs predicted that by 1986 42 per cent of status Indians in B.C. would be residing in settings off reserves. Andrew Siggner and Chantal Locatelli, "An Overview of Demographic Social and Economic Conditions Among B.C.'s Registered Indian Population," Research Branch, Department of Indian and Northern Affairs, Ottawa, 1980, p. 11. It has also been estimated that the number of non-status Indians, most of whom reside in towns and cities, exceeds the population of registered Indians in B.C. by 20 per cent. See Gene Elmore et al., "Survey of Adoption and Child Welfare Services to Indians of B.C.," Report to the B.C. Department of Human Resources, 1974.

16

CHILDREN'S RIGHTS:
AN EVALUATION OF THE CONTROVERSY

Donald J. MacDougall

INTRODUCTION

Groups seeking political, social and legal recognition of particular interests often emphasize the importance of the interests being claimed by describing them as "rights." Social reformers have traditionally used "natural rights" arguments to justify social changes or to advance claims to individual freedom of action. More recently, different segments of our society, considering themselves unfairly treated, have forcefully advocated their wish for better treatment. This has led to movements such as those for women's rights, native rights and children's rights. When the term "rights" is used in this context it may include, but is not limited to, rights which are enforceable in a court of law.

The children's rights movement can be traced back at least as far as 1852 when a short article on "The Rights of Children" was published.[1] The child-saving movement at the turn of the century increased social awareness of the needs and interests of children.[2] The 1959 United Nations Declaration of the Rights of the Child[3] and the books of Farson[4] and Holt[5] have focused professional attention on the topic. No one opposes the idea of rights for children— but there is considerable debate about what legal and social rights children should have and how those rights should be secured. As Professor Teitelbaum wryly observed:

> [W]hatever the issue, neither side opposes the rights of children. On the contrary, each insists that it and only it understands and proposes to serve the interests of youth. "Rights of children" now occupies a position held in a more devout age by religious categories such as "Christianity" and "God"; everyone is militantly in favour of the idea, but only if correctly defined and properly observed in practice.[6]

UNITED NATIONS DECLARATION OF THE RIGHTS OF THE CHILD

The United Nations Declaration of the Rights of the Child illustrates some of the difficulties involved in defining children's rights. It lists some ten basic principles including:

Principle 2
The child shall enjoy special protection, and shall be given opportunities and facilities, by law and by other means, to enable him to develop physically, mentally, morally, spiritually and socially in a healthy and normal manner and in conditions of freedom and dignity. In the enactment of laws for this purpose, the best interests of the child shall be the paramount consideration.
Principle 6
The child, for the full and harmonious development of his personality, needs love and understanding. He shall, wherever possible, grow up in the care and under the responsibility of his parents, and, in any case, in an atmosphere of affection and of moral and material security; a child of tender years shall not, save in exceptional circumstances, be separated from his mother.

Obviously the United Nations Declaration embodies an ideal, or Utopian, concept of childhood rather than a set of legal standards capable of immediate application in the real world. Any Bill of Rights is likely to be phrased in general terms. But the terms used in the United Nations Declaration of the Rights of the Child are so vague as to be indeterminate. What standards are to be used to determine whether a child is developing "in a healthy and normal manner"? And how are we to resolve conflicts between the child's need for "love and understanding" and his need to develop "morally, spiritually and socially"? Idealistic statements of objectives serve a necessary function. They provide standards against which we can measure our achievements. But they are likely to be ineffective in improving the actual living conditions of children because the objectives are too easily dismissed as unrealistic and impractical.

Even the United Nations statement of general principles produced some controversy:

The USSR representative, in discussing this text, and also later when some of the principles of the Declaration were being debated, argued that the child could not be adequately protected without the cooperation of the State and society and that only the State could guarantee many of the rights set forth. The USSR believed also that the text should contain provisions indicating measures that governments should take to give effect to the Declaration. . . .

Most Third Committee Members, however, could not accept the amendments as presented. It was argued that the family — especially the parents — and not the State, should be primarily responsible for the child's welfare. Moreover the Declaration should state principles without entering into the question of their implementation.[7]

The issue in this debate was the role and importance of the family as a social institution in western democratic societies. In countries such as Canada the family still carries the primary responsibility for the protection and socialization of children. Any attempt to legislate the rights of children has implications for the complex interplay between the interests of: the individual child; the family; and the state.

In the United Nations a compromise was reached. The Declaration "calls upon parents, upon men and women as individuals, and upon voluntary organizations, local authorities and national Governments to recognize these rights." The specific references to "parents" and "voluntary organizations" were added on the initiative of the Netherlands.[8]

The discussion in the United Nations provides a reminder that "children's rights" should not be discussed in a vacuum. They need to be related to the broader social and political values of a community. Given ideal circumstances the family provides a setting in which an individual can reach his or her peak of personal development or fulfilment. But many families fall short of that ideal. Sometimes the family becomes an institution that limits and inhibits personal development. Sometimes, too, the family is a violent place in which individuals are physically injured and psychologically scarred. Family relationships are unstable. Divorce rates are already high, particularly in British Columbia and Alberta, and there is no evidence that they have reached a plateau or begun to decline. An increasing percentage of households are headed by single parents — many of whom are themselves young and immature.

The impact of alternative lifestyles on the quality of child care is still a matter of debate. But they force a re-examination of the basic assumption—that in Canadian society the changing family has the primary responsibility for the protection and socialization of children. Some will consider the children's rights movement as a necessary response to the failure of the modern family to meet the needs of children. Others will view the movement as a naive and damaging challenge to a system that has been generally effective. From a social planning viewpoint, several responses are possible. A conservative option would note the stresses on the modern family and provide services to supplement and support it. A more radical option would emphasize the relationship between the individual child and the community, with the family reduced to playing a subsidiary role. In recent years parental rights have been whittled away. Academics talk of the fragmentation of parental rights[9] and "the ascendancy in any case of the welfare of the child in almost every case where a parental right came into conflict with the welfare principle,''[10] but Canada, like other democratic societies, has not deliberately planned an alternative to the family. Government and non-governmental services are still considered supplementary to the family. Development of an alternative model would involve fundamental decisions about the social and political values in Canadian society.

If the family is to continue to have the primary role, provision must be made for those families that are utter failures and the many more that need extensive community support if they are to function at a satisfactory level. The danger is that governments will publicly espouse the primacy of the family but neglect to provide the alternatives that are needed when the family fails or is in difficulty.

Finally, it must be noted that the United Nations Declaration of the Rights of the Child is basically paternalistic. It is concerned with the "best interests" of the child rather than his wishes. The child was perceived as someone in need of special protection because of his physical and mental immaturity. It was left to later writers to develop the idea that a child is an individual who should have some control over his own destiny.

AUTONOMY FOR CHILDREN?

Some advocates of children's rights (sometimes called liberationists[11]) argue that children should have the same rights as adults. They recognize that there are natural limits on what children might wish to do or are capable of doing, but they seek to free children from the protective authority of their parents and other persons in authority. This position seems more persuasive in relation to adolescents, who often have considerable autonomy in any event, than in relation to very young children. The liberationists, however, are reluctant to accept age as a relevant differentiating factor.

Frequently the rights claimed for children are freedoms, rather than rights in a technical legal sense. For example Holt, an educator, argues that children of any age should be given the right to vote, to work for money, to buy and sell property, to choose their education, to travel and to live away from home.[12] Farson, a psychologist, emphasizes the child's right to self-determination:

> The issue of self-determination is at the heart of children's liberation. It is, in fact, the only issue, a definition of the entire concept. The acceptance of the child's right to self-determination is fundamental to all the rights to which children are entitled.[13]

According to Farson children should have sexual freedom, financial independence, and the right to choose where they wish to live. Obviously those objectives cannot be realized unless children have rights that adults do not have. Farson contemplates that families would be under an obligation to support their children,[14] and this would be a source of the child's economic power.

The position of the liberationists has been criticized. Freeman has described their arguments as "politically naive, philosophically faulty and psychologically wrong,"[15] Psychological research raises significant questions about the decision-making capacity of children — including adolescents.[16] Even if adolescents are capable of making most decisions without significantly harming themselves, there may be social arguments for restricting their autonomy. Teitelbaum notes that there is an apparent conflict between (1) the need to socialize an individual; and (2) the demand for individual autonomy. A healthy society will pursue both goals.

> On the one hand, it is expected that children will be acculturated; that is, they will learn cultural values in general and conform their conduct to social rules in particular. They must, in short, become knowledgeable members of the community. At the same time the end point of these processes is adulthood, upon which the child becomes a full citizen who must have developed a capacity for choice and autonomous action. Failure in either direction is a most serious matter. A child who does not learn social values and rules cannot join the society in which he must live; a person without capacity for independent choice cannot usefully participate in that society.[17]

In the U.S. children have been successful in establishing that they have certain basic rights that are constitutionally protected. The U.S. Supreme Court has proceeded on a cautious case-by-case approach analysing the interests involved in each case. For example, the decision in *Planned Parenthood v. Danforth*[18] that a pregnant teenager may secure an abortion without parental consent was distinguished in the later decision, *H.L. v. Matheson.*[19] One can reasonably anticipate a number of cases testing the extent to which the Canadian Charter of Rights and Freedoms has incorporated "liberationist" philosophy into Canadian law. Already some provisions of the Juvenile Delinquents Act have been challenged as contravening the Charter.[20] In 1985, section 15 of the Charter came into effect. It provides: "Every individual is equal before and under the law and has the right to the equal protection and equal benefit of the law without discrimination and, in particular, without discrimination based on . . . age." Under section 1 the rights given by section 15 are subject "to such reasonable limits prescribed by law as can be demonstrably justified in a democratic society." These provisions will force the courts to make some fundamental decisions about the legal position of children in Canadian society.

OTHER APPROACHES

Geiser suggests that advocates of children's rights fall into four distinct groups.[21] They share a common concern for children but differ over how the interests of children are best advanced. Different groups emphasize: (1) children's liberation; (2) children's needs; (3) the welfare of children; or (4) due process for children.

Children's Liberation. Advocates of liberation, such as Holt and Farson, argue that children need "consistently enforced legal rights equal to those of adults. They need freedom, democracy and full citizenship."[22]

Children's Needs. Many child advocates, especially those working through professional organizations, have issued needs manifestos listing the rights that children should have. Different professional groups identify somewhat different needs. Some emphasize the child's physical and psychological needs. Educators would add other education-related needs. Yet others would emphasize the special needs of particular classes of children (e.g., the handicapped). Only a Utopian community could respond to the needs of every individual child in that community. But these advocates do provide a positive, if somewhat idealistic, set of community goals for children. Inevitably any attempt to translate those goals into legally enforceable standards will involve the introduction of practical limitations and qualifications.

The Welfare of Children. There seems no reason to distinguish between children's welfare and their needs. Surely one ensures a child's welfare by satisfying his needs? The difference between the "welfare" group and the "needs" group is over the role of the family. The welfare advocates note that the anticipated results of professional intervention in the family are not always realized in fact. Goldstein, Freud and Solnit[23] argue that a child needs "the privacy of family life under guardianship by parents who are autonomous" and that state intrusion "is invariably detrimental."[24] Consequently, they would limit state intervention to a few strictly defined situations where the risk to the child outweighs the risk of state intervention.

Due Process Advocates. Due process advocates have more limited goals. Their object is to ensure that critical decisions affecting children are not made in an arbitrary fashion but only after a proper consideration of the child's interests. They seek to impose systems of checks and balances either by incorporating procedural safeguards into legislation or by invoking court review of decisions by parents or professionals. Critics accuse them of introducing too much "red tape" and unnecessary legal technicality. The justification is that children, because of their relative helplessness, need these procedural safeguards more than adults.

Exploring the various viewpoints within the children's rights movement demonstrates the complexity of the issue. Clearly there are important philosophical differences between the groups. It would be wrong, however, to exaggerate the importance of those differences or to minimize the values that they share. All seek to advance the interests of children. The cumulative impact of the different groups has raised the level of public debate about the legal position of children and had a subtle influence on policy-makers, lawyers and judges.

IMPACT ON CANADIAN LAW

It would be a difficult task, and beyond the scope of this paper, to make a comprehensive review of how the children's rights movement has affected the development of Canadian law. Canadian legislatures have not been any more successful than the professionals in reconciling all the interests involved. Nevertheless, some general comments can be made.

In the criminal law field it is easy to trace the influence of due process advocates. Judges have added a due process gloss to the current Juvenile Delinquents Act, and the new Young Offenders Act recognizes that young people should have special rights and guarantees in addition to the same rights that adults have to due process of law and fair and equal treatment. The result is an extensive system of controls. Indeed the Young Offenders Act is open to the criticism that it is a Criminal Code for children that does not adequately consider their needs or welfare. No doubt the emphasis on due process is the result, in part, of developments in the U.S. where the *Gault* decision[25] precipitated an extensive review of the juvenile justice system. The influence of due process philosophy can also be seen in the child legislation of some provinces (e.g., Ontario) which provide judicial review of placement decisions.

In the area of private law legislative policies are more mixed. On the one hand, there is a trend towards extending the period of parental financial responsibility, which is consistent with a respect for the family structure. But there has been no effort to extend parental powers to correspond with parental obligations. Rather, parental rights are being whittled away, mainly by the powers given to professionals to intervene in the family but partly through the development of independent rights for children. Cynically, it would appear that legislative policies are influenced more by financial considerations than by any consistent philosophy about the relationship between the child, his family and the state.

It is probable that judges have been influenced by the debate over children's rights, but Canadian judges traditionally limit their judgments to the issues presented in a particular case and eschew doctrinaire statements of general principle. Where parents withhold consent to necessary medical treatment (e.g., a blood transfusion), child welfare legislation usually authorizes an official to intervene and arrange the treatment. Where the prognosis is poor, the problem becomes more complex. In the *Dawson* case,[26] the parents of a six-year-old child with severe brain damage refused to consent to an operation to relieve pressure on his brain. Their expectation was that without the operation the child would die. Provincial Court Judge Byrne held that the operation was "extraordinary surgical intervention" and not "necessary medical attention" within the Family and Child Service Act (B.C.). Indeed she held that the operation would constitute cruel and unusual treatment within section 12 of the Canadian Charter of Rights. In subsequent proceedings before McKenzie, J., in the B.C. Supreme Court, evidence was led that if the operation was not performed the child might not die but live in increasing distress. In authorizing the operation, McKenzie, J. stated:

> I am satisfied that the laws of our society are structured to preserve, protect and maintain human life and that in the exercise of its inherent jurisdiction this court should not sanction the termination of a life except for the most coercive reasons. The presumption must be in favour of life. Neither could this court sanction the wilful withholding of surgical therapy where such withholding could result not necessarily in death but in a prolongation of life for an indeterminate time but in a more impoverished and more agonizing form.
>
> I do not think that it lies within the prerogative of any parent or this court to look down upon a disadvantaged person and judge the quality of that person's life to be so low as not to be deserving of continuance.[27]

Most children's rights advocates would agree that this was now an appropriate case for state intervention. However Goldstein, Freud, and Solnit would leave such decisions to parents unless "the anticipated result of treatment is what society would want for every child — a chance for normal healthy growth or a life worth living."[28] Where that condition cannot be met, they consider there is no reason to believe that judges or professionals can make a better decision than the parents. However Goldstein, Freud, and Solnit also approve intervention where parents, by acts or omissions, cause serious bodily injury to a child. It may be that the distress suffered by the child in the *Dawson* case would bring this principle into operation.

The case illustrates how easily conflicts can emerge between the interests of (1) the individual child; (2) his family; and (3) the state. The judgment of McKenzie, J., does not refer to "children's rights" but it proceeds on the basis that a severely handicapped child has the same basic rights as other individuals in Canada. Enforcement of those rights, however, depends on the willingness of someone to initiate litigation. It was fortuitous that the *Dawson* case came to court. In many similar cases decisions not to treat are made by parents and physicians.[29] The *Dawson* case is an important reaffirmation of the rights of a child and it should influence medical practice. It is clear, however, that Canada has not established a system that guarantees that all children, including handicapped children, receive necessary medical treatment.

THE FUTURE OF CHILDREN'S RIGHTS

To repeat a point made earlier in this paper, the children's rights movement seeks rights that include, but extend beyond, rights that are enforceable in a legal sense. This is important because no legal system has the ability to ensure that a child's needs will be met or his welfare protected. The limitations of the legal process must be acknowledged.[30] The needs and capacities of children vary greatly, depending on the age and maturity of the individual child. Children need love and affection, guidance, and training. The socialization process is a complex one that is not easily converted to a system of legal rules and regulations. The law can require minimum standards of conduct, but it cannot regulate the intimate relationship upon which the healthy growth and development of the child depends. A child's legal rights will always fall short of his needs. It would be unkind to abandon him to his rights.[31] Recognizing this the children's rights movement makes an extra-legal appeal. It asks adults to recognize children as individuals and to respond to their needs. It seeks to shape community attitudes as well as specific legal rules.

Within the movement there is a continuing debate about the best method of advancing the interests of children. Teitelbaum is right to emphasize the need to reconcile the socialization of the child with a respect for his autonomy, but we lack the knowledge required to determine the most appropriate role of the family and other professionals in the life of the child. It is tempting to call for further research but it should be frankly admitted that the issues may be so complex as to defy any simple solution. If this assessment is correct, efforts to create a comprehensive, legally enforceable Bill of Rights for children are unrealistic. In the near future there will be an opportunity to assess the effectiveness of the Canadian Charter of Rights and Freedoms in protecting children's rights.

Meanwhile there is a need for legislation more limited in scope but more specific in content (e.g., on access to medical care; access to legal services; student rights; employment rights; welfare rights). Even in these limited areas, decisions will have to be made in the face of controversy and the absence of desired empirical evidence. In such a situation wisdom dictates a conservative approach — that we continue to rely on, and support the family, but provide alternatives for the children of failing families. That choice presupposes a particular set of social values. Others may choose different values. Central to the debate should be our conception of the characteristics of a society in which we would wish to live and which we hope to create. Our basic social and political beliefs will determine our attitudes to children, their needs, and their rights.

NOTES

1. See M.D.A. Freeman, "The Rights of Children in the International Year of the Child," *Current Legal Problems* 33 (1980): 12.
2. See A.M. Platt, *The Child Savers: The Invention of Delinquency.* (Chicago: University of Chicago Press, 1969).
3. *United Nations Yearbook 1959,* pp. 192-99.
4. R. Farson, *Birthrights.* (New York: Macmillan, 1974).
5. J. Holt, *Escape from Childhood.* (New York: E.P. Dutton, 1974).
6. L.E.Teitelbaum, "Foreword: The Meaning of Rights of Children," *New Mexico L.R.* 10 (1980): 236.
7. *United Nations Yearbook 1959,* p. 194.
8. Ibid..
9. See the articles by Susan Maidment, "The Fragmentation of Parental Rights" *Cambridge L.J.* 135; and J.M. Eekelaar, "What Are Parental Rights?" *L.Q.R.* 89 (1973): 89.
10. Maidment, p. 135.
11. See, for example, R.L. Geiser, "The Rights of Children," *Hastings L.J.* 28 (1977): 1044.
12. Holt, p. 18.
13. Farson, p. 27.
14. Ibid., p. 154.
15. Freeman, p. 17.
16. See M.S. Wald, "Children's Rights: A Framework for Analysis." *U.C.D. L.R.* 12 (1979): 274-75.
17. Teitelbaum, p. 253.
18. (1976), 428 U.S. 52, 96 S. Ct. 2831, 49 L. Ed. 2d.788.
19. (1981), 450 U.S. 398, 101 S. Ct. 1164, 67 L. Ed. 2d.388.
20. See N.C. Bala, "Constitutional Challenges Mark Demise of Juvenile Delinquents Act." *C.R.* 30 (1983): 245.
21. Geiser, p. 1044.
22. Ibid., p. 1049.
23. J. Goldstein, A. Freud, and A.J. Solnit, *Before the Best Interests of the Child.* (New York: Free Press, 1979).
24. Ibid., pp. 8-10.
25. *In re Gault* (1967), 387 U.S. 1, 87 S. Ct. 1428, 18 L. Ed. 2d.527.
26. *Re D(S),* [1983] 2 W.W.R. 597 (B.C. Prov. Ct.), [1983] 3 W.W.R. 618 (B.C.S.C.).
27. [1983] 3 W.W.R. 618 at 629.
28. Goldstein, p. 91.
29. J.E. Magnet, "Withholding Treatment from Defective Newborns: A Description of Canadian Practices," *Legal Medical Q.* 4 (1980): 271.
30. D.J. MacDougall, "Children and the Law: The Limited Effectiveness of Legal Process," in I.F.G. Baxter and M.A. Eberts, eds., *The Child and the Courts.* Toronto: Carswell, 1978: pp. 185-202.
31. See B.C. Hafen, "Children's Liberation and the New Egalitarianism: Some Reservations about Abandoning Youth to their Rights," *Brigham Young U.L.R.* (1976): 605.

17

THE DYNAMICS OF CHILD WELFARE:
A REPORT OF A STUDY IN PROGRESS

Lawrence Shulman

During the past ten years, I have been investigating communications, relationship, and problem-solving skills which appear to be related to effective social work practice.[1] Interest in the question of method, that is, what it is social workers actually do when they work with clients, is related to my belief that this is a crucial variable often ignored in social work studies.[2] While focusing on the activity of the workers, I realized that they only accounted for a part of the outcome. For example, the client's motivation and capacity for change plays an important part in the process. Any attempt to understand practice would need to focus on the dynamic interaction between worker and client, each affecting and being affected by the other.

This complicated interaction between worker and client does not, however, take place in a vacuum. It is set within an agency setting, and it is influenced by a host of factors. For example, worker caseload, supervision, agency practices, and staff morale can all have a powerful impact upon the moment by moment movements of a social worker dealing with a client. Even the most skillful workers are limited in their impact if they have little time to see clients or are always seeing them while they are under stress.[3] The agency system will also affect the client and his or her ability to become involved constructively. For example, in the child welfare setting, agency policy on visiting children in care may either encourage parental involvement or turn parents away.[4] Thus, our attempts to study practice are complicated further by the fact that we are examining a system (worker-client) set within another system (the agency), with each affecting the other.

On a third level, the agency and the client can also be viewed as set within the context of the larger community and society. For example, child welfare practices in a given setting are strongly affected by the operation of the court system, the availability of resources (for example, group homes for teenagers), and decisions by the political system on funding. For the client, availability of community and family resources and socio-economic factors (for example, employment, income, race) may all play some part in influencing outcomes.

Therefore, to understand the dynamics of such a process, it is necessary to integrate an interactional approach which focuses on the dynamics of the helping process between worker and client, with an ecological approach, which takes into account the influence of the systems within which the interaction takes place.

This paper is a report of such a study in progress. While the approach to theory-building described has some usefulness in developing a generalized theory of social work practice, the specific case described is drawn from the child welfare field.

BUILDING A THEORY OF CHILD WELFARE PRACTICE

The approach to theory-building used in this study was drawn from the work of Zetterberg.[5] He suggested the development of sets of propositions consisting of "determinent" and "resultant" elements, each linked by terms which described their relationship. For example, the literature indicates that parental visiting of children in care (determinent element) correlates positively with the incidence of children returning to their own homes (resultant element).[6] This information can be translated into a proposition as follows: "More frequent parental visiting of children in care increases the chances of a child returning home." In preparing for this study, the literature was reviewed to identify propositions already supported by research or which appeared to be promising. The researcher used his practice experience and his years of consulting work with child welfare agencies to identify other propositions. Finally, the initial model, consisting of eighty such propositions was discussed through key informant interviews, both individual and group, with participants at all levels of the process (executive directors, managers, supervisors, social workers, alternate care-givers, clients, judges, lawyers, Native Indian organization staff, and social workers, foster parent association leaders, and so forth). This four-month process led to a further refinement of the model and the development of many additional propositions which the key informants suggested as important to understanding.

For example, to return to the proposition related to parental visiting, a related proposition is the following: "Investment of social worker activity during the first two years of contact leads to an increased level of parental visiting."[7] Thus, we now have two linked propositions. In the first, the determinent element of worker investment of activity leads to a resultant element of increased parental visiting. In the second proposition, increased parental visiting becomes a determinent element for a new resultant, an increased chance of the child returning home. By connecting these related propositions, we can begin to develop a theoretical model of the dynamics of the child welfare process, translated into testable terms.

Another important idea employed in the theory-development stage of this project was borrowed from Rosenberg, a sociologist.[8] He proposed employing third variable analysis to examine the effects of a third variable on the relationship between two other variables. In the example used thus far, it was suggested that increased investment of worker activity in the first two years of contact would lead to an increased level of parental visiting. In order to deepen the understanding of this process, a third variable, worker-client relationship needs to be introduced. Thus, the effects of worker activity on client visiting may be mediated by the quality of this relationship, with a positive working relationship increasing visiting and a negative relationship having the reverse effect.

Diagram 1

AN OVERVIEW OF THE THEORETICAL MODEL

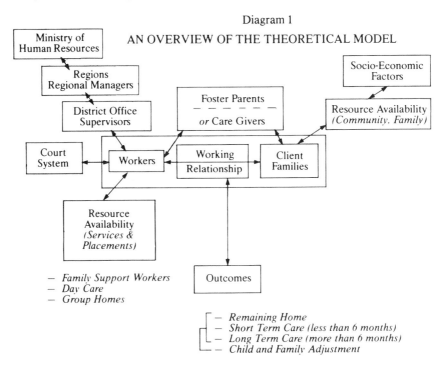

In order to develop a theoretical model of such a complex process, it was necessary to determine its major components. Diagram 1 provides an oversimplified picture of the theory. At the centre of the model is the interactional element of worker and client with their working relationship a crucial element leading to the outcomes of the process. The other elements form the ecological context in which worker and client are operating. For example, the worker is seen as affected by the setting of service (agency), in this study, a district office with a supervisor. The district office and supervisor are in turn affected by their contextual setting, a region administered by a regional manager. This administrative unit is set in a macro-area with an executive director and agency wide-policies, which, in turn, are affected by the political system.

On the family side, resource availability, both community and family, is an important part in influencing the family's ability to respond to the social worker's interaction. For example, a Native Indian mother who is isolated from her family and sources of support from her band may have a much more difficult time in dealing with her children than one who has such support. This factor may be somewhat modified by the availability of urban Native Indian support services (friendship centre, court workers, homemakers, and so forth).

In the larger context, socio-economic factors are also seen as having a profound effect on the client. For example, families experiencing (or fearing) a job loss in difficult economic times will experience increased stress, which, in turn, may lead to increased incidents of family violence. Race has been shown to be associated with lower income, poorer housing, and poorer health, all of which can lead to stress, which, in turn, can lead to family disruption. Any effort to understand the dynamics of child welfare practice without examining related socio-economic issues will be focusing on a symptom while possibly ignoring a crucial set of determinent elements.

To return to Diagram 1, three other major systems are incorporated into the model-building process. These consist of the court system, resources available to the agency (for example, placement resources, family-counselling services), and finally, the alternate care givers (foster parents and child care workers). Propositions have been developed to help explain the interactive effects of each of these factors on the process. These range from simple ones, such as the length of time it takes a court proceeding to be completed which may be related to the number of lawyers involved to more complex sets of propositions about the interplay between alternate caregivers, social workers, and parents.

The advantage of attempting to examine such a large, complex process at one time is that it allows for observation of patterns of relationship which may not be obvious by focusing on only one area. For example, my work has focused on the communication and relationship skills of the helping professionals and their impact on developing positive working relationships and the ability to be helpful to clients.[9] In the current study, I examine hypotheses about a parallel process which may exist throughout the different levels of a complex administrative system. Stated simply, I will be exploring the idea that a social worker's ability to be genuine and empathetic with clients and to create an atmosphere of trust will be affected, among other factors, by the ability of his or her supervisor to do precisely the same things in their relationship. In turn, the supervisor's ability to provide this support will, in part, be affected by the impact of the next level of administration. The general concept is that of a flow-through effect in which a tone set by the political system governing the agency can be passed down through the system to influence the worker's interaction with a specific client. In turn, a worker who can be supportive to a parent, may find this to be a crucial ingredient in helping the parent to be more supportive to his or her child. By trying to examine the whole, instead of focusing on the separate elements, insights on the dynamic nature of the process may emerge.

OVERVIEW OF THE STUDY

The study is being conducted in the Ministry of Human Resources of the Province of British Columbia, Canada. The ministry is divided geographically into five macro-areas, each administered by an executive director. Macro-areas are further divided into regions (twenty-one in the province) headed by regional managers. Regions are organized by district offices administered by supervisors. Each district office is responsible for administering both the child welfare and the financial assistance programmes in their area.

This study includes ten of the regions (48 per cent) selected to provide a representation of the province as a whole (that is, urban, suburban, and rural). In February 1983, six project field staff began visiting the seventy district offices in these ten regions to review family files which had opened or reopened in the office since December 1982. Field staff returned to read new files in April and June. By the final file reading, 969 families were identified as potential subjects. Immediately after each field visit, clients were sent a letter from the Research Division of the ministry asking if they wished to participate in the project. The names and addresses of only those families agreeing to participate were shared with the central project office staff. Of the possible sample group, 348 (35 per cent) agreed to be in the study. Of this group, 43 were dropped from the sample for a variety of reasons, (for example, client change of mind, social worker non-participation, unsuitability, or inability to trace after a move). Thus, the final sample included 305 families with a total of 449 children identified as at risk.

Of this group, approximately two-thirds consisted of the type of child welfare case which usually involves physical or sexual abuse, or neglect, or the general inability of parents to care for their children (for example, serious health problems). The children in this group are often age twelve and under. The second major grouping, about one-third of our sample, could better be described as the teen-parent conflict problem usually occurring with children age thirteen and over. In these cases, abuse or neglect may not be present; however, a breakdown in the parent-child relationship may lead to the teen leaving home. In British Columbia, this type of child welfare case is increasing and the provincial percentage matches that of the sample (one in three cases).

Data Gathering Procedures

Home interviews were conducted with most of the families in the study with a few completing a parallel questionnaire. Sixty teenagers in the families were contacted in the same way. Follow-up questionnaires were sent to parents and teens approximately one year later. These two procedures provided all of the client-report data.

Staff members at all levels of the ministry were surveyed by mailed questionnaires at the start of the study. These obtained data on individual staff members (for example, supervisors and workers rated each other on their skills and their working relationship), on administrative units (for example, district office morale and the effects of cutbacks on services in a region), on community systems (for example, the supportiveness of the court system and the working relationship with the local foster parent association), and more. Some staff were re-surveyed on some crucial factors at periodic times during the study (for example, supervisors were surveyed every three months on the impact of a restraint programme introduced in the province). Similar information on the systems was obtained by surveying foster parents, their associations, and Native Indian workers and associations.

In addition to staff and system data, information was obtained on individual families from the social workers involved, family support workers, the foster parents or other alternate care-givers. Data on the families and individual children was also obtained from the central records of the ministry (for example, court judgments, days in care). Ministry records were also used to obtain data on administrative regions (for example, child population, number of children served, percentage of children in the region entering care).

LIMITATIONS OF THE STUDY

There are a number of limitations which need to be taken into account when the findings are reviewed. First, is the self-selection of the sample of families. Perhaps the two-thirds of the potential population who did not participate differs significantly from the one-third which did. Analysis of the brief data available on the non-respondents will be undertaken; however, this remains an important limitation. It is also possible that some staff may have screened out cases they found to be more difficult. While there was some evidence of this in specific district offices, it did not appear to be widespread. Initial analysis of the sample indicates that it is generally representative of the total ministry population on a number of important variables (for example, percentage of teen-parent conflict cases, attitude towards the ministry, number of children entering care). Further analysis will have to focus on this question region by region.

Other limitations have to do with the reliability and validity of the instrumentation used. To date, twenty-four separate questionnaires, interview guides, and checklists have been developed for this project. A number of core items (for example, communications and relationship skills) have been drawn from questionnaires used in earlier studies. These items now have a positive history of evidence of reliability and validity. Data on further reliability will be obtained and reported on for these items as well as the new ones employing traditional means of analysis (for example, Cronbach's alpha will be computed for all scales, construct validity will be explored).

While other limitations will be discussed in the full report, the major limitation of the impact of the government cutbacks to child welfare and other social service programmes and the dramatic responses by the general community and public servants (for example, the strike in November 1983) have to be given heavy weight. While these cutbacks came after the first phase of the project and thus did not interfere with that data, they must be seen as having a major impact on the work which followed. So our ability to generalize from findings of longer range outcomes to other populations which have not experienced this trauma is limited. Since the impact of the cutbacks has been different for various units of the system, at different times, this can be incorporated into the analysis. In addition, many cases were completed and closed during Phase One of the study and were isolated from the cutback effects. These cases can be compared to those opened late in the intake period, which may have felt the full impact. However, these events, which occurred in the middle of the study, have had an important impact in the design. However, it is possible that by being opportunistic in responding to this reality, we may end up with a different study, one at least as important as that first proposed.

DATA ANALYSIS

One aspect of the data analysis will involve taking the overall theoretical model and breaking it down into its general component parts. For example, one part of the analysis will focus on the impact of district office factors and supervision on worker activity with clients. Another part of the analysis will focus on the interaction of worker activity with clients and client factors and their relation to selected outcome measures. Using the techniques described earlier and guided by the propositions of the theory, constructs will be tested, and the results used to endorse the proposition, reject it, or rethink its significance. In earlier efforts, I have found that my most significant learning came when cherished hypotheses were not supported. It forced a rethinking of the underlying assumptions that often led to a deeper understanding of the process and the development of new and sometimes more sophisticated insights.

In addition, traditional forms of analysis will be undertaken. For example, analysis of variance will be used to determine factors which appear to distinguish the three major outcome groups in the study: those whose children never went into care, those who entered short-term care and returned home, and those who remained in care for more than six months. As another example, urban, suburban, and rural district offices can be compared.

Finally, data from the study will be used to develop a computer simulation model which incorporates the major propositions of the study and which can be used to predict outcomes if these variables are manipulated. This simulation model may prove to be a useful tool for line workers, supervisors, and administrators, all of whom must make practice and policy decisions based upon available data. If the simulation model is then used to construct simulated experiments (for example, what happens if specific special services or more skilled workers are provided to selected populations?) and the results of these simulated experiments are then replicated in actual field trials, then a degree of external validity of the simulation model will be evidenced which will increase its usefulness as a predictive tool. The use of the simulation approach is a secondary form of analysis, but one which offers an interesting area for investigation.

ELABORATING THE THEORY: SOME ILLUSTRATIVE FINDINGS

In order to illustrate some forms of data analysis, I have selected a small segment of the study and some of the initial findings within it for discussion. The focus is on the agency context which affects the worker-client interaction and, in particular, on the supervisory relationship. Table 1 lists some of the hypotheses associated with this component.

In order to deepen understanding of how supervision mediates the effects of agency practices upon eventual worker activity, we must examine the supervisor/worker/client component in more detail. The starting places are the degree of stress felt by the supervisor and the manageability of the job. Some supervisors find the job both stressful and manageable, and so it is necessary to consider both factors jointly. When supervisors find the total job more manageable and less stressful, they can be more available to their workers. In addition, the supervisor is more likely to define his or her role as including ongoing supervision and consultation, rather than simply

TABLE 1

SUPERVISOR/WORKER/CLIENT COMPONENT

Determinant Elements	Resultant Elements
1. The less stress a supervisor feels and the more manageable the job	a. the more available the supervisor will be for workers, b. the more evident will be the supervisor's communications and relationship skills, c. the more likely that the supervisor will define the role as "supervision and consultation."
2. The effects of the determinant element of hypothesis 7 on the associated resultant elements are mediated by	a. the supervisor's experience and education, b. the supervisor's access to support and ongoing training, c. the supervisor's perception of his or her role.
3. The more a supervisor who defines the role as "supervision and consultation" is available for the worker, and employs communication and relationship skills	a. the more likely that the supervisor/worker working relationship will be more positively perceived by the worker, b. the more likely that the supervisor will be perceived as more helpful by the worker, c. the worker's perception of the supervisor's emphasis in the area of agency practices will parallel the agency's emphasis.
4. The effects of the determinant elements in hypothesis 9 on the resultant elements in 9b and 9c are mediated by	a. the supervisor/worker working relationship, b. the worker's education and experience.
5. The more effective a supervisor is in employing communications and relationship skills with a worker	the more effective the worker will be in employing the same skills with the clients.
6. The effects of the determinant element of hypothesis 11 on the associated resultant element are mediated by	a. the stress and manageability of the worker's caseload, b. the worker's education and experience, c. the availability of support from fellow workers.
7. The more a worker perceives his or her supervisor as effective in communicating staff views to administration	a. the more likely that supervisor/worker relationship will be more positively perceived by the worker, b. the more likely that the supervisor will be perceived as helpful.

more management or liaison. Finally, the supervisor with more time will be better able to relate to staff, employing a variety of communications and relationship skills, such as picking up indirect cues of worker problems and empathizing with the feelings of staff. If a supervisor feels overwhelmed, he or she may find it difficult to empathize with precisely the same feelings on the part of the workers.

The association between stress/manageability and availability, skill, and implementation of the consultation role will be mediated by three other variables. These are the supervisor's experience and education, access to support and on-going training, and concept of role. For example, some supervisors with enough experience and support may find it possible to be more available for workers and to relate more skilfully in spite of higher stresses. Others, who are perhaps new to the role, find that any level of stress can interfere with their ability to relate effectively with staff.

If a supervisor defines the role as including supervision and consultation, is available to the worker, and employs effective skills, then these will all contribute to a more effective working relationship with the worker, and, in turn, the supervisor will be perceived as more helpful. In addition, the combination of these three factors will provide a medium through which the supervisor will be better able to communicate his or her emphasis on practices with families. This association between skill, role definition, and availability with the outcomes of helpfulness and communication of emphasis may vary according to the worker's education and experience. More experienced workers, for example, may feel less need for more intensive supervision; thus, workers' experience and education will mediate the association.

Another crucial aspect of this component of the model is the hypothesis that the supervisor will often serve as a model for effective communication and relationship skills in action. Thus the worker may be influenced in the way he or she deals with clients by the way he or she is dealt with by a supervisor. In my supervision workshops, for example, I have often noted that the same skills required to help a defensive client feel more comfortable and less resistant are helpful in supervising a defensive worker. One way to help a worker become more empathetic with clients is to empathize with the worker's struggle to be supportive. The hypothesis is that effective use of communication and relationship skills with workers will lead to more effective use of the same skills by workers. This process is mediated by the stress and manageability of the worker's caseload, the worker's education and experience, and the availability of support from fellow workers which may, at times, supplement or serve as a substitute for supervisory support.

Finally, a key factor influencing the development of the supervisor/worker relationship will be the worker's perception of how well the supervisor represents his or her views in dealing with administration. This factor will also influence how helpful the worker perceives the supervisor to be. Studies of supervision not directly related to work with families and children in care have supported this hypothesis.

The supervision/worker/client component described thus far was developed at the starting point of the study — that is, the propositions as they stood before the key informant interviews. The data supporting or questioning these propositions is currently under analysis. However, two interesting and related additional issues arose during discussions with workers prior to the start of the study. These were the amount of stress experienced by workers when apprehending children and the stress experienced when workers had to recommend that a child become a permanent ward. In one moving workshop, it became clear that workers had strong emotional reactions to this part of their work, reactions which they rarely shared with each other or their supervisors. The general assumption was that if they were competent workers and the facts in the case were fairly straightforward, they would have less trouble in taking these actions. The reality is that it is never easy.

In particular, workers indicated the greater difficulty is in moving for permanent wardship, since even when apprehending, they always feel the possibility of returning the child to the family. While full analysis of this component of the study remains to be done, some initial findings are shared here. In one of the questionnaires completed by the supervisors, they were asked to evaluate each of their workers in a number of areas, two of which were the amount of stress experienced in making an apprehension and the stress experienced in requesting permanent wardship. The item was stated in the positive, indicating that these activities were particularly difficult for this worker, and the supervisor responded on a scale ranging from (1) strongly agree to (5) strongly disagree. The workers were asked to rate themselves on the same questions.

Table 2 compares the responses of supervisors with those of their workers. There were 131 supervisor ratings of workers on this item (there were 68 different supervisors responding) and 142 workers rated themselves. The table graphically reveals a difference in perception of the difficulty involved. While almost 40 per cent of the workers strongly agreed that they experienced particular difficulty in apprehending children, only 5 per cent of the supervisors gave that response. When strongly agree and agree are combined, the percentages are 80 per cent for workers and only 15 per cent for the supervisors.

On the issue of stress involved in requesting permanent wardship, reported in Table 3, the results differ slightly. Workers reported that requesting permanent wardship was somewhat less stressful than apprehending. A total of 57 per cent strongly agreed or agreed that it was stressful, compared to 80 per cent on the apprehension question. The difference in the supervisors' perceptions was still present, since none of the supervisors strongly agreed that it was stressful for workers and only 15 per cent agreed. On these overall figures, there appears to be evidence of a communications gap between supervisors and workers.

To examine this gap more tightly, individual supervisor/worker scores on these items were compared. An index of disagreement was computed by simply subtracting the workers' score from their supervisor's assess-

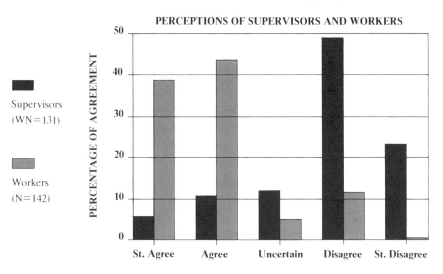

Table 2
WORKER APPREHENSION STRESS

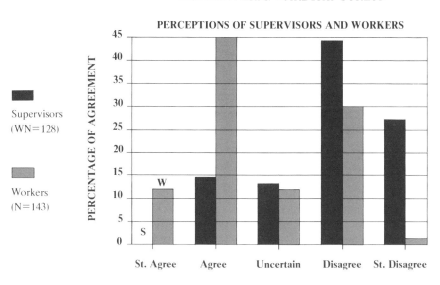

Table 3
WORKER PERM. WARDSHIP STRESS

ment. Scores could range from (-4), which indicated the supervisor strongly disagreed with the statement (1) and the worker strongly agreed (5), to ($+4$), indicating the worker strongly agreed and the supervisor strongly disagreed. A score of (0) would indicate perfect agreement between supervisor and worker, whatever the response (for example, both strongly agreed).

Only 12 per cent of the supervisor/worker pairs had a zero difference in agreement on the question of stress of apprehension. The index of disagreement was heavily weighted on the positive, indicating supervisors were reporting disagreement with the existence of particular stress while their workers were agreeing that apprehension was stressful. The percentages were as follows: 17.5 per cent were one scale off; 22.5 per cent were two scales off; 34 per cent were three scales off; and 7 per cent were four scales off.

The comparison of individual worker and supervisor scores on the issue of stress related to permanent wardship revealed similar directions in the differences; however, the perceptions were closer on this item. Twenty-three per cent of the pairs had zero disagreement in their ratings, while the percentages of differences were as follows: 22 per cent were one scale off; 25 per cent were two scales off; 20 per cent were three scales off; and 1 per cent were four scales off.

While the analysis is still in a preliminary stage, the initial findings suggest supervisors are not in touch with their workers' sense of stress in apprehending children and requesting permanent wardship. If support from a supervisor or colleague in this area proves to be important in assisting a worker in dealing effectively with these decisions, then these findings suggest the possible need for on-going attention to these issues both in general discussions with staff as well as in specific case discussions with workers.

Further analysis will also explore the associations between supervisor factors and the size of the index of disagreement. For example, is there a pattern that distinguishes supervisors who are closer in agreement with their workers when compared to those who are not? Does this relate to supervisor skill, experience, or education? How does the state of the working relationship affect these scores? Is there an association between a good working relationship, openness in the relationship, and the creation of a safe atmosphere where workers feel free to risk their mistakes and the communication gap in these areas? Or, are there worker factors which contribute to the differences rather than supervisor variables? It may be, as this researcher suspects, that in many cases it is the indirectness on the part of the worker which leads to the communication breakdown between worker and client. If this is supported, is there anything a supervisor can do to create the conditions for maximizing the possibility of worker honesty and self-disclosure?

This researcher also believes that the parallel process described earlier may prove to be important, that is, that supervisors who have access to on-going support and feel that they are operating in a safe and open atmosphere may be those who are more ready to provide the same for their workers. The parallel process will be examined at the next level as well. That is, the impact of these factors on the ability of the worker to create the conditions where clients can be honest about their feelings in these same, very stressful areas.

CONCLUSION

This paper is a report of work in progress. As such, its findings should still be viewed as very tentative. However, I have tried to present a summary of the overall study as well as an illustration of the approach to data analysis which will follow. Social work practice in general, and child welfare practice in particular, is a complicated process to analyze and understand. This study will provide some tools and findings to assist in the on-going task of strengthening theory-building efforts.

NOTES

1. For publications of related research, see: Lawrence Shulman, "A Study of Practice Skill," *Social Work* 23 (1978): pp. 274-81; Lawrence Shulman, producer. *The Helping Process in Social Work: Theory, Practice and Research* (Montreal: Instructional Communications Centre, McGill University, 1976); Lawrence Shulman, *A Study of the Helping Process* (Vancouver: University of British Columbia School of Social Work, 1977). (French translation: Ottawa: Cdn. Assoc. of Schools of Social Work, 1979); Lawrence Shulman, *The Skills of Helping Individuals and Groups* (Itasca, Ill.: F.E. Peacock Publishers, 1979).
2. Eileen Gambrill and Kermit T. Wiltse, "Foster Care: Plans and Actualities," *Public Welfare* 32 (1974): 12-21.
3. Lawrence Shulman, *The Input of Reduced Caseloads on Preventative Services* (Vancouver: University of British Columbia School of Social Work, 1977).
4. David Fanshel and Eugene B. Shinn, *Children in Foster Care: A Longitudinal Investigation* (New York: Columbia University Press, 1978); Henry S. Maas, "Children in Long Term Foster Care," *Child Welfare* 48 (1969): 321-33.
5. H.A. Zetterberg, *On Theory and Verification of Sociology* (Toronto: Bedminster Press, 1965).
6. Fanshel and Shinn.
7. Ibid.
8. Morris Rosenberg, *Logic of Survey Analysis* (New York: Basic Books, 1978).
9. Shulman, 1976, 1977, 1978, 1979.

18

THE CHALLENGE OF CHILD WELFARE

Brian Wharf

None of the writers of the preceding chapters were specifically asked to include a critique or evaluation of child welfare policy and practice in Canada. But many did and the unanimity of their conclusion is striking. Consider the following:

1. Callahan's review in Chapter 1 argues that child welfare is a residual crisis-oriented system that has been characterized by "public apathy and government parsimony." Callahan further notes that child welfare as a field of service has not developed a coherent philosophy or policy of service and, in fact, has devoted little if any time to addressing values and ideologies.

2. In her chapter, Martin establishes that child welfare agencies deal disproportionately with children in poverty and, indeed, have always done so. Nevertheless, agencies have not documented the impact of poverty on children, nor sought to identify ways of ameliorating the impact.

3. Bagley describes the increase in sexual abuse of children, but concludes that the practice knowledge and skills required to deal with this complex problem have yet to be developed. Hence, while new problems face child welfare agencies, practice has not changed.

4. In their chapters dealing with native children, MacDonald, McKenzie, and Hudson claim that the efforts to "help" these children have resulted in cultural genocide.

5. Levitt and Robinson argue that even in its most residual and limited function of providing substitute care, child welfare in B.C. and in most Canadian provinces has not developed either a subsidized adoption programme or permanent planning systems for children in care. Both have the potential for bringing about significant improvements in practice.

6. In his chapter, David Cruickshank, formerly the director of research for the Berger Commission, traces the impact of the commission's work

on child welfare legislation in Canada and other countries. Cruickshank acknowledges his bias — his total agreement with and commitment to the recommendations. Thus, he applauds the decision of the State of Victoria in Australia to require the state to provide services prior to apprehension. In Canada, only Ontario, New Brunswick, and Manitoba have revised child welfare legislation to reflect prevention and a concern for the rights of children.

However, as Hepworth and Wharf point out, child welfare ministries across the country have reduced the number of children coming into care by developing an array of support services designed to assist families experiencing difficulties. In addition, McDougall argues that the action of the B.C. ministry in intervening in the Dawson case represents a conviction on the part of child welfare authorities or ministries that children have rights and must be protected. But with the exception of these few positive developments, the fundamental challenge facing the field of child welfare is whether it will continue to operate in a residual capacity or emphasize prevention and seek to place child welfare within the context of family and community.

The child welfare field has always functioned under several handicapping features. In the first place, child welfare is a provincial responsibility, and in most provinces it is provided through large and multi-function ministries. Until recently, provincial governments have not assigned a high priority to the broad field of social welfare and within social welfare ministries, child welfare is but one of many responsibilities, with income assistance being assigned the highest priority.

Secondly, locating the responsibility for child welfare within provincial ministries effectively precludes the participation of citizens in the policy and practice of child welfare. Simply put, child welfare does not have an informed and committed constituency to advocate additional resources or plead for change. Only Ontario, Quebec and Manitoba have organized services in a way that allows for the involvement of citizens. Ontario retains the pattern of Children's Aid Societies organized on a county basis. Quebec has developed an integrated system of health and social services across the province, and citizens are elected to both local and regional boards which oversee the provision of service. Manitoba has recently established six child and family centres in metropolitan Winnipeg. Each centre is governed by an elected board of citizens and will be required to develop a range of preventive services.

Thirdly, as many of the chapters in this book argue, practitioners in child welfare are in the classic conundrum of "When you are up to your neck in alligators, it is hard to think about the need for draining the swamp." Practitioners, like their clients, are imbedded in crises and find it next to impossible to reflect about needed improvements.

The point has been made many times that in service structures where both statutory and non-statutory services are provided, the demand for the former will always, and especially in times of scarce resources, serve to divert attention from the latter. Thus, in B.C. the well-intentioned efforts of the NDP government in 1972 to integrate financial assistance, child welfare, and family counselling have resulted in priority being assigned to the first, to the relative exclusion of the third. In order to prevent the erosion of non-statutory services and to provide opportunities for practitioners to initiate innovations in practice, separate structures are required.

Only once in a very long time does a Berger Commission appear with a mandate to review practice and recommend changes. And implementing the massive changes recommended by the Berger Commission would have required a fortuitous blend of timing, resources, and a positive reception by the politicians.

A fourth factor is that academics in social welfare have neglected child welfare in recent years. Perhaps because of the coercive aspect of child welfare or because of the severity of the problems facing the clientele, academics have focused research and reflections on the voluntary rather than the involuntary client. However, a number of contributors to this book are currently engaged in research in the field. Professor Pence is the director of a nationwide day-care study, and Callahan is investigating the feasibility of establishing a nationwide data base to record the factors involved in the apprehension of children. Professor Shulman's work on effective practice is described in Chapter 17, and four other contributors, Hudson, MacKenzie, MacDonald and Wharf have been reviewing the approach of Native Indian Bands to child welfare services. These activities may well presage a renewed interest in the field of child welfare by academics.

WHAT CAN BE DONE

Despite the existence of a number of national voluntary organizations in the field of child and family welfare, such as the Canada Council on Children and Youth, the Vanier Institute on the Family, and the Canadian Council on Social Development, and the efforts of the federal and provincial governments, a vacuum exists with regard to data collection, standard setting, and policy development in child welfare.

Data Collection. As noted in Chapter 1, the child welfare community in Canada lacks basic data on the number of children in care by province, the reasons, and the trends. Why do the provinces of Newfoundland, Quebec, Alberta, British Columbia, and the Yukon/NWT have more than 1 per cent of the total number of children in the province in care? What factors account for this relatively high percentage — the number of poor families, the number of native children, the extent and development of the social services? All or none of these factors? In the absence of systematically recorded data of such variables as poverty, these will continue as questions which barely penetrate the consciousness of the child welfare community, rather than as major issues for attention and resolution.

It would be appropriate for a federal agency such as Health and Welfare Canada or Statistics Canada to assume the responsibility for collecting data. The federal government now contributes 50 per cent of the cost of child welfare services, and a national ministry should undertake the task of compiling data on child welfare in Canada. From a technical point of view it would be relatively simple to design a nationwide reporting system which would, at a minimum, contain the following ingredients: the number, age, race, and other salient characteristics of children and families being served by the child welfare field where children were *not* taken into care; the same data with regard to children in permanent and temporary care; children discharged from substitute care and returned to their parents; and the number of children placed for adoption and subsidized adoption.

However, simple as the design aspect of a reporting system might be, conversations with senior staff members of Health and Welfare Canada indicate that gaining agreement from provincial governments to implement such a scheme would be difficult. Previous attempts have foundered on the rocks of provincial autonomy, and some pressing incentives may be required to encourage provincial ministries to co-operate in a national reporting scheme.

Standard-Setting, Accreditation and Evaluation. Standards in any field of service can be developed and tested on either an internal or external basis. Accreditation requires an external review of standards and a determination of whether the programme or agency is living up to these standards. Evaluation is concerned with the determination of effect — what is the outcome of a particular programme — and effectiveness — is the outcome superior to that which could be produced by other programmes. Again, evaluation may be conducted internally or by an external agency.

Regardless of whether one refers to standard-setting, accreditation, or evaluation, precious little is evident in Canada. Child welfare agencies may set standards, may test those standards, and may evaluate programmes, but the results of these are usually confined to the agency and are not released in either annual reports or other publicly available forms. And there is no organization, public or private, provincial or national, which has as a main purpose the accrediting of child welfare services. Without attention to these functions, there is no way of knowing which programmes are effective and should be replicated and which are ineffective and should be discarded. And the consequences of no standards and no accrediting mechanism is precisely what Elizabeth Robinson points out in her chapter — namely, that provincial child welfare ministries can continue to provide services without establishing permanent plans for children in care.

Responsibility for the development of standards of service and the accreditation function might be jointly assumed by provincial ministries and the Canadian Council on Children and Youth. Some provinces, notably Ontario, have already begun work on standards of service, and these might serve as prototypes for other provincial ministries. Envisaged here is the establishment of standards in foster care provision, in the support services such as homemaker and family support programmes, and, perhaps most significantly, standards which set out targets for reducing the number of children in care.

Again the principal difficulty lies not in designing standards, but in obtaining approval for implementation by the provincial ministries, and given the wide disparities which exist between provinces, nationwide standards would be undesirable. A beginning might be made by following the example of Canadian Schools of Social Work within the broad context of a national association and a national accrediting function. The curricula of the Canadian schools vary greatly, from those seeking to prepare generalists for rural practice to those focusing on specialized skills at the Masters and Doctorate levels. Recognizing that forcing all schools into a common mould would be undesirable, the essential and compelling feature of the accrediting function in social work education is that schools are required to define objectives and specify how these objectives are being reached.

Establishing accreditation in child welfare would require agencies to develop objectives, including the establishment of targets to be reached and how these targets are to be achieved. Thus, reducing the number of children in care by a certain percentage would require the development of programmes of family support and tracking their impact. The second step in accreditation consists of reviewing written material and site visits to interview staff and clients. It provides a way of reviewing existing programmes and the potential. Accreditation in this form constitutes a viable form of evaluation — a continuing review of programmes by both operating agencies and an outside organization. The outside review function could be undertaken by the Canadian Council on Children and Youth or by an organization created specifically for this task.

Policy Development in Child Welfare. Perhaps the most important aspect of Canadian child welfare is its residual nature and the absence of efforts to reconceptualize and redefine the field. Several factors suggest that the need for a redefinition is urgent. In his chapter, Pence presents a convincing case that the need for day care is not simply a whimsical abdication of parental responsibility, but an absolute requirement in an industrial society where the majority of parents works. A cultural lag is evident in Canada between the reality of employment and the perception of politicians and other leaders that day care is a frill required by only a few people.

Pence goes on to argue that the need for day care provision is so great that it is inappropriate and unrealistic to expect the public purse to meet these demands. Just as European countries have, Canada must recognize that the responsibility for day care has to be broadly shared among industry, education, and community groups. The development of industrial social services in Europe is well established and has several important contributions. It provides some choice for consumers, lessens reliance on the public sector, and increases the opportunities for innovation and competition in the social services.

A second argument calling for a redefinition of the field was alluded to at the beginning of this chapter — the child welfare field deals disproportionately with children of poor families. A recent report by the Metro Toronto Social Planning Council establishes this point.

> In cold statistical terms Ontario children make up 42% of those on public aid. If parents are maintained in poverty because of the inadequacy of public programs, then their children will have a greater likelihood of being poor when they become adults.[1]

As pointed out in a number of chapters in this book, society is prepared to make certain provisions available as public utilities to all families, rich or poor, but it is not prepared to ensure that families enjoy the most basic right of all — the right to an adequate income. In fact, children of poor families are provided with adequate support only when they are removed from their families and placed in substitute care. The cost of maintaining a child in even the most basic form of foster care far exceeds the cost of supporting a parent and a child together.

Third, and most importantly, child welfare has largely operated as a back up and mop up operation and has not sought to redefine its function to one of supporting families. This position is supported both by writers in the field and by provincial politicians. For example, Brenda McGowan and William Meezan, following their work in assembling a text on child welfare policy and practice in the U.S., come to the following conclusion:

> We believe it is unrealistic to expect the child welfare field to expand its boundaries to the point where it could assume the responsibility of providing for the welfare of all children, and we would urge a renewed emphasis on its original function of providing services to children whose developmental needs cannot be fully met by their own families, even with the assistance of the community support services available to all families and children. In other words, we view child welfare as essentially a residual service system.[2]

Their position is similar to that taken by Costin and Rapp in the third edition of a popular U.S. text on child welfare.[3] However, this residual stance runs counter to the position taken by other writers. Kamerman and Kahn argue the case for a broader framework and context than traditional child welfare services. The task is to develop family support services within a personal social service system, to include both services of the developmental-socialization type and those that will offer help to individuals in the early stages of difficulties when family integrity is more readily preserved.[4]

There is then a basic lack of agreement regarding the appropriate functions for child welfare. The residualists argue that the provision of substitute care is an important and demanding responsibility which requires the existence of distinct structures. The proponents of this position are not against preventive, supportive services, but they believe that these services should not be part of the child welfare system. The opposing position holds that boundaries between fields of service are artificial and unhelpful — needed is a conceptualization of services which provides assistance to families and individuals in need and which supports them before they experience problems.

The position taken here is that families and children might be better served if the term "child welfare" and the field as a discrete segment in the social services were eliminated. As long as child welfare functions in a purely residual fashion, it will continue to legitimize a pattern of services which essentially denies assistance until family breakdown has occurred. Even more paradoxically, the field has viewed the substitute care of children as being desirable and has devoted infinitely more resources to this function than to the task of supporting families.

It is instructive to compare this stage of development with that prevailing in health. Thanks to the conceptual breakthroughs of reports such as the Lalonde document, *A New Perspective on the Health Care of Canadians*, it has finally begun to be recognized that the primary determinants of health are the environment and lifestyle.

> Self-imposed risks and the environment are the principal or important underlying factors in each of the five major causes of death between age one and age seventy, and one can only conclude that, unless the environment is changed and the self-imposed risks are reduced, the death rate will not be significantly improved.[5]

In fact, what has traditionally been referred to as the health care system is a sickness care system. Improvements in health have been largely achieved by changes in the environment and lifestyles and in the identification of specific preventive vaccines developed through years of research.

Applying a similar conceptualization to the social well-being of families would identify such factors as employment and income as being of primary importance. It would accord significance to family planning, parent education, day care, and family supports — the kind of assistance which was earlier found in extended families. It would give third ranking to the aspects of the child welfare field which now rate as the first priority — assistance to families in crisis and foster and other forms of substitute care.

Chapter 12, which deals with prevention, recommended that:

1. income assistance should be provided by the federal government in order to eliminate disparities across the country and to be clearly recognized as a response which is largely required because of the failure of the market to provide employment.

2. child welfare services should become part of an integrated human service system which would consist of both substitute care and support services for families, would include the frail elderly requiring day care, and would connect with out-patient health care.

3. the responsibility for this integrated human service system should be divided between provincial governments and local communities. The former would be responsible for establishing policy, standards of services and budgets, for evaluation, and for the operation of specialized services. Local communities would then take on the task of delivering services. A fundamental challenge is the determination of the kinds of administrative structures and the mix of services required in communities. Given an option, some communities might prefer to provide personal social services through a combination of recreational and industrial auspices. Others might prefer the model of the outpatient health and social service centre. Administratively, some communities might elect to govern their services through city councils, while others might opt for elected boards following the example of boards of education.

It cannot be emphasized too strongly that we do not know whether integrated or separate services are more effective; if integrated, what mix is preferable, or what kind of administrative structure is the most appropriate for the human services. We desperately need information regarding the effect of services that come only from deliberately planned diversity and careful attention to evaluation.

This discussion would be incomplete without noting that the province of Quebec has carried out some of the above. Following the recommendations of the Castonguay-Nepveu Commission, Quebec integrated health and social services, assigned income assistance to a separate ministry, and developed local and regional social services centres governed by citizen boards. The Quebec experience has been reviewed, but little material is available in English.[6] It does, however, appear that the provincial government has been reluctant to delegate budgetary authority to the regional and local centres and that considerable difficulty has been experienced in sorting out which services are regional and which are local.

It should also be acknowledged that the integration of services is not without its critics. From the perspective of a physician specifically concerned with adolescents, Roger Tonkin argues forcefully that the particular needs of this age group require specialized personnel employed by agencies established with the express purpose of serving adolescents. The argument is persuasive, but it must be recognized that to implement the suggestion would result in a further fragmentation of an already complicated interagency scene. An alternative would see age-related specialists working out of integrated human services centres rather than the development of separate service systems.

A second and more powerful attack on integration comes from representatives of minority groups who view a tightly-integrated service system as collusion. Thus Myrna Whitehawk in an address to a Native Workers' Conference in Regina describes case conferences where professionals meet to share information and develop treatment plans as representing a conspiracy against the best interests of the native client. In Whitehawk's opinion, such conferences merely pool the collective ignorance of white middle-class professionals and exclude the values and traditions of native clients. Whitehawk goes on to argue that clients or their advocates should be present at case conferences.

In any considerations of service integration, the principle of affinity should not be forgotten. This principle argues for the identification and protection of certain values which are of crucial importance to native and religious groups. Thus the existence of a separate Catholic agency means to Catholics that their values concerning birth control and abortion will be respected. The principle of affinity is a powerful argument in support of the case for community coherence.

It is unlikely that any improvements will occur until a constituency for child welfare is developed. Ontario is the only province to rely on privately organized societies to deliver child welfare services. Each of the fifty odd CAS's in Ontario has a board of directors, and the rotating membership on these boards means that Ontario has developed over time a large number of citizens who are well informed about and committed to the cause of child welfare. It may be coincidence, but Ontario also has the lowest number of children in care of any province and by a considerable margin. Ontario has also devoted time and energy to developing standards for child welfare and to developing research and demonstration projects. In short, Ontario is the only province with a child welfare constituency, and it is, by any yardstick, a leader in the field.

Bagley makes the telling point that "child welfare authorities themselves are generally cautious and conservative. Former victims themselves must lead a community based movement for the development of open and comprehensive counselling and help services which can reach all of those currently being abused, as well as former victims still suffering impaired mental health as a result of earlier abuse."[7]

While leadership from victims should be welcomed, I think the task of reconceptualizing and reforming the field of child welfare is too complex and forbidding to be entrusted to any single group. Rather, the task should be shared among a number of groups, including politicians, volunteers, professionals, and victims. It is particularly important that the federal and provincial governments not restrict their interest in child welfare to sporadic royal commissions, but assign it high priority on the policy agenda. And this will be aided by reconceptualizing child welfare as part of a human service system which can make a positive contribution to communities.

The current era, which is dominated by conservative governments and scarce resources, is not the most propitious time to attempt basic reforms of the human services. At first glance there is little or no congruence between the residualist philosophy of conservative governments and the kind of progressive, innovative work represented by Kahn, Kamerman, Froland,[8] and many other leading theorists in social welfare. And there are, of course, many differences, but stripped of the loaded adjectives, both groups would agree that where natural helping is possible, it should occur, where it can be supported this should happen, and where partnerships between the formal helping agencies and informal support groups can be developed, this is desirable.

> Human services have come full circle, reaching back to the beginnings of organized human services to find the basis for a renewed partnership with people who are helping one another in their everyday lives. This shared philosophy emphasizes the principles of self-determination, self-reliance, and mutual aid, which serve as a frame of reference for staff in providing help. In working with clients, this may involve looking at an individual's abilities and strengths.[9]

In addition, the current interest of many governments in transferring functions to the private sector may afford some intriguing possibilities for partnership arrangements between the provinces and local community agencies. In particular, voluntary organizations and educational institutions must begin to give attention to some of the questions and issues which will perplex human services in the future. Developments such as genetic engineering will have implications for child care and rearing which professionals in the human service field have not yet begun to speculate about. For example, couples now unable to have children of their own and wishing to adopt must undergo a screening process and a waiting period to determine if they are acceptable for adopting a child. Will the same requirements be made for couples who eschew the adoption route in favour of artificial insemination? Should children conceived in this way learn about their "natural" parents? Who will be responsible for keeping the records and for informing children?

It seems apparent that human services in the future will be riddled with ethical and moral dilemmas, both on the policy and the practice level. Yet neither the educational nor the operating establishments have done much to help practitioners sort through these dilemmas. While we have recognized that the human service professional of the future will need to be comfortable with the technology of computers, we have yet to face the reality that the technical skills of helping clients confront and unravel moral dilemmas will pose greater challenges. A few hospitals in the U.S. have employed ethicists, whose function is to assist staff to sort through ethical puzzles regarding euthanasia and abortion. Such assistance is badly required in other aspects of the human services.

To this point the courts have been the only source for considering moral dilemmas. But again, as Professor McDougall points out, "It was fortuitous that the Dawson case came to court. In many similar cases decisions not to treat are made by parents and physicians." And the difficulties posed in these dilemmas is exemplified by the fact that the first court ruling in the Dawson case was in favour of the parental argument that the infant should not have the operation.

The point is that child welfare has always been a field plagued by value judgments, and this will increase in the future. It makes sense then to begin to assist staff in the field, whether at a policy or practice level, to develop some additional competence in addressing these dilemmas. Ethicists can certainly help, as can judges, lawyers, and social service staff who have taken a special interest in ethical issues.

In short, improving and reforming the present child welfare system will require the sustained and committed efforts from a number of sources. At a minimum it will require that

1. Child welfare agencies establish standards of service, accrediting mechanisms and evaluation procedures, and policy and research institutes.

2. Child welfare agencies direct attention to data collection and to research in order to determine the potency of the various factors responsible for children coming into care.

3. Governments follow the examples of Quebec and New Brunswick which have folded the child welfare system into larger and more comprehensive human service systems.

4. Voluntary organizations such as the Canadian Council on Children and Youth and the Vanier Institute develop the capacity to analyse the impact of new policies in related fields (taxation, employment) on families. The basic conceptual work for family impact statements has been done by Kahn and Kamerman, but there have not been any efforts to implement these impact statements on the Canadian scene.[10]

Finally, it is essential that a national organization assume responsibilities for analysing policy and practice, for initiating research and demonstration projects, and for acting as a clearing house of information about new developments. The field of child welfare needs the knowledge and the stimulation which can be gained from carefully designed projects aimed at preventing children from coming into care and from thoughtful analysis of present practice. For example, David Henry claims that present policies in adoption are based on a fundamental error — that children of one set of natural parents can assume the identity of a second set — and argues that only permanent care-taking arrangements are possible and desirable.[11] Such arguments deserve careful consideration because they contain the potential for basic reforms in child welfare and represent the kind of radical analysis which should occur on a regular and continuing basis.

NOTES

1. *And the Poor Get Poorer: A Study of Social Welfare Programs in Ontario,* A joint project of The Social Planning Council of Metropolitan Toronto and the Ontario Social Development Council (Toronto: The Council, 1983), p. 62.
2. Brenda McGowan, and William Meezan, eds., *Child Welfare* (Itasca, Ill.: Peacock Publishing, 1983), p. 505.
3. Lela Costin, and Charles Rapp, *Child Welfare Policies and Practices* (New York: McGraw-Hill, 1984).
4. Sheila Kamerman, and Alfred Kahn, "Child Welfare and the Welfare of Families with Children," in *Child Welfare,* ed. McGowan and Meezan, p. 161.
5. Marc Lalonde, *New Perspectives on the Health Care of Canadians* (Ottawa, 1974).
6. Frederic Leseman, *Services and Circuses, Community and the Welfare State* (Montreal: Black Rose Books, 1984).
7. Chris Bagley, "The Sexual Abuse of Children," ch. 4.
8. Kamerman and Kahn, and Charles Froland, Diane Pancoast, Nancy Chapman, and Priscilla Kimboko, *Helping Networks and Human Services* (Beverly Hills: Sage Publishing, 1981).
9. Ibid., p. 124.
10. Sheila Kamerman and Alfred Kahn, *Family Policy* (New York, Columbia University Press, 1978).
11. David Henry, in the videotape produced by the *Taking Control Project,* Faculty of Social Work, University of Regina.

SELECTED CANADIAN REFERENCES

Adams, Howard. *Prison of Grass*. Toronto: General Publishing, 1975.

Albert, S. James. *Children and the State*. Proceedings of a Conference, 16-18 April 1978 at the School of Social Work, Carleton University, Ottawa, Ontario.

Allen, His Honour Judge H. Ward. *Judicial Inquiry into the Care of Kim Anne Popen by the Children's Aid Society of the City of Sarnia and the County of Lambton*. 4 vols. Toronto: Queen's Printer, 1982.

Anderson, C., and P. Mayes. "Treating Family Sexual Abuse: The Humanistic Approach." *Journal of Child Care* 2 (1982): 31-47.

Armstrong, Pat and Armstrong, Hugh. *The Double Ghetto: Canadian Women and their Segregated Work*. (Toronto: McClelland and Stewart, 1978).

Badgley, R. (Chairman). *Report of the Committee on Sexual Offences against Children*. Ottawa: Government of Canada, 1984.

Bagley, C. *Child Sexual Abuse: Annotated Bibliography of Studies, 1978-1980*. Calgary: Rehabilitation and Health Monographs. No. 3. Calgary: University of Calgary Press, 1984..

———."Child Sexual Abuse and Childhood Sexuality: A Review of the Monograph Literature 1978 to 1982." *Journal of Child Care* 3 (1982): 100-21.

———."Child Sexual Abuse: Annotated Bibliography of the Journal Literature, 1978 to 1982." *Journal of Child Care* 4 (1983).

———."The Gentle Revolution." *Starting Over: Newsletter of Sons and Daughters United*, Calgary Chapter. P.O. Box 116, Station J, Calgary, Alberta.

———."Mental Health and the In-family Sexual Abuse of Children and Adolescents." *Canada's Mental Health* 32 (1984): 17-23.

———, and Ramsey, R. "Research Problems and Priorities in Research of Suicidal Behaviours: An Overview with Canadian Implications." *Canadian Journal of Community Mental Health*, in press.

———, and McDonald, M. "Adult Mental Health Sequels of Child Sexual Abuse, Physical Abuse and Neglect in Maternally Separated Children." *Canadian Journal of Community Mental Health* 3 (1984): 15-26.

Bissett-Johnson, A. "Step-Parent Adoptions in English and Canadian Law." In Baxter, I.F.G., and M.A. Eberts, *The Child and the Courts*. Toronto: Carswell, 1978, pp. 335-58.

British Columbia Daycare Action Coalition. *Report of the Ministerial Task Force*. 5 November, 1981.

British Columbia Federation of Foster Parents Association. "A Brief on Subsidized Adoption." Vancouver, B.C., Jan. 1977.

Bross, Allon, ed. *Family Therapy: A Recursive Model of Strategic Practice*. Toronto: Methuen, 1982.

Callahan, M., and M. Martin. "Developing Consumer Information — A Strategy for Service and Policy Change." *The Social Worker* 49, no. 4 (1981): 161-73.

Callahan, M., and Wharf, Brian. "Demystifying the Policy Process: A Case Study of the Development of Child Welfare Legislation in B.C." Victoria: University of Victoria School of Social Work, 1982.

Canada. Indian and Northern Affairs Canada. *Indian Conditions: A Survey*. Ottawa: Government of Canada, 1980.

———. *Program Circular on Child Welfare Policy*. Ottawa: May 1, 1982.

———. *Report of the Child Core Task Force on B.C. Indian Child Care*. May 1982.

Canada. *Report of the Special Committee of the House of Commons on Indian Self-Government in Canada*. Ottawa: Queen's Printer, 1983.

Canadian Council on Children and Youth. *Admittance Restricted: The Child as Citizen in Canada*. Ottawa: The Council, 1978.

Canadian Council on Social Development. *Guaranteed Annual Income: An Integrated Approach*. Ottawa: The Council, 1973.

Cardinal, Harold. *The Unjust Society*. Edmonton: Hurtig, 1969.

Cavanagh, Mr. Justice J.E. *Board of Review: The Child Welfare System*. Alberta, 1983.

Chisholm, Ruth. *Family Service Survey*. Vancouver: Children's Aid Society, 1972.

Christian, Wayne. Speech to Native Child Apprehensions Conference, Saskatoon, September 1981, as reported by Richard Thatcher, "Stop Stealing Our Children." *Canadian Dimension* 16, no. 6 (1982): 3.

Clague, M., Dill, R., Seebaran, R. and Wharf, B. *Reforming Human Services: The Community Resource Board Experience in B.C.* Vancouver: University of British Columbia Press, 1984.

Commission on Emotional and Learning Disorders in Children. *One Million Children.* Toronto: Leonard Crainford, 1970.

Community Task Force on Maternal and Child Health. "Adoption: The Issue of Bonding in the Adoption of Newborn Infants." Winnipeg: March 1981.

Currie, Janet, and Pishalski, Fred. *Loosening the Fabric.* Victoria: The B.C. Association of Social Workers, Southern Vancouver Island Chapter, and the B.C. Childcare Services Association, August, 1983.

Doehler, Ruth. "Can a Case Be Made for Subsidized Adoption?" *Journal of Ontario Association of Children's Aid Societies* (May 1970).

Dosman, Edgar. *Indians, The Urban Dilemma.* Toronto: McClelland and Stewart, 1972.

Elmore, Gene et al. "Survey of Adoption and Child Welfare Services to Indians of B.C." Report to the B.C. Department of Human Resources, 1974.

Falconer, N.E., with K. Swift. *Preparing for Practice, The Fundamentals of Child Protection.* Toronto: Children's Aid Society of Metro Toronto, 1983.

Farquharson, A. "Self-Help in the Provision of Child Welfare Services: The Stoney Creek Indian Band." A paper presented to the Conference on Self-Help and Mutual Aid in Contemporary Society, Dubrovnik, Yugoslavia, 10-15 September 1979.

Forward, S., and Buck, C. *Betrayal of Innocence: Incest and its Devastations.* Toronto: Macmillan, 1978.

Frank, A.W. III, and Foote, C.E. "Formulating Children's Troubles for Organizational Intervention." In *The Canadian Review of Sociology and Anthropology* 19 (February 1982): 111-122.

Graham, Betty. "The Director of Child Welfare, Ontario Comments on Subsidized Adoption." *Journal of Ontario Association of Children's Aid Societies* (May 1970).

Health and Welfare Canada. Health Education. "Adolescents Face Stressful Life Changes." A report prepared by the Health Promotion Directorate. Fall 1983.

Hepworth, H.P. "Child Welfare Services in Longitudinal Perspective." *Canadian Journal of Social Work Education* 6, no. 1 (1980).

———. *Foster Care and Adoption in Canada.* Ottawa: Canadian Council on Social Development, 1980.

———. "Trends and Comparisons in Canadian Child Welfare Services." Paper prepared for presentation at the First Conference on Provincial Social Welfare Policy, University of Calgary, Calgary Alberta, 5-7 May 1982.

———. "Family Policy in Canada: The Case of Mothers' Allowances." In *SPAN Newsletter,* no. 4 (June 1981).

Hill, S. "Child Sexual Abuse: Selected Issues." M.S.W. thesis, University of Calgary, 1982.

Howell, Mary. *Helping Ourselves.* Toronto: Fitzhenry and Whiteside, 1977.

Hudson, Peter. *Report on the Preventive Services Project of the Family and Children's Services of the District of Rainy River.* Winnipeg: University of Manitoba School of Social Work, March 1980.

Hudson, Peter, and Brad McKenzie. *Evaluation of Dakota Ojibway Child and Family Services.* Prepared for Dakota Ojibway Child and Family Services and Evaluation Branch, Department of Indian Affairs and Northern Development, June 1984.

Inventory of Canadian Research. A Research Report Prepared by the Tree Foundation, Solicitor General of Canada and Minister of National Health and Welfare, 1981.

Johnson, Laura C. and Dineen, Janice. *The Kin Trade—The Day Care Crisis in Canada.* Toronto: McGraw-Hill Ryerson, 1981.

Johnston, Patrick. *Native Children and the Child Welfare System.* Ottawa: Canadian Council on Social Development, 1983.

———, and Stephen Novosedlik. "Child Welfare and the Native Peoples of Canada." Paper presented to the Canadian Association of Schools of Social Work Annual Conference, Ottawa, Ontario, 1-4 June 1982.

Jones, A., and Rutman, L. *In the Children's Aid.* Toronto: University of Toronto Press, 1981.

Kellough, Gail. "From Colonialism to Economic Imperialism: The Experience of the Canadian Indian." In John Harp and John R. Hofley, *Structured Inequality in Canada.* Scarborough: Prentice-Hall, 1980. pp. 343-77.

Leon, J.S. "The Development of Canadian Juvenile Justice: A Background for Reform." In *Osgoode Hall Law Journal,* 15, no. 1 (June 1977): 71-105.

Lero, Donna. *Factors Influencing Parents' Preferences for, and Use of Alternative Child Care Arrangements for Pre-School-Age Children.* Ottawa: Health and Welfare Canada, 1983.

Leseman, Frederic. *Services and Circuses, Community and the Welfare State.* Montreal: Black Rose Books, 1984.

Levitt, K.L. "A Canadian Approach to Permanent Planning." In *Child Welfare* 60, no. 2. (February 1981): 109-112.

Luke, Catherine. "Community and Mobility: A Comparative Study of Single Parents in Victoria West and James Bay." Ministry of Human Resources, Victoria, 21 September, 1979.

MacDonald, J. The Spallumcheen Indian Band and Its Impact on Child Welfare Policy in British Columbia. Unpublished paper. Vancouver, B.C., April 1981.

MacIntyre, J. McEwan. "Subsidized Adoption—Love Plus Money." In *Perception,* (December 1977):32.

McParland, Brian. *Forty-nine Children. A Project to Free Children for Permanent Placement.* Victoria: Ministry of Human Resources, 1979. (M.S.W. thesis, University of British Columbia, 1977.).

———. *Forty-nine Children: One Year Later.* Victoria: Ministry of Human Resources, 1979.

Magnet, J.E. " Withholding Treatment from Defective Newborns: A Description of Canadian Practices." *Legal Medical Quarterly* 4 (1980): 271.

Manitoba Court of Appeal. "The Children's Aid Society and the Big Grassy Indian Band." 28 January 1982.

Manitoba Métis Federation. *Position Paper on Child Care and Family Services.* Winnipeg, Manitoba, 15 May 1982.

Manitoba Working Group on the Emotional Abuse of Children. *Proceedings: Think Tank on the Emotional Abuse of Children.* Winnipeg Health Sciences Centre, 1981.

Matheson, K. Douglas, and David. C. Neave. "Directions in Research." *Canadian Welfare* 46 no. 6 (November/December 1970).

———. "Child Separation in B.C." Unpublished M.S.W. thesis. Vancouver: University of B.C., 1971.

Mohr, J.W. "The Future of the Family, the Law and the State." The People's Law Conference: The Family and the Law. Ottawa, Ontario, 9-10 April 1984.

Morse, B. "Native and Metis Children in Canada: Victims of the Child Welfare System." In G. Verma and C. Bagley, eds., *Race Relations and Cultural Differences: Educational and Cultural Perspectives.* London: Croom-Helm, 1983.

National Council of Welfare. *In the Best Interests of the Child.* Ottawa: The Council, 1979.

———. *Poor Kids.* Ottawa: The Council, 1975.

———. *Report on Women and Poverty.* Ottawa: The Council, 1979.

Native Council of Canada. Crime and Justice Commission. *Metis and Non-Status Indians.* Ottawa: Supply and Services Canada, 1978.

Ontario, Ministry of Community and Social Services. Children's Services Division. *Consultation Papers: Children's Services, Past, Present and Future.* Toronto: the Ministry, 1980.

———. *The Children's Act: A Consultation Paper.* Toronto: Ministry of Community Social Services, 1982.

Palmer, Sally. "Government Commitment to Child Welfare as Shown by the Monitoring of Services." *Social Worker* 50 no. 1 (Spring 1982).

Poulos, S. *Foster Care Study: Factors Associated with Placement Stability.* Vancouver: Children's Aid Society of Vancouver, 1972.

Puxley, Peter. "The Colonial Experience." In Mel Watkins, ed. *Dene Nations. The Colony Within.* Toronto: University of Toronto Press, 1977.

Quebec. Commission of Inquiry on Health and Social Welfare. *Report of the Commission.* (The Castonguay Nepveu Report) Quebec City: Official Publisher, 1976.

Robertshaw, Corinne. *Child Protection in Canada.* Ottawa: Health and Welfare Canada, February 1981.

Robinson, Elizabeth. "The Case for Subsidized Adoption: The Concept and a Model for Implementation." Unpublished Master of Social Work Term Paper, University of British Columbia School of Social Work. Vancouver, B.C. April, 1980.

Royal Commission on Family and Children's Law. *Reports.* Vancouver, 1973-75.
Ryan, Thomas, J. *Poverty and the Child.* Toronto: McGraw-Hill Ryerson, 1972.
Ryan, William. *Blaming the Victim.* Toronto: Random House, 1976.
Ryant, Joseph et al. *A Review of Child Welfare Policies, Programs and Services in Manitoba.* Winnipeg: Government of Manitoba, 1975.
Saskatchewan Department of Social Services. *The Child and Family Services Act: Legislative Proposals.* Regina: Queen's Printer, January 1975.
———. *Review of the Family Services Act: A Discussion Paper.* Part Two: Adoption/Foster Care Issues and Proposals. Regina, November 1983.
Schlesinger, B. *Sexual Abuse of Children.* Toronto: University of Toronto Press, 1982.
Sealey, Bruce and Verna Kirkness, eds. *Indians without Tipis.* Winnipeg: William Clare, 1973.
Shaw, Susan. *Better Day Care for Canadians: Options for Parents and Children.* Ottawa: Canadian Advisory Council on the Status of Women, 1982.
Shulman, Lawrence, producer. *The Helping Process in Social Work: Theory, Practice and Research.* Montreal: McGill University Instructional Communications Centre, 1976.
Shulman, Lawrence. *A Study of the Helping Process.* Vancouver: University of British Columbia School of Social Work, 1977.
———. *The Input of Reduced Caseloads on Preventative Services.* Vancouver: University of British Columbia School of Social Work, 1977.
Shulman, L., Robinson, E., and A. Luckji. *A Study of the Content, Context and Skills of Supervision.* Vancouver: University of British Columbia, 1981.
Siggner, Andrew, and Locatelli, Chantal. "An Overview of Demographic Social and Economic Conditions among B.C.'s Registered Indian Population." Ottawa: Department of Indian and Northern Affairs, Research Branch, 1980.
Social Planning Council of Metropolitan Toronto and the Ontario Social Development Council. *And the Poor Get Poorer: A Study of Social Welfare Programs in Ontario.* Toronto: the Council, 1983.
Social Planning Council of Metropolitan Toronto. *Social Infopac,* 2, no. 4 (October 1983).
Sorrenti-Little, L., Bagley, C., and S. Robertson. "An Operational Definition of the Long-term Harmfulness of Sexual Relations with Peers and Adults by Young Children." *Canadian Children: Journal of the Canadian Association for Young Children* 9 (1984): 1.
Splane, R.B. *Social Welfare in Ontario, 1791-1898.* Toronto: University of Toronto Press, 1965.
Stanbury, W.T. *The Social and Economic Conditions of Indian Families in British Columbia.* Report prepared for the B.C. Royal Commission on Family and Children's Law, Vancouver, 1974.
Thomlinson, R.J. *Case Management Review: Northwest Region Department of Social Services and Community Health.* Alberta, September 1984.
Tonkin, R.S. "Adolescent Manual." Vancouver: Hemlock Printers, 1982.
———. "Child Health Profile — 1981." Vancouver: Hemlock Printers, 1981.
———. "Child Health Profile: Mini Series No. 2. Violence in Adolescence." Vancouver: Hemlock Printers, 1981.
Turner, David. "Community and Prevention: The Case of Rose Blanshard Court." *Corrections Branch Newsletter.* (Fall 1976).
Wharf, Brian, *Community Work in Canada.* Toronto: McClelland and Stewart, 1978.
Zenter, Henry, ed. *The Indian Identity Crisis.* Calgary: Strayer Publications, 1973.
Zetterberg, H.A. *On Theory and Verification of Sociology.* Toronto: Bedminster Press, 1965.

CONTRIBUTORS

Chris Bagley, Burns Professor of Child Welfare, University of Calgary

Thomas Berger, Professor, Faculty of Law, University of British Columbia

Marilyn Callahan, Associate Professor and Director, School of Social Work, University of Victoria

David Cruickshank, Professor and Associate Dean, Faculty of Law, University of Calgary

H. Philip Hepworth, Coordinator, Policy and Development, Health and Welfare Canada

Peter Hudson, Associate Professor and Director, School of Social Work, University of Manitoba

Ken Levitt, Social Worker, Vancouver, B.C.

John A. MacDonald, Associate Professor, School of Social Work, University of British Columbia

Donald McDougall, Professor, Faculty of Law, University of British Columbia

Brad McKenzie, Associate Professor, School of Social Work, University of Manitoba

Marjorie Martin, Assistant Professor, School of Social Work, University of Victoria

Alan R. Pence, Assistant Professor, School of Child Care, University of Victoria

Elizabeth Robinson, Social Worker, Vancouver, B.C.

Brian Shields, Social Worker, Victoria, B.C.

Lawrence Shulman, Professor, School of Social Work, Boston University, Boston, Mass.

Roger Tonkin, Professor, Faculty of Medicine, University of British Columbia

David Turner, Assistant Professor, School of Social Work, University of Victoria

Brian Wharf, Professor, School of Social Work, and Dean, Faculty of Human and Social Development, University of Victoria

Barbara A. Whittington, Assistant Professor, School of Social Work, University of Victoria

INDEX